Shallow  Grave
in Trinity County

Shallow Grave in Trinity County

Harry Farrell

St. Martin's Press ❧ New York

Library of Congress Cataloging-in-Publication Data

Farrell, Harry.
    Shallow grave in Trinity County / Harry Farrell. — 1st ed.
        p.   cm.
    Includes bibliographical references (pp. 307–308) and index.
    ISBN 0-312-17009-2
    1. Abbott, Burton W., d. 1957.   2. Bryan, Stephanie.   3. Murder—Investigation—California—Berkeley—Case studies.   4. Trials (Murder)—California—Berkeley—Case studies.   5. Bryan, Stephanie.
    I. Title
    HV6534.B44F37   1997
    364.15'23'0979467—dc21   97-14780
                                                                  CIP

Book design by Maura Fadden Rosenthal

First Edition: November 1997

10   9   8   7   6   5   4   3   2   1

FOR
GRACE ELAINE

CONTENTS

PART ONE
THE DISCOVERY

PART TWO
THE FATEFUL DAYS

PART THREE
BEFORE THE TRIAL

INTRODUCTION

For the ninth-grade girls at Berkeley's Willard Junior High School, the last period of the day was gym, and on cold, blustery days they were tempted to cut class and head home early from the playing field. Their teacher therefore usually called the roll at both the beginning and the end of the hour. That is how police were able to confirm that Stephanie Bryan was indeed where she was supposed to be between 2 and 3 P.M. on Thursday, April 28, 1955.

The morning had been mild, but that afternoon a west wind off the bay was stacking the clouds up against the hills, and rain was forecast by nightfall. At five minutes past three the shower bell rang. Whether the girls were being watched from afar as they trooped back to the locker room in their gym shorts, we can only guess. What we know is that the fourteen-year life of Stephanie, the shy daughter of an esteemed local physician, had but few hours left.

In 1955 fear did not rule the streets of Berkeley, or most other American cities. It was a time of civility and good cheer. The country was at peace. The front-page news that April was a message of hope about the new Salk vaccine for polio. People were whistling "The Yellow Rose of Texas"; jukeboxes blared that "Love Is a Many-Splendored Thing"; and carefree teenagers danced to "Rock Around the Clock."

Willard Junior High, barely seven blocks south of the University of California, was a favored school for the children of Berkeley's intellectuals, whose homes surrounded the campus. As we shall see, Stephanie's homeward walk would take her through a dense buffer of trees—a miniature forest scarcely a hundred feet across—separating a Berkeley business district from the stately homes of her neighborhood, just where the foothills begin to rise. On bright days, with sunlight filtering through the foliage overhead, the path through this sylvan strip possessed a charm such as one might expect in a Disney movie. But on this day of wind and overcast, the scene must have been forbidding.

Along that wooded path, someone lay in wait for the doctor's daughter. Who? That is what our story is about.

The atrocities Stephanie would suffer in her final hours were the same as those in many sad episodes since, through which America has learned the names of other little girls such as Polly Klaas and JonBenet Ramsey. Polly's kidnapping and murder, also in northern California, was in some ways a reenactment of what had happened to Stephanie thirty-eight years earlier. But the Bryan case violated the tranquility and confidence of its era, and it thus carried a horror seldom matched since. It held Californians transfixed for two years.

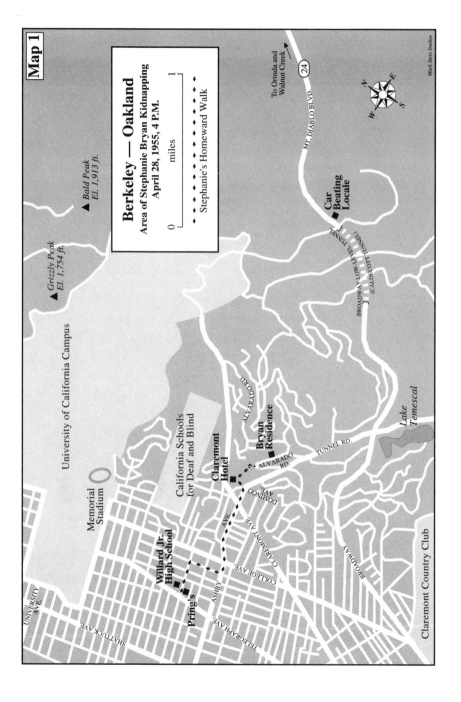

Map 1

Berkeley — Oakland
Area of Stephanie Bryan Kidnapping
April 28, 1955, 4 P.M.

0   miles   1

♦ ♦ ♦ ♦ Stephanie's Homeward Walk

Grizzly Peak
El. 1,754 ft.

▲ *Bald Peak*
El. 1,913 ft.

University of California Campus

Memorial Stadium

UNIVERSITY AVE.

SHATTUCK AVE.

Willard Jr. High School

Pring's

TELEGRAPH AVE.

ASHBY

COLLEGE AVE.

CLAREMONT AVE.

California Schools for Deaf and Blind

Claremont Hotel

DOMINGO AVE.

ALVARADO

Bryan Residence

ALVARADO RD.

TUNNEL RD.

Lake Temescal

BROADWAY

Claremont Country Club

BROADWAY LOW LEVEL TUNNEL
(CALDECOTT) TUNNEL

Car Beating Locale

MT. DIABLO BLVD.

24

To Orinda and Walnut Creek

N W E S

Mark Stein Studios

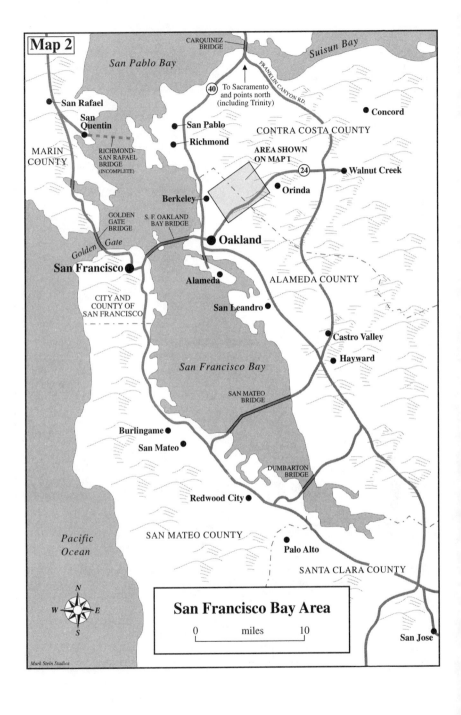

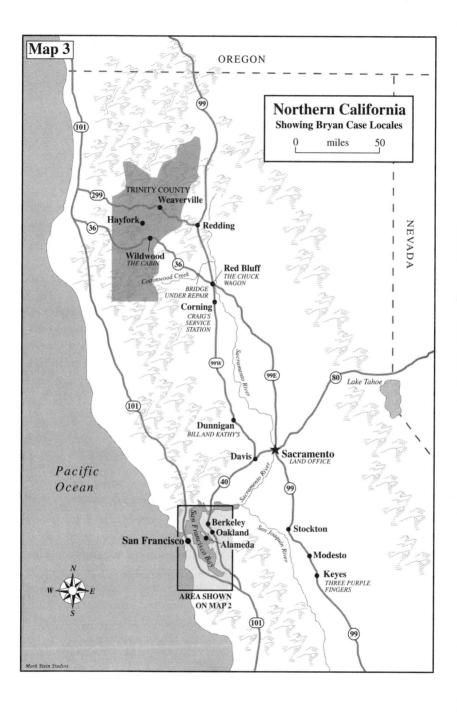

PART ONE

The Discovery

1

The Box in the Basement

It was six-thirty on the midsummer evening of Friday, July 15, 1955, when Georgia Abbott descended the stairs to the basement of her white stucco house in Alameda.

She had just come home after a long day on the job at the Morton Beauty Salon, a neighborhood shop that drew its clientele from the town's upper crust. Georgia, a fun-loving, titian-haired woman, was thirty-three years old.

In the cellar she hunted for a costume hat—a black, 1920s-style cloche—for a comedy skit at a forthcoming hair-styling contest of the Oakland Cosmetologists Association. Georgia, the association's president, had done the same act before and stored her costume away.

Amid the basement clutter were boxes of old clothes, and she searched through several without success. Then she opened a cardboard carton stamped on the side with the name of the detergent it had once held: "All."

It might as well have read "Pandora."

Upstairs Georgia's husband, Burton, was broiling steaks for dinner. His mother, Elsie Abbott, was there too; she had moved in with her son and daughter-in-law the previous January. Her presence added problems to a household that already had more than its share.

Burton Wilbur Abbott, often called "Bud," was twenty-seven—six years younger than his wife, who was the family breadwinner. He was enrolled as an accounting major at the University of California's nearby Berkeley campus. He was a slender, pale man with intense gray-blue eyes behind horn-rimmed glasses. As *San Jose Mercury News* reporter Charles Cruttenden would write, "He gives the impression of a pencil standing on end." No fewer than three journalists would take note of his long, white hands and slender fingers with flawlessly manicured nails—hands whose quick, abrupt gestures punctuated his conversation. His eyes were intelligent, but cold in a way that negated an otherwise engaging smile. His pencil-line mustache was light brown.

While Georgia was in the basement, the doorbell rang. It was a friend, Otto Dezman, whose wife, Leona, was the owner of the Morton Beauty Salon and Georgia's boss.

"Otto, you're just in time for dinner," Abbott greeted him.

Dezman, a retired navy chief warrant officer, held a copy of that evening's *Oakland Tribune,* carrying a photograph taken of Georgia and a friend to publicize the hair-styling contest. Alongside it on the page was a picture of the movies' Francis the Talking Mule; "Francis takes a better picture than Georgia," Dezman jested. Abbott laughed, and shouted down to his wife through the furnace register, "Georgia, your picture's in the paper!"

It was only a few minutes later that Georgia came running up the stairs, visibly shaken, screaming "Abbott! Abbott!"—a form of address she had picked up years before, during her service in the Wacs.

In the "All box," as it came to be known, she had found two cocktail aprons and some of her husband's clothing—shorts, socks, T-shirts, all of which she recognized. She had packed these herself the previous March. But in the bottom of the carton lay a strange new item—a red leather purse she did not recognize. Her curiosity aroused, she had opened it. Inside were three pennies, a white plastic comb, two bobby pins, a green and gold Papermate ball-point pen, a blue wooden pencil and pink rubber eraser, an unfinished letter written on notebook paper to someone named "Teddy," and a red leather wallet. The latter contained stamp-size photographs of several girls, a picture of a pet dog, and a Junior Red Cross card bearing the name "Stephanie Bryan," which at first was also unfamiliar. Then Georgia looked at another card—a special privilege pass from Willard Junior High School in Berkeley, identifying Stephanie as a student there.

"I saw the card with Willard Junior High, and then it clicked," Georgia later told the police. "That's when I turned white. Goose pimples stood out all over me."

Fourteen-year-old Stephanie Bryan, the oldest child of a Berkeley doctor, had been on the front pages of California newspapers for the past two and a half months. On Thursday, April 28, she had vanished on her way home from school, and there was still no clue to her fate. Thousands of $2,500 reward posters, tacked up throughout Northern California, had acquainted residents with her smiling, dimpled face; her features conveyed friendly intelligence and poise.

As Georgia emerged from the cellar, she held the Willard card in her right hand and the purse in her left. In the kitchen she confronted Burton, Elsie, and Dezman.

"Isn't this the girl who disappeared in Berkeley?" she demanded, pointing to Stephanie's name. She still wasn't sure. Burton took the card and examined it.

"Oh, that purse must belong to one of your girlfriends," he said.

The purse's contents were passed around the room. Everyone there handled them before Dezman belatedly warned, "Don't ruin the fingerprints."

None of them could answer Georgia's question—was this the missing girl? Dezman was the first to respond, according to most accounts, including his own.

"Well, the way to find out is to call the Berkeley police," he said.

Burton's mother instantly objected. "If you call the police, there will be publicity."

Later Burton would claim that it was he who had suggested calling the police. He also said it was he, not Dezman, who looked up their number in the phone book—a critical variance from the recollections of others. It was Georgia who finally placed the call to Berkeley police headquarters, where it was taken by Sergeant Victor Vieira.

"I was down in the basement and I found a purse," she told him. "It has a junior high school I.D. in it, with the name of Stephanie Bryan."

The words galvanized the sergeant.

"What color is the purse?" he asked.

"Red."

"Who else is there with you?"

"My husband and a friend and my husband's mother."

"Don't touch anything," Vieira instructed, already too late. "We'll be right over."

"Was it her?" Burton called from the kitchen when Georgia hung up.

"Yes."

"Well, let's eat," Burton responded. "The steaks are getting cold."

"I could go out and get drunk," Dezman said. Taking his cue, Burton produced a bottle.

In obedience to Vieira's admonition, Georgia gathered the purse contents, avoiding further finger contact, and placed them on the dining room table to await the police.

Within an hour some ten officers, including three FBI agents, would arrive.

Burton acted totally perplexed.

"How could that purse have gotten down there?" he wondered aloud. "Why *our* house, of all the houses in Alameda? If I'd had anything to do with that girl's disappearance, I'd have burned the purse."

Then, offering the germ of a frame-up theory never substantiated and still debated, Burton added, "The only thing I can think of is that someone's trying to put us on the spot." But neither then nor later did he offer any idea of who the framer, if any, might be.

While awaiting the police, Burton recalled that he had found the light burning in the garage, which led to the basement, a couple of afternoons earlier.

"Did you leave it on, Georgia?" he asked.

"No," she said.

For her part, she reminded her husband of a thudding noise they had heard about midnight the previous Wednesday, seeming to come from the basement and followed by scraping that sounded like a screen door opening. Burton had declined to investigate, so Georgia had left their bed and gone down herself but found nothing amiss. Finally she had concluded that the noises were caused by her pet budgie, which had just had its wings clipped and kept hitting the wall while flying clumsily about the house.

At this point in the conversation the doorbell rang. It was not the police but DeVere King, a longtime friend of the widowed Elsie, who had a date to take her to dinner. They quickly left together, taking with them the Abbotts' four-year-old-son, Chris, who would stay with friends for the remainder of the evening. They had escaped, so to speak, just in time. Barely had they departed when police headquarters called back with the admonition that no one was to leave.

During the whole episode, Dezman would later tell the FBI, Burton went on devouring his steak, though no one else touched the dinner. Burton's appetite would become a matter of some consequence in the ensuing investigation.

At about seven-thirty the first police car arrived, followed within the hour by two others. Much of the night was taken up with the questioning of all present. During the interrogations both Burton and Georgia were cooperative. At the outset, however, the officers were confused, as Inspector Charles O'Meara would write in his report:

> While Georgia Abbott was relating her information, her husband was saying very little. While Dezman was injecting himself vigorously into the conversation, she [Georgia] was calling on him for corroboration in such a manner that those present thought Dezman was her husband until proper introductions were made.

Burton was asked where he had been on April 28, the date of Stephanie Bryan's disappearance.

He had no difficulty answering. That Thursday was two days before the fishing season opened. He had driven alone some 275 miles north to open the family's summer cabin in the remote, rugged mountains of Trinity County.

"What time did you leave?" asked Officer Willard Hutchins, who took the lead in the questioning.

"About eleven o'clock that morning," Burton said.

Stephanie had not vanished in Berkeley until four that afternoon.

Hutchins, a careful observer of human behavior as well as a skillful questioner, later wrote: "Abbott seemed nervous, used nervous gestures, forced laughter, and so on. All of the actions of Mrs. Abbott seemed normal. Mr. Abbott to the contrary appeared to have a forced calmness."

The "calmness" would fail to impress J. Frank Coakley, Alameda County's district attorney. He would later inform a jury that while the questioning was under way, Abbott "sat on the couch working a crossword puzzle. [His] behavior was that of a person trying too hard to look innocent, of a person overacting his part. The defendant, incidentally, while in high school was interested in dramatics and took part in plays."

Not until Hutchins's questioning was over did the police turn their attention to the purse on the dining room table, and Georgia showed them where she had found it. O'Meara at once ordered a thorough search of the premises for "anything else belonging to Stephanie Bryan, including her body."

As the main body of officers left the house at ten-thirty, O'Meara detailed Hutchins to stay, guarding whatever evidence the dwelling might yet conceal. During the night no one was to enter the basement or its adjoining garage. Nor was anyone to go near the Abbotts' two cars—a green-and-cream 1955 Pontiac hardtop convertible used mainly by Georgia, and a gray-green 1949 Chevrolet sedan in which Burton commuted to his U.C. classes.

After the officers left, Dezman drove the Abbotts in his car to pick up Chris at the friend's home where Elsie and DeVere King had left him for the evening. Hutchins remained at the Abbott residence until about eleven-thirty, when he was relieved. At headquarters it had been decided that an investigative team including Hutchins should head for the Northern California wilds to search the Abbotts' cabin.

Hutchins needed a ride back to Berkeley, and Dezman offered to drive him. During the ride, Hutchins gained the impression that Dezman was contemptuous of Abbott, and that "possibly Dezman and Mrs. Abbott were quite close"—an offhand observation that would foreshadow a critical motif in events to follow.

After taking Hutchins to Berkeley, Dezman returned to the Abbott home after midnight, bringing another bottle. With sleep evading them, he and Abbott played chess until after dawn.

2

Case J-22219

It was Gertrude Stein who damned Oakland several decades ago with her remark that "there's no 'there' there." She was, of course, contrasting it with its cross-bay neighbor San Francisco, an urban jewel superbly situated by the Golden Gate, between the ocean and the bay.

This ridicule was unjust. Oakland was a vibrant city in its own right, with thriving businesses, ample industry, a pulsing waterfront, cultural amenities, plenty of sports, and good living. Its "there" is different from San Francisco's but it exists.

Yet Ms. Stein may have had a broader point. The eastern shore of San Francisco Bay—the "East Bay," to locals—remains a place of unfocused sprawl. A dozen individual municipalities, Oakland being the largest, run together amorphously for twenty-five miles along the narrow coastal plain between the bay and the steep Oakland-Berkeley hills.

Among these towns only Alameda—an island in the bay—is set apart from its neighbors by geography. Alameda is separated from Oakland by a ship channel; three bridges and an underwater tube are all that connect it to the mainland. By contrast, the line between Oakland and the university town of Berkeley to the north is virtually imperceptible, either on the ground or on the map.

Ashby Avenue is a principal east-west artery in Berkeley, and following it three miles inland from the bay leads one to the landmark Claremont Hotel. Against a backdrop of wooded foothills, the gables and cupola of this sprawling white structure are visible for miles. It commands a breathtaking panorama of San Francisco, its bay, and its bridges.

In 1955 the Claremont was a mecca for socialites, a magnet for vacationers, and a favorite for conventioneers. Just to the southeast of the hotel a tract of rolling foothills was covered with lovely old homes—in one of which, a six-bedroom Moorish-style house at 131 Alvarado Road, the Bryan family lived.

Alvarado Road might better have been called a "lane"; it was not a major thoroughfare but a narrow, winding residential street shaded by tall sycamores. Dr. Charles Silas Bryan, a radiologist at Oakland's Peralta Hospital, had brought his family there from Massachusetts in 1953. Mary, his wife of seventeen years, was a Radcliffe graduate who had once been a research assistant to a Harvard professor. She was the caring mother of five children, of whom Stephanie Randolph Bryan was the oldest.

Steffie, as her family called her, had been born in Boston on October 12, 1940. She was a small girl, five feet two and about 108 pounds, with milk-white skin, dark-brown glossy hair, hazel eyes, and gleaming white teeth. She was a ninth grader at Willard Junior High, an exceptional student.

Crossing the threshold into womanhood, Stephanie was not overdeveloped physically. Midway through her fifteenth year, she had been menstruating for only two months. She enjoyed dancing and was taking piano and ballet but had yet to attend her first social dance.

"Stephanie doesn't make friends easily," a schoolmate would tell officers. Yet she was not friendless; she was part of a group of five girls at school who ate lunch together almost every day.

She was not active in clubs or athletics. Rather, she was a bookworm, interested in puppets and baking cookies, for which she used her own special recipe. She loved pets and had two dogs, one of them a diminutive poodle named Hoagie.

Her brother Sam, four years younger, would later describe her as an introvert, not antisocial but introspective. Even at home she enjoyed privacy, staying in her room much of the time. By contrast, Sam was extroverted and gregarious.

Although the Bryans were a close-knit family, a certain Spartan restraint pervaded the household. By 1955 most American families had television, but the Bryans were among the holdouts who did not own a set.

"Frugality had nothing to do with it," Sam recalled. "It was just that that was not how we spent our time. If you wanted entertainment, you read a book."

Lesley Emmington, a girlhood chum of Stephanie's, much later remembered the Bryans as New Englanders "bound and driven by pedigree." Stephanie's middle name, Randolph, and Sam's real first name, Rutledge, were taken from statesmen of the Revolutionary era, both probably Bryan forebears. Moving to California had been traumatic for the family because the standards they had cherished in the East meant so little in the West.

"They were ducks out of water," Lesley said. "In everything, they worshiped quality. If it was leather, it had to be the finest leather. If it was a book of Beatrix Potter, it had to be the first edition of Beatrix Potter. If it was the first course to a dinner party, it had to be oysters. The skirts that the girls wore had to be pure wool. The Bryans were not trying to high-hat us, but they just lived on a different plane."

Mary Bryan was a methodical mother. Stephanie, whose last class at school ended at three-fifteen, was expected home at four o'clock—a rule she understood and dependably obeyed. Therefore, on Thursday, April 28, when she had neither appeared nor called by four-fifteen, Mary began to worry and started telephoning her daughter's friends.

The girl's delinquency, though minor, was particularly vexing to her mother because that evening the Bryans were due to attend a garden show in the Oakland Auditorium with friends. Mary needed to be on her way well before six o'clock, when the group was to assemble at Dr. Bryan's office. Stephanie was aware of these arrangements.

Ironically, as Mary Bryan was phoning Stephanie's friends one after another, it did not occur to her to call a girl named Mary Ann Stewart. Mary Ann was one of the first girls Stephanie had befriended at Willard after transferring there in 1953 from Friends Academy, a private school in South Dartmouth, Massachusetts.* Formerly Mary Ann had lived near the Bryans, but she had moved some distance away so did not often accompany Stephanie home anymore.

As call after call produced no word of her daughter, Mary Bryan's agitation grew. At four-thirty she phoned Willard Junior High, but the switchboard was closed. Finally, at about six-fifteen, she went to the school herself and searched the halls, but no one there knew anything of Stephanie's whereabouts.

Dr. Bryan got his first inkling of the trouble when his wife failed to appear to go to the garden show. When he called home to find out what was wrong, the phone was answered by his mother-in-law, Cora Marks, who lived with the family.

"Stephanie's not home yet," she said. "Mary has gone to try to find her."

When Mary returned home soon thereafter, deeply disturbed, she returned her husband's call and then got friends to drive her to his office. From there, at 6:43 P.M., he called in the first report of Stephanie's absence to the Berkeley police. The case was given the number J-22219, and it was assigned to Officer Willard Hutchins. It would monopolize his time and effort for almost the next full year.

(Ironically, a hint that something was wrong had reached the *Berkeley Daily Gazette* city desk some two-and-a-half hours before the doctor's first call to the police—perhaps even before Stephanie's mother had grown alarmed. Not long after four o'clock, City Editor Everett Johannes had taken a spate of phone calls from excited citizens, all with substantially the same

---

* Sending her children to a public school across town in Berkeley at first troubled Mrs. Bryan, who asked Lesley's mother, Margaret Emmington, "Don't you worry about your children attending school on the other side of College Avenue?" Mrs. Emmington responded, "Why would I worry about that?"—an answer that would cause her regret after Stephanie's tragedy.

message: "Hey, I just saw some guy beating hell out of a girl in a car!" Johannes had checked with the Berkeley police at once, but at that point they had known nothing of such an incident. The worst of the irony was that when the *Gazette* received its calls, Stephanie was probably alive; by the time of her father's report at 6:43 she may well have been dead.)

Abandoning the garden show plans, the Bryans returned to the school, where Hutchins awaited them. With him they explored every room but found no trace of their daughter. Then they proceeded to the Claremont Hotel, knowing that Stephanie often used a shortcut across its grounds on her way home. Their search there went on until midnight, when they went home to await the daylight that would enable them to continue.

Meanwhile Berkeley police had been combing the neighborhood— checking soda fountains, skating rinks, movie houses, and hospitals. They made a house-to-house canvass along Alvarado Road and talked to the Claremont's manager, turning up nothing. An all-points bulletin listing Stephanie as a missing juvenile was issued at 9:45 P.M.—three hours after Dr. Bryan's first report.

Stephanie's habitual shortcut took her along a garden path on the Claremont property and then across the parking lot. The far side of the lot was bordered by a woodsy thicket of lush old trees ensnarled in vines—a planned buffer between the hotel grounds and the residential neighborhood beyond. Through this growth the landscapers had cleared a path leading uphill from the parking area to an outlet on Alvarado Road almost within sight of the Bryan residence. Over time, arching tree branches had turned this path into a wooded tunnel perhaps ten feet wide and a hundred feet long. It might have looked like an enchanted forest scene, but it was also—detectives later concluded— a place where anyone lurking among the trees could go unnoticed.

In using this shortcut, Stephanie was not flouting her parents' wishes; Mary Bryan herself considered this route a commonsense alternative to a dangerous street with heavy traffic. Stephanie's walk from the shortcut to her home usually took about ten minutes.

The Berkeley police would expend countless man-hours tracing Stephanie's movements on the day she vanished. A little after eight that morning, on his way to work, Dr. Bryan had dropped off Stephanie and her sister Cheryl at Willard Junior High. Cheryl, two years younger than Stephanie, was a seventh grader. The sisters had attended all their classes that day and encountered each other in the hall at least once, after lunch.

Sergeant Basil Rebstock and Officer Don Kent spent most of Friday, April 29, at Willard, talking to Stephanie's classmates. Her final class the day before had been gym, where several girls remembered seeing her. Evelyn

Burton's gym locker was next to Stephanie's, and they had dressed together. Evelyn recalled Stephanie's full petticoat.

Mary Ann Stewart, the girl Stephanie's mother had neglected to call, gave Rebstock and Kent their most productive interview. At three-fifteen the bell had rung, dismissing classes for the day, and Mary Ann had joined Stephanie by chance on her homeward walk, as she was headed for a lesson at the Berkeley Tennis Club that adjoined the Claremont. Stephanie was complaining, Mary Ann told the officers, because her mother would not let her have a formal gown for an upcoming May Day event at school.

"Maybe she just decided to run away," Rebstock suggested.

"Oh, no, she's not that type," Mary Ann responded, voicing an opinion shared by several other girls interviewed. Stephanie's disappointment about the formal was a trivial thing, really, all concurred.

"Try to remember, did you notice any suspicious persons or cars that might have followed you during your walk?" Rebstock asked Mary Ann.

"No, nothing like that."

Willard Junior High was (and is) situated on the Berkeley flatlands at Telegraph Avenue and Stuart Street, seven blocks south of the U.C. campus and more than a mile from the Bryans' foothill residence. On that dark afternoon the girls' route took them three blocks south from the school to heavily traveled Ashby Avenue, then east on Ashby to the Tennis Club with three stops along the way.

Their first stop was at a branch of the Berkeley Public Library, where Stephanie checked out two books, *Sue Barton, Staff Nurse* and *Two's Company.* Library records confirmed that the books had been issued to her at exactly three-thirty.

From the library the girls continued east to the Elmwood Pet Shop, just a few doors off Ashby on College Avenue. Stephanie was saving from her allowance to buy a parakeet, and on this day she bought a booklet, "Everything About Parakeets." The shop's proprietor, Frank Sullivan, remembered selling it to her for twenty-five cents.

Finally, still farther east on Ashby, Stephanie and Mary Ann popped into the Dream Fluff Donut Shop for a couple of doughnuts to munch on as they continued along the street. At the intersection of Ashby and Domingo, a stone's throw from the Tennis Club and the Claremont, they parted at four o'clock or a little after. Much later, on the witness stand, Mary Ann was questioned about this parting:

"Did you have any conversation?" the district attorney asked.

"Yes, one of us said good-bye, and the other said, 'I'll see you tomorrow.' "

"Did you ever see her again?"

"No."

Nor did anyone else who knew her.

———

Talking to Stephanie's schoolmates and parents, Rebstock and Kent put together a meticulous description of the girl at the moment she vanished. Her dark hair, which hung to her shoulders in her best available photograph, had recently been cut to ear-length. The change had been so striking that when the photo was later used on a reward poster, it was retouched to suggest the shorter coiffure.

Stephanie had been dressed that Thursday in a navy-blue cardigan over a white Orlon slipover sweater. Her turquoise pleated skirt covered a white slip and several half-slips—green, pink, and white. She wore white nylon bobby socks and brown-and-white saddle oxfords. Her panties were of stretchable knitted nylon; her "Olga Originals" white Du Pont nylon brassiere, size 34-A, bore the label of I. Magnin's in San Francisco.

She had been examined two months earlier by an Oakland optometrist and fitted with glasses; she was supposed to wear them at all times but often went without. Mary Ann told the police, however, that on her last walk home she was dutifully wearing them. The glasses had slightly corrective lenses and gray-blue plastic top rims.

Stephanie was not thought to have been wearing any jewelry. For makeup, she most often wore bright-red Pond's "Honey" lipstick and colorless Revlon "Adheron" nail polish.

When she had left for school in the morning, her father said, she was probably carrying no more than a dollar in change. He doubted that her red purse, passed down to her by her mother, would have contained more than twenty-five cents at the end of the day.

The first brief press reports that a Berkeley girl was missing appeared in the Friday afternoon newspapers. At ten minutes past noon a young, red-haired navy pilot, who had read one such story in an early edition, appeared at Berkeley police headquarters and said he wished he had come sooner. His name was Allen Hill, and he was then assigned as an NROTC instructor at U.C. What he told of seeing the previous afternoon explained the vague alarms city editor Johannes had received at the *Gazette,* gave the police their first substantial (albeit fragile) clue to Stephanie's fate, and kept Case J-22219 from sinking into limbo.

Little more than two miles southeast of the Claremont Hotel, an eastern extension of Ashby led into Mt. Diablo Boulevard. This artery linked Oakland with its eastern suburbs in Contra Costa County by way of the half-mile-long Broadway Tunnel.*

---

* It is now called the Caldecott Tunnel.

Hill and his wife, Jacqueline, had been westbound on the boulevard, headed for Berkeley, about four-fifteen on Thursday afternoon. As they were approaching the tunnel, they had seen an eastbound car whip off the pavement onto the shoulder in a cloud of dust.

"A girl appeared in the open left rear window of the car," Hill said. "She had a frightened look on her face, and she yelled 'No!' very loudly. There was an individual moving rapidly from the front seat to the back, and the brown-haired girl, I'd say ten or twelve years of age, was abruptly pulled away from the window and down."

Hill said the car was a four-door 1950 or 1951 Chevrolet, medium gray with a "very oxidized" flat finish, a torpedo back, and blackwall tires. His first impulse had been to stop and help, but heavy, speeding traffic had precluded this. He and his wife had decided they would report the incident to the first officer they saw, but none had appeared as they continued home.

Stephanie's smiling picture appeared on the front page of the *San Francisco Chronicle* on Saturday morning, April 30, with a story that was alarming but far from sensational. It was headed "Berkeley Girl Disappears, Kidnap Feared," but the headline was only one column wide, and the tone of the story was muted.

For several days to come, Stephanie's disappearance would be treated officially as a missing-persons case, not a crime.

3

The Bloodsuckers

At ten minutes before midnight on Friday, some thirty-two hours after Stephanie vanished, the telephone jangled in the Bryan residence. Jarred awake by the bell, Dr. Bryan flipped a switch to activate a tape recorder that the Berkeley police had placed on his line.

In 1955, such an installation was no small undertaking. Tape recorders had been in use for a decade, but the technology was still fairly primitive. Minirecorders and cassettes were far in the future. The machine at the Bryan home, a bulky reel-to-reel job, was not police property but supplied by a private laboratory, and Pacific Telephone had sent an expert to supervise the hookup. The work had not been completed until after 10 P.M., little more than an hour and a half before the phone rang. With the reels spinning, the doctor answered.

"Hello."

"I understand you have a missing girl," a male voice said. From the tone and inflection, Bryan judged the caller to be black.

"That's right."

A prolonged, unintelligible mumble followed. After a time Bryan hung up and immediately, on another line, reported the call to Sergeant Vieira at police headquarters.

Four minutes later the doctor's phone rang again, and again he turned on the recorder. The voice was the same, but this time more distinct.

"Dr. Bryan?"

"Yeah."

"Do you want to see your daughter?"

"Yes."

"Bring five thousand dollars here on Eighth and Brush."

"Eighth and what?" Stephanie's father, only two years away from Massachusetts, had not yet familiarized himself with East Bay street geography.

"Eighth and Brush."

"How do you spell that?"

Spelling, it became obvious, was not the caller's forte.

"B-R-E-S-H."

"B-R-E-S-H? What city is it in—Oakland?" the doctor inquired.

"Yeh."

"Where in Oakland?"

"West Oakland."

"I'm new around here. Where is West Oakland?"

"Right down on this side of East Oakland." The caller's voice conveyed disdain for his educated victim. "Do you know where the Tenth Street Market is?"

"Tenth Street?" To be certain there was no misunderstanding, Dr. Bryan counted out the numbers: "One, two, three, four, five, six, seven, eight, nine, *ten?*"

"Come down to Eighth and Bersh," the caller said again, now mispronouncing the name. ("Bersh," at least, was the way the word was later transcribed.)

"What about the Tenth Street Market?" Bryan asked anew.

The caller ignored the question. "Bring it to Eighth and Brush Street."

"What do you want me to bring?"

"Five thousand dollars and you see her alive. Don't bring no police or nothing."

"Do you have any proof you've got her?"

"Yeh, do you want to talk to my proof?"

"I sure do." Dr. Bryan's heart pounded. Was it possible that within a few seconds he would hear Stephanie's voice?

It was not to be. At this point the caller, seemingly holding his hand over the phone, consulted with another person whose words were unintelligible in the background.

Finally Bryan said, "Hello?"

"Yeh," the caller responded.

"What is the proof?"

"Ain't no proof. Just a chance you going to have to take. When you bring it, she will be turned loose."

"Turned loose where?"

"Just bring it. Don't try to stall for no police now," the caller warned again. "If you want to see her, just bring it. If anything goes wrong, it will be your daughter's life, not mine."

"O.K. Thanks," Bryan responded.

"Mmmm-m-m, uh-huh."

There was a click at the other end of the line.

Deeply shaken, Bryan instantly reported again to the Berkeley police, who were by now on full alert. In the minutes between the two phone calls Vieira had passed the news of the ransom demand to three of his superiors—Captains Addison Fording and Laurence Laird and homicide Inspector

William Robinson. He also had notified the neighboring police department in Oakland, where men were now standing by, ready to move.

"Are you ready to keep the rendezvous?" Vieira asked the doctor. "Can you handle it?"

"Certainly."

"Then stay right there. We'll be right over."

Inspector Art Lyman, Officer Hutchins, and Policewoman Marian Clark soon arrived at the Bryan residence. Overall, ninety minutes were consumed setting up the rendezvous arrangements. It was 1:30 A.M. when the doctor set out for Eighth and Brush Streets in Oakland, driving his own car, a dark-green 1949 Buick sedan. He carried a dummy package simulating $5,000 in small bills. Beside him in the passenger seat rode Officer Clark, playing the role of Mrs. Bryan. Lyman and Hutchins, with a radio, were hidden in the back, lying prone on the seat and floor below window level.

In plain clothes, Sergeants Vieira and Ralph Bischop and Officer Phil Mower set out for Eighth and Brush in Bischop's nondescript civilian car, timed to arrive unobtrusively ahead of Dr. Bryan's vehicle. The Oakland P.D. meanwhile dispatched an inspector, two radio officers, and a uniformed patrolman to the area.

A little before 2 A.M. the Bryan automobile reached the rendezvous site. The doctor parked at the southwest corner of the Eighth and Brush intersection, and the waiting began. After about five minutes two black men passed on foot, walking south on Eighth Street. Dr. Bryan got out of his car and took a position on the sidewalk nearby. Ten more minutes passed; then he saw one of the earlier passersby approaching.

"Are you the doctor who's supposed to deliver a package here?" the man asked.

On a prearranged signal from Bryan, all the Oakland and Berkeley officers closed in. The startled questioner, who offered no resistance, was arrested instantly. He turned out to be an eighteen-year-old former mental patient at Sonoma State Hospital. His story changed from minute to minute.

First he said a white man, who was parked with a young girl in a car two blocks away, had given him 50 cents to pick up a package from Bryan. Lyman, Bischop, and Vieira drove the suspect to his home nearby and searched it. They found nothing incriminating, but in the presence of his sister and her boyfriend the man's tale fell apart totally. He admitted plotting the shakedown with a friend, a twenty-five-year-old unemployed fry cook, who was the supposed mastermind of the idea. He offered to finger the fry cook, but a street search for him throughout West Oakland was fruitless.

Dr. Bryan declared the arrested man's voice identical to the telephone caller's, and he was booked by the Oakland police and then transferred to the jail in Berkeley. There a platoon of reporters and photographers had gathered after learning a suspect had been taken.

Perfunctory interrogation convinced the police that the suspect had nothing to do with Stephanie's disappearance, nor was he an agent for the kidnappers. It quickly became apparent that he was merely a weak-brained outsider trying to cash in on a crime crafted by someone far more cunning.

Charged with attempted extortion, the young man appeared May 3 in Berkeley Municipal Court, where his bail was set at $10,000. He came to trial four months later before Superior Court Judge Chris B. Fox, who heard the case without a jury and found him guilty. He faced five years to life in state prison, but eventually was returned instead to Sonoma State Hospital.

His accomplice, the fry cook, was arrested in the deep South in late May, three weeks after his failed crime. His case dragged on for almost a year before he went on trial for attempted extortion. With a jury of seven men and five women already seated, he suddenly changed his plea from innocent to guilty.

In their sorrow, the Bryans now became targets for other such bloodsuckers throughout California. On Saturday, April 30, the police placed a mail cover on everything addressed to the family. Three days later, on May 3, an anonymous, semiliterate letter postmarked in Oakland the previous evening appeared:

> *Bryan*
>   *don't be idiotic This is not a hoax. Don't contact any law enforces if you expect to see your girl in the near future.*
>   *Your instruction are—on Tuesday May 3 have $8,000 to $10,000 no less than $8,000 no more than $10,000 in 5-10-20—wrap it in a small box than go to the T and D theatre be in the last row of the television lounge at 9:45 There you will be contacted Give the box to your contact He will give you instruction Follow them and you will reach your child.*
>   *Don't contact any one it will take the package a while to reach me but your child will be okey if you follow instruction. If the man that contact you in the theatre is followed the instructions won't do any good.*
>   *Wear—brown hat—put pipe in mouth, don't drive your car I have my reasons for waiting before contacting you Things have been carefully planed so don't be foolish Follow instructions.*

Dr. Bryan appeared at the theater as directed, again carrying a dummy package, with Berkeley and Oakland police covering him. But no contact was made. A second letter, postmarked May 4, arrived two days later:

> *You tipped law They can't help you Only I can. You will get instructions.*

Together the two letters had one important impact on the Bryan investigation. Until now the FBI had taken part only unofficially, but under the Lindbergh Act the use of the mails for extortion made this clearly a federal case. J. Edgar Hoover immediately threw the full resources of his Bureau into the effort to find Stephanie.

The FBI lab in Washington discovered no latent fingerprints on either of the letters. Of nine prints on the envelopes, six belonged to a police sergeant who had handled them. The remaining three could not be identified.

Extortionist mischief broke out again in early July, at a time when a thirteen-year-old Alameda girl named Karen Boyington was also missing. She had vanished May 22, but the police did not yet believe her to be a victim of foul play.

On July 6 similar notes demanding cash arrived at both the Bryan and Boyington residences. Both envelopes had been postmarked at 10:30 A.M., July 5, in South San Francisco. Whether the writer was the same one who had asked the Bryans for the theater meeting in May, the ante had been raised. The new note to them, signed "NONA," was only two lines long:

> *If you want your child back send me $12000 I'll send you a letter "When to send and where."*

In like vein, the message to the Boyingtons—signed "LIZ, the Tiger"—read:

> *Get me $8000. I will send you the right time to send the money I have got your daughter.*

These notes also were forwarded to the FBI lab. For the moment it came up with little that was helpful.

Six weeks later, in late August, the mystery grew when the San Francisco FBI office received an envelope postmarked in Harbor City, a Los Angeles suburb some four hundred miles to the south.

Inside was a puzzling two-page handwritten letter to an unknown woman or girl. Perhaps the writer, after composing it, had had second thoughts about mailing it, for both pages were crumpled as if once consigned to a wastebasket. Whoever had retrieved them had tried to smooth them out. The letter read:

> *My Dearest Canice:*
> *Well here I am writing you after my long delay, until today I couldn't help it.*
> *How's things there, as for me, everything is so boring and lonesome because I'm scared.*

I'm sure you got the money for helping with the Bryan Kid, the same as I.
Mom said that if you didn't worry the law they ask questions but everything
is O.K. and I'm glad. . . .
Until I hear from you again

> *God keep you safe*
> *Laminack*

In the envelope along with this letter was a plain white, unlined half-sheet of paper measuring five by eight inches, with a hand-printed notation:

The FBI lab concluded that the Laminack envelope and its enclosures were the handiwork of the same person who had written earlier to the Boy-

---

Laminack		
	815 B--- St.	
		SF
Youth Guidance		
	Center	
		SF
182 P--- St.		
		SF

---

ingtons from South San Francisco. The crumpled Laminack letter was specifically the work of "LIZ, the Tiger"—whoever she might be—who had signed the Boyington letter. It was a reasonable inference that she was also "NONA," the Bryans' tormentor. The Bureau's handwriting and fingerprint experts could offer no clue as to her identity, though they did rule out many possibilities.

For the Berkeley police, the tantalizing line in the Laminack letter was *"I'm sure you got the money for helping with the Bryan Kid, the same as I."*

What did that mean? Nobody knew.

Nor does the author, four decades later. In the thousands of Bryan case documents that still exist, no other reference to Laminack is found. It is a page in the history of the case that remains blank.

4

Purple Fingers

Stephanie had been missing barely twenty-four hours when Sergeant Vieira picked up his phone and heard a woman's voice: "My name is Emma Lee Van Meter."

"Yes, ma'am, what can I do for you?"

"Well, maybe I saw that little girl who's missing."

Mrs. Van Meter lived in Walnut Creek, a well-to-do suburb a dozen miles east of Berkeley in Contra Costa County on the other side of the hills.

"Thursday afternoon," she related, "I was on my way home, driving east through the tunnel. The traffic was heavy, stop and go. I looked at my watch, and that's how I remember what time it was. It was about twenty minutes to five."

From her eastbound perspective on the road, Mrs. Van Meter had observed the same scene Lieutenant Allen Hill and his wife had witnessed while traveling west: an eastbound automobile spinning off the highway so violently that it stirred up the dust of the unpaved shoulder, about a quarter of a mile past the tunnel's east portal.

"There was a girl with dark hair in the rear seat," Mrs. Van Meter said, "thirteen or fourteen years old. Her face was pressed against the rear window, and she was screaming and crying. I heard her scream three times—loud, horrible screams. The driver turned around, leaned over the backseat, and started beating the girl with his fist. I saw him strike her two or three times."

Vieira decided it was unlikely that the woman on the phone could know of the similar sighting by Lieutenant Hill. Nothing about that had been in the papers yet.

"Can you describe the car?" Vieira asked.

"It was a dark-colored sedan, not very new. Maybe about 1950." Mrs. Van Meter wasn't sure of the make—maybe a Pontiac. But she was positive it had a sloped back.

Not too different from what Hill had said.

"What did the driver look like?"

"He was a white man, about forty I'd say, medium build. He was wearing a brown coat."

Soon after passing the struggle scene, Mrs. Van Meter had noticed two men standing by the road, alongside a sedan with the California State Seal on its doors. She had stopped and implored them to go back and help the girl in trouble. Instead, they had promised to call the Highway Patrol. (Though they never did, Vieira ascertained when he checked later.) Thoroughly shaken, Mrs. Van Meter had remained parked at the roadside a few minutes before driving on home.

In the ensuing days, no fewer than a dozen additional observers of the events on Mt. Diablo Boulevard came forward with eyewitness accounts.

Perhaps the most vivid was that of Percy Dappen, a gardener with the Berkeley Parks Department, who had left work about four-ten and headed for his home in Lafayette. As he passed the Claremont Hotel traveling east, a gray-green, 1949-vintage Chevrolet roared out of the hotel grounds. A frail, slender man with a "vicious, mean look on his face" was at the wheel, with a young girl as his passenger. Eastbound on Tunnel Road, the driver swerved into the westbound lane to pass Dappen, shouting insults and risking a head-on collision with an oncoming car. Dappen saw the Chevy's right-hand door swing open as it passed the intersection of Tunnel and Alvarado Roads. The girl seemed to be trying to jump out, but the driver pulled her back and slammed the door. (At the time, that location held no special significance for Dappen. Only later, from the newspapers, did he learn that Alvarado Road was where Stephanie Bryan lived.)

In creeping traffic midway through the tunnel, the Chevy driver began honking his horn, setting up a loud, cacophonic reverberation. Emerging from the tunnel, Dappen saw him pull off the road and start to beat the girl, much as described by others.

"I recall seeing him with both hands raised, as with probably some sort of small club in his hand, swinging down with a terrific speed," Dappen said.

Six employees of the Marchant Calculating Machine Company, headed home from work in two carpools, had seen something similar. So had Rachel Dotson, a schoolteacher; Mrs. Lorene Yetter, a pregnant Walnut Creek woman returning from a doctor's appointment; and four men riding eastbound together—James Thomas McDonald, Sam Marshall, Terrell Goodman, and Wayne Holcomb.

The latter four first noticed the old, torpedo-shaped Chevrolet or Pontiac while in the tunnel. It was two cars ahead of them, weaving in and out of its lane, alternatively slowing and speeding. Then they witnessed the battering episode, and reported it to Highway Patrolman Charles Harry Jaeger when they saw him farther down the road. Jaeger headed back west watching for the offending car but could not find it. Somehow the driver had made a clean getaway, presumably with the terrified little girl still riding as his captive.

———

Every detective, traffic cop, and insurance adjuster knows that multiple observers of the same event, all well meaning, often give vastly conflicting descriptions of it. The beating incident on Mt. Diablo Boulevard was a classic case in point. Time estimates for it ranged over a span of more than an hour. Mrs. Van Meter's recollection of the girl's face "pressed against the rear window" contradicted the statements of Hill and Mrs. Yetter that the window was open. Dappen, Mrs. Dotson, and two of the Marchant carpoolers, Edwin Briggs and Fay Clark, placed both assailant and victim in the front seat.

Guesses about the driver's age varied from twenty-five to fifty. Marshall's description of a slight-built assailant with a "receding hairline" conflicted with Mrs. Yetter's memory of "dark, bushy hair that fell forward when he leaned over." One of the Marchant employees, Howard Boardman, said the man was a husky 200-pounder, and another, Russell Chivers, described him as "swarthy, either Mexican or Portagee, with black hair and sunglasses." Most witnesses said the driver was wearing jeans and a leather jacket or other hunting clothes, but according to Dappen he "was well dressed, wearing either a sport coat or a suit coat and a white shirt, also a bow tie." Mrs. Van Meter's description of the girl's "shoulder-length hair" was contrary to police knowledge that Stephanie's hair had been bobbed.

To the investigators trying to reconcile the conflicts, most troubling of all was the certainty of the six Marchant employees that the assault had taken place at about three-thirty. They fixed the time by when they had quit work. Yet at three-thirty Stephanie had still been safe, checking out her library books in Berkeley. Moreover, the location of the attack, as pinpointed by the Marchant group, was three-tenths of a mile from where most of the others placed it.

Could there have been two separate struggle incidents? If so, did they involve the same assailant? Did they even involve the same girl?

Despite their discrepancies, the conflicting observations convinced the police that an assault of *some* nature had indeed occurred. *Some* young girl had been slapped around, or worse, by *some* man. No witness had gotten the license number of the assailant's car; in Dappen's version of the incident, the rear plate of the suspect's car was missing.*

By Monday morning, May 2, Stephanie had been gone for eighty-seven hours. In the newspapers, the story was still on the front pages, but its excitement value was inevitably waning. The *Chronicle* had it well below the fold, and the lead angle was in fact incidental to the Stephanie Bryan mystery. An all-day search on Sunday had turned up no new clues about the girl

---

* Much later, when Burton Abbott's auto was impounded, his rear plate was intact.

but had revealed the desiccated corpse of a toothless old woman in a section of sewer pipe lying on the ground alongside Tunnel Road. She had been there at least a year. Missing-persons files shed no light on her identity, and police took her to be a suicide. Her head rested on a purse that contained five silver dollars. Apart from this oddity, the *Chronicle's* Stephanie story was dull and pessimistic: "Police admitted they are now completely without leads concerning the girl's whereabouts."

Many casual newspaper readers were still only vaguely aware of the Stephanie Bryan case. Among them were David Tyree, an electrician, and his wife, Effie. Before 7 o'clock that Monday morning they left their home in the Contra Costa County town of San Pablo to drive their son, Ernest, to school in Concord some fifteen miles inland. The Tyrees had moved from Concord just recently, and the boy was finishing out the year at Loma Vista Junior High there before changing schools.

At age sixty-seven, David Tyree was described by a friend as "a cantankerous, ornery old man." He was uncommonly old to be the father of a junior high school boy, but such he was. On Sunday night he had taken a laxative, and en route to Concord he felt an urgent need to relieve himself. So on a remote stretch of winding Franklin Canyon Road, about four miles east of Highway 40, he stopped the car, climbed over a fence, and headed into the brush.

Returning a few minutes later, Tyree noticed a book on the road shoulder, about two feet off the pavement, and picked it up. Because it appeared to be a schoolbook, Tyree handed it to his son; it seemed the natural thing to do. The boy ripped off the protective jacket, which was tattered and soiled, and threw it away. When he got to school, a little after 8 o'clock, he tossed the book into his locker.

As the days passed, new clues about Stephanie were few and meager but assiduously pursued:

• There were inevitable "sightings" of the girl over a wide area. She was variously reported wearing a black suit in Marin County, aboard the Western Pacific Zephyr in Stockton; trudging along a rural road in Kern County 250 miles to the south; in company with four men between Novato and Petaluma; and high on drugs in an Oakland brothel.

• A nut caller to Dean Mattox, a San Francisco radio personality, promised news of Stephanie if he would include a code signal on his next broadcast. He was instructed to say, "I'd like to hear from my chum from the Owl Drug Store."

• A food storeroom helper at the Claremont Hotel informed the police that its incinerator had not been cleaned since two days before Stephanie's disappearance. "It would reduce flesh just like a crematorium," the man said. The incinerator contents were sifted but yielded nothing.

• Tips began pouring in from victims of stalkers, molesters, pedophiles, and perverts. Patricia Cobb, a thirteen-year-old friend of Stephanie's, told of a black man with a chain around his neck who lurked near the California School for the Blind in Berkeley. Another girl reported seeing a man of identical description twice near Stephanie's home.

One by one, all these leads fizzled. But the searching for the girl, alive or dead, went on. Beginning Tuesday, May 3, five thousand fliers bearing Stephanie's picture and dental chart were mailed to law enforcement agencies throughout eleven western states.

On Wednesday, Colonel Alfred Budd Marks flew in from Grosse Pointe, Michigan. He was Stephanie's uncle—Mary Bryan's brother—and the commander of the Michigan Air National Guard. Two of his pilots followed him. In a borrowed observation plane Marks overflew the hill country between Berkeley and the 3,849-foot summit of Mt. Diablo* seventeen miles to the east. He was dismayed by what he saw: "about a thousand miles of small backwoods roads that might need exploration." The following day the colonel returned to the skies in a helicopter.

Although the East Bay was a megalopolis of close to a million people, in 1955, it retained certain small-town virtues, including a neighborhood mentality. People who lived there were concerned with one another to a degree not often found in large cities. This attitude was due in no small part to the East Bay's commanding newspaper, the *Oakland Tribune*. Although oriented globally and nationally (befitting a paper whose publisher's son** aspired to be President of the United States), the *Trib* never forgot its grass roots. It went after the big stories but also, a reporter from that time would recall, "covered every dog fight and PTA meeting."

Thus when Stephanie Bryan disappeared, genuine anguish ran deep through the Bay Area community, and volunteers turned out by the hundreds to join the search for her. On Sunday, May 8, there were twelve hundred in the field. The Boy Scouts, Explorer Scouts, Dads' Clubs, and the Council of Scouts' Fathers joined the Sheriff's Mounted Patrol to scour thirty-two square

---

* A surveyor's monument atop Mt. Diablo ("Devil Mountain"), a commanding peak visible for up to a hundred miles, is the base point for geographical surveys throughout Northern California.

** William F. Knowland, minority leader of the United States Senate in 1955.

miles of hills and canyons on a fifteen-mile front. From eight that morning until four-thirty in the afternoon they beat the bushes. Six National Guard Jeeps combed the rougher terrain.

A few yards off Mt. Diablo Boulevard and a mile east of the tunnel, not far from where the car struggle had been observed, a blood-spattered bed-spread was found. Its link to Stephanie would remain dubious, however, because, ironically, Dr. Bryan did not know his daughter's blood type. Not even Baker Memorial Hospital in Boston, where Stephanie was born, had a record of it.

For the Bryans, this was a time not only of anxiety and grief but also of rigorous mental demands. By now foul play was assumed, and the doctor endured a grueling interview with three FBI agents who came to his home on Thursday, May 5.

"Can you suggest any suspects—no matter how unlikely?" asked Special Agent William Whelan, head of the Bureau's San Francisco office.

Dr. Bryan replied thoughtfully. He had no real reason to suspect anyone, he said, but he mentioned a shell-shocked war veteran who worked at a nearby service station; a certain newsboy his daughters considered "repulsive," though he didn't know why; and a rather odd male accompanist at the studio where Stephanie took ballet.

"Tell us about your daughter," Whelan said. He wanted every detail of her past and present. The agents elicited such specifics as a small strawberry birthmark on the nape of her neck and a vaccination scar on her left hip. She bore no surgical scars, her only surgery having been a tonsillectomy. At fourteen she retained the juvenile habit of biting her nails. Near-constant dental care had given Stephanie an exceptionally fine set of white, even teeth. Besides amalgam fillings in practically all her molars, she had four inlays, two of plastic and two of gold.

The agents compiled a list of Stephanie's relatives, including her siblings (Sam, Cheryl, Estelle, and Beatrice), her grandparents, and aunts, uncles, and cousins scattered from Rhode Island to Alaska. The doctor guessed that Kay Yonekura, a classmate at Willard, was her "best friend."

"How about boys?" one of the agents inquired.

"She doesn't seem to have any interest in boys at all. She has never had anything that could be called a date. We have never permitted her or any of the children to be out alone at night."

"Did she correspond with anyone?"

"I think she wrote to a girl named Macomber and one named Bliss. They went to Friends Academy with her."

"Doctor," Whelan said, "there's one more painful matter we have to talk about. Are you prepared to pay a ransom?"

"We'll pay whatever it takes."

"You're ready to pauperize yourself?"

"Of course. But I can't believe they took her for money. I'm not a wealthy man by any means. Why would any kidnapper think so?"

Whelan glanced around the room. "Well, this is a pretty fine house you have here."

Indeed it was. The facade, rising three stories from the street and dominated by huge arched windows and overhanging balconies, conveyed an impression of spacious elegance.

"I suppose so," the doctor conceded. "The house is where our money's tied up, but we needed a big place for the family. Otherwise we don't live like rich people. My car is almost seven years old."

"Do you come from a wealthy family?" Whelan inquired.

"Mary's brother—Colonel Marks, who's out here now from Michigan to help with the search—is married to a tremendously wealthy woman. But hardly anyone knows we're related to him. This is the first time he's visited us in years."

"Have you had any publicity that might lead someone to think you were wealthy?"

"No. The only time we've been mentioned in the paper lately was last month when Mary had a party here for the Radcliffe College alumni. There was a note about it in the society column."

"If you do get a ransom demand, Doctor, how much can you pay? What are your resources?"

Stephanie's father paused, considering.

"Well," he replied at length, "I suppose ten thousand dollars wouldn't be too great a strain. Colonel Marks has told us that he and his wife will guarantee any check we have to write."

"How much could they guarantee?"

"I'm guessing. Maybe fifty thousand. Maybe much more than that."

Another pause.

"I've got to tell you, though," the doctor continued, "Mary and I have discussed this, and we won't pay a ransom without positive assurance that Stephanie will be returned. If we hear from the kidnapper, I'll try to stall. I intend to tell him I have practically no liquid assets and will have to borrow on my insurance or get the money from friends at the hospital. It should be reasonable to ask for at least a day to get the money together."

Dr. Bryan and his wife had worked out a plan to make sure, before paying any ransom, that Stephanie was alive:

"We're going to ask for a dated note in Stephanie's handwriting. We'll ask that she write all about the camping trip we took last summer. She remembers all the details, and nobody else would know them."

"It might help us to know your itinerary on that trip," Whelan suggested.

The doctor consulted some records. Two days after the Fourth of July in 1954, the Bryans had set out in the family car for California's far northern mountains and forests. They had spent two nights at Clear Lake and five at Richardson Grove before proceeding to Patricks Point on the coast above Eureka. From there they had driven east through the rugged and scenic Trinity Alps to Lassen Park, where they camped for five or six more days before returning home. It had been a wonderful time.

"We need to talk to Mrs. Bryan also, Doctor," Whelan said as the session ended.

"Not today, please," Dr. Bryan pleaded. By now it was midafternoon, about time for Stephanie's three school-age siblings—Cheryl, Sam, and Estelle—to come home. The FBI men agreed to return the next morning.

In the eight days since their daughter's disappearance, the Bryans had made a determined effort to keep the household on an even keel. The remaining school-age children still attended classes each day, and the mother and father tried to function effectively as parents. They were only partially successful.

"They were very upset," Sam Bryan would recall in 1993. "I remember being home in the evening, just a big flurry of activity, I can remember all this going on around me, but I can't remember anything that was said. We children were kept in the dark as much as we could be. They should have told us what was going on. What it means to me is that my parents kept it all inside."

Even in happy times Dr. Bryan had often seemed distant and forbidding to his children—at least to Sam, at age ten.

"My parents shrank away from the world," he later would conclude. "My dad had been a basketball player in school, but he never played basketball with me, and I wasn't allowed to play baseball."

During the uncertain weeks after Stephanie's disappearance, however, the doctor tried earnestly to lower whatever barriers of aloofness he had unwittingly erected between himself and his children.

"One night Estelle, Cheryl, and I went out with my dad to put up reward posters," Sam remembered. "We ended up way out in the Delta someplace and stopped at a hot dog stand where we all had hot dogs 'with everything.' I had never had onions before, as far as I know. It was unheard of!"

After four decades, that carefree stop for wieners somewhere amid the tortuous roads and marshy islands of the Sacramento–San Joaquin Delta remained a memory precious to Sam Bryan.

During the sad summer that followed, the doctor also took his three oldest remaining children on their first pack trip into the High Sierra, trying to recapture some of the joys of the previous year's camping vacation. Mary was left behind to care for three-year-old Beatrice and face alone the demands imposed by the continuing criminal investigation.

In their talks with Stephanie's mother, the FBI men focused on the girl's intimate life and personal relationships, exploring seemingly trivial matters that might prove important.

Diligently Mary searched closets and dresser drawers for duplicates of the girl's garments, including her white nylon stretch socks, panty girdle, bra, and inner sweater. All were turned over to the agents. Also found were three nametags like those sewn into the missing girl's clothes, special tags from a shop in Harvard Square in Cambridge, Massachusetts, with the name "Stephanie Bryan" woven into them.

Three of Stephanie's school notebooks, which Mary also produced, bore examples of her penmanship and hand printing. Another specimen of the girl's schoolwork, supplied by Willard Principal H. N. McClellan, was an original composition she had handed in on April 22, six days before she vanished. She had titled it "There's a Song in My Heart."

Seventy-five miles southeast of Berkeley, the tiny community of Keyes was a dot on the map between Modesto and Turlock in Stanislaus County. It was one of the numerous villages straddling Route 99—in 1955 the main north–south artery on the vast flat floor of the San Joaquin Valley.

About 8 o'clock on Wednesday evening, May 4, a gray Pontiac sedan of 1949–50 vintage pulled up to the pumps at Bob's Service Station in Keyes, on Route 99's northbound frontage road. As the attendant, twenty-five-year-old Mack Jensen,* approached the vehicle, he saw what looked like three human fingers protruding from the crack of the trunk lid. They were on the right side, about eighteen inches from the lid's forward edge. Not believing his eyes, Jensen bent down for a second look.

That the fingers were real, he was certain—small and slender, purplish in color, with white nails. Without forethought he stepped back and shouted to the man behind the wheel:

"Dammit all, fellow, you got somebody's hand caught back here!"

Instantly the driver, a dark-haired man Jensen judged to be thirty-five or forty, slammed the car into gear and sped away, leaving burned rubber on the pavement and heading east on Christine Avenue, a crossroad. Jensen tried to get the license number, but the vehicle had no rear plate.

From Paul's Bar, adjoining the service station, Jensen called the police in nearby Turlock, who logged the complaint at 8:05 and relayed it to the Stanislaus County sheriff's office in Modesto. Undersheriff Harry Oliver, on duty, put out an all-points bulletin for the suspect automobile and kept five patrol cars on duty all night searching for it.

The all-points bulletin sent both a wave of shock and a glimmer of hope

---

* Fictitious name.

through Berkeley police headquarters. Could the fingers have been Stephanie Bryan's? This might be the first break in the mystery that until now had defied Berkeley's best efforts. Jensen's description of the car matched closely, if not precisely, that given by witnesses to the Mt. Diablo Boulevard scuffle. Chevrolets and Pontiacs looked a lot alike.

At forty minutes past midnight, Sergeant Bischop and Willard Hutchins set out from Berkeley on a long ride to Keyes, much of it over treacherous, windswept mountain roads. They arrived at 2:30 A.M. and found Undersheriff Oliver and Inspector Larry Martin waiting to brief them. As the early-morning hours crept by, the sheriff's cars scouring the countryside were reporting in, all results negative.

"Let's put the story on the civilian radio," one of the officers suggested. "Maybe someone in the boondocks will recognize the automobile Jensen saw."

This too was done, but with no response.

After their briefing, the Berkeley officers went on to Bob's Service Station to talk to Jensen—who alone had seen the purple fingers. He made a poor first impression on Hutchins.

"The complainant does not appear, to me at least, to possess normal intelligence," Hutchins wrote in his report. "He is highly nervous, has tremors, becomes emotional when questioned closely, and all in all appeared to me as unstable."

Nevertheless, Jensen's story remained constant with a ring of truth.

"You're sure you saw real fingers, that there wasn't some kind of dummy or doll in that trunk?" Hutchins asked him.

"Oh, no, sir. Those fingers were real all right," Jensen insisted.

"Did you touch them?"

"No, only looked."

"Did you see blood on them?"

"No."

"Which fingers of the hand were they?"

"Either the last three or middle three fingers, not the thumb. I could see them almost to the second knuckles."

"Which hand did they belong to, right or left?"

"I couldn't tell."

"What can you tell us about that Pontiac? You say it was gray. Light or dark?"

"Medium gray," Jensen replied.

"And it was a sedan. Two-door or four-door?"

"Probably a two-door."

"Any spotlights, special lights, aerials?"

Jensen couldn't remember about those. On another matter, however, he held a firm opinion: Automatic transmissions had been available on 1949 and 1950 Pontiacs, but Jensen was sure the suspect car was a stick-shift model. He distinctly remembered hearing the gears grind loudly as the driver made his getaway.

This was corroborated when Hutchins examined the tire tracks of the fleeing vehicle. There was a skip in the trail of burned rubber, indicating the instant during the manual shifting when the wheels had ceased to spin.

Jensen described the driver as heavyset. He had seen the driver's broad chest and shoulders. He had no idea of the man's voice.

Earlier Hutchins and Bischop had suggested to the sheriff's men that the episode might be a hoax—with Jensen as the victim, not the perpetrator. Was he the butt of someone's joke? The local officers who knew him considered this possibility remote.

After questioning Jensen, the Berkeley officers talked to the bartender at Paul's, from which he had made his original call to the Turlock police.

"That man was really scared when he came in here," the bartender said. "He wasn't faking."

Still, Jensen's story bordered on fantasy. Was it even possible for the fingers to have protruded from the trunk in the manner Jensen described?

At the local Pontiac agency, Bischop and Hutchins learned that trunk lids on 1949 and 1950 Pontiacs would remain in the down position even if not latched, and they could be closed on human fingers without much damage or even much pain. By experimenting, the officers concluded that for anyone's hand to have been in the the position Jensen described, the wrist and forearm would have had to cross over in front of the spare tire. While it would have been difficult to stuff a corpse into a trunk that way, it was certainly possible.

Bischop and Hutchins devoted Thursday afternoon to a massive search of the Keyes countryside. They visited everywhere a car or body might have been hidden—the spots where hot cars had been found or loot discovered in the past. They checked idle industrial plants in the area.

In tiny Keyes, word of the big police search spread rapidly. Reports of "suspicious" observations finally began to stack up on the sheriff's desk. Hopes for a break in the case rose in early afternoon when a nine-year-old boy, Jimmy Burnes, told school friends he had seen a man get out of a car in front of his house, run to the rear and slam the trunk, and drive off at high speed. Jimmy was pulled out of class and questioned, but the officers ultimately decided that what he had seen, if anything, was a drunken neighbor.

While checking out all Pontiacs registered in the area, the Berkeley officers found a slope-backed one with the right side of the trunk lid warped and bent. They experienced a brief flush of excitement. However, the story of the woman who owned the car—that she had bent her trunk lid while improperly positioning her spare tire—turned out to be both true and provable.

Fighting fatigue, Hutchins and Bischop began the long drive home, arriving in Berkeley twenty-five sleepless hours after leaving on their mission. At one-thirty Friday morning the exhausted Hutchins turned in his six-page, single-spaced report. Although he still had doubts about Jensen's intelligence, he was convinced of his truthfulness.

"I feel the complainant did indeed see fingers," he wrote. "I am of the opinion that it is a valid complaint. At any rate I cannot disprove it."

Eight days had now passed since Stephanie's disappearance, and the police were still not far from square one.

The Mt. Diablo Boulevard struggle was amply established, but neither the man nor the girl involved had been positively identified. It was a good guess that Stephanie's assumed abductor had taken her east, but where east? On a road leading to Keyes? Perhaps.

On Monday, May 9, the investigators got their first real break.

In San Pablo, after reading something about Stephanie in his newspaper, David Tyree suddenly remembered the textbook he had found a week earlier on Franklin Canyon Road. At last he went to the police with the story and told them he had given the book to his boy, Ernest. Officer Hutchins went to Ernest's school and obtained the book from his locker.

Its title was *Modern French Course, Book I.* In it Hutchins found the handwritten name "Stephanie Bryan."

5

The French Book

The weather had been clear on Monday morning, May 2, when David Tyree recovered the French textbook from the shoulder of Franklin Canyon Road. And the volume itself had been dry except for some dew on the jacket—despite the fact that it had rained in Franklin Canyon most of the weekend, at least through Sunday morning. So clearly Stephanie Bryan's book had been left there no earlier than Sunday afternoon—three days after her disappearance.

Where, then, had it been—and where had she been—during that interval?

Besides Stephanie's name, the book bore that of Evelyn Prisk, her French teacher at Willard, and in the upper left corner was the pen-printed notation "Francais, H-9." A slip on the flyleaf identified the book as Number 100 in the school's inventory.

The FBI sent the French book to its lab in Washington for fingerprint examination, with disappointing results. Fourteen latent fingerprints and palm prints were found, all on the inside pages, but seven of them belonged to Jo Anne Kido, now a student at Berkeley High, who had formerly used the book at Willard. The rest defied identification, matching none in the Bureau's files; at this point the lab had no specimens from Stephanie for comparison. All the fingerprints were of small fingers.

The FBI had officially entered the Bryan case on orders from Washington one day after the second extortion note clearly established federal jurisdiction. This was the sort of high-visibility, high-emotion case that Director J. Edgar Hoover loved. It aroused the deep passions of decent citizens who identified with the family of the wholesome young girl who was missing—the victim of who knew what atrocity. Because of the paucity of clues, the reason for Stephanie Bryan's abduction was shrouded in mystery, but her nubile attractiveness suggested a sex motive that inflamed the public. The case cast Hoover's agents as white knights.

The Bureau's first action, upon its formal intercession, was to stake out two of its men, Richard E. Luebben and James C. Connors, in the Bryan residence—a step proven in past cases to have dual value. Not only did it give the Bureau a front-line command post, but the agents' friendly presence helped stabilize the distraught family. Luebben and Connors would remain in the house on Alvarado Road for eleven days. One agent shared the room of ten-year-old Sam Bryan, who would remember him forever as a friend in time of need.

"The FBI man was the only one who paid any attention to me," Sam told the author in 1993.

Laboratory expertise was one of two major assets that the FBI brought to the investigation. The other was an enormous infusion of manpower, augmenting the strained resources of the Berkeley Police.

The Bureau could and did throw its agents into the Bryan case in platoon strength. On May 5 and 6 they checked and cleared 159 registered sex offenders in Alameda and Contra Costa counties. During a second sweep seven weeks later, an additional 135 men with sex-crime records were tracked down in the Bay Area—all again having confirmable evidence of innocence.

The FBI also deployed its huge resources in a long-shot effort to identify, by process of elimination, the car seen by so many but identified by none in the girl-battering episode. On May 9 the Bureau called in all witnesses to the incident on Mt. Diablo Boulevard for a joint brainstorming session. Pictures of various automobiles were shown them, and they were asked to plumb their subconscious for clues they might have disregarded. The response, while minimal, gave the agents hope.

Jacqueline Hill, who with her husband had been the first to report the scuffle, dredged up a fleeting impression that one letter of the license might have been Y or V. Other responses strengthened a consensus on Y. With only this slim hunch to go on, Agents Paul J. Malone and Edwin P. Park went to the Department of Motor Vehicles in Sacramento.

"How many California license plates contain a Y?" they asked.

"About ninety thousand, mostly in Southern California" was the discouraging reply.

This was before the time of instant computer searches. Malone and Park spent two days combing manually through the Y registrations for Chevrolets in the Bay Area. They eliminated trucks, convertibles, and station wagons. With their final list in hand, they headed back to Berkeley, and G-men were deployed throughout all nine Bay Area counties, interviewing every Y plate owner. The whereabouts of each at 4 P.M. on April 28 was checked out, with special attention to those in the U.C.-Berkeley area.

A list of eighty-eight Chevy owners cleared of suspicion was attached to the agents' report. How many possible suspects they found went unrecorded.

On the sixth day of the Bryan mail cover a strange letter appeared, post-marked at the little town of Los Gatos in the foothills of the Santa Cruz Mountains fifty miles to the south. Its ostensible sender was one Harold A. Hansen, who operated something called the Welget Health Center. It invited Dr. Bryan to visit Hansen "in regard to the whereabouts of Stephanie Bryan." The doctor turned the message over to the FBI, and Special Agent D. Ray Quinn was dispatched to Los Gatos.

Hansen examined the letter and declared, "This is not from me; I've never seen it before. But I think I know who sent it."

The actual writer, Hansen said, had to be Amelia Benton* of Palo Alto, a patron of the health center. Quinn recognized the name; Stephanie's father had already received several rambling, incoherent letters on other matters from Miss Benton.

"She's psychopathic," Hansen told Quinn. "She believes that I am God and she is the son of God."

Hoover's men again demonstrated their doggedness when a man named Carl Nigh, preparing to sell his blue 1949 Oldsmobile, was observed washing it at the foot of Fifth Avenue in Oakland. The observer reported what looked like bloodstains on the car's upholstery.

"Yeah, that's blood," Nigh acknowledged when an agent approached him. "My brother got it there while he was screwin' his lady in the front seat. She was a virgin—a thirty-one-year-old virgin."

The brother, John Nigh, readily confirmed the encounter:

"Yeah, I banged her on the first day of her period. It was in a drive-in movie in El Cerrito. Ask her; she'll tell you."

And she did. The "virgin" turned out to be a cooperative married woman, identified by the FBI only as "Mrs. Gordon." Cheerfully she gave a blood sample to confirm that the stains on the car seat were hers.

Nigh's innocence in the Bryan case was further proved when he was found to have kept a doctor's appointment at 4 P.M. on April 28, the precise hour of Stephanie's disappearance.

The investigation of the drive-in lover would have ended at that point, had not the agents, in their thoroughness, talked to some of his other girlfriends. One of them happened to mention that John Nigh was a pistol enthusiast and that she had accompanied him twice to target practice at a nearby rock quarry.

---

* In this chapter the names Amelia Benton, Carl Nigh, John Nigh, Mrs. Gordon, Brewster, Francis M. Poston, Sally Smith, Jimmy Joe Henderson, Abbie, and Terry Dawson are fictitious, but they represent real persons and the situations involving them are factual.

Early on the next Monday morning no fewer than twenty-one FBI agents swooped down on the quarry and searched all day—finding nothing. The report they submitted ran 256 pages, ending in the meek conclusion "In view of this information, John Nigh is eliminated as a suspect in this case."

At four-thirty on Saturday afternoon, May 7, a man named Brewster phoned the Berkeley police with a story that instantly grabbed their attention. On April 28, he said, he had been working as a gardener for a Mrs. Eggerson, who lived about four blocks from the Bryan home. While there, he had seen a girl he now recognized from news photos as Stephanie, riding in a gray 1951 Pontiac sedan between two neighborhood men known to him as "Christie" and "Jamison."

Brewster's report touched off a flurry of investigation, with many interviews. Finally an FBI agent took him to the house where he claimed to have worked, and they rang the doorbell.

"I've never seen this man before," declared the woman who answered.

When questioned anew, Brewster admitted he had never worked in Berkeley. He definitely had seen Stephanie with his friend Christie, he insisted, but not while gardening; he had seen them as he emerged from a house of prostitution.

"I made up the part about Mrs. Eggerson to keep my wife from finding out," he confessed.

For four more days the FBI stayed on Brewster's case, and an agent was sent across the bay to reapprehend him in Marin City. On the ride back to Berkeley, he changed his story again.

"I wasn't in no whorehouse," he said. "A white bartender got this black hooker for me, and I screwed her in the backseat of his car."

"Can you identify the bartender or the prostitute?" the G-man asked.

"I don't think so."

"Where did the act of intercourse take place?"

"I don't know, man. Do you think I was payin' attention to that?"

Brewster was turned over to Dr. Douglas M. Kelley, a police psychiatrist (whom we will meet again in another context). The doctor decided the man was "a pathological liar and a hysterical personality" who could make himself believe things that never happened.

A forty-four-year-old bachelor who had once lived near the Bryans, Francis M. Poston, became a suspect only because he drove a gray automobile and a neighbor reported him. Although his car was a 1946 Packard, totally unlike the vehicle described by the Mt. Diablo witnesses, Poston got the full FBI treatment.

At some past time, Francis had suffered a nervous breakdown. He now lived alone in another part of Berkeley and for the past few months he had been employed as a messenger at the University of California.

To be sure, Poston was a strange fellow. His boss at U.C. told an FBI agent he talked to himself a lot and seemed deeply mired in personal problems; he was the butt of many office jokes. It was unknown what time he had left work on the afternoon Stephanie vanished, but he usually stayed on the job until four-thirty.

"By the way," his boss added. "Francis has asked for a week's leave, starting May 20. He says he wants to get married."

The agent's next stop was a county office where Poston had worked for five years until fired in 1953. His troubles there had begun when he complained to his supervisor that certain women coworkers were sending "sex vibrations" through his body.

"What I need to know," he told the supervisor, "is whether these women have complained about sex vibrations from me?"

The answer she gave him is not on record, but it did not solve his problem. Several months later he asked that his desk be changed because the sex vibrations from the girl sitting opposite him were intolerable. At that point his resignation was demanded.

In the end, Poston was totally cleared as a Bryan case suspect. He had no history of violence and no record as a sex offender, and on the late afternoon of April 28 he had been at a Berkeley auto dealership having his car fixed.

In Redwood City on the San Francisco Peninsula, the police considered Sally Smith "a person of extremely low morals." Yet she supplied good tips from time to time, so they listened respectfully on May 11 when she came to them about the Bryan case. Sally considered Jimmy Joe Henderson, the ex-con husband of her sister Abbie, a likely suspect.

On Saturday evening, May 7, Abbie had called Sally in distress and asked a favor: Would Sally and her husband drive the Hendersons up Highway 40 to retrieve their disabled car? Jimmie Joe had abandoned it near Dixon, about seventeen miles south of Sacramento, with a flat tire.

The Smiths had driven the Hendersons to Dixon the next day. The crippled Henderson automobile was a gray Chevrolet, although several years older than the 1950-ish model sought by the Bryan investigators. What had aroused Sally's suspicion was a pair of girl's panties she found under the seat, stained with blood—lots of blood.

Understandably, Sally's discovery had brought on a caustic scene between Jimmy Joe and his wife. Making no pretense of fidelity, he told her the panties belonged to "some woman I picked up and had trouble with."

The wiring under the Chevy's dashboard had been torn loose, and beneath the front seat Sally had found an empty wine bottle and a blood-covered pair of men's shorts. Abbie had identified the latter, gaudily printed in red, green, white, and blue, as her husband's. The Henderson car had been towed to a service station in Dixon, but Jimmy Joe had refused to go in. In the three days that had elapsed since, Sally told the Redwood City police, she had had no further contact with Abbie or her husband.

"Do you really think your brother-in-law kidnapped Stephanie Bryan?" an officer asked her.

In response she shot him a grim look. "He's the type of person who could have done it," she said.

A ripple of interest followed a May 12 discovery in Richmond, an industrial port on the bay north of Berkeley and Contra Costa County's largest city. Two young girls playing in a park there (coincidentally Alvarado Park, sharing the name of the Bryans' street) found twelve-inch block letters fashioned from streambed moss spelling "HELP STEP." FBI agents concluded the message was the work of "some youthful perpetrator."

In contrast to the East Bay's urban coastal strip, the mountains and bucolic valleys just a few miles to the east were close to nature, and folks there knew nature's signs of death. From this rustic area during the month of May, ominous reports repeatedly reached the Bryan case investigators.

A man named Alan MacDonald called the Berkeley police on May 13 to tell of buzzards circling for the past two days near a road above the Orinda Golf Course—Orinda being the next town east from the Mt. Diablo car-beating locale. Could the birds be feeding on a human body? A week later an anonymous caller reported buzzards again, this time hovering above Dimond Canyon. Two FBI agents searched the area, discovering only the carcass of a deer.

Then came a call from the chief of police in the tiny Contra Costa town of Pinole. Nearby on Pinole Valley Road, he said, was a multiracial shanty-town known as Old Adobe. Recently an old man had died there and his dog had howled for several days. Now the same dog was baying again in a wooded area nearby, and neighbors had reported the stench of a body, although no vultures had been seen.

Special Agent James E. Treher accompanied the Pinole chief to the area, where a painstaking search turned up nothing. The odor was no longer noticeable. But for the next forty years a report on the matter would be preserved in the Alameda County District Attorney's office in a file folder labeled "Howling Dog at Old Adobe."

Throughout May, inevitable "sightings" of Stephanie continued all across America. A Petaluma woman, Minnie Edenburn, believed she had seen her in San Francisco's Greyhound bus depot. Recognizing Stephanie from news pictures, Mrs. Edenburn had spoken to the girl, who supposedly had admitted her identity. By the time the report could be checked, however, the girl was long gone.

Two days later and much farther afield, the police in Fall River, Massachusetts, were called by Mrs. Agnes Carvalho, who had known Stephanie in 1952 before the Bryans moved to California. From her second-story window, she was sure she had just seen Stephanie about 200 feet away, walking with a young man. They had driven off to the north together in a light-blue sedan.

Two weeks after Stephanie disappeared a San Pablo produce dealer, Charles F. Munds, came forward with a story that would generate controversy as the case proceeded. Munds, a lean, intense man of middle age, ran a fruit stand on Highway 40,* the main road north to Sacramento. His first report, to the San Pablo police, was tentative and got scant attention. About eight forty-five on the night of April 28, he said, two young Mexicans in a beat-up two-door sedan, dark green or black, had stopped at his place to buy cigarettes. Seated between them was a pretty, short-haired Caucasian girl with a scarf around her head. (Another time he called it a "hair net.") The girl showed no emotion, nor did she try to leave the car. Now, fourteen days later, Munds believed she was Stephanie Bryan.

"I thought it was odd that a white girl should be with this type of men," he said.

Why had he waited so long to tell about it?

He had not thought much about the incident, he said, until the discovery of Stephanie's textbook on Franklin Canyon Road. David Tyree, who had found it, was one of Munds's customers.

After Dr. Bryan held a press conference May 18 to offer a $2,500 reward for information on his daughter's whereabouts, Munds's identification of the girl with the Mexicans became much more positive.

"It was Stephanie all right, I'll tell you that," he declared after examining a reward poster. "That's the girl, unless there's another in the world that looks just like her. She just sat there looking straight down the road. Maybe she was scared."

The *Detroit News* carried a story about the reward in a late edition on May 19. Four hours after the paper hit the streets, an unknown man placed a collect call to the Bryan residence from a pay station near Briggs Stadium, the home of the Detroit Tigers.

The caller identified himself to Mary Bryan as "Mr. Stefan"; the FBI ran

---

* Now I-80.

checks on dozens of people with that or similar names in the stadium area, which included Detroit's skid row. Nothing of value or significance was developed, but the Bureau's report on the phone call ran to eleven pages, single-spaced.

An ex-mental patient, Victor Louis Christy, fifty-four, became a Bryan case suspect because of an unsigned letter to the police. The anonymous correspondent wrote that the one-time Oakland upholsterer drove a car closely matching that seen on Mt. Diablo Boulevard.

Christy had recently been discharged after treatment for psychosis at Agnews State Hospital near San Jose, where he now worked for the Food Machinery and Chemical Corporation. Officer Hutchins found him in a seedy San Jose hotel room. FMC confirmed, with his time card, that he had been on the job until 4:31 P.M. the day Stephanie vanished. His car, moreover, was a black 1954 Ford with a yellow top, totally unlike the suspect Chevrolet.

The investigation of Christy would have been insignificant in the context of the Bryan case—had it not been for unforeseen events to come.

Terry Dawson, a schoolmate of Stephanie's from a well-known family, had been the bane of his teachers at least since age nine, when he shot a woman with a pop gun. His later misdeeds on the school grounds involved shooting a BB gun, shooting firecrackers, shooting slingshots, and throwing a rock through a window. On one occasion, when Terry had been held back a year, he had taken his report card to the school office, set it afire, tossed the burning match into a wastebasket, and gleefully watched the blaze.

By the age of fifteen he already had a rap sheet longer than most, with offenses including joyriding in a stolen car, burglary, and stealing money from a man's trousers while he was playing tennis. Terry's probation officer described him as a "psycho" and a "terrific liar."

Now the Berkeley police began hearing that Terry was boasting a lot, claiming to have dated Stephanie Bryan regularly and taken her to bed more than once. On May 31 Hutchins found the boy on a Berkeley street and confronted him with the story.

"Sure, I fucked her," Terry said, his stance full of braggadocio.

"If you tell us the truth, and if you had nothing to do with her disappearance, we won't snitch to your dad," Hutchins promised him. Terry's father was a well-known and formidable man.

Terry's story was that he had become involved with Stephanie about February or March, when they had had two secret movie dates on Saturdays. Both times, he said, they had met inside the theater, and after each show he had remained there while she departed alone.

"What pictures were playing?"

Terry couldn't remember.

"Who were the actors?"

He didn't know.

He told Hutchins that later, on a day when he had played hooky from his classes at Willard, he had met Stephanie after school, taken her home, and led her to his bedroom. At first she had been reluctant, he said, but soon she had undressed. Then she had put her clothes back on, but with urging she had stripped again and their first act of intercourse had taken place. Afterward she had left for home by herself.

"What time of day was this?"

"Four or four-thirty in the afternoon."

"What color was her underwear?"

"I don't remember."

"Tell me about her body."

Terry couldn't think of anything special.

"Was she a virgin?"

"As far as I know."

The boy was only warming up in his narration, which he was clearly enjoying. Not long after this first intimacy, he said, he had gone to the Bryan home for the first and only time, on a Thursday afternoon, and rung the doorbell. A boy five or six years old had answered and told him Stephanie wasn't there.

"What street does she live on?" Hutchins asked.

Terry couldn't give the name.

Once, he boasted, Stephanie had told him, "I would run away with you and get married if you wanted."

Although highly suspect, Terry's story was too pertinent to be ignored. He supplied too much believable detail.

"There is no doubt in my mind that he lies," Hutchins wrote in his report, "but I cannot separate any grain of truth from the mass of lies, and I cannot disprove any of his statements."

Confronting Stephanie's heartsick parents with this tale of her alleged unchastity was a duty Hutchins dreaded—but he need not have feared the interview. Mary Bryan's stoical calm and her systematic management of her household now served her well. Without emotion, she totally demolished Terry Dawson's erotic fantasy.

"If Steffie had been more than ten or fifteen minutes late on any school afternoon, I would have known it and I would remember it now," she stated positively.

Further, she said, if Terry had rung the Bryan doorbell and one of the children had answered, either she or Stephanie's grandmother would have checked it out personally. As for the Saturdays in February and March, Mary had recollections and records that made Terry's claim of movie rendezvous impossible.

In Burlingame, a high-toned residential suburb on the Peninsula south of San Francisco, Mrs. Georgia Harrop went to the police on July 7 and asked Sergeant William L. Rowland if she could speak confidentially.

Certainly, he said.

Mrs. Harrop was a drapery shop proprietor who had done some work for a friend named Willis Henry Magennis, fifty-six, across the bay in San Leandro. What she had observed and heard while riding with him in his station wagon worried her.

Magennis had told her he previously owned a Chevrolet or Pontiac but "had to get rid of it in a hurry." On the seat of his wagon, a brand-new 1955 model, Mrs. Harrop said she had seen a revolver to which he variously referred as "Old Betsy" or "the persuader." The wagon's odometer showed only 1,900 miles, much of which Magennis said had been rolled up on a recent trip north. The distance he mentioned was six hundred miles, but Mrs. Harrop was unsure whether he meant one-way or round trip.

On this journey, Magennis had told her, he had taken some books— "French classics," he called them—for the teenage son of a friend. To reach the friend's home he had crawled through a fence and, while doing so, had dropped a book.

"I think it had her name on it," Magennis had said.

Could "her" be Stephanie Bryan? Mrs. Harrop wondered. She further quoted Magennis as saying, "Some things I took up there I didn't give them; I buried them."

Her report was substantial enough to compel the district attorney's office to look into it. Magennis worked for a paper company in San Francisco, and his time cards showed he had been there until 4:38 P.M. on April 28. He could not have kidnapped Stephanie at 4 o'clock.

As the mystery went into its third month with no promise of solution, the Reverend James Fritchman appeared at the FBI office in San Francisco. He identified himself as the pastor of the Spiritual Army of God, Inc., and the owner of the Open Door Healing Center, both in Oakland.

"I am inspired," he declared. "I deal directly with a Divine Source."

Eight days earlier, Fritchman said, a spirit named Kandion had informed him that Ebba Bolton, his Healing Center colleague, would soon be enlightened about Stephanie Bryan's fate. Now, that very morning, the spirit had returned! Fritchman produced a paper bearing in his own handwriting the message Ebba had received:

The man who kidnapped Stephanie Bryan is about forty years old, ferret-like face, ruddy complexion, pale blue eyes, blond hair, known as Mac. Body placed in sack weighted down with rocks, thrown in slough, Napa road to Sacramento. Steep bank, roots of trees over water, sack caught in roots.

The frustrated agent who accepted Kandion's revelation placed it in the FBI's thickening file of Bryan case tips. At this point it seemed as plausible as anything else the file contained.

PART TWO

The Fateful Days

6

The House on San Jose Avenue

Burton Abbott had scarcely concluded his all-night chess game, after the discovery of Stephanie Bryan's purse, when his doorbell rang. Inspector O'Meara and FBI Special Agent Marvin Buchanan confronted him.

"We need your signature on this, Mr. Abbott," Buchanan said, handing him a mimeographed FBI form.

By signing it Burton would consent to a search of his premises without a warrant. The wording specified that the consent was voluntary and given "without threats or promises of any kind."

After scanning the form hastily, Burton cheerfully wrote his name in the precise, legible hand of an accounting student, adding a flourish on the crossbar of the final two t's. Georgia signed a similar paper, and O'Meara witnessed the twin documents, noting the time as 9:15 A.M.

Within minutes three Berkeley officers—Sergeant Vieira, Inspector Robinson, and Lieutenant Hank Whaley—arrived with shovels. At 9:45 they were joined by FBI Special Agents Richard Nichols, Robert Barthol, and Phil Nottingham, who began probing, digging, and sifting the soil of the Abbott cellar floor.

Whatever physical evidence the domicile at 1408 San Jose Avenue might conceal, it also harbored much anguish and emotional turmoil. The converging paths that had brought Burton and Georgia Abbott together in this white stucco house had not been easy.

Burton Wilbur Abbott was born in Portland, Oregon, on February 8, 1928, the younger of two sons in his family. His father, Harold Mark Abbott, was a lumberjack, and when Burton was two years old the family settled in the little village of Sequim on Washington's rugged, heavily forested Olympic Peninsula. There, where wildlife abounded, Burton learned to hunt and fish—pursuits that would figure crucially in the last crisis of his life. In 1933 his father deserted the family and to the best knowledge of friends was never heard from afterward. By 1955 he was listed as deceased.

Burton's mother, Elsie Belle Abbott, was an intelligent, strong-minded, high-principled woman, twenty-four years old at the time of his birth. Her father, Wert Moore, was a teacher and college professor.

Elsie taught her boys reading and writing at home, even before their school years. She raised them in the Methodist Church, and Burton faithfully attended Sunday school as a child, winning medals for attendance, though as he came of age he would become a backslider.

In 1937 Elsie moved the family to Stockton, California, a lusty town of factories, canneries, and stockyards abutting the rich farmlands of the San Joaquin River Delta. There the Abbotts moved in with Elsie's sister May, whose husband, Cyril Smith, was a police sergeant in charge of the vice detail.

Elsie and her sons remained in the policeman's household for about three years. By his own account, Smith became a surrogate father to the boys, and it was he who dealt with Burton's early questions about sex. The years in Stockton were a time of growth and emergence for Burton. He adjusted easily to his surroundings, made new friends, enjoyed competitive sports, and sang in the Stockton Boys' Choir.

Burton's mother worked as a seamstress to support her sons. Then in 1939, in a move unsuspectedly fateful, she took a job as a fabric worker at the Alameda Naval Air Station—an installation that would crucially affect Burton's life until his final hours.

Elsie resettled with her boys in Oakland. She and a widowed sister, Mona Marsh, took an apartment on Rawson Street, a few blocks from a bridge leading to Elsie's Alameda island workplace. Their bus driver brother, Wilbur "Bud" Moore (from whom Burton took both his middle name and nickname), moved into another apartment across the hall. The Moores were a close-knit family.

Burton entered Oakland's Frick Junior High School in December 1940. His grades were mostly Bs, with an A in art, and he was active in the student government as homeroom councilor and grounds commissioner. School records describe him as "efficient, courteous, rather retiring, sensitive, well-liked by students."

While at Frick, Burton went to dances and had his first date. He graduated as a ninth-grader in June 1943, and that fall, at age fifteen, he entered Fremont High School as a sophomore.

Fremont's records on Burton noted, "General appearance, posture, skin, teeth, eyes, ears, throat, all '9' [presumably on a scale of 10]." He was always "spotlessly clean, well-mannered, and pleasant."

He became an avid reader. He scored 127 on an IQ test (up from 106 at Stockton three years earlier), but his grades were erratic. They ranged from As in Spanish and drama to Fs in world literature and chemistry. Other typical grades were Bs in geometry, mechanical drawing, and American literature; Cs in written expression, typing, physics, U.S. history, and U.S. government; and Ds in Latin, oral expression, English, and trigonometry. In the high school ROTC, he earned an A in his first semester and Bs thereafter.

A girl named Martha, who went to both Frick and Fremont with Burton, remembered him as a "nice boy, a good student, and very friendly." Although she never dated him, she later said "any girl would have been glad to go out with him because of his personality." He loved to dance.

Dramatics was Burton's forte. He was student director of a high school play, and his drama teacher thought him "likeable, full of fun and life." Fremont's school paper, *The Green and Gold,* carried his picture in the cast of *Ever Since Eve,* and he also played in *She Stoops to Conquer.*

In 1945 the fall term play was a onetime Zasu Pitts vehicle called *Ramshackle Inn,* with Burton playing a romantic character accused of murder but ultimately exonerated. During a dress rehearsal, he prolonged a kiss with Maxine Bauman, a girl in the cast, to the point where her boyfriend, Alfred Cambra, broke into a jealous rage and attacked him on the stage. Later Cambra claimed to have beaten him up, but the teacher called it "all good fun."

Burton graduated from Fremont High on June 21, 1946, and entered Oakland's Central (later Laney) Trade School, taking sheet metal work with a grade of A.

In high school he had many dates but never became serious about any one girl. A San Quentin sociologist would later write, "He experienced his first heterosexual relationship when he was sixteen, with a girl of similar age. He describes this as a pleasurable experience, though laughingly confesses to feeling disappointed because he was anticipating more enjoyment from the act. He claims several later heterosexual experiences previous to marriage." To the prison interviewer, Burton pointedly denied any homosexual experiences or "undue or sexual interest in young girls."

When Burton and his brother, Mark, began to show interest in girls, they appeared to face a formidable obstacle in the person of their mother.

"She disliked other women and made this quite plain," Ada Flenner, their landlady at the Rawson apartment, would later tell a police officer. "She seemed to resent any girls or women who might be interested in the boys."*

Mark showed his anger at this, but Burton would refuse to argue with his mother and just walk away. Elsie was instrumental in having Mark join the navy, Mrs. Flenner said, "because of too many girls in the neighborhood. She broke Mark up with two girls that I know of."

The issue of matriarchal jealousy and domination was to recur time after

---

* Elsie strongly denied such an attitude in a 1955 interview.

time as the Bryan case unfolded. Georgia would tell the police Burton was a "mama's boy"; when they were planning to marry, she said, Elsie had thrown every stumbling block possible in their path.

Another of Mrs. Flenner's complaints was what she deemed pornographic interest on the part of the Abbott boys. Once she found a cache of books on crime, nudism, and sex in the Abbotts' garage, and she asked Mark to remove them.

"I'll have to talk to Burton," he responded. "They belong to him."

Finally Mrs. Flenner destroyed the books herself.

During his school years, Burton worked at several jobs. He carried a *Tribune* route and, in the summer of 1943, became an office boy at the Atlas Imperial Engine Company at fifty cents an hour, later promoted to accounting clerk at sixty-five cents. In 1946 he had a job handling empty lug boxes at a San Leandro cannery, making $1.05 an hour.

On October 3, 1946, three and a half months after graduating from high school, Burton enlisted in the army, beginning a short, ill-fated military experience. At the Camp Beale induction center he falsified his qualifications, claiming to have been an ROTC lieutenant and to have completed one semester at U.C.-Berkeley as a business administration major. These embellishments, which passed unnoticed at the time, would return to haunt him nine years later.

From Camp Beale he shipped out to antitank school at Fort Knox, Kentucky. In February 1947, after serving only four months, he was diagnosed with pulmonary tuberculosis and sent to Fitzsimmons General Hospital in Denver. He was routinely promoted to private first class in July but was busted back to private one month later for failure to stay in bed as ordered. He was honorably discharged from the army on October 22, 1947.

On his return to Oakland Burton was admitted to nearby Livermore Veterans Hospital, where he remained for nine months. It was at Livermore that Georgia, six and a half years his senior, entered his life.

Georgia Evelyn Schorch was born August 4, 1921, in Kanopolis, Kansas, into a family that boasted a small measure of fame; movie actor Otto Kruger was her second cousin.

While she was still a child, Georgia's parents moved to Northern California and took over the management of the rustic Wildwood Resort deep in the mountains of Trinity County. Her father bought an old mining claim on nearby Hayfork Creek and erected a cabin—destined to become, twice, a site of misery and horror.

The area was bucolic, rugged, remote, and isolated—a fine place for a child of Georgia's adventurous bent, especially after she befriended an early-day

pilot who had a farm not far away. He taught her to fly before she was out
of grade school.

"When I was eleven or twelve years old, I could land his plane in the pasture right there," she would remember.

Georgia spent her high school years in San Anselmo, in more populous but
nonetheless rural Marin County across the Golden Gate from San Francisco.
That village nestled below Mt. Tamalpais, a formidable feature commanding
the North Bay geography.

Nineteen forty was a memorable year in Georgia's life for several reasons.
Her father died, and by the terms of his will her mother received a two-thirds
interest in the cabin on Hayfork Creek. The remaining third went to a man
named Lloyd K. Snyder, who had married Georgia's cousin. Within a few
years Snyder would unwittingly set the stage for the final act of the Stephanie
Bryan horror story.

Also in 1940, on June 18—two months before her nineteenth birthday—
Georgia ran off to Reno with Mark Costanza,* twenty-four, just back from
a three-year army hitch in Hawaii. Although the marriage lasted seven years,
it was a disaster from the first day. The newlyweds lived together less than
three weeks, with his parents in Petaluma, before Georgia walked out and
headed north for the sylvan scenes of her childhood.

A Berkeley police investigator who interviewed Costanza during the
Bryan investigation wrote, "He says that in the seven years they were married, Georgia allowed him only one act of intercourse, and that not on the
wedding night. However, according to Mark, Georgia extended her favors to
many other men. She drank considerably in bars and was often out all night."

Five months after their marriage, Mark was drafted back into the army and
would serve for the duration of World War II. While he was stationed in Illi-
nois, Georgia rejoined him for a time, Mark said, but resumed her cheating.
When he got orders to sail for Europe, she asked him for money to return
to California.

"No," he told her, "use your body like you always have."

They never saw each other or corresponded again. From other sources
Mark learned that she had enlisted in the Women's Army Corps. After the war,
in 1947, he received divorce papers from Reno and did not contest them.

Georgia's time in the Wacs, from 1942 to 1944, paralleled Burton's later
tour of army duty. Like Burton, she never rose above Pfc.

"They never would promote me," she said in 1994. "I had a stiff-as-a-stick
captain, and she disliked me intensely. I don't know why, but she did. Maybe
it was because I was smarter than she was."

---

* Fictitious name.

While waiting to go overseas, Georgia caught pneumonia, and her condition, like Burton's later, was diagnosed as tuberculosis.

After her discharge she gravitated again to the little cabin on Hayfork Creek and stayed there in 1946, in what was regarded as a common-law relationship with a lumberman named Frank, who had a record of petty theft and check-bouncing.

When Wildwood old-timers were quizzed about Georgia by the Alameda County cops much later, they remembered her as a "rough character" and "fast liver" who "put away quite a bit of liquor." One woman recalled rumors of her getting drunk at the Wildwood Inn, stripping before the men present, and walking home naked.

Then Reno beckoned, and Georgia took a job as a blackjack dealer. This interlude was brief, for in March 1947 her health worsened and she entered the Livermore Veterans Hospital. There Burton shortly joined her in the ranks of the T.B. patients—"lungers" in the hospital parlance.

They were married on June 12, 1948.

Seven years later, preparing for Abbott's trial, officers would spend countless hours talking to the doctors, nurses, and fellow patients who had known Burton and Georgia at Livermore. What about their character? Their habits?

The answers were as varied as those who gave them. From the nurses especially, many recollections of Burton were favorable.

"He was an ideal patient," said nurse Beulah Packard, "the nicest boy we had on 5-M." Another nurse remembered that Abbott "always said please and thank you."

Georgia, however, was an enigma. In the wards her reputation was that of a man-crazy chaser. When Abbott became engaged to her, there was a lot of kidding that she had "got herself a young man to teach the tricks to."

If Abbott's nurses thought highly of him, many of his fellow patients did not. One of them, William Smiley, considered him "self-centered, selfish, talkative, argumentative, with a one-track mind; he was always sure that he was right." Another, Arthur Bibbee, thought he was prone to deceive himself, believing the things he said whether they were true or not.

Abbott was generally seen as intelligent, however. "He was the best chess player, card player, pencil sketcher, and leather worker in the hospital," one fellow patient said. His sketches included nudes but were not pornographic. He was good with his hands and did well in a therapy program that included woodworking, radio announcing, and photography. He liked light opera and was an avid reader who went through eight to twelve books a week, including Boccaccio's *Decameron,* the works of Erskine Caldwell, and historical novels.

There were diverse opinions of Burton's sexuality. Ex-patient Vic Magina had a theory that "lungers" in general were an "oversexed and a rather happy lot," but he considered Abbott an effeminate exception: "not an obvious fruit, but not a man's man."

There was no real evidence that he was homosexual. Maurilio Palacie, a young Mexican artist who had known him at Livermore, thought he was a "pussy eater." Palacie said someone had advised Burton to grow a mustache to improve his oral copulation performance with women by giving him something to tickle them with. Abbott had taken the advice.

Elsie Abbott's domination of her son cropped up often in his fellow patients' recollections. Burton had seemed to rejoice in her treating him as a child. Smiley recalled that his mother made him a pair of pajamas and a silk bathrobe, which he wore with flair.

The first years of married life for Burton and Georgia were not easy. Each was receiving a monthly disability payment of $138, giving them $276 to live on. Burton's tuberculosis and other lung problems hung on, and he was in and out of Livermore repeatedly; two long inpatient stays lasted more than a year. Some of his ribs were removed, and the upper lobe of his left lung was excised.

During this period the Abbotts occupied a succession of apartments in Oakland and for a time moved in with Elsie in a neat tract home she had bought not far away in Castro Valley.

About 1949 Georgia enrolled in an Oakland cosmetology school, where she befriended Leona Dezman. By 1951 Leona had acquired her own establishment, the Morton Beauty Salon, and persuaded Georgia to come to work for her. By then both Georgia and Leona were skilled professionals.

At about the same time, the Abbotts became across-the-hall neighbors of Leona and her husband, Otto, who were destined to play crucial roles in their lives four years down the road.

In the early nomadic years of the Abbotts' marriage, their friends perceived it as a relationship beset by serious sexual difficulties. Burton, the obsessive talker, blabbermouthed their problems to anyone who would listen, including his hospital friends, his cop uncle, and his mother. Ample confirmation would be uncovered by Bryan case investigators who interviewed these people.

Early on, Abbott told Arthur Bibbee at the hospital that he had had only one normal sex act with Georgia but six acts of oral copulation. Burton's policeman uncle in Stockton, Cyril Smith, told one of District Attorney Frank Coakley's inspectors that Georgia wanted intercourse "every night and two and three times a night" and Burton could not keep up with her.

The FBI's report of an interview with Elsie was in a similar vein: "She indicated that he [Burton] is having marital troubles and she blames it on the wife. She claims that Georgia Abbott is oversexed and very demanding."

In further corroboration, we know what Georgia herself told the Berkeley Police about Burton. Inspector Robinson wrote:

> With regard to his personality and personal traits she stated that he has no sex drive, is not very romantic; that he cannot accept responsibility, so she and his mother do everything for him, make all the decisions, run the household, do all the work including mowing the lawns—both of them acting as mother towards him. She said that in a sense they, and she especially, have helped rob him of what manhood he may have had; that she nags him frequently because of his lack of drive and because he shows no sexual or romantic interests. She said that once or twice per month is a maximum for intercourse.*
>
> She described his temperament as never angry. He never raises his voice, never has a temper tantrum, even when nagged by her. She said he has never shown interest, to her knowledge, in other girls or women [and is] apparently interested only in his studies. She thinks of him as a good student but a person without any inherent reasoning capacity.

Yet a woman who had lived briefly with Georgia while Burton was back in the hospital told police of a party where Georgia passed around a half-dozen nude photos of Burton and herself. In one of them she was lying on a bed and Burton was approaching with an erection. In others they were copulating. Georgia told the group she and Burton had taken the pictures themselves, using a camera timer, and that Burton had developed them in the hospital's darkroom.

From numerous sources, investigators would continue to hear that Georgia turned regularly to other men for the sexual favors Burton could not supply. Cy Smith was one of several who suspected an affair between Georgia and Otto Dezman. Chester and Verna Ensign, who had been the Abbotts' neighbors when they lived across the hall from the Dezmans, said the Otto-Georgia liaison was a matter of common talk. Coakley also received undercover reports that Georgia was "seen a great deal" with Mark Abbott.**

---

*   The FBI's version of the interview says "three times per month."
** In 1994 the author questioned Georgia about these alleged liaisons:
    Q. They claimed you and Dezman had an affair.
    A. No, no-no-no-no, never. Not with my friend's husband—and she was my friend before he was....
    Q. What sort of a guy was Mark?
    A. Quiet, very quiet.
    Q. Did you like him?
    A. Yes.
    Q. Didn't they say that you were having an affair with him, too?
    Q. They thought I was having an affair with everybody in Oakland, I think (laughter).
    Later, in a separate interview, Dezman was equally emphatic in denying any romantic involvement with Georgia.

Gloria Olsen,* a one-time neighbor of the Abbotts, told police that while Burton was in the hospital Georgia was "after all the other husbands in the area"—including hers. When Gloria had complained, she said, Georgia had told her, "I can get any man I want; why don't you just put a rope around him?"

An outright admission of adultery with Georgia came from Al Dixon,** a friend of Mark's who worked at the Naval Air Station and considered himself a close friend of the whole Abbott family. He told Officer Hutchins that during one of Burton's hospitalizations, he had become intimate with Georgia after movie dates and "generally took her to his room for acts of intercourse."

Georgia and Burton became parents of a son, Christopher Wesley Abbott, on September 30, 1951. Just prior to Chris's birth, Cy Smith said, Burton had talked about divorcing Georgia, but when the baby arrived he "decided to give it another chance."

Burton Abbott first applied for admission to the University of California in September 1948, three months after his marriage, listing his probable major as advertising. He did not make the cut at that time, however, being informed by letter that because of a D grade at Fremont High, he had a scholarship deficiency of three units. He was advised to make up the shortage at another college or to enroll in U.C. Extension, and he chose the latter, taking economics, geology, and algebra. Illness forced him to drop out twice, but eventually he completed all requirements and was admitted to U.C.'s regular session in September 1953. He attended under Public Law 16, a specialized G.I. Bill for the disabled.

Abbott's 1953 and 1954 grades at Cal were As, Bs, and Cs in a curriculum that included economics, geology, anthropology, mathematics, French, philosophy, and business administration. His Veterans Administration counselor was "very satisfied" with his progress.

After six years of shuffling from one apartment to another, the Abbotts finally moved into their rented house at 1408 San Jose Avenue in mid-November 1954. It was a quiet street on which modern houses mingled with the stately, flawlessly maintained Victorians of elite Alameda families. Franklin Park, a landscaped city playground, was directly across from number 1408. The Abbotts' dwelling was within easy walking distance of Georgia's job at the beauty parlor.

Georgia, Burton, and three-year-old Chris had only a few weeks of family privacy in this home before Elsie moved in with them. She did so after

---

*   Fictitious name.
** Fictitious name.

turning over her Castro Valley bungalow to her son Mark when he took a bride at the end of December.

Despite the undeniable problems and tensions in the Burton Abbott household, there had been encouraging signs that things were settling down, getting better. Chris's birth had been a turning point. Burton was doing well at the university. Georgia was good at her job and well paid. She recently had been installed as president of the Oakland Cosmetologists Association.

Now, suddenly, all of this was in jeopardy.

About the time that the FBI men and police arrived Saturday morning to begin their search of the Abbott premises, Georgia made a quick phone call to the beauty shop.

"I'll be a little late," she said. "Something has happened here at home."

When she did get to work, she did not go into the details. To Lou Kirkpatrick, another hairdresser who worked there, she seemed "very much upset," but to a client whose hair she fixed later in the day, she appeared "calm and quite unconcerned."

By word of mouth, radio, television, and newspapers, the discovery of Stephanie Bryan's purse became known to thousands within hours. One who heard it was Zella Prager, who ran the Select Cleaners next door to the Morton Beauty Salon. Zella was a former chorus girl and vaudeville performer, drawn to Georgia by their common interest in theatricals. At midday she went over to the beauty shop and found Georgia working on a customer.

"I heard the news on the radio," she said.

"What did you hear?" Georgia asked without stopping her work.

"You found something."

"Yes, I'll tell you about it later."

"I'll pray for you and loan you money if you need it," Zella promised without being asked.

All day that Saturday, as the search of the Abbott house proceeded, the curious assembled outside, creating a circus atmosphere on the genteel street. At times the crowd grew to five hundred or more. Uniformed police, plainclothesmen, and FBI agents came and went, and U.C.'s eminent criminalist Paul L. Kirk arrived to examine the Abbott automobiles. District Attorney Coakley and his assistant, Folger Emerson, put in appearances. Fire trucks arrived—for what purpose no one knew—and parked in the street. Floodlights were brought in so that the work could continue into the night. Reporters and cameramen hovered, asking many questions but getting few answers from the tight-lipped lawmen.

Al Reck, an old-time cop-shop reporter who was now a legend as "the greatest city editor of them all" at the *Tribune,* showed up. His practiced eye settled on a new patio in the Abbott backyard, created by Burton in June as an anniversary present to Georgia. It was paved with wooden blocks scrounged from a lumber company in San Leandro.

"Stephanie's body is under the blocks. That's a shrine," Reck decided, and ordered the police to "dig it up." In deference to his awesome stature in journalism and in the community, they did—but this time his hunch was wrong. Under the blocks was nothing but dirt.

FBI Agents Nottingham, Barthol, and Nichols, working in the Abbott cellar, had the most arduous search assignment. The basement ran the full length of the house front to rear and was divided into halves by a concrete footing wall that supported the floor joists. Only the easterly half was paved. The sandy soil of which Alameda Island essentially consisted was exposed in the other half—sand so loose it could be dug into with the fingers. All day long, with special probes, the agents poked into it, testing inch by inch for foreign objects.

Burton remained cool and unruffled as his home was turned inside out and his handiwork dismantled. He complained only that the excavating interfered with his sleep, which he said was important for a frail man with a tubercular history and a lung lobe missing. During the day he carried on with normal chores as best he could. At some point he signed and dated a form enrolling Chris at Alameda's Oak Park Child Care Center.

A little after 4 P.M. Burton voluntarily accompanied Inspector O'Meara and FBI Agent Donald Hallahan to the latter's office in the Oakland Post Office Building for interrogation. At about the same hour Georgia, having returned home from work, was taken to police headquarters for a separate interview with Inspector Robinson and Agent Buchanan.

At that point the police described both Burton and Georgia to the press as "most cooperative."

Less than a half hour after the Abbotts departed, Agent Nichols's probe hit an obstruction at a depth of about eight inches in the sand of the basement's rear area. The location was six to eight inches out from the concrete footing, directly opposite the third stud from the corner. Nichols summoned Agent Nottingham as a witness and then dug in to determine the nature of the foreign object. Within a few minutes he held it in his hands: the book *Sue Barton, Staff Nurse,* which Stephanie Bryan had checked out of the library half an hour before she vanished.

Immediately beneath *Sue Barton* was Stephanie's other library book, *Two's Company,* and under that the booklet "Everything About Parakeets" that she had bought at the pet shop.

Carefully the agents continued their probing and sifting. Shortly they recovered a green spiral notebook bearing Stephanie's name and a cream-colored composition book with the words "Francais" and "Exercises" on the cover. Next found, a short distance away, were Stephanie's glasses, with their blue plastic top frames, and finally a white brassiere bearing the labels "Magnin" and "Du Pont nylon." Also nearby were a length of insulated wire and a soiled piece of white cloth with a blue print in a long-arrow-and-ball pattern.

At the Alameda police station, unaware of these discoveries, Georgia was self-possessed and confident as her interview with Robinson and Buchanan began. Briefly she gave her life history and related the difficulties in her marriage. She told what she knew about Burton's trip to the Trinity cabin on April 28, and she supplied detail about her discovery of the purse.

As the session was winding up, word of Nichols's basement-floor discoveries was relayed, outside the interview room, to the questioners. They paused to digest the information and then returned to Georgia.

"Mrs. Abbott," Buchanan said, "we have something very serious to tell you. You'd better prepare yourself for it."

Georgia responded with an uneasy, inquiring look, and Buchanan gave her the news about the finding of Stephanie's books, bra, and glasses.

She went white. There was a momentary silence, and then she gasped: "He could have done it! He must have done it if they found that stuff in the basement."

It was one of the few times—perhaps the only time—that Georgia would ever openly express doubt of her husband's innocence. She later called Buchanan and specifically retracted that part of her statement.

Elsie Abbott was likewise under questioning by an FBI-police team late that Saturday afternoon.

To her inquisitors she repeatedly and emphatically asserted her son's innocence, until she too was informed in midinterview of the basement findings. She lapsed momentarily into hysteria and then cried: "If Burton did this thing, I wish he were dead. He would be better off!"

Like her daughter-in-law, Elsie would never let such a doubt escape from her lips again.

7

Burton's Story

Burton Abbott's manner, if not actually cocky, was certainly casual at four thirty-five that Saturday afternoon when he first confronted the law in a formal interrogation setting. He was much aware of the fact that he was not under arrest, and he acted as if the interview were going to be a piece of cake. When advised of his right to an attorney, he insisted he did not need one.

"I am perfectly willing to talk about this case," he said, "because I am innocent and have nothing to do with it."

He declared he had never seen Stephanie Bryan in his life, did not know her family, and had been barely aware before the previous night that a girl was missing. Emphatically and specifically he disclaimed knowledge of how her purse and wallet had come to be in his cellar. The first and only time he had seen them, he said, was when Georgia had brought them upstairs.

In the eyes of the law, however, Burton was already in deep trouble.

"Abbott is a definite suspect and can't be considered anything else," Berkeley Police Captain Laird had told reporters. Even as Burton sat there across the table from Special Agent Hallahan and Inspector O'Meara, the overnight editions of Sunday papers carrying Laird's statement were hitting the streets.

O'Meara, a blunt, balding, six-foot-tall cop who had come up through the ranks, was now in command of the Bryan case, although it was outside his normal purview. His usual duty was in intelligence, ferreting out subversion—always a preoccupation in Berkeley, with U.C.'s supercharged left wing. Some of his fellow officers said he "saw a communist under every bed." O'Meara was a crack pistol shot, a rough, tough operator overall.

With Burton's blanket denial on the record, Hallahan and O'Meara wanted to know about his trip to Trinity County on Thursday, April 28, the day of Stephanie's disappearance.

He said he had gone north for two purposes: to open up the family cabin, which had been closed for the winter, and to be on hand for the opening of trout season on Saturday, April 30. The jaunt had been planned for some time, and his mother, his wife, and their baby-sitter knew all about it. The plan was that his brother, Mark, and Mark's wife, Mary, would join him at the cabin on Saturday. Burton identified the baby-sitter as Hilda Frakes.

"What time did you leave home?" O'Meara asked.

"About ten or eleven o'clock," Burton replied, introducing an alibi timetable that would be the heart of his defense. As the case proceeded, it would become both crucial and suspect.

"What were you wearing?"

To the best of his memory, Burton said, he had worn blue jeans on the trip north, with a green-and-red-plaid flannel shirt "that I always take because it's warm." He also took a "chocolate brown" leather jacket with a fur collar, and dark-brown field boots.

"Any hat?"

"No, I only have one hat and that's an old rain hat. It's pretty well gone by the wayside now."

Burton said he was driving his gray-green 1949 Chevrolet, having gassed it up on Wednesday night, the eve of his departure, at a Standard station on Webster Street in Alameda. He had a distinct recollection of that.

"On Wednesday nights we go dancing," he explained; he and Georgia had been taking lessons. On the evening of April 27 they had left the car at the service station to have a tire fixed and the tank filled, and they had picked it up after the dance.

"Georgia says I am quite a wallflower when I have to do some of the modern dances—samba, rumba," Burton interjected.

They had come home from the dance about nine-thirty or ten-thirty. The car was already loaded for the next day's trip, its trunk containing a Coleman stove, an oil lantern, a canvas cot, cooking utensils, and three sleeping bags. In the backseat was a box of groceries Burton had purchased that day at the Lewis Store near the beauty salon. He said he had taken no rifles, hunting knives, or other weapons.

Hallahan and O'Meara asked him to remember, if he could, the route he had taken out of town.

After stopping briefly at the beauty shop to say good-bye to Georgia, he said, he had left the Alameda island by way of the Posey Tube,* a tunnel beneath the inner harbor ship channel, emerging onto Harrison Street in Oakland. He traced his route through the Oakland street grid, along Harrison, Eighth, and Cypress Streets and finally the Eastshore Freeway, which took him to Richmond. There he had connected via San Pablo Avenue to Highway 40, the main route inland to the Sacramento Valley.

The one-way distance to the cabin was some three hundred miles. Burton said he had followed Highway 40 over the Carquinez Bridge to Davis and then turned north on Highway 99W.** The next hundred miles led through

---

* Named for the engineer who built it.

** Roughly the route of today's I-5.

the flat orchards, fertile fields, and little towns of California's great Central Valley. At Dunnigan in northern Yolo County he had stopped for lunch about three o'clock, he said.

"Do you know the name of the restaurant?" he was asked.

"It had two names—a woman's and a man's name, something like Ruby and Bob's." (Later Burton would call the place "Bob and Ray's" and "Ruth and Bob's" before getting it right: "Bill and Kathy's.") "It was a ranch-style building with a shed roof and redwood siding, with a twelve-by-twelve timber out front for a bumper stop. The food there is excellent."

Burton said his next stop was for gasoline at a Shell station on the southern outskirts of Corning, a town nestled among olive groves and known for its olive oil refineries.

"About what time you did buy the gas at Shell?"

"I would say four-thirty or a quarter of five."

If this timing checked out, it would mean that Burton had been somewhere between Dunnigan and Corning, as far as two hundred miles north of Berkeley, at the four o'clock hour when Stephanie vanished.

"Did you get anything at Corning besides gas—oil, or water?"

"I am positive I went into the men's room. I didn't buy oil. The attendant said the oil was fine. I do know that."

"Why did you stop at Shell, instead of using your credit card at Standard?" Hallahan asked.

"My wife had been complaining about my credit card bills. Before I left, my mother had given me $15 in cash; so I used that money instead."

This answer reinforced the investigators' growing perception that in the Abbott family it was the women who ruled. Sometimes at loggerheads, sometimes in uneasy alliance, Georgia and Elsie vied endlessly for the attention and love of the passive Burton.

"Maybe you used cash because you didn't want anyone to know where you were at the time," O'Meara suggested. Burton dismissed this idea as ridiculous.

"The brand of gas made no difference to me," he said.

From Corning, he had continued north to Red Bluff, where he recalled stopping for dinner at a restaurant on the west side of the road at the south end of town. It was still daylight, he said, probably about six o'clock.

(As Abbott retold his alibi story during successive interrogations, his time estimates for stops on his trip north would vary by up to forty-five minutes. Were the discrepancies random or were they evidence of a fabrication?)

"Can you describe the place you stopped in Red Bluff?"

"It is down off the highway pretty well—a small place, just a wooden-front, flat building; some type of service station. They have a counter, a U-shaped counter."

"You don't recall the name?"

Again Burton was uncertain. "It had something to do with chicken—the Chicken Fry Spot maybe?"

By now the grilling had been going on for three hours, during which, at some point, Hallahan had been called out and informed about the basement burial of Stephanie's books, bra, and eyeglasses. Now he sprung this on Burton and demanded, "How do you account for it?"

Once more Burton professed total puzzlement.

"This makes the whole thing even more impossible," he protested. "Why would these things be buried and the other things be put in a box?"

Hallahan, convinced that Abbott was lying and that his protest was an act, decided it was time to talk turkey with him.

"Burton," he said, "think of the ordeal that girl's parents are going through. If you have any compassion at all, tell us where she is. You owe that much to the Bryan family."

For the only time in the interview, for a single instant, Abbott lost his veneer of cool reasonableness.

"I don't give a damn about the Bryan family," he snapped. *"When do we eat?"*

As the grilling resumed, Burton continued his recitation of his route to Wildwood.

At Red Bluff, State Route 36 branches off Highway 99 to the west. It was in 1955 a narrow, lonely road, unpaved in places as it rose from the floor of the Sacramento Valley into wild mountains. The climb was gentle at first, through grassy hills mottled with patches of scrub oak. Then the terrain changed; the road became steeper, with occasional ponderosa pines thrusting their tall crowns above the oaks in an ever-thickening forest. At intervals, tortuous side roads took off for isolated places with names like Rat Trap Gap and Sunday Gulch.

As day turned to dusk with rain and snow, Burton followed this desolate westward route for sixty miles. It was about 8 o'clock, he said, when he reached the Wildwood Inn, which he knew well, and stopped for a drink before proceeding to his cabin nearby.

The inn was a rustic structure of weathered vertical siding, with a tar-paper roof deteriorating from age. The forest came down to the edge of the little clearing on which it stood. Inside ten or twelve stools faced a long bar. Behind it a NO CREDIT placard vied for attention with another proclaiming, in bold letters: WE RESERVE THE RIGHT TO REFUSE SERVICE TO ANYONE. To the rear was a dining area, and outside, close to a prominent privy, was a solitary Shell gas pump. A few rentable cabins were scattered through the nearby trees. This humble tavern was the social center for the mountain folks from miles around.

As he entered the place that Thursday evening, Burton said, he was briefly greeted by the rough-hewn innkeeper, Delbert Cox, behind the bar. He had known Cox for a couple of years. The two or three other customers present were strangers. Burton had one drink, a bourbon and soda as he recalled, and left after about twenty minutes. He said he arrived at the cabin about a quarter to nine.

In the rude cabin, which abutted a narrow dirt road scarcely wide enough for cars to pass, the furniture was hanging from the rafters, to which it had been wired the previous fall to keep it from invading rats.

"I got the cabin all straightened around," Burton related. "I pulled everything off of the double bed and put the mattresses on, because my brother and sister-in-law were coming up. I filled the Coleman lantern and the Coleman stove and got out the groceries and unpacked the car, and then I went to bed, about ten-thirty I think."

Burton said he rose about 8 o'clock and fixed a breakfast of bacon and eggs and coffee, then shoveled away some dirt that was causing the doors of the cabin garage to stick. After finishing with that, he had visitors; two men and a woman came along in a green pickup, wanting to know the best place around for bear hunting. Burton referred them to an expert, Jesse Laffranchini, who ran the hotel in Hayfork some fifteen or twenty miles farther along the road. The pickup took off in that direction. Another passing vehicle that morning was the truck of traveling produce dealer Robert Wetzel, who stopped and talked for a while. Burton didn't buy anything, however.

The weather grew worse. About 2 or 3 P.M., as Burton remembered it, he was "feeling sorry for himself," so he returned to Del Cox's place for what would be a memorable boozing session. At the bar he met and began drinking with Tom Daly, who worked at the Wildwood Lumber Company mill. Tom was a carpenter by trade, but knew something about accounting, Burton's own field.

"We had quite a lot in common," Burton recalled. "He was a nice fellow."

"What does Tom look like?" O'Meara asked.

"He is tall, thin, about forty I guess. He has almost coal-black hair. He wears dark horn-rimmed glasses."

For the next five hours that dismal Friday afternoon, Abbott and Daly scarcely stopped drinking. Burton had seven or eight tall bourbon and sodas. After a break about 7 or 8 o'clock for a dinner of T-bone steak, french fries, and salad, they started drinking all over again.

"Still bourbon and soda?"

"I don't know what it was, some sweet drink though, and that kind of set me off," Burton said. "We talked and talked and talked." He estimated his tab at $15 or $16.

"That would be a lot of drinking," O'Meara observed. "How much do they charge for drinks at Cox's?"

"Fifty cents."

Burton was not sure what time the imbibing had broken up but thought it was a little after midnight. "We were the only two in the bar and Del Cox wanted to leave. I asked him could I have some gas before I go, and I drove the car up to the pump and he put the gas in. I guess I was pretty high and Tom was wondering if I was going to make it, but Cox didn't seem to give a damn. So off I went. Well, I made it home, honestly, and I got the car into the garage, and I got into the darn cabin and then it hit me. I remember taking off my jacket, and I know I got my shoes off. I was positive I had taken my pants off, but I guess I didn't."

Fully clothed, Burton got into his sleeping bag and collapsed on the couch in a drunken stupor.

Early in the boozing marathon, about three o'clock Friday afternoon, Burton had called home and talked to Mrs. Frakes, the baby-sitter.

"Tell Mark and Mary that the weather is terrible and I don't think they should come," he had instructed. "But it's up to them. If they do come, they'd better bring chains."

Mrs. Frakes had relayed Burton's warning, but Mark and Mary had ignored it. They arrived at the cabin about 3 A.M. Saturday after an eight-hour drive from their home in Castro Valley. They found the cabin door open and Burton passed out on the couch. Their efforts to rouse him were futile.

Burton woke up about 8 o'clock Saturday morning, discovering the arrival of his brother and sister-in-law. He was hung over, craving Alka-Seltzer. His condition startled Mark, who had never seen him drunk before.

That Saturday, Burton told Hallahan and O'Meara, he and Mark spent much of the day fishing, and that night went to bed about 10 o'clock. On Sunday morning, May 1, they repaired a broken wooden step outside the cabin and remained there until noon, when they all started home, driving convoy-style in their separate cars with Mark and Mary leading most of the way.

"Tell us your route," Burton was asked.

For most of the distance, he said, they had traveled the same roads he had taken on the trip north, with a stop at Willows this time for dinner and gas. But through Contra Costa County they had taken a shortcut ("the zigzagest route you ever did see") to Mark's house in Castro Valley.

Hallahan and O'Meara exchanged knowing glances, but said nothing,

when Burton said the shortcut took them along Franklin Canyon Road—
where David Tyree had found Stephanie Bryan's French book.

Burton must have congratulated himself at this point on coming through the
questioning unscathed. He had furnished a detailed, seemingly unassailable
account of his whereabouts and actions before, during, and after the time of
Stephanie Bryan's disappearance.

But he had not taken into account the depth of the investigation already
completed in the past twenty-four hours by a platoon of officers working behind the scenes. Suddenly the interrogators challenged him in a way he was
not expecting.

"You told your brother Mark that you detoured through Sacramento on
the way to the cabin. That doesn't square with what you've just told us.
What about it?"

A momentary frown flickered across Burton's face, but he quickly re-
gained his composure.

"Oh, I forgot!" he replied matter-of-factly, prefacing an explanation that
seemed to make sense. Mark Abbott, he said, wanted a cabin site of his own
at Wildwood, and he had asked Burton to find out how to file for a site on
an abandoned mining claim. Earlier Burton had made inquiries at the Bureau of Land Management in San Francisco but had been referred to its
Sacramento office.

He now corrected himself about turning north at Davis. Instead, he said,
he had continued on Highway 40 another fifteen miles or so, all the way into
Sacramento, and stopped at the land office there.

"But they were so crowded I didn't wait," he said, "I felt, golly, it's going
to be dark by the time I get to Wildwood. And I don't like to get there when
it's dark, because almost every time we go up to the cabin, almost every year,
it has been broken into."

"What time did you go to the land office in Sacramento?"

"Early afternoon—one-thirty maybe, one o'clock, something like that."

"Did you talk to anybody there?"

"No," Burton said, "it was so darn crowded, I think everybody was filing
claims for uranium mines throughout the darn state. So I said the heck with
this, I won't fool with it. I turned around and got in the car and headed back
to Davis junction."*

From there, Burton said, he had proceeded north on 99W, along the route
he had described before. He estimated his Sacramento detour had taken "an
hour, an hour and a half, maybe a little longer."

---

* Burton sprinkled his speech liberally with "darn," "heck," and "golly," but as we have seen he sometimes
lapsed into profanity when annoyed.

"Where is the land office in Sacramento?" he was asked.

"In a big gray stone building across from the post office."

"In the middle of a block or on a corner?"

"In the middle of a block."

"What floor is the land office on?"

"The second floor, I think. I remember walking upstairs."

"Describe the office, please, Mr. Abbott."

Burton said it was a square room, with a counter about thirty feet long across the front. At Hallahan's request, he drew a sketch of the interior layout.

Now his interrogators sprung another surprise. Burton's statement about gassing up his car in Alameda on the eve of his trip had been positive and precise. How was it then, O'Meara wanted to know, that he had to fill up again the next day at 20th and Harrison Streets in Oakland, using his Standard Oil credit card? The station at that corner was twelve blocks off the route by which he claimed to have left the city.

Burton showed a trace of fluster.

"I don't remember that purchase at all," he said. "It doesn't make sense, because that would have taken me out of my way."

"You have no recollection at all of getting gas at 20th and Harrison? Is that it?"

"Not that I can recall."

"All right, Mr. Abbott. Now on May 2, the day after you got back, you returned to Contra Costa County and bought gas again at Tank Farm Hill. What were you doing out there?"

Tank Farm Hill, named for gasoline refinery tanks dominating its landscape, was close to the bay between Richmond and Pinole. The road there, if followed for several more miles, could have taken Burton back to Franklin Canyon Road.

"I went there looking for cheap used tires," Burton said. "I had no classes between eleven o'clock and one o'clock at the university; so I took a ride out there."

He had found no tires at the price he wanted, so he had returned to the campus after buying the gas. In answer to a direct question, he averred he had gone nowhere near Franklin Canyon.

The grilling had now gone on for five hours with only a half-hour dinner break. Hallahan, still hoping for a confession, decided this was the right moment to step up the pressure, tighten the screws.

"Burton," he said, "just supposing—just supposing you had killed that girl. You'd have a helluva problem on your hands. How would you get rid of the body? Would you dump her in a river or a lake somewhere? Or along some road? Would you hack her to pieces? What would you do?"

As he posed his questions, Hallahan expected, if not a confession, at least an anguished cry of protest. Instead Burton gave a cold and analytical response, devoid of the slightest emotion.

"Under the circumstances, I'd probably bury the body," he said. "I'd find someplace like a bank with loose rock or shale, and I'd push the body down the bank and then shove the loose material down over the top of it."

"How would you carry the body? Stephanie was a small girl, but still she weighed more than a hundred pounds."

"I'd probably carry her like I'd carry a deer."

With the body on the ground, Burton explained, he would lie back against it, hooking his arms around an arm and a leg. Then he would rock back and forth until he rolled over on his stomach, and then raise one knee and straighten up with the body across his shoulders.

Abbott gave the answer as coolly as if he were taking an exam at the university. He admitted nothing.

Hallahan's psychological ploy had failed, but he and O'Meara did not ease up. Next they wanted to know the route Abbott customarily took from his home to the U.C. campus.

Abbott traced a route along the streets of Alameda, Oakland, and Berkeley. O'Meara noted that in Berkeley it included sections of College and Ashby Avenues, passing the library, doughnut shop, and pet shop where Stephanie had stopped on her last walk home. It also took Burton past the Standard Station at 20th and Harrison Streets where he had purchased gas on April 28. Yet in itself none of this was especially incriminating; the route was a logical one for a student commuting from Alameda.

"Who are your friends at the university?" Burton was asked next.

"I have no close ones. We don't socialize with anybody on campus."

"Maybe you're screwing a girlfriend on the side out there?" O'Meara suggested.

"No, since I've been married I haven't had sex with anyone but my wife."

The interview terminated at 10:55 P.M.—six hours and twenty minutes after it had begun.

"Can I go home now?" Burton asked.

"Well, Mr. Abbott," O'Meara said, "the D.A. also wants to talk to you. He will tell us whether to arrest you or not."

Again voluntarily, Abbott agreed to a nocturnal confrontation with District Attorney J. Frank Coakley. It would be just a short ride from the post office to the massive Alameda County Courthouse.

To understand where Coakley was "coming from" in 1955 (to use an apt expression of later vintage), one must consider both his personal and political background.

He was born in 1897 into a devout Irish Catholic family of three boys and two girls, all high achievers. Two of the sons—Frank and his brother Tom—went into law; the third became a priest.

Frank attended St. Mary's College at Moraga, just east of Oakland—not far from where the search for Stephanie Bryan would be centered four decades later. After World War I service in the navy, he finished his education at Stanford and U.C., joining the thin ranks of those with loyalties to both of these fiercely competing schools.

Not long after passing the bar, Coakley went to work in the Alameda County District Attorney's Office, where he would remain for virtually his whole career. It was a small office in the 1920s, led by an ambitious young lawyer whose name was Earl Warren.

In a county then riddled with corruption, Warren went after powerful and petty crooks alike, sending several grafting politicians, including the sheriff, to prison. As his assistant, Coakley carried much of the prosecutorial load. By the time he took over the D.A.'s office on his own in 1947, he knew every trick in the book. Perry Mason's creator Erle Stanley Gardner, after watching him in action, wrote "Coakley is just about as clever a fighter and as two-fisted a fighter as I have ever seen in a courtroom."

Warren meanwhile went on to become governor of California and Chief Justice of the United States. He and Coakley would remain friends throughout their lives.

In 1955 Coakley was already an icon in American law enforcement, the founding president of the U.S. District Attorneys Association. Fighting crime was his obsession. Two descriptive words often applied to him were "bulldog" and "stubborn."

Off the job, he was a gregarious, convivial family man, a joiner who thrived in the Elks, the Knights of Columbus, the Naval Reserve, and the St. Mary's Alumni. His politics were Republican, as was natural in the circles where he moved. He was generally perceived to yearn for the broader and higher political planes that his mentor Warren would attain.

Only thirty-five minutes had elapsed since the conclusion of Abbott's interview at the FBI office. At 11:30 P.M., he entered Coakley's office to face for the first time the man who now held his life in his palm.

It was not extraordinary that Frank Coakley should be at his desk at the near-midnight hour. He often worked that late, a nocturnal habit his family had learned to endure.

"Well, we'll start in with asking your name," Coakley said as the session began. His opener could not have been more easygoing.

It's open to question whether the D.A.'s casual approach was purposeful or the result of fatigue. Coakley was known to enjoy a drink with dinner; had he perhaps passed the hours awaiting Burton's arrival with another nip or two? The transcript of the interrogation suggests that he was not at his sharpest and best. As he took Abbott through his story anew, he was sometimes imprecise and repetitious. Trying to establish the time of Abbott's return from the cabin, for example, he mused, "That would be Saturday night and Sunday, Sunday, Sunday, Sunday night, yes." Later he wanderingly inquired, "When you drove, when you drove, when you arrived home, where did you put the car?" Abbott could be forgiven if he sized up the district attorney as a dodderer. But was the district attorney's loose performance intentional—a disarming ploy?

Overall, Coakley's interrogation was effective. Although he elicited no damaging admissions from Burton, he probed several sensitive areas that the earlier inquisitors had passed over.

At one point Burton mentioned that after leaving Red Bluff, heading westward toward the cabin, he had encountered a delay at a bridge across the South Fork of Cottonwood Creek. Oddly, Coakley zeroed in on this offhand remark.

"Where was this you say you stopped?"

Burton's drifting answer was wordy, complex, and ambiguous, but Coakley seemed content to let him ramble.

"Oh, as I just started on the road, there was a big sign," he said, "and the sign said the road was under repair, and I got to the bridge, and the bridge, they are rebuilding it. I can't remember whether it was going in or going out that there were people working there, and they waved us through."

Abruptly taking a new tack, Coakley asked, "Do you ever drive out through the Broadway Tunnel?"

"I have, but it's very seldom that I go out there."

"When you do, why do you go through there and out that way?"

"This last time we were going to Orinda for an installation dinner for my wife. She was being installed as president of the Oakland Cosmetologist Association."

"Have you ever been down around Modesto?" Coakley asked, obviously thinking about the three human fingers that had protruded from the trunk of the Pontiac in Keyes.

"I have been through Modesto."

"When were you through there the last time?"

"It was several years ago. We were on our way to a vacation in Mexico."

Another sudden shift:

"On Thursday, the twenty-eighth of April of this year, at any time that day were you around the Claremont Hotel?" Coakley asked.

"No."

"Were you any place in that vicinity?"

"Not that I can recall. Sometime during the week, though, I bought gas in Berkeley." Although that had been a vacation week at the university, Burton said he had gone there to return some library books.

"Do you ever drive up around the Claremont Hotel?"

"No, Georgia and I have been there once, maybe twice. I don't know. I do recall one time we have been there."

"When was that approximately?"

"A couple, three years ago. It was another one of the cosmetologists' doings. It was a big thing."

"You have never been there any other time? You don't go by there to and from the university?"

"No."

Now it was five minutes before one o'clock on Sunday morning, and Coakley, giving no hint of his intentions, airily terminated the interview: "All right. Well, that's all."

On the way home, sometime around one-thirty, Abbott must have felt another surge of self-assurance. Coolly, cooperatively, and convincingly—even cheerfully—he had stood up for almost eight hours to the best interrogative efforts of the vaunted FBI, the Berkeley police, and the district attorney. None of them had laid a glove on him. Otherwise Coakley would have had him locked up. Or so it seemed.

On San Jose Avenue floodlights still blazed outside the Abbott house. Since the discovery of Stephanie's books, bra, and eyeglasses, the digging for other of her possessions—or her body—had not stopped. Flower beds had been uprooted, and ten FBI agents were still shoveling sandy soil out of the cellar, sifting it spadeful by spadeful. The entire unpaved half of the basement floor had been excavated to a depth of two feet. Nothing more had been unearthed, however.

With lawmen swarming through and around the dwelling, it was plain that the Abbotts would get no rest there. Otto and Leona Dezman were standing by to offer aid and comfort—Leona having just flown in during the evening from a beauticians' convention in Louisville. The Dezmans invited Burton and Georgia to spend what was left of the night at their house, and the offer was gratefully accepted.

8

"One Slight Change"

To Georgia Abbott, her husband's declaration that he needed no lawyer because he was innocent made no sense at all. Not that she necessarily disbelieved him (though she must have wondered); but she was six years his senior, had batted around more, and was wiser in the ways of the world.

In the wake of his grilling, the Sunday papers were naming Burton as the hottest suspect in a crime that had public outrage at white heat. If he was too arrogant or naive to obtain help for himself, Georgia decided she would obtain it for him.

Two houses from the Abbott home stood the big Victorian dwelling of the socially and politically prominent Anderson family. Chesley Anderson, who owned a mortuary, was a member of the Alameda City Council. His wife, Jean, was Georgia's trusted friend, both as a neighbor and as a customer at the beauty shop. It was to her that Georgia now turned.

"I'm scared," she told Jean. "What shall I do?"

"We'd better get Stan Whitney right away," her neighbor replied.

The Whitneys, like the Andersons, were entrenched members of the Alameda establishment. Stanley D. Whitney, fifty-seven years old at this time, headed the much-favored law firm of Whitney & Hanson. Although in court he sometimes appeared stuffy and pugnacious, elsewhere he was an outgoing man who loved to socialize, an extrovert who loved to sing in public settings. He belonged to the Elks Club, which pretty much ran Alameda's politics, and he had been city attorney in the 1940s. His flourishing private practice occupied the second floor of a commanding building on the main street, and the best people in town were his clients. His much younger partner, John Hanson, had grown up in Alameda and was well thought of by old-timers.

On this fateful Sunday, Jean Anderson knew, Whitney was attending a social event at the high-toned Encinal Yacht Club. She drove there and pried him away, and by midafternoon he had consented to defend Burton Abbott against whatever charges he might face. He would not collect much in the way of fees, but the case promised a supreme challenge and a huge publicity dividend.

True, it also posed a major professional problem for Whitney. Early in his career he had done some public defender work, but for years his practice had been mainly civil. He knew much more about torts, probates, and divorces than about indictments and criminal procedure.

Well, he would deal with that deficiency later.

Before four o'clock on this Sunday afternoon, Abbott was back in the D.A.'s office for another round with Frank Coakley—less than fifteen hours having elapsed since their first confrontation. Despite his bravado the previous day about not needing a lawyer, Burton now seemed pleased to have Whitney at his side. Nothing in the record tells us why this repeat interrogation had been convened, but Coakley's opening question suggests that Whitney, after meeting his new client, had requested it.

"Well, now," the prosecutor began, addressing Burton, "we were talking about this matter of your going into Sacramento on the twenty-eighth of April. There is something you wanted to correct?"

Burton had lied the previous evening, and now he appeared frantic to set the record straight. Whitney took over the questioning to lead his client through a painful admission of falsehood.

Abbott was abject. "I am sorry," he said. "I told the officers that I had gone to the land office to see about a claim for my brother. Actually I went to Sacramento and drove around, but I couldn't find the place. It was getting later and later and later, and it got darker. So I said the heck with it and continued on to the cabin."

As we know, Burton had gone so far as to sketch for Agent Hallahan a supposed floor plan of the land office. Now he was saying he had never been there at all. His drawing was a fake.

Whitney asked him why he had fabricated his story.

It was because he had already told the same falsehood to Mark, he said: "I just don't lie to my brother—but I did. I had told him that I would go to the land office because he wanted me to. I had said, 'Sure, Mark, I'll do it.' But when I couldn't find the darned place, instead of spending more time to look for it, I didn't."

In short, Burton had lied to the cops to preserve his credibility with his brother. Not very smart for someone in deep trouble.

At this point Whitney turned the questioning back to the district attorney. The fuzziness of Coakley's rambling interrogation the night before was gone now.

"What time did you arrive in Sacramento?" he asked Burton.

"I would say one or one-thirty. It could just as easily be two-thirty."

"Did you drive there directly from your home without stopping?"

"No stops."

"How fast do you drive?"

"Fifty-five miles an hour—I don't mean in town. The trip to Sacramento takes two or three hours."

Coakley wanted more detail about Burton's unsuccessful search for the land office once he reached Sacramento.

"You said you had been told it was opposite the post office. Did you look there?

"There is an office building there."

"One story? Or more than one story?"

"I don't recall. Been so long ago."

"Do you recall the color of the building?

"Gray."

"I am simply trying to help you," Coakley said. "Would you be willing to go back up there?"

"Yes, I would."

"Did you get out of your car any time in Sacramento?"

"No, I didn't get out of my car."

"You came back out of Sacramento driving west. What time of day was it?"

"Three o'clock, thereabouts."

Coakley betrayed no great concern about Burton's admission of falsehood. The next morning's *Chronicle* would quote him as saying Abbott had made "one slight change" in his story. Apparently neither Abbott nor Whitney sensed that they had handed the prosecutor a time bomb that would explode in their faces months later.

Suddenly, without warning, the district attorney shifted to a totally different line of questioning, as would be his pattern throughout the interview.

"Before last Friday night did you know anything at all about the Stephanie Bryan case?" he asked again—essentially the same question Burton had answered several times already, emphatically in the negative.

"I don't recall ever reading it or anything like that," Burton said. "I think that my mother, my wife, and I said something about it. On one occasion, my wife said something about there was a reward put out. That was about it. We are not prone to read newspapers."

Burton elaborated that he had subscribed to no newspaper until the previous February, when he had entered a U.C. course in labor unionism and had to keep up with what was happening in that field. He had then subscribed to the *Examiner.* He sometimes bought the Sunday *Tribune* as well for the comics and crossword puzzles.

His insistence that he scarcely followed the news caused Coakley to wonder. It seemed implausible, coming from a person of Abbott's intellectual pretensions.

Coakley evinced exceptional interest in Burton's consumption of alcohol. Harking back to his phenomenal drinking session at Wildwood, he inquired, "How did you feel the next morning?"

"Other than a brilliant hangover I felt fine."

"May I ask what your drinking habits are? As a rule do you drink as heavy as you did that night?"

"I have on occasions. The cabin is the one place I figure that it's okay to drink. There are no policemen around and you can't get pinched for drunk driving. Whenever we go up there—you can check with my wife's family—we do drink. As far as frequenting the bars in the Bay Area, I don't. Whenever we went to a Cosmetologists Association meeting, we drank."

"About how much, would you say?"

"I could drive home."

Whitney cut in to make the question more precise: "Two or three drinks?"

"Maybe five," Burton said.

"Bourbon?" Coakley asked. "Bourbon and soda?"

"It really depends on the weather. If it's extremely hot, I would rather take vodka, but if it's cold, bourbon."

"What is your habit with respect to drinking around home?"

"We seldom have liquor in the house except when we have guests in."

"When you drink, how does it affect you? Do you find it exhilarating?"

"I become quite talkative, ramble on and on."

"Quarrelsome?"

"Maybe argumentative, but I am usually quite happy if anything."

"What I am getting at," Coakley said, "is whether or not there is any change in your personality or your behavior. Do you get into trouble of any kind?"

Burton attempted a small quip. "I become a little more affectionate—like my sister-in-law, I might go over and hug her."

Coakley changed the subject again, returning to what had seemed a trivial matter at the previous night's interview—Abbott's crossing of the Cottonwood Creek bridge on the road to Wildwood.

"When you got to the bridge, what did you observe, if anything?" the prosecutor wanted to know.

"They had planks across it. I seem to recall seeing some trucks parked—state highway trucks or something like that, and a fellow with a red flag or lantern or something like that. He waved me onto the bridge, and I went on."

"Was your car the only car there at that time?"

"It is an isolated spot. If a dozen cars pass in a day you are lucky. As to this specific incident, I don't know whether the men were there waving us on then, or when we came back through there. It was Thursday, and that is a day people work; on Sunday they don't work, unless there is a guard or someone."

"How many times did you cross that bridge?"

"Twice—once in and once back."

Coakley posed half a dozen questions about the appearance of the flagmen, but Burton had few definite recollections.

Answering a question about an earlier trip to the cabin in 1954, Burton mentioned that he had missed the deer season, leading Coakley in a new direction of inquiry.

"Are you a deer hunter?"

"Not much of a deer hunter. We used to go up there and park alongside the road and do the hunting. Or we would go down to the apple orchard about a quarter of a mile from the cabin and shoot the deer in the apple orchard. As far as getting out and traipsing through the woods—no, I am not a traipser."

"Do you have a gun?"

"My wife has a gun, a 30-30 Winchester, 1904. My brother has a .22 and a Japanese rifle."

"Other than your wife's gun, do you own any weapons of any kind?"

"No weapons of any kind."

"No knives?"

"Butcher knives. I have a couple of large old hunting knives, but I scarcely know where they are. I may have a few pocket knives. I have fishing knives."

In his wandering interrogation, the district attorney was like a mining prospector picking away at random in an uncertain vein. Now the vein yielded an unexpected nugget.

"Did you obtain anything else that you would have to buy, in preparation to go to the cabin?" Coakley asked.

"My fishing license."

"When did you get that?"

"I'll take a look," Burton responded, pulling out his wallet. He shuffled through its cards and papers until he found what he was looking for. As he put his wallet away he handed the license momentarily to his own lawyer, who examined it and then passed it to Coakley.

"Just for your information, Frank," Whitney said, "—to keep the record straight, this was purchased at the Alameda Sporting Goods Store. It is dated May 26."

A frown furrowed Abbott's brow and his mouth tightened. He knew that the fishing season had opened April 30.

"You mean to say I went up there without a fishing license?" he gasped.

Turning to other matters, Coakley continued his wandering exploration.

"When your brother and his wife arrived at the cabin Friday night, did that awaken you?" he asked Burton.

"He said he tried to wake me up."

"What was the condition of the cabin the next morning?"

"Pretty much of a mess, after Mark got his gear in there."

"Before he arrived, what was its condition?"

"All straightened. I cleaned it up Thursday night."

"It was all squared away?"

"Yes, it was quite clean."

If to Burton and Whitney this seemed a senseless rehash of previous questioning, that suited Coakley fine, for he had just sprung a trap. Clearly Burton was unaware that Mark had already told the FBI he and his wife were appalled by the disorder of the cabin when they got there. Burton had failed on his promise to prepare it for them; their bed was still hanging from the rafters.

This new lie reinforced the prosecutor's impression of Burton Abbott as sneaky and deceitful. Whether it was material to the crime at hand, Coakley had no way of telling right then. So, giving no hint of the ploy he had used, he chose this moment to adjourn the interview.

"That is all," he said cheerfully. "You gentlemen run along."

It was now five-forty-three on Sunday afternoon. For the second time Abbott left the D.A.'s office a free man. In the foyer, however, he confronted for the first time the assembled forces of the press. Half a dozen reporters shouted questions at him, and cameramen began clicking their shutters.

Whitney, escorting Burton through this gauntlet, had dealt with news people often, both in court and as a public official. So, repressing annoyance, he stood aside for several minutes while the flash bulbs popped. Then he stepped forward commanding, "Okay, fellas, let's knock it off."

All the photographers complied except one, a man from the *Chronicle* who tried for one more picture, and Whitney's irritation instantly flared into anger. Impulsively he grabbed an ashtray from a table at his side and hurled it at the offender, damaging his camera. It was an inauspicious beginning for Burton Abbott's relations with the press, which would be following his every move and weighing his every word from then on.

Perhaps to mitigate this fiasco, Whitney presented his client the next morning in what must have been one of the smoothest, most extraordinary performances ever given by a suspect in a capital crime. It amounted to a full-scale press conference in the Abbott living room.

The *Tribune* was instrumental, perhaps at Whitney's instigation, in setting the event up, but it was open to journalists of all Bay Area papers. *Trib* reporter Paul Lewis and photographer Kris Kjobeck called for Whitney at his home about eight-thirty and drove him to his office, where he picked up a wire recorder. Tape recorders were not yet widely available. Then they delivered him to the Abbott home, where the press conference got under way at nine-forty-five.

Flawlessly dapper in a dark sport coat, light-colored slacks, and white shirt with a cheerfully splotchy cravat, Burton sat on the couch between Georgia and Whitney as he faced the Fourth Estate. An aspiring actor since high school, he was convincing in the role of a man pained by unjust accusation. He fielded questions for forty-five minutes, repeating much of what he had been telling the police all weekend. He had saved one new morsel of hard news for the reporters, however: He had agreed to take a lie detector test later that morning.

"I have not evaded or concealed anything," he declared. "I have made my statement voluntarily to Mr. Coakley. I have given the police the jeans and shirt and jacket I wore up north last April. I just feel, let's get this thing all finished and over with. I have nothing to do with Stephanie Bryan. I never knew her or her family. I have not the slightest idea how those things got down there in the basement.

"I don't have to submit to this test today, but I want it gotten over with. My conscience is clear. I'm a little bit leery, but let's go ahead and shoot the works. I would have liked to go to school today; there's an exam in accounting. But I want to get this over with."

Throughout the weekend Whitney's young law partner, John Hanson, had been on vacation a hundred miles south of Alameda, out of touch with his office, on the serene and scenic Monterey Peninsula. About the time Burton was beginning his news conference, Hanson picked up that morning's *Chronicle* and was flabbergasted by what confronted him on the front page: a photo of Whitney taken a split second after he had hurled the ashtray, which was caught in midair coming straight toward the camera. Whatever the damage to the camera, the film within had not been ruined.

This spectacular picture was Hanson's first notice that he himself was now involved in what would become the hottest criminal case Alameda County had ever seen. Later, after he was back from his vacation, the aggrieved photographer showed up at the Whitney & Hanson law office demanding recompense.

"Go to hell," Hanson told him.

9

The Trinity Mystique

To most Californians, even in the 1990s, Trinity County is a remote realm with an awesome mystique. It is a parcel of considerable dimensions, almost a hundred miles north to south and in most places thirty miles wide. Its area is almost three times that of Rhode Island.

Lying far to the north of the state's great cities, its terrain is precipitous, forested, and forbiddingly rugged. It touches neither the ocean nor the great Central Valley nor the Oregon line. No important north-south highway traverses it, and the nearest railhead is thirty miles to the east. Fishermen and hunters know Trinity County, and lumbering thrives there, but most Californians have never set foot on its soil.

Its first settlers were attracted by the fur trade and by gold. It is the sort of place that breeds independent people, proud of their heritage, clannish, and wary of strangers.

Lost Horizon author James Hilton, visiting in the 1940s, pronounced the idyllic county seat of Weaverville "the closest approximation on earth to Shangri-la." Yet episodes of violence and eerie atrocity have regularly punctuated Trinity's past. The pioneers who massacred and scalped nineteen Indians are venerated in local annals, and one of the scalps was on display for a decade in Weaverville museum.

Drollery flourishes in Trinity County. It may be apocryphal, but some old-timers swear that a graveyard there has a tombstone reading

Here lie the bones of my daughter Charlotte,
Born a virgin, died a harlot.
For twelve full years she preserved her virginity:
A long, long time in the County of Trinity.

In 1955 Trinity County's population was about 6,400—roughly two persons per square mile. Here the Stephanie Bryan case would reach its hideous climax.

Berkeley police officers Willard Hutchins and Ralph Schillinger left at midnight Friday for Wildwood, barely six hours after Georgia found Stephanie's purse. Speeding northward, they were the vanguard of a vast army of cops, lawyers, and journalists who would invade the Trinity countryside in the days, weeks, and months ahead.

The cabin that the officers found, when they arrived not long after day-break Saturday, was depressingly crude. They did not need to break in; the lockless door was secured only by a wire wrapped around a nail. There was a potbelly woodstove for heat and the Coleman stove to cook on, but no electricity, telephone, or plumbing.

Erected by Georgia's father in the 1930s, the cabin was a grim landmark to the mountain folk. Seven years before the Bryan case, it had been the scene of another atrocity.

Its occupant then was a sometime-miner named Lloyd K. Snyder,* the for-mer husband of one of Georgia's cousins. Although regarded as a wino, he was well liked by most people in the area. In 1947 he invited another alcoholic miner, Ray Latham, to batch with him.

Latham turned out to be an ornery, unwashed slob, and the two men, snowed in together during the 1947–48 winter, grew to detest each other. During an argument, Latham threatened to slit Snyder from end to end. The latter, catching a mirror view of Latham brandishing a butcher knife, grabbed a shotgun, turned, and shot him dead.

Because he was snowbound without communication, Snyder could nei-ther summon the sheriff nor remove the corpse. So to dispose of it, he hacked it to pieces with an ax, apportioned the parts into six packages, and buried them outside the cabin. When the snow melted, he decided silence was his wisest course.

Latham was little missed, and the crime might have gone unnoticed were it not for a spunky little rancher named Harold "Bud" Jackson. In the rough-and-ready area of Trinity mountain life, few men were more respected. Jack-son was a local native and in truth much more than a rancher. He was also a miner, a deputy sheriff, a county road boss, and above all a "cat hunter"—a man who tracked and killed the mountain lions that preyed on farmers' live-stock. He understood instinctively the ways of the wilds and the animals therein.

Not long after the snow melted in early 1948, Jackson came along Hay-fork Creek with his hunting dogs, Shorty and Spot. As the hounds neared the place where Snyder had interred Latham's parts they set up a dreadful bay-ing, but at the time Jackson assumed they had merely picked up the scent of lions passing through.

Latham's demise still might have passed without notice had not Snyder gone to the post office to claim his late companion's mail. His manner

---

* Unrelated to the late Lloyd B. Snyder, who moved to Weaverville with his family around 1970.

aroused the suspicions of the postmistress, and she went to the sheriff, who in turn sent Jackson to investigate. With his dogs, Jackson returned to the spot of their previous howling and in less than an hour uncovered the chopped meat that had once been Ray Latham.

Snyder was convicted of second-degree murder and sentenced to five years to life. Because he was so popular, some said the jury might have let him off had he not compounded the homicide by dismembering his victim. On leaving for San Quentin, he signed his share of the cabin over to Georgia's older brother, Robert Schorch, who became owner of record.

In the eyes of many mountain people, the cabin was still tainted, and some shunned the blameless Schorch family for continuing to use it. Georgia's brother-in-law, Edwin Jeppesen, feared that sooner or later someone would torch the place.

Now in 1955, the Berkeley cops learned with interest, Snyder was again free. He had been paroled on April 7—exactly three weeks before Stephanie Bryan's disappearance.

Hutchins's and Schillinger's search of the cabin was a depressing duty. The photographs they took conveyed the inhospitality of the place. Georgia's father had wasted not a nickel on anything that could be called an amenity. The carpentry was shoddy: walls of rough-hewn planking nailed to a few haphazard vertical and diagonal timbers. Neither plaster nor paint graced the interior. Whitewash applied long ago had flaked away. The furniture consisted mainly of a beat-up kitchen table with four cheap, unmatched chairs, a couple of cots with lumpy mattresses, and a couch that no self-respecting secondhand dealer would allow on his floor.

Had Stephanie Bryan been abducted to this mean hovel? For hours the two officers combed the interior, vainly seeking an answer. Then they went underneath, into a sloping cellar created by the cabin's hillside location. There they found a four-foot iron bar and several shovels, which they used to excavate the dirt floor. As tools the shovels were far from ideal; one was short-handled and the other had a one-inch nick out of the blade.

Hutchins and Schillinger kept digging until Saturday night closed in on them, then resumed the work for most of Sunday. Late Sunday afternoon they called their headquarters to report that they had found nothing of interest and would return to Berkeley.

From the day the FBI had entered the Stephanie Bryan investigation in May, its dedication to the case had been total. So by this Sunday the Bureau was fully activated in Trinity County as well as in the East Bay. Special Agent Jim Griffith was preparing to deploy twenty-four men on foot to search fifty or sixty miles of Highway 36, all the way from Red Bluff to the top of the grade above Wildwood. Twelve men would tramp along each side of the road, beating the brush that might hide Stephanie's body.

Meanwhile, Griffith joined Hutchins at the Wildwood Inn to interview the owner, Del Cox, who remembered well the drinking session of Abbott and Tom Daly on Friday, April 29.

Hutchins asked the critical question: "Was that the first time you had seen Abbott this year?"

"Yes, I'm sure it was," Cox said. "I shook hands with him and gave him a big greeting, and then I introduced him to Daly."

"What time was that?"

"Sometime in the middle of the afternoon."

"Abbott says he had stopped here the night before that, Thursday, and had a drink on his way to his cabin."

"No, I don't remember that. I'm sure I didn't see him until Friday."

While Hutchins and Griffith were questioning Cox, Schillinger and another FBI agent, William B. Dillon, checked out Daly. His memory coincided with Cox's, and he pinned down the date of the drinking marathon with a pocket diary.

"I had lunch that Friday about noon at the cookhouse at the mill," he said. "Then I went to my trailer and cleaned up, and I went to Del Cox's place and started with a beer. This fellow Abbott came in fifteen or twenty minutes later."

Abbott was wearing faded blue jeans, a shirt of some light color, and regular shoes or rubber fishing boots, Daly recalled. From the boisterous greeting Cox gave him ("Where the hell have you been keeping yourself?"), Daly had gained a clear impression that the two had not seen each other for a long time.

So now the parallel recollections of Cox and Daly demolished the critical time frame of Abbott's alibi. Back in Berkeley, when a *Chronicle* reporter inquired whether the alibi was standing up, Inspector O'Meara gave a guarded reply:

"It stands up for Friday, Saturday, and Sunday, but for the key date, Thursday, April 28, we're still not satisfied. We can't corroborate Abbott's story for that day, but we haven't found any proof that it's false either."

After Burton Abbott's Monday morning press conference, he was driven to Berkeley police headquarters to take the lie detector test for which he had volunteered. Still sportily attired, he played it for all it was worth in public relations. He gladly posed for photographers with the polygraph strap around his chest and a blood pressure cuff on his arm. His countenance reflected neither unconcern nor despair, but studious concentration. Behind him in several of the pictures stood balding, bespectacled Inspector Albert Riedel, who would conduct the test. Riedel was known as one of the most skillful polygraph operators anywhere. For the Abbott interrogation he would be joined by an equally eminent scientist, Dr. Douglas M. Kelley, a U.C. professor who had been the chief U.S. psychiatrist at the Nuremberg war crimes trials.

When the first lie detector session ended, two and a half hours after it began, a much-chastened Abbott emerged. His face was pale, his buoyancy gone. The *Chronicle* described him as "weary and silent."

"Abbott was obviously tiring badly, and we broke it up because of his physical condition, to let him get a good night's sleep before continuing," Riedel explained. He alluded to breathing difficulties having to do with Burton's tuberculosis and lung surgery.

On Tuesday the polygraph examination resumed; when it was over, Riedel told reporters, "It was an exceptionally slow process. Abbott could stand up under only about fifteen minutes of high-pressure questioning at a time."

"High-pressure" was a well-chosen adjective. Abbott, who had remained cool under the earlier questioning by Hallahan, O'Meara, and Coakley, had come totally unglued in the face of Riedel and Kelley. He later complained that the lie detector test was "worse than a Red Chinese brainwashing."

Although Riedel made excuses for Burton's fatigue when speaking for print, he had been merciless in his interrogation.

"He spent two hours asking me just two questions," Abbott told a *Chronicle* reporter. "He asked one question thirty-two times and the other question forty-two times."

One segment of Riedel's interrogation was keyed to the investigation simultaneously under way in the northern wilds. He showed Abbott a map of California on which were drawn vertical and horizontal lines dividing the state into quadrants. In turn he pointed to each, asking "Is Stephanie's body here?" "Is she here?" "Is she here?" In each case, Burton disclaimed any knowledge, but when Riedel came to the northwestern sector, which included Trinity, the polygraph betrayed tension and alarm. Burton's respiration line flattened out ominously, as if his breathing had stopped.

Then Riedel drew new cross-lines, dividing each map quadrant into four smaller parts, and repeated the process. As the geographical focus narrowed, the polygraph's needles showed Abbott's agitation compounding. Finally Riedel felt certain that the corpse of Stephanie Bryan lay within a tiny map area close to Wildwood.

To Riedel's satisfaction, the map grid technique also elicited the scene of Stephanie's death. Abbott reacted profoundly when Riedel's pointer touched an inconspicuous spot in the Contra Costa County hills between San Pablo and Pinole, scarcely ten miles from where the girl had last been seen.*

---

* More than fifty officers were deployed to the location Riedel indicated and searched some two thousand acres. The fact that they found nothing did not shake Riedel's conviction that this was the murder scene.

The wooded pathway between the Claremont Hotel and the residential area where the Bryan family lived. *(Courtesy of Harry Farrell)*
(inset) Stephanie Bryan. Her hair was cut to a shorter length before her disappearance. *(Courtesy of* San Jose Mercury News*)*

Burton and Georgia Abbott's rented home at 1408 San Jose Avenue in Alameda; Georgia's Pontiac is in the driveway. *(Courtesy of Alameda County District Attorney's Office)*

Officers Steven Soishno and Russ Johnson dig for clues in the sandy soil of Abbott's basement. (Oakland Tribune *photo courtesy of Alameda County District Attorney's Office)*

An unidentified police officer displays the All detergent box in which Stephanie Bryan's purse was found in the basement of the Abbott home. (Oakland Tribune *photo courtesy of Alameda County District Attorney's Office)*

Stephanie Bryan's brassiere, which was found in Abbott's basement. *(Courtesy of Alameda County District Attorney's Office)*

Georgia Abbott in happier times: She is shown (right) at a luncheon of the State Cosmetologists Association in Long Beach, 1952. *(Courtesy of Otto Dezman)*

Burton "Bud" Abbott at the press conference in which he professed his innocence, with attorney Stanley Whitney. (Oakland Tribune *photo courtesy Alameda County of District Attorney's Office)*

Otto and Leona Dezman in a photo probably taken a short time before the case broke. Otto was with the Abbotts when Georgia found Stephanie's belongings. *(Courtesy of Otto Dezman)*

The lie-detector test: Abbott with Inspector Albert E. Riedel of the Berkeley Police Department. (Oakland Tribune *photo courtesy of Alameda County District Attorney's Office)*

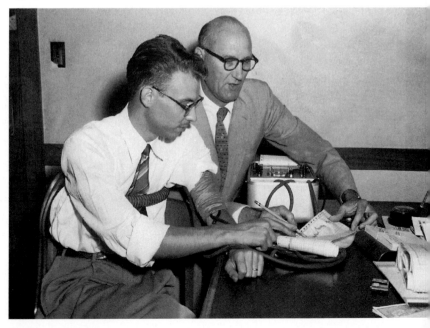

The Wildwood Inn, where Abbott claimed to have stopped on the night of the kidnapping, and where he had his marathon binge the next afternoon. *(Courtesy of Alameda County District Attorney's Office)*

Burton Abbott displays the hunting clothes he claimed he wore on his mysterious Trinity trip. His attorneys distributed the photo to newspapers in northern California, hoping someone would recognize him and confirm his alibi. *(Oakland Tribune photo courtesy of Alameda County District Attorney's Office)*

Abbott's gray-green 1949 Chevrolet: Note the turtleback design and sun visor. *(Courtesy of Alameda County District Attorney's Office)*

The cabin at Wildwood. *(Courtesy of Alameda County District Attorney's Office)*

The cabin interior, looking from front to back. *(Courtesy of Alameda County District Attorney's Office)*

Harold "Bud" Jackson, the Trinity County "cat hunter" who found Stephanie's grave with his hounds. *(*Oakland Tribune *photo courtesy of Alameda County District Attorney's Office)*

tephanie Bryan's grave as it was iscovered, before the exhumation ad begun. *(Courtesy of Alameda County District Attorney's Office)*

Stephanie's exhumation. District Attorney J. Frank Coakley is at rear center (behind man holding ax); Berkeley Officer Willard Hutchins is at far right foreground. *(Courtesy of Clare Coakley Klinge)*

A photo taken during the exhumation shows Stephanie's ankle and saddle shoe clearly (top). *(Courtesy of Alameda County District Attorney's Office)*

Burton Abbott in handcuffs on the night of his arrest, with Inspector Riedel and Jack Fink, the arresting offficer. *(Courtesy of Jack Fink)*

The prosecution: Folger Emerson (left) and J. Frank Coakley. *(Courtesy of Clare Coakley Klinge)*

Earlier Abbott had told Riedel he was broke and his family would have to pay for his defense, so now the inspector took a Dutch uncle approach: "What I can't understand, Burton, is why you want your brother to spend his last dollar when we both know you're guilty?"

Abbott became thoughtful for a moment and then mused, "Yeah, it's tough on the family, but as long as there's a chance I should take it. You're right, but I still want to have as much of a chance as possible."

"Well, then, you admit you're guilty?"

In that blunt form, Riedel's question struck Abbott like lightning, cutting short his reverie.

"Hell no, I didn't do it!" he shouted, bolting from his chair. "I'm shutting up. I've said too much already."

Dr. Kelley, the Nuremberg psychiatrist, now took his turn at trying to pierce Burton's shell. "Your situation is hopeless. What are you going to do?" he asked.

"A miracle will save me," Abbott replied.

"What miracle?"

"I haven't the faintest idea, but something has always saved me when I'm in trouble."

Dr. Kelley was later quoted as saying that of all the persons he had examined professionally, "Hermann Goering and Burton Abbott were the most self-centered."

Not everyone shared Riedel and Kelley's certainty of Abbott's evil.

"Anybody who had access to his basement is still a suspect," police Captain Addison Fording told reporters.

The list of people with access to the basement of the house in Alameda was longer than one might suppose. Entry to the cellar was through the garage, whose rear door was never locked. Besides family members, friends and neighbors had been in the basement from time to time, as had Clyde Wood, the landlord, and several housekeepers and baby-sitters. Moreover, the garage had been a polling place in an election on May 24, with three board members present all day and about 150 voters coming and going.

Landlord Wood, a retired railroad man, had free run of the house whether the Abbotts were home or not; so he was among the first persons grilled, but he quickly exonerated himself. On the afternoon Stephanie vanished, he had been stranded at his own home without a car while his wife drove a friend to a circle meeting at the Presbyterian Church. Then after supper the

---

Two weeks later a convincing tipster (with no knowledge of the polygraph findings) told the Berkeley police that at about 5:15 P.M. on April 28 he had seen a man who looked like Abbott eating a ham sandwich in a steak house on San Pablo Dam Road within a mile or two of the spot Riedel had pinpointed.

Woods had gone with other friends to an Odd Fellows and Rebekahs meeting to hear a speaker discuss "The Women of the Bible." Wood incidentally gave the Abbotts high marks as tenants. "I'd hate to lose them," he said.

From others too the police heard favorable opinions of Burton. Among those who totally rejected his guilt at this point was Leona Dezman, Otto's wife and Georgia Abbott's employer.

"I can't believe he had anything to do with Stephanie Bryan," she said in a statement that would return to haunt her. Like Georgia, Leona remembered Burton's good-bye stop at the beauty parlor as he was leaving for Trinity on April 28. She thought it was "just before noon"—four hours before Stephanie had vanished. He was wearing blue jeans.

Pressed by the FBI to identify any other possible suspects, the Abbotts could not come up with anyone.

"Do you have any enemies, anyone with cause to frame you?" they were asked.

"None that we can think of."

"Any prowlers or Peeping Toms in the neighborhood?"

"We did have some lewd phone calls," Georgia said. "I reported them to the Alameda Police Department." Then, her memory jogged, she also recalled her burglar scare the previous Wednesday night—the thudding she ultimately had ascribed to her pet budgie's flying into unseen objects in the dark.

"Are you a bird lover?" Agent Buchanan asked her.

"I've got a book on budgies. I borrowed it from a customer at the shop."

Interesting, Buchanan mused, considering that Stephanie was a bird fancier too.

With the Bryan investigation entering its twelfth week, Berkeley police officers had now put in 2,100 hours of overtime on the case. As platoons of detectives had fanned out through the area, one place that had drawn their attention was Pring's Doughnut Shop,* a tiny Telegraph Avenue café half a block south of Willard Junior High and about eight blocks from the U.C. campus. It was a popular hangout for Willard youngsters, and Stephanie had stopped there almost every day for an ice cream cone or a cherry phosphate.

FBI agents showed pictures of Burton Abbott to people at Pring's, who instantly recognized his likeness. He was a regular who came in several times a week, always neat, always mannerly. Waitress Elmyra Mills liked him because he always left a tip, a rarity at Pring's. He ordinarily wore collegiate sport

---

* Not to be confused with the Dream Fluff Donut Shop on Ashby Avenue, where Stephanie had stopped on her last homeward walk.

clothes, but Elmyra recalled that he had once left a leather jacket in the shop and later reclaimed it. She had looked through the pockets for some identity object but had found only a pack of chlorophyll gum and about eight Kleenex tissues.

Abbott seldom conversed with other customers, but another waitress, La Verne Malloy, said he would usually read the morning's *Chronicle* and they would discuss the day's news. No one could remember whether he and Stephanie Bryan had ever been in the shop at the same time. Dolores Pring, who ran the place with her husband, guessed they probably had been, but if so he had paid no special attention to the girl or anyone in the junior high school crowd.

Coakley, reading the reports from the doughnut shop later, was intrigued by Miss Malloy's remark that Abbott regularly read the *Chronicle*. This did not jibe with what he was insisting now, that he scarcely followed the news at all.

On the day of the Pring's interviews, the same inconsistency came to the attention of Clarence Severin, Coakley's captain of inspectors, while he was chatting with Richard Felgenhauer, a court bailiff who had been a Livermore patient with Abbott.

"I can't understand why Burton claims he never reads the papers," Felgenhauer said. "At Livermore I subscribed to the *Tribune* and I think he did also. He would read the whole paper every day, either his own copy or mine."

The FBI interrogation of Burton's mother was assigned to Agent William Poole, working with Berkeley Officer Bill Plantz. Elsie was a cooperative subject, recounting in much detail her son's return from Trinity on May 1. She remembered him as being exhausted, unshaven, and complaining loudly about the bad weather and rotten fishing, but otherwise in good spirits. His car was mud-caked, and as Burton unloaded it he had dumped his dirty clothes and fishing gear in the basement. As always, it had fallen to his mother to pick up after him.

Elsie's narration was inconsequential until she mentioned returning to the cellar sometime later to look for a couple of missing chenille bedspreads. Going through a carton of old clothes, she revealed matter-of-factly, she had both seen and examined Stephanie's purse a couple of months before Georgia found it. She had thumbed through the wallet, looked at the snapshots, and seen the name Stephanie Bryan, which had meant nothing to her at the time. She had hastily scanned and refolded Stephanie's unfinished letter to "Teddy."

Supposing Stephanie to be a friend of Georgia's, Elsie had replaced the purse in the "All box" and put it out of her mind. When Elsie had seen the box, it was on the basement floor, although it was on a shelf when Georgia found the purse in it later.

"Can you be more exact about the date you saw the box, Mrs. Abbott?" Plantz asked.

"It was probably the first week in May."

Elsie had innocently disclosed two crucial facts, which her questioners instantly perceived: The purse had been in the cellar within a few days after Burton's trip and also well before the May 24 election. In eight words Elsie had both tightened the evidence against her son and eliminated the election board members and voters as suspects.

In San Francisco's stately Hearst Building, Bill Wren was troubled by the failure of the Wildwood searchers to turn up a single clue. Why had they quit so soon?

Wren was the tough managing editor of the *San Francisco Examiner,* an aggressive morning paper in a city where competition raged among four scrappy dailies. For these vying papers, the Bryan story was raw meat. Wren's news instincts told him the nub of the story was in Trinity County and everyone was missing it. On Tuesday he assigned reporter Ed Montgomery and cameraman Bob Bryant to find it, and they flew to Trinity late that afternoon.

Montgomery was a serious, bespectacled journalist—a loner who had worked a lot of tough police and court yarns and corruption exposés. One of the latter had won him a Pulitzer Prize. Bryant likewise was tops in his field; in 1945 he had taken the press pool pictures of the Japanese surrender aboard the *U.S.S. Missouri.*

In their small plane the *Examiner* men landed at a little airfield near Hayfork, rented a car, and drove to Wildwood to reconnoiter. Just before dusk, standing on the road about 250 yards north of the cabin, Montgomery got a momentary whiff of what he knew as the smell of death, but he couldn't tell where it came from. A few minutes later, with a shift in the breeze, he caught it again. Then it was gone.

He and Bryant drove to the Hayfork Hotel, arriving late that night. There, from someone in the bar, they heard for the first time the story of Lloyd Snyder and how Bud Jackson's dogs in 1948 had sniffed out Ray Latham's dismembered body.

"Is Jackson still around?" Montgomery asked.

"Sure."

"Does he still have dogs?"

"He sure does."

Early Wednesday morning Montgomery and Bryant found Bud Jackson where he was grading a county road with his bulldozer.

"We'd like to hire you and your dogs to search around Abbott's cabin," Montgomery told him.

"I'll be glad to help you, but I can't start till tonight after work."

They agreed to meet at Jackson's ranch at day's end.

Jackson would be helping the *Examiner* team in a private capacity, not as a special deputy. So during the afternoon, to head off any accusation of private interference in a criminal investigation, Montgomery informed Deputy Charles Wyckoff, the head of the sheriff's station in Hayfork, of what he had in mind.

"You're wasting your time," Wyckoff said. "My men have been over and over that ground, and so have the Berkeley cops and the FBI. There's nothing there."

Wyckoff offered no objections, however.

In the five days since the discovery of Stephanie's purse, no newsman had pursued the story more tenaciously than *Tribune* cameraman Russ Reed, who had won Abbott's confidence with small favors. Before Burton had turned his fishing clothes over to the police, he had asked Reed to take his picture wearing them. Abbott's lawyers had sent the resulting photo to the newspapers in Sacramento, Redding, and Red Bluff, in the hope that some reader might remember having seen him in April and confirm his alibi.

On this Wednesday, Burton decided to decompress from his interrogation ordeal by going to the movies with his brother Mark and Edwin Jeppesen, and he invited Reed to come along. They met at a restaurant for a bite before the matinee, and although Burton's name and face had been on the front pages all week, no one recognized him. At Oakland's T & D Theater, they took loge seats for the double bill, *Francis in the Navy* and *Ma and Pa Kettle at Waikiki*. Abbott laughed heartily throughout.

During the afternoon Reed mentioned that he and a *Tribune* reporter would take a working trip to Wildwood on Friday, two days hence. Would Abbott like to come along?

"Would I!" he exclaimed. "Maybe I can find someone to clear me."

As Abbott and Reed parted after the show, neither had an inkling that as they spoke, an opposition news team was already at Wildwood unloading bloodhounds from Bud Jackson's truck.

The truck, bearing Jackson, Montgomery, Bob Bryant, and a friend of Jackson's known as "Pop" Coleman, had reached Abbott's cabin a little before six-thirty. With them were Shorty and Spot, the same hounds that had found Ray Latham's remains. Now the dogs were seven years older but still keen and agile, as was Jackson himself. At age forty-three he was thin and wiry but well muscled. He had on work clothes and a white Stetson.

On arriving at the cabin, the group found they were not alone. Two reporters from the *Redding Record-Searchlight* were there too, poking around. The small, remote Redding paper posed no real competitive threat to the *Examiner,* but still Montgomery glumly realized he would not have a clean scoop on any story the evening produced.

Released from their pens on the truck, Jackson's dogs explored the immediate area of the cabin for five minutes, sniffing at the ground between the structure and the creek to the rear. Then they headed downstream to the north, to about where Montgomery had caught the elusive scent twenty-four hours earlier. Now, however, the dogs gave no response there. Next they splashed across the creek and penetrated deep into the woods. For three-quarters of a mile they followed the stream's east bank southward before returning to the cabin.

An hour and five minutes had passed since the start of the search, with no reaction whatever from the hounds. Montgomery had about decided that Deputy Wyckoff was right; he was on a wild goose chase. As darkness began to settle, however, a slight breeze arose and he turned to Jackson with a final plea:

"Can we take the dogs back one more time to where I got that whiff last night?"

"Okay," Jackson said.

The dogs had almost reached the point Montgomery meant when Shorty stopped suddenly, thrust his nose in the air, and looked inquiringly at his master.

"Go get it!" Jackson commanded.

The hounds bounded up the mountainside across the road from the cabin, vanishing into dense brush and manzanita that blanketed the ground. At places the incline was so steep that Jackson, striving to follow, had to pull himself up by grabbing at tree roots. The others brought up the rear.

About three hundred feet up the hillside, the dogs started to run around and around excitedly in ever-tightening circles. Finally, at a place where the earth seemed disturbed near a manzanita thicket, a few feet from the base of a towering ponderosa pine, Spot lay out on the ground and began a mournful whimper. The soil emitted a heavy, saturating stench.

Jackson went back to the cabin and returned with the nick-bladed shovel. Using it, he scraped a little soil from the extreme north end of the dug-up area. As he did so, a brown-and-white saddle shoe came into view, and the decayed flesh of a small ankle.

10

"String Him Up!"

That evening Elsie Abbott was home alone in the house on San Jose Avenue. The moviegoers had not yet returned, and Georgia was at Coakley's office for another interview. When the phone rang a little after seven, Elsie answered and heard a businesslike male voice.

"My name is Frank Purcell. I'm a reporter for the *Examiner,* and I'd like to come and talk to you folks for a little while. Is this a convenient time?"

"This is Burton's mother, and I'm here by myself right now," Elsie replied. "Please call back in a half hour or so."

When Purcell did so, Mark Abbott answered—he and Burton having returned from the theater in the meantime. Purcell repeated his request, and Mark said, "Come on over."

Later Coakley would angrily demand to know why Purcell had sought the interview on that particular night. The vague answer he got was that the *Examiner* was "developing a newspaper exclusive." Unfolding events, however, would suggest that Purcell's assignment was actually a stakeout.

His editor, Bill Wren, knew that Ed Montgomery was up in Wildwood searching for Stephanie's body with bloodhounds. Wren almost certainly dispatched Purcell to Burton's home by design, to position him strategically in case Montgomery's efforts succeeded.

Purcell arrived at the Abbott door about eight-thirty and joined the family in the living room.

"Where's your wife?" he asked Burton.

"She was called to the D.A.'s office. Stan Whitney is with her."

"If possible I'd like to wait until they return before I start talking about the idea I have," Purcell said. "I want everything to be absolutely clear and on the table."

Was Purcell stalling for time? For the next half hour, he and the family talked mostly of inconsequentials.

About nine o'clock Georgia and Whitney arrived, and Georgia took a chair in the corner of the room. Whitney seated himself on the couch with Burton. Almost at once the doorbell rang. Mark went to see who it was; a minute later he told Purcell, "It's someone to see you."

If the reporter had indeed been stalling, his timing was flawless. On the front porch Purcell found another *Examiner* staffer, George "Eric" Erickson, with whom he spoke briefly. Then he reentered the house, bringing Erickson in and introducing him to all present.

"Folks, Mr. Erickson has some news for us," he announced.

"I am sure we will all be very glad to hear it," chirped Whitney, who strove for good cheer in the worst of times.

"I don't know whether you will or not," Purcell said. "Go ahead, Eric."

Erickson quietly addressed himself to Burton: "The body of a girl about fourteen—a girl resembling Stephanie Bryan—has been found near your cabin."

"Near the cabin!" Burton cried out—an ejaculation more than a question.

Elsie reached out to her son and said simply, "Oh, Bud!" Georgia rose from her corner chair and moved to Burton's side.

"It can't be!" Abbott gasped. Then: "How far from the cabin?"

"I don't know," Erickson replied. "I don't have any details."

"I can't understand it," Abbott said. "It just can't be!"

Erickson was incredulous. "You maintain that you don't know how the body got there?"

"I don't know *anything* about it," Burton screamed. "I'm sticking with my story. I—did—not—do—it."

By now Purcell had picked up the Abbotts' telephone and was describing the scene to a rewrite man in the *Examiner* newsroom. Meanwhile a third *Examiner* man, photographer Seymour Snaer, had appeared and caught a shot of Georgia, in tears, holding Burton's hand. When Snaer took a second photo, showing the agitated suspect seated between his primly coiffed wife and his anguished mother, Abbott's anger flashed: "Don't use that!"

The plea was to no avail. The picture, with Burton wagging a hostile finger at the camera, ran in the next morning's paper.

The *Examiner* informed the Berkeley Police Department of the body's discovery at approximately the same time it broke the news to the Abbotts. O'Meara, when notified at 9:30 P.M., was furious that a newspaper had dared invade his investigative turf. Minutes later, however, he sent an emergency teletype to Alameda Chief of Police George Doran:

PLEASE PICK UP BURTON ABBOTT, 1408 SAN JOSE AVENUE, YOUR CITY, AND HOLD FOR 187 PC.

Section 187 is the murder section of the California Penal Code. Alameda Police Inspector Jack Fink and Lieutenant Joseph Bertrand got to the Abbott house a little after nine-forty.

"You are under arrest," Fink told Burton, who put up no resistance. However, fastidious as always, he went to the bedroom, changed his shirt and necktie, and selected a coat and hat before leaving to be booked at Alameda police headquarters.

Whitney and Mark accompanied him to the station, where reporters bombarded him with questions.

"I know it looks black for me, but I didn't do it," Burton told them. "My mind is a blank as far as this is concerned. It's a complete blank." He rattled on and on until Whitney shut him up.

He cooperated as the Alameda police fingerprinted him and took his picture front and profile, a process requiring only minutes. He was then handed over to O'Meara, who had arrived from Berkeley with Inspectors John Pedersen and Al Riedel—the latter Abbott's nemesis of the polygraph sessions.

O'Meara frisked his prisoner, snapped handcuffs on him (the first time he had been manacled), and led him to a waiting Berkeley police car. The transfer to the Berkeley police station was an eight-mile ride. After arriving at about ten-thirty, Burton was led in through a side door and taken to the third-floor jail.

He remained unruffled—not least because he was unaware of ominous calls already swamping the police switchboard downstairs, The messages were all of a kind:

"The bastard doesn't deserve a trial." "String him up!" "Let's have a necktie party." "LYNCH HIM!"

Officer Schillinger was posted at the bottom of the staircase leading to the jail, with orders that were explicit: "No one goes up there—no visitors, no reporters, nobody."

The press was told that Abbott was under a suicide watch.

Back at the Abbott residence, meanwhile, Georgia made one lone phone call, to Zella Prager, her theatrical friend who had offered prayers and money.

"They've found the body, Zella," Georgia said. "Have you heard?"

"Yes, I have." Already the news from Trinity County was on the radio throughout the state.

"Your offer may be needed now," Georgia told her friend. "It looks bad."

Again a crowd was gathering outside the house. Police speedily erected barricades at both ends of the block, closing it to vehicular traffic.

At two minutes before 11 P.M., Abbott again found himself seated across the table from a team of questioners, two of whom—O'Meara and FBI Agent Buchanan—he already knew. They were joined this time by Assistant District Attorney Folger Emerson, a veteran prosecutor of crimes from fraud to homicide. At age forty-eight, Emerson was an intense, scholarly man with receding wavy hair. Horn-rimmed glasses gave him an owlish look.

Physically the setup for this interrogation was much the same as Burton had already encountered, but now the dynamics were radically altered. He was no longer submitting voluntarily; now he was a prisoner. Less than three hours had elapsed since the discovery of Stephanie's grave far to the north.

"You understand why you are here?" O'Meara opened.

"Yes, sir, I do," Abbott said

"Why are you here?"

"I'm being charged with the murder of Stephanie Bryan."

"Did you do it?"

"No, sir, I did not do it."

Thus Abbott signaled that he was not going to fold. The officers would get no easy confession or cooperation from this slight young man.

"What else do you know about the murder of Stephanie Bryan?" O'Meara asked.

"I know an awful lot about it now."

"Who told you about the murder of Stephanie Bryan?" O'Meara mercilessly repeated the chilling "murder" phrase.

"You did; all the officers did."

"Did anyone tell you tonight about the murder of Stephanie Bryan?"

"Yes, an *Examiner* reporter. I don't know his name. He came in and said a body was found somewhere near our cabin."

"Do you know how that body got there?"

"No, I do not know how that body got there."

"Did you carry that body there?"

"No, I did not carry that body there."

"Did you help carry that body there?"

"No, I did not help carry that body there."

"Do you know what Stephanie Bryan looks like?" O'Meara inquired.

"Yes, I do."

"On any occasion, have you talked with that girl?"

"Not that I know of."

"Have you had any occasion to see her any place in Berkeley?"

Again: "Not that I know of."

Relentlessly O'Meara bore in, repeating each question in a dozen variations: Had Stephanie ever talked to him? Had he ever seen her near the Claremont Hotel? Or around the tennis courts? Or walking home from school? Or waiting for a bus? Or walking around the streets? Had he ever picked her up? Had she ever been in his automobile?

In each case Abbott answered in the negative.

"Now on April 28, 1955, what did you do?"

Suddenly Abbott tried to draw a curtain on the interview: "I would rather not say anything else until I have talked to Mr. Whitney. Stan—Mr. Whitney—told me not to say anything, and here I have been talking."

In that belated outburst, Abbott revealed a trait that would ill-serve him in what lay ahead—that of ignoring his lawyers' instructions and undercutting their best efforts. An egotistical belief that his interrogators and prosecutors were his intellectual inferiors, whom he could outwit, would lead him to disobey his attorneys repeatedly. His compulsion was to talk and talk when silence was golden.

Folger Emerson now entered the give-and-take for the first time, speaking softly, almost deferentially, assuming the "good" role in this "good cop-bad cop" scenario.

"Do you mind if I ask you a question?" he began tentatively. "It doesn't pertain to April at all. You said an *Examiner* reporter told you this evening that this body had been found. Exactly what did he tell you?"

"It's so hazy right this minute."

"Did he tell you whether the body had been buried or not?"

"I don't recall. I think all he said was that a body had been found near the cabin."

"Did he say how near?"

"I don't recall."

"Have you ever received any information as to where the body was found with relation to the cabin—what direction it was?"

"No, I have not."

"Have you received any information as to whether the body was buried or covered with something?

"Yes, I have."

"What have you heard about that?"

Suddenly Abbott realized that within the course of five answers he had diametrically contradicted himself. Again he said, "I'd rather not say until I talk to Stan."

Emerson ignored Abbott's request for his lawyer as if it had never been uttered. This was eleven years before the U.S. Supreme Court's *Miranda* decision,* and a suspect's safeguards against self-incrimination were loosely defined if at all.

"Whom have you talked to besides the *Examiner* reporter?" Emerson asked.

Burton answered at some length regarding several *Examiner* reporters with

---

* To be written by Coakley's friend and former boss Earl Warren, as chief justice.

whom he had spoken, including Purcell, another he knew only as Sam, and another "great big, tall fellow." Hardly realizing it, Abbott had been sucked back into a responsive posture.

"Well," Emerson asked, "did Purcell talk to you about where the body had been found?

"I don't know."

"Did these other reporters talk to you about it?"

"I don't know who told me anything. They told me that a body had been found near the cabin and that was all. It was a madhouse just about then."

"What information do you have right now, from any source, about where the body was found? How far from the cabin? What direction?"

"Well, somebody—I'm not going to tell you how far it was because I don't know who told me, but . . ."

Under pressure, Abbott was becoming increasingly self-contradictory and incoherent.

"All I want to know is what you were told," Emerson reiterated.

"Well, I don't know. Somebody said 200 yards, 300 yards, I don't know. And somebody said 250 feet. That seems to stick in my mind, but I don't know. I seem to recall getting two different stories."

"Did somebody tell you whether the body was buried, whether it was in something, or whether it was covered by something, or how it was found?"

Now for the third time Abbott pleaded for his lawyer. "Can I talk to Stan before I make any more statements?"

"Well, you can," Emerson answered, "but he isn't here now."

"I'd just like to call him. If he says go ahead, I'll go ahead. But he has told me, 'Don't say anything, don't talk to any officers.' "

O'Meara cut in, feigning astonishment: "You've been talking to officers right along!"

Skillfully the interrogators were playing Burton's natural bent to keep his mouth going against his lawyer's admonition to keep it shut.

"It's not that I don't want to talk to you, Mr. O'Meara," he said. "I just want to make sure than Stan knows what's going on."

"Let me ask you this," Emerson interrupted. "Did Mr. Whitney give you his advice before or after you heard that the body had been found?"

"He has told me so many times, never to talk to anyone."

Emerson goaded him on: "You see, the situation has changed considerably with this body being found. Now you have said many times in the past few days that you want to cooperate with the authorities."

"Well, I still do," Abbott declared.

"But wait a minute! As soon as the body is discovered, you apparently don't." Emerson's tone was becoming harsher.

Abbott attempted to respond in kind: "You seem to have some reason for being afraid of my talking to Mr. Whitney. That's what I keep thinking. Stan doesn't have to come out here. I'll answer any questions two minutes after I talk to him on the telephone. You can listen in if you want to."

On and on the inquisition continued, with O'Meara picking up on Emerson's line of persuasion: "You have talked before, all about your trip, answering the very same questions. You felt capable of handling the situation then. Why didn't you call the attorney then and talk to him?"

"Well, it just dawned on me."

Sensing that the young suspect was close to a breaking point, O'Meara turned up the heat.

"How do *you* think that body got there?" he demanded. *"You* were up there in April when Stephanie disappeared. *You* were fishing on those dates, and drinking in the bar on those dates, and visiting with your relatives on those dates, and *you* are completely familiar with the property and its immediate surroundings. How do *you* think a body got on that property?"

"Can I just call Mr. Whitney first?" Abbott beseeched. Finally his self-preservation instinct was overriding his inclination toward glib repartee.

"Yes, you can," Emerson assured him once more, "but let me say something. You are an intelligent man, Mr. Abbott. You sat here for maybe ten, fifteen minutes answering Inspector O'Meara's questions, and then, to use your own words, something 'dawned on you.' The thing that dawned on you was the purpose of the questions we were asking. I think you realize at last that you can't talk to us any further without incriminating yourself."

"I don't feel that way at all," Abbott said.

"What I really want," Emerson said slowly, emphasizing each word, "is the true story of what happened to this girl."

"And I'm giving you everything I know."

"I don't think you are."

The interrogators took a break about half an hour before midnight. O'Meara went downstairs to brief the reporters keeping vigil there.

"What's Abbott's attitude, Inspector?" asked the *Tribune's* Rose Glavinovich.

"He's just as complacent as ever. We are getting exactly the same responses that we got when we started to question him last Saturday," O'Meara said. He neglected to mention Abbott's belated demands for his lawyer. Nor did he inform the reporters that upstairs, Burton had been turned over to a tougher team of questioners whom he already viscerally hated: Inspector Riedel, the "Red Chinese brainwasher," and Dr. Kelley, the Nuremberg shrink.

Despite his earlier press statement that Burton's lie detector test was "inconclusive," Riedel now told Abbott he had flunked it hopelessly. (The polygraph apparatus was nowhere in sight now, however, as Riedel and Kelley launched into almost three more hours of accusatory questioning.)

When Kelley took over the interrogation, he painted a vivid word picture of Stephanie's corpse. In hideous detail he described its decay and told how a bear or other animal had molested it. If his aim was to shake Abbott's composure, however, he failed. After listening to the nauseating recitation with no sign of contrition or even sorrow, Burton turned to O'Meara, who had reentered the room, and snapped, "Damn you, O'Meara, where is that ham sandwich you promised me?"

Not until 2:45 A.M. did the session end. Burton's last words, before he was locked in a cell for the first time, were: "Tell my wife and my mother I didn't do it."

In the Bryan home on Alvarado Road, Stephanie's parents had been showing home movies to their four surviving youngsters when police arrived to inform them, in gentler manner, of Stephanie's fate. The children, from three through twelve in age, were sent to bed before the news was broken. A little later the Bryans, seated on their living room sofa, talked briefly to reporters.

"We've been prepared for this—for a long time," said Dr. Bryan, the grieving father. Mary spoke sadly of the three sisters and brother Stephanie left behind, observing "We'll have to tell them before they find out from somebody else."

"Do you want to talk to Burton Abbott to find out more about what happened to Stephanie?" a reporter asked.

"I have no desire to see Mr. Abbott," Mary answered coldly. "He doesn't exist for me."

"I wish they'd turn him over to me," the grim-faced doctor interjected. He went on to elaborate on his feelings:

"It is a surprise that I haven't been red mad," he said. "If I had been faced with the possibility of a situation like this six months ago, I presume I would have been so mad I couldn't see. But my emotion now is bigger than that; it is a cold feeling, not a hot anger."

What did the doctor think should happen to Stephanie's killer?

After pondering the question he replied thoughtfully, "I don't think that the punishment aspect is as important as a matter of removing someone who will repeat if given another chance. There should be a deterrent also to anyone else with similar thoughts. Those are the important reasons why such a man should be removed from the world completely. He is no good to himself or anyone else. He is a miserable creature, like a cancer that should be cut out and given to a pathologist."

11

The Exhumation

During the five days since the discovery of Stephanie's purse in Abbott's cellar, Frank Coakley had never wavered in his conviction that her body would be found in Trinity County.

"He just had that feeling. He had a bag packed in his car, ready to leave as soon as he got the word," his widow, Kathleen, recalled in 1993.

As district attorney, Coakley could have left the front-line duty of the Bryan investigation to his inspectors, but he was deeply involved at an emotional level. His daughter Clare, then a coed living at home, sensed that she herself was an important reason for her father's passionate participation in the case: "He had a daughter not too far from Stephanie's age."

The Coakleys were at dinner Wednesday night in their hillside home overlooking forested Moraga Canyon when the phone rang and Frank answered it. He took the call in his den, a pine-paneled room no more than ten feet square, filled with mementos of his legal, civic, and naval careers.

When he returned to the table with the news of the body's discovery, the meal ended abruptly. Coakley returned to the telephone to call the Trinity sheriff's office with orders that the grave remain untouched until he got there. He was leaving at once, he said.

Every major development in the Bryan case seemed to occur at day's end, requiring someone to take a long, tortuous journey at night. Despite Coakley's anticipation of this trip, it took him several hours to round up the people he needed, and it was 2 A.M. when his car finally rolled northward. Inspector Charles Ryken, a mainstay of his staff, was at the wheel. Riding as passengers were Stephanie's dentist, Dr. Reginald Hanson, with her charts, and Dr. George Loquvam, an Oakland pathologist retained for the autopsy. The nonstop trip to the desolate grave site took more than six hours, until 8:20 A.M.

At the end of April this lonely place had been sodden with cold rain and melting snow. Now, as Coakley and his aides huffed and puffed up the steep hillside (all but Ryken in dark business suits), the red soil beneath their feet was bone dry and hard-packed. Already the sun had been climbing for more than two hours into a cloudless sky, boding a torrid day ahead.

Coakley gazed down upon the crude grave, roped off as he had ordered. It was an inhospitable resting place, a narrow excavation dug with evident haste. It was shallow for certain; he could plainly see the exposed saddle shoe at the north end. At another point he could perceive a bit of turquoise fabric—the color of the skirt Stephanie had worn on her last school day.

In the twelve hours since the bloodhounds had discovered this grave, law enforcement had been galvanized at every level. Deputy Wyckoff had been the first officer besides Bud Jackson to reach the site, and with him now to welcome Coakley were Trinity Sheriff Harold Wilson with two other deputies, Coroner E. C. Chapman, three FBI agents, and four Berkeley policemen.

During their nightlong vigil the local officers, versed in wild country wisdom, had been critically studying the scene. Jackson pointed out to Coakley the newly disturbed area where an animal had molested the grave.

"A bear did that," he said. "A cat wouldn't do it, and I don't think a coyote would do it. Lots of bear up here—black bears and brown bears both."

Nearby were bear tracks and strips of cloth, unweathered and unfaded, appearing to be freshly exposed.

"Bears have great big claws," Jackson told Coakley, "and tearing that cloth would be easy. The digging the bears did, just recently, made enough odor for my dogs to pick up."

Jackson next led Coakley to a pack rats' nest not far away, in which he had discovered bits of cleansing tissue.

"Pack rats will carry things around with them—knives, clothes, toilet paper," he said. "They could have taken that tissue from down around the cabin."

Whoever had buried Stephanie had tried another site first. Jackson showed Coakley where someone had started to dig at the base of the nearby pine tree but apparently given up after hitting the roots. The loosened clods there still bore the imprint of the nick-bladed shovel from the cabin.

Coakley was struck by the isolation of the grave. The trees and the dense manzanita on the hillside blocked vision and muffled sound from the little-traveled road below. This spot could have been a hundred miles into the wilderness. Later measurements determined the actual distance from the cabin to the grave, by a zigzagging trail, to be 339 feet. The average grade was 25 percent.

At eight-thirty Dr. Loquvam took command at the grave site, and with the permission of Coroner Chapman began the disinterment as some thirty-five persons—mostly reporters, police, and FBI men—watched in silence. The work was slow, exacting, and oppressive, taking two hours and forty minutes and lasting well into the scorching heat of midday.

Wyckoff and other deputies did the heavy labor, using the nick-bla led and short-handled shovels from the cabin and an army entrenching tool from Berkeley. First a trench was dug around the grave, much deeper than the grave itself. Soil samples, which would later become crucial, were taken at each level as the pit deepened. Finally Stephanie's body lay upon a sort of earthen pedestal in the middle of a much larger excavation.

As originally dug in haste, the grave had been only about six inches deep at the point where Stephanie's shoe appeared. It had been even shallower, scarcely five inches, where her right pelvic bone and thigh bone protruded, with degenerated tissue clinging to them.

To remove the hard red clay in contact with the body, Loquvam used neither tools nor instruments. To loosen the clods, he worked with his fingers only. Berkeley police photographer Roland Sherry shot pictures at every step, making a complete photographic record of the exhumation.

As the body came into view little by little, Stephanie was found to be lying on her left side, her right knee and thigh slightly flexed, her left leg extended. At the grave's deepest point, fifteen to eighteen inches of dirt had covered her head. Loquvam first exposed her right arm, markedly degenerated within the sleeve of her dark-blue cardigan. Shovelfuls of dirt, which had been wet when the grave was filled, were caked against the sweater, retaining an impression of its weave.

Coakley at once perceived the soil condition as an indicator of the time of death: The heavy rains of April 29 and 30 had been the last of the season, so at no later time would the earth of the refilled grave have retained shapes and fabric textures. To the D.A. it was now beyond question that Stephanie had been buried within two days after her disappearance on April 28. Bud Jackson and Sheriff Wilson concurred.

"Abbott put her in the ground on that wet Friday morning, I'm sure," Jackson said. "I think he dug the grave in daylight, and after he finished he went right to the bar."

To the assembled reporters, Coakley announced, "There is no doubt in my mind that Burton Abbott is the murderer." He revealed that even as he spoke, a formal murder complaint was being prepared in Berkeley and Stephanie's father would sign it.

Some of the exhumation witnesses were nevertheless inclined to accord Abbott a benefit of doubt. Particularly puzzling to them was how this frail young man, with a lung lobe and several ribs missing, could possibly have carried Stephanie's 108-pound body up the hill. The feat would have taxed some men in good health.

On the other hand, Coakley's driver Charlie Ryken saw no incompatibility between Bud Abbott's physical disability (such as it might be) and the grave's altitude.

"The question is, where did she die?" he said. "I think she died at the grave site. He didn't have to drag or carry her; he walked her up the hill. She was hit over the head and just dropped in the hole."

Although Ryken's hypothesis conflicted with Riedel's belief that Burton had murdered Stephanie in the Contra Costa hills, it was a viable theory accepted by many.*

Stephanie's remains were badly decomposed. Her wadded mouth had been sealed with adhesive tape, her skull bashed in. Besides the turquoise skirt and blue cardigan, her white Orlon sweater, slip, and three half-slips still clothed her, but her brassiere was missing, as expected. Her panties had been slashed from her body and knotted around her neck.

With the corpse fully exposed, the trench alongside the grave was widened. Coroner Chapman placed his basket on the trench floor, and gently the remains were slid and rolled into it from their earthen mound. Deputies carried the basket to a hearse on the road below.

Ryken again took the wheel of the car bearing Coakley, Loquvam, and Reginald Hanson as it followed the hearse, bound for Redding where the autopsy would take place. The route ahead was fifty or sixty miles, much of it over narrow, winding, unpaved mountain roads.

By now the sun was nearing the zenith, and the rigors of the night and morning were taking their toll on the district attorney and his party. The men were midway through their second day without sleep, without breakfast, and with no lunch in sight. The tension, the six-hour nocturnal drive, the strenuous clamber up the mountainside, the stench of death, and the hours in the broiling sun were catching up with them. There was special concern for Dr. Hanson, the dentist, who was diabetic.

"Man, it was hot!" Ryken recalled forty years later.

When the car crossed a river a few miles out of Wildwood, Loquvam said, "That looks good to me!" and all agreed. Ryken pulled off the road, and the four men, stripping to their shorts, jumped in. They were in trouble at once, having overestimated the stream's temperature and underestimated its current.

"We hit that cold water, and zingo! I was down," Ryken remembered. "I couldn't swim because the water had too much force. I don't know how we ever got back."

Eventually the naive adventurers managed to pull themselves out of the river, recover their clothes, and dress—and none too soon, for dentist Han-

---

* The author, who visited the grave site in 1994, shares the view that whoever killed Stephanie marched her there under her own power. The climb up the hillside was indeed rugged, even on a sunny day without a hundred-pound burden.

son was pale and faint. His breath grew short as his pulse quickened, and he broke into a cold sweat. His blood glucose depleted, he was sliding into diabetic shock.

"I thought we might lose him," Ryken admitted later.

Someone in the car gave Hanson a candy bar, and as he munched it, his symptoms began to recede. Ryken hit the gas pedal and raced on toward Redding—not for McDonald's mortuary where the body lay, but for a hospital emergency room. There the dentist got an insulin shot.

The ill-considered swim and the time-consuming hospital detour had used up the better part of the afternoon. Not until two-forty-five did Loquvam commence his postmortem examination, with Ryken assisting him at the slab. Nothing in Ryken's experience had prepared him for autopsy work, but he had learned to view death impersonally.

Hanson was still under the weather, but remained at the autopsy table long enough to complete a full examination of the victim's dental work. He recognized it at once. The girl's upper central incisors had plastic fillings; two lower left molars had gold inlays, and there were nine other fillings, all silver. The match with Stephanie's chart was precise. When the dentist finished his examination, not the least possibility remained that the girl on the slab was anyone but Stephanie Bryan.

In the first phase of the autopsy, Loquvam removed Stephanie's apparel with extreme care, to minimize damage to skin, tissue, and organs underneath. Painstakingly he logged each garment and noted its condition. Her shoelaces were still tied. Her white bobby sox were dirt-stained but intact within the shoes, although rotted at the ankles. Numerous stress tears were apparent in the buttocks area of her turquoise skirt, but its zipper, on the left side, was closed. Her three bouffant half-slips—white, pink, and green— were similarly torn, but her full-length slip and both sweaters were intact. Loquvam took particular note that the slip's shoulder straps were unbroken.

Stephanie's dark-brown hair was matted with the red clay of the grave. Loquvam described her scalp pathologically as "a soft glutinous mass of graywhite degenerating tissue, with hair tangled and enmeshed." All soft tissue was gone from the face, except for a bit of one cheek. The nose, ears, lips, chin and forehead had degenerated, exposing the facial bones and lower jawbone. As Loquvam and Ryken washed the skull, the hair and scalp tissues fell freely from it.

The skull: Stephanie's murderer had battered it ruthlessly, sadistically, striking blow after blow with a heavy weapon—probably a ball-peen hammer. It was clear that the fractures were not gunshot wounds. There were two large holes in the back of the skull at ear level, the largest measuring 6 by 7 centimeters (2 1/4 by 2 3/4 inches) in each direction and the other only slightly smaller. A lineal fracture was 12 centimeters (almost 5 inches) in length.

Whether Stephanie had been alive when attacked, Loquvam could not tell. Chunks of the cranium had been driven into the brain and ground to bits, literally pulverized. Within the cranial vault, small amounts of gray-white degenerated brain tissue remained.

The soft tissue of Stephanie's neck had totally decomposed, exposing her cervical vertebrae. Had she been strangled, either before or after her skull was beaten in? There was no way to tell. Her panties were loosely knotted around the neck now but could have been tight before the decomposition. Loquvam listed strangulation as a possible secondary cause of death.

The panties had been removed with two slashes of a sharp instrument—a vertical stroke at front center, ripping the fabric from the waistband to the left thigh, and a horizonal stroke that would have exposed the pubic area. Stephanie's breastbone, collarbones, ribs, and thoracic vertebrae were all exposed, but none of them was fractured. Several chest organs, still within the thoracic cavity, had decomposed into unidentifiable blobs.

Degenerated skin remained on the left side of Stephanie's back. Parts of her left shoulder and arm were covered by gelatinous adipocere, a waxy substance produced when tissue decomposes in moist conditions. Her right arm was devoid of soft tissue.

"The right humerus, radius, and ulna," Loquvam wrote in his report, "are lying free in the sleeve of the blue sweater. After removing this garment, the bones lie free on the examining table. The left shoulder joint is intact, held by the altered soft tissues. The left forearm, wrist, and hand are degenerated, similar to the right. No fractures are noted."

Stephanie's thighs remained partially covered by dried skin, brown-black in color, covering red-pink degenerating muscle. All soft tissue was missing from her stomach and right side, and her left side and back were in advanced stages of degeneration. None of her abdominal organs could be identified, except a three-inch section of the large bowel containing soft fecal material.

The internal genitalia were wholly gone, and the external sex organs were degenerated except for a small part of the right labia majora, which had also taken on a parchment-like texture. Thus it would never be possible to tell whether Stephanie Bryan had been raped.

The discovery of the body by reporter Montgomery, a layman rather than a lawman, "really pissed off the police," Coakley's son Tom would remember long afterward. "They didn't like that, and my father, I don't think he liked it. My father was never enamored of newspapermen, because they tended to be on his tail a lot."

O'Meara, the pugnacious Berkeley police inspector in charge of the Bryan case, was especially upset. In a report written later he suggested that after finding the grave, Montgomery "had sat on this information in order that his newspaper could have a scoop"—an allegation disproven by the speedy time frame of events that evening.

Three thousand miles away, in Washington, D.C., FBI Director J. Edgar Hoover was livid that a civilian had succeeded where his own men failed. The three agents who had searched for the body in Wildwood were summarily exiled to the Bureau's "Siberia" of Butte, Montana.

"J. Edgar back in those days was very dramatic," one officer said later. "Those agents did nothing wrong, but you know the FBI's story about Butte: If things went bad, that's where your ass went."

Coakley's concern about the *Examiner's* coup was more substantive than mere loss of face. Although the newspaper had informed Burton Abbott and the Berkeley police of the body's discovery at approximately the same time, Burton had gotten the word *before the police came to arrest him.*

An innocent suspect would have no knowledge whatever about the location and condition of the body. Thus any slip Abbott might make revealing such knowledge would be devastatingly incriminating—unless the newsmen had supplied him with details.

Had they? Precisely what had Abbott been told? The prosecutors needed to know. Therefore, on this Thursday afternoon while Coakley stood by the autopsy table in Redding, Folger Emerson back in Oakland was grilling the *Examiner's* reporters. How much had they blabbed?

Emerson questioned George Erickson in a formal setting at the Courthouse with a stenographer making a verbatim record.

"All right," the assistant D.A. began, "we are talking about last night, Wednesday, July 20, and your visit to the home of Burton Abbott. What time did you get there?"

"Shortly after nine o'clock."

"You yourself didn't tell him anything about the body except that it was found somewhere near the cabin?"

"That's right."

"Did you tell him whether or not the body was buried?"

"I did not, because I wasn't aware how it was found."

"Did you tell him anything about how the body was clothed?"

"No, I didn't know myself."

Emerson wanted to know next whether Purcell had given Abbott any such information.

"Yes," Erickson acknowledged freely, "after phoning the *Examiner* office he came back and had a complete description as to where the body was and how far it was."

Later, reviewing the transcript of his own interview with Abbott the previous night, Emerson found that as hazy as Burton's rambling had been, it reflected only what Erickson and Purcell had told him.

From start to finish, the Bryan case was exceptional for its degree of press participation.

In more recent cases it has become the habit of the media to range far beyond the reporting function, becoming kibitzers, interpreters, critics, and umpires. In the Bryan case, however, the interplay between the press and the legal process was more pervasive than in even so sensational a case as that of O.J. Simpson. Journalists repeatedly crossed the line separating observers from newsmakers. They pursued and discovered clues, developed evidence, tracked down missing witnesses, and became witnesses themselves. Ed Montgomery's spectacular exploit of finding the grave and establishing the corpus delicti was only the most obvious manifestation of such involvement.

If Montgomery's coup for the *Examiner* was embarrassing to the police and the FBI, it was more so to the *San Francisco Chronicle,* which would later attempt a far more controversial countercoup.

The *Tribune's* activist role in the Bryan case began with assistant managing editor Stanley Norton, who happen to be one of Dr. Bryan's patients. Within a day or two after Stephanie vanished, while the police still officially regarded her as a runaway, Norton pressured them to take a more serious view and begin their massive search.

Sometimes Coakley appeared to regard journalists as his own lackeys. At one point he assigned an inspector "to get copies of all [Bryan case] photographs taken by all newspapers, published or otherwise." While some editors cooperated, others deemed the request an insult to their independence.

Throughout the investigation and trial, Coakley would remain intensely concerned about press reaction and what the newspapers were doing on their own. He regularly sent undercover men to eavesdrop in bars and eateries frequented by journalists. From a place across the street from the *Tribune,* one such spy fawningly (but probably accurately) reported to him:

> Most of the patrons were from the *Tribune.* The only thing I could pick up, from one of the females, was that the pool shows Coakley will win the case by a landslide. I was informed that circulation is up approximately 15 percent. This is all free publicity for the district attorney, and it will remain that way for the rest of his life, win, lose, or draw. For the next ten years, every time his name comes up it will be associated with the trial of Bud Abbott.

PART THREE

Before the Trial

12

"The Hottest Thing Since Sliced Bread"

The Berkeley Police Department, serving a town of some 100,000 people in 1955, boasted resources that many metropolitan departments envied. On the University of California campus, around which the city had grown up, were some of the world's foremost scientists and specialists in disciplines crucial to police work. They were available to the Berkeley police on call. We have already met Dr. Douglas Kelley, psychiatrist, and Dr. Paul L. Kirk, founder of U.C.'s criminalistics program.

As a microchemist for the Manhattan Project in World War II, Kirk had helped develop the first speck of plutonium for the American nuclear arsenal. As a defense consultant in Cleveland's celebrated Sam Sheppard wife-murder case, he had submitted a 10,000-word affidavit on blood evidence that helped overturn Sheppard's conviction.

Kirk did not even bill the City of Berkeley for his services. Sometimes he passed along his police assignments to graduate students in his university classes to give them hands-on experience.

The association between the Berkeley Police Department and the university had a long and important history. Early in the century Berkeley's chief of police had been August Vollmer, dean of the U.C. Police School and a towering figure nationally in police education. He had inspired and demanded from his department a professionalism that remained a source of pride and strength in the 1950s, long after he was gone.

"Our morale was terrific," remembers ex-cop Ralph Schillinger, who worked on the Bryan case. "We were like the marines. We thought we were the hottest thing since sliced bread."

Criminalist Kirk, a dark-haired, intense man of slight stature, was destined for a pivotal role in the Bryan investigation. He first strode onto the scene at Abbott's home late Saturday, the day after Georgia found the purse: a dapper figure in loose-fitting tweeds, a pipe clenched in his teeth, carrying two suitcase-size boxes of equipment. While the police and FBI were digging up the basement, Kirk headed straightaway for the older of the two automobiles in the driveway and garage, a gray-green, torpedo-back 1949 Chevrolet,

California license 1L53486. This car, driven mainly by Burton, matched closely the description given by the witnesses to the April 28 girl-beating east of the tunnel (though it lacked the "Y" license plate some of them thought they had seen).

Kirk took sweepings from the front and rear seats and floors of the Chevy, hairs and fibers from the trunk mat, iron scrapings from the trunk, and miscellaneous items including a brown leather jacket, a pair of leather gloves, a pipe, a ruler, a green-and-yellow pencil, and a soiled Kleenex.

Forty years later we can only speculate about the character of the "sweepings" and "scrapings." From police reports it would seem that Kirk's first examination of the car on July 16 was essentially perfunctory. If not, why did he search it again on July 19 and still a third time on August 5, after it was stored in the Alameda County garage?

The vehicle was not vacuumed thoroughly until the second inspection and the seats not removed until the third. These later examinations produced several interesting items, including a lug wrench (a possible murder weapon), several school assignments in Abbott's handwriting, a newspaper clipping about psychiatry, and a one-column newspaper headline reading "Puppets and Props." (Mrs. Bryan had told the police earlier that Stephanie was a puppet enthusiast and had staged shows of her own.)

Had Paul Kirk, the famous scientist, been guilty of a slipshod inspection of the automobile on that first Saturday when the evidence was freshest?

Probably not. A valid legal consideration may have led him to defer critical parts of his examination. In that year, 1955, the *Cahan* decision of the California Supreme Court drastically tightened the exclusionary rule against illegally acquired evidence, and it was so new that no one yet knew precisely what it meant. Kirk was aware that the other searchers turning the Abbotts' home inside out were working without a warrant, only with the loosely written waivers given by Burton and Georgia. Did he purposely postpone the crucial phases of the car search until he had a warrant in hand? Did he foresee—rightly—that evidence taken that first day would later be challenged in court? A specific warrant for seizure of the Chevy was not issued until July 21.

The Abbotts' other automobile, principally used by Georgia, was a new, green-and-cream 1955 Pontiac Star Chief Catalina. It could not have been used in the Stephanie Bryan kidnapping; Burton and Georgia had just taken delivery of it from Kehoe Pontiac Motors in Alameda on May 13, two weeks after the girl disappeared.

The police, however, desperately wanted to examine the old car the Abbotts had traded in at that time; it was also a Pontiac, a gray 1950 model which could easily have been mistaken for a Chevy by the tunnel witnesses. Moreover, it was an exact match for the auto that Mack Jensen had reported

May 4 at his service station in Keyes, with three small fingers protruding from the trunk.

Berkeley officer Donald Kent located the Abbotts' old Pontiac in the possession of Albert Lee Clouse, an Oakland fireman; it had stood on the Kehoe used car lot less than two days before Clouse bought it. Fortunately, from the investigators' viewpoint, it had not been cleaned, either inside or out. From its interior and trunk Kent recovered a stainless steel needle, fragments of leaves, a black cloth, a white button with thread attached, a small block of wood, a pair of green rubberized plastic gloves, a soiled Kleenex, a pearl bead and a pink one, and two pieces of pink chenille fabric. The latter were shown to Elsie Abbott, who said emphatically they were *not* from the chenille bedspreads she had been seeking when she had first noticed Stephanie's purse in the cellar in early May.

Everything found in the old Pontiac was bundled up and shipped to the FBI laboratory in Washington, which confirmed just about what anyone could have told by looking at the stuff. In the Bureau's stilted prose, the laboratory "advised" that "no blood was found on any of the specimens. No latent fingerprints of value were developed." There were "several human head hairs" ranging from blond to medium brown in the left green glove, which had been in the trunk, and on cloths under the front seat; but their source could not be determined. Under the microscope, all but two of the hairs were "dissimilar" to Stephanie's, and even those two were different in color. As a cosmetologist, Georgia of course regularly handled hair of every hue, both natural and dyed.

In the ensuing days of his investigation, Kirk analyzed a vast and varied volume of physical evidence: soil samples from the grave and elsewhere, sand from the Abbott basement, Stephanie's hair and garments, two sleeping bags, Abbott's clothing, boots, and fishing creel; and numerous articles from the cabin, including furniture, three shovels, an iron bar, and a pair of ice tongs.

When Kirk asked for specimens of Abbott's hair, the district attorney sent Inspector Russell Ryan to raid his jail cell. Ryan seized a pair of pajamas, two pairs of slacks, a sport coat, a pair of blue-striped shorts, a pair of socks, three blankets, two sheets, and a pillowcase. From the pajamas Kirk obtained arm and leg hairs; on the sport coat and in the right pocket of one pair of slacks, he found numerous head hairs. Pubic hairs were obtained from the shorts.

"It may be weeks before we can say whether this material yields any clues," Kirk told the press. His findings would remain Coakley's best-kept secret. Abbott's lawyers would get no inkling of them until the trial, when they would be introduced with memorable effect.

For Abbott's attorney, Whitney, the onrush of events was overwhelming. In these few mid-July days his professional practice was turned upside down, his personal life disrupted, and his community image altered in ways he could not have imagined. A week earlier he had cherished the security, comfort, and quiet respect accorded a "small-town" lawyer. Now he found himself in the eye of a hurricane of revulsion. Millions were weighing his performance as defender of a suspect already pronounced guilty by the district attorney. Some deemed Abbott a scapegoat or victim, but countless others instinctively reviled him.

Whitney needed help urgently. This former municipal attorney, whose practice now ran to wills and contracts, required someone at his side who had jousted in the slippery arena of criminal law. He turned to Harold Hove, another denizen of the Alameda City Hall.

Hove, a solidly built, blunt-faced man with wavy hair, was forty years old, seventeen years Whitney's junior. He had earned his law degree at Gonzaga University in Spokane and soon thereafter entered the FBI for an eventful career in Detroit, Washington, D.C., and San Francisco. During World War II he had won acclaim in treason prosecutions of Americans who sheltered German POW escapees. In 1945 he had quit the Bureau to start a criminal law practice in Oakland. He was a family man with three children.

Whitney and Hove had several meetings over a period of days, while the latter pondered joining the Abbott defense.

"I was begging him not to do it," recalled his widow, Alice Hove, in 1994. "I felt a lot of empathy for that girl [Stephanie] and her family."

For the defenders, the Abbott case loomed as a bruising battle against intimidating state resources and a supreme test of their skills. It would pay little and would drain their energy for months to come. There would be excitement, exhilaration, and fame, but with these went the risk of humiliating failure. Yet Hove ultimately decided to take the risk. He and Whitney became Abbott's team in the courtroom, with Whitney's young partner, Jack Hanson, handling behind-the-scenes chores.

The first court maneuver Whitney and Hove undertook was a habeas corpus petition challenging Alameda County's jurisdiction to prosecute their client. They asserted that "the proper county in connection with all proceedings" was Trinity, where the body was found.

The habeas corpus action was summarily denied; on its face it seemed a specious ploy. The California Penal Code clearly provided that a crime taking place in two or more counties could be prosecuted in any of them. To the press, Hove explained that the petition was merely groundwork for seeking a change of venue later.

Far to the north, the prospect of trying Burton Abbott in Trinity County sent a surge of excitement through the little county seat of Weaverville. Trinity District Attorney Stennett M. Sheppard shared Coakley's certainty of Abbott's guilt.

"To hold the trial in Trinity County offers immense possibilities for publicity," the *Trinity Weekly Journal* editorialized. "While the expense would be prohibitive, we can't help licking our chops over the chance of being the stage for a national drama."

On Saturday evening, July 23, a young Oakland housewife named Jean Trimble answered her phone and was surprised to hear Georgia Abbott's voice. They had once been friends and fellow patients at Livermore, but they had long been out of touch, partly because Jean's husband disapproved of the Abbotts and their lifestyle.

"Jeanie," Georgia said now, "we need several thousand dollars to pay the lawyers by Monday, and you are the only ones we can think of where we might get several thousand right away. Mark has mortgaged his home, and goodness knows I've sold everything I can think of, so I don't know what I could give you for collateral, but we sure need the money."

Jean thought quickly and told Georgia her money was tied up, but she would talk to her husband. If there was any possibility of a loan she would call back the next day.

She did not call back.

During the two weeks after Abbott's emergence as a suspect, and especially after the finding of Stephanie's body, Coakley's mail sack grew fatter each day. Dozens of citizens from across the country felt compelled to offer tips, insights, and advice ranging from the provocative to the absurd:

- "Take Abbott to view the body in the McDonald funeral home in Redding. Watch his reactions. Might help decide whether he is the guilty party."
- "Both Burton and Stephanie were interested in birds. Could it be possible the girl got into his car and went to his house to see his bird and was attacked and injured so that he had to do away with her."
- "Butt ends of fishing poles make good weapons."
- "The young high school crowd in the Bay Area is saying that Abbott dated steady with a girl in high school who is a dead ringer for Stephanie Bryan. Her picture is in the yearbook. Good luck!"
- "Return of the eye: Murderess Pobati remained impressed on the eye of the murdered person and could easily be recognized by examining the retina." (Alas, Stephanie's eyes no longer existed.)

Not all writers offered aid. A man in Ukiah wanted to buy Abbott's cabin. A man named Vickery admonished, "Mr. Persecutor, stop braying like a jackass. You know the young man is not guilty." A Veterans Administration hospital patient in New York declared, "I killed Stephanie because she was rude. I am pathologically inclined and 'nuts' too. Who can say otherwise?"

Psychics, mystics, and believers in the occult had a field day. One anonymous writer suggested that Coakley retain Duninger, a TV mind reader, to "come here and read Abbott's mind." Another writer told the district attorney, "You have the right man in Abbott. I've been psychic for years. Those people who have been murdered come to me. Stephanie Bryan said Abbott is the man."

From an ex-nurse in San Francisco came a three-page, single-spaced type-written letter—a fascinating reconstruction of the crime, blending fact, fantasy, and astrology. The woman wrote:

> *According to the astrological horoscopes of Stephanie Bryan and Burton Abbott, she had been under surveillance by her abductor for some time. He lay in wait for her at various times until she became familiar with his being there. In her chart it shows that she was destined to die at the hands of someone whom she trusted and had become infatuated with, only in a platonic way. . . . This secret love not only caused her sorrow but also cost her life.*

The nurse went on to describe imaginatively how Burton lured Stephanie to his home and "suddenly stripped off her sweaters and tore off her brassiere and started to kiss her body . . . When the time came for him to kill her, he took delight in beating her, and at each blow he got a thrill of power and strength and relief of his pent-up emotions."

The nurse volunteered her services to help convict "that lying, snaky pedophiliac," telling Coakley: "I would be willing to analyze Stephanie's horoscope for the jury. I would prefer to be a surprise witness and go before the jury after all the testimony is in and after Abbott's attorneys have exhausted what they have to present. Then I could come forward with a giant horoscope, tack it to a blackboard, and proceed. The truth will triumph in the end."

A particularly puzzling and seemingly insignificant piece of mail was postmarked in Redwood City at two o'clock on Sunday afternoon, July 24. The envelope—the printed business stationery of a San Francisco real estate broker named Alma Ogel*—was empty except for a small brown card on which someone had written "Berkeley, Calif.," nothing more. Scotch-taped to the card for no apparent reason was a small rubber band.

In the D.A.'s office Captain Severin examined the strange missive, scratched his bald head, returned the card to its envelope, and added it to a

---

* Fictitious name.

growing stack of useless communications. Many weeks later he would have cause to dig it out.

In the wake of the *Examiner's* triumph of finding Stephanie's grave, other papers stepped up their activist roles in the Abbott case. Now it became the *San Francisco Call-Bulletin's* turn to score.

On Tuesday, July 26, Berkeley police picked up a tip that the newspaper was about to unveil an eyewitness who could place Burton Abbott in Berkeley as late as 3:30 P.M. April 28—only thirty minutes before Stephanie was last seen.

On a hunch, Officer Kent sped to Pring's Doughnut Shop, the rumored locale of the sighting. His instinct proved sound; at the counter sat *Call* reporter Bob Hall, conversing with his mystery witness, William J. Russell, a thirty-year-old typewriter repairman. Several newspapers, it turned out, had been on Russell's trail for days, but until now he had been unknown to the police. Russell, who worked for the Berkeley School Department, was a regular at the doughnut shop. Kent took him to headquarters for interrogation.

"Everyone knows me in Pring's," he said. "I've been taking my coffee breaks there for a year."

"Have you ever seen Bud Abbott there?" Kent asked.

"Oh, sure, we'd talk about the news. I used to loan him my paper." Like others previously interviewed, Russell remembered Abbott's interest in a *Chronicle* story about a "flying manhole cover" helicopter. Another time Russell and Abbott had discussed a report about a woman who had thrown a baby out a window, and Burton had observed, "It takes all kinds of people to make a world."

"Abbott was an odd guy," Russell said. Although the two of them talked often, Burton sometimes would ignore Russell in the café as if he were a total stranger.

On Wednesday, April 27, Russell had been asked by Eleanor Rice, the Willard Junior High typing teacher, to fix a Woodstock typewriter in her room. He had removed a faulty part, and Mrs. Rice told him she needed it replaced the next day, to be ready for Willard's open house that evening. Thus Russell was certain it was Thursday, April 28, when he had returned to the school and completed the repair. Mrs. Rice's typing room was not in use while he did so, he said; he thought it was during the school's eighth period, between 2:27 and 3:15 P.M.

From the school, Russell had walked half a block down Telegraph Avenue to his car, which was parked almost in front of Pring's, and had gone in for a cup of coffee, probably between 3:00 and 3:20. There was only one other customer in the place—Burton Abbott.

"Are you *absolutely sure* this was April 28?" Kent prodded.

Russell considered carefully before answering: "I can't *swear* it, but there is no doubt in my mind about it. I'm as sure as I could be of any day."

Russell's certainty about the date grew as he recalled other details. He remembered that Burton was "dressed for roughing it" in blue jeans and a fur-lined leather jacket. Previously, like others at Pring's, the typewriter man had always seen Abbott in his campus togs, usually slacks and a white shirt with rolled-up sleeves.

In the doughnut shop that afternoon, Abbott had said nothing to Russell, nor had he even nodded as usual, even though for at least part of the time they were the only patrons present. They had left about the same time, Russell a little ahead of Abbott, and gotten into their respective cars. Russell did not remember seeing Abbott drive away.

From the doughnut shop, Russell had driven to his mother's house nearby and later picked up his wife, Carol, a secretary at the Crown Zellerbach Corporation, when her work day ended at four-forty-five. Recalled details and records kept by both the mother and the wife confirmed this timetable.

Later, from the witness stand, the repairman's story would become crucial. It would also cause much grief for the defense, for the prosecution, and not least of all for Russell himself.

13

Behind Closed Doors

Burton had been behind bars less than a week when Harold Hove sought out his mother, Elsie, and urgently admonished her, "Get out of the country! Go somewhere, go to New York, get as far away as you can, where nobody can find you."

In blind obedience (for Hove did not give her a reason) Elsie went underground. She thus dodged a subpoena that Coakley was trying to serve on her. He wanted to confront her before the grand jury, which would convene on Wednesday, July 27, to consider Burton Abbott's indictment. Ironically Burton's mother, if she could be made to testify, could strengthen the state's case immensely.

In particular Coakley was itching to ask Elsie about her declaration that she had seen Stephanie's purse in Burton's basement in early May, more than two months before Georgia found it there. In the excitement right after Georgia's discovery, Elsie had chattered about this to everyone in sight, seemingly oblivious to the trouble it boded for her son. She had first volunteered the information to the three FBI agents digging up the basement. Later she had repeated it in a formal interview and then told Georgia about it.

If what she said was correct, Stephanie's things had arrived in the Abbott cellar almost immediately after her disappearance. But at this point Elsie's disclosure was still hearsay. Coakley wanted her to repeat it under oath before the grand jury.

If there was anyone Coakley more wanted to bring before the jury than Elsie, it was Abbott himself. He had not totally abandoned hope of prying a confession from the defendant. To this end, he extended Burton a special invitation to testify, using Riedel as his emissary.

Riedel visited Burton in his cell in Berkeley, telling him "I have a message from the district attorney. The grand jury will meet the day after tomorrow. It is your privilege to appear, if you so desire, and tell your story. I have two questions: First, do you want to appear?"

Abbott held up one of his lawyer's business cards and replied, "Call Mr. Hove."

"Second question, will you appear?"

Abbott held up the card again and gave the same reponse.

Sixteen grand jurors answered the roll at 10 o'clock on Wednesday morning as the panel convened behind closed doors in the Alameda County Courthouse. The massive, majestic structure, with art deco lines of the 1930s, stood on the shore of Lake Merritt, the placid jewel of downtown Oakland's largest park.

Besides presenting hard legal evidence, Coakley wanted to give the jurors an overview of the Bryan case in human terms, fitting together all the pieces of the puzzle known so far. As his first witnesses, he called three of those who had observed the April 28 car scuffle on Mt. Diablo Boulevard. Their testimony held the jurors transfixed. Of the three, Sam Marshall painted the most vivid word picture:

"A man in the front seat swung around to the right. I think he had his knees on the front seat. In the rear I saw a small person, who I presumed to be a girl or a small woman. I saw her fall back, and her feet come up so the tips of her toes were above the window sill of the car. The man was reaching as if to choke her."

The next two witnesses, Mary Ann Stewart and librarian Lydia Barton, presented a vividly contrasting picture of a carefree Stephanie less than an hour before the assault Marshall had described: a girl on her way home from school checking out library books, visiting the pet store, buying a doughnut snack. Mary Ann, Stephanie's school chum, was compelling as she said the date of the events was fixed in her mind because it was her mother's birthday. Mrs. Barton identified Stephanie's signature on her library card.

Stephanie's mother presented a patrician image as she came next before the grand jury, attired in a severely tailored suit and close-fitting hat. Mary Bryan's finely chiseled, intelligent features were composed, but it was a composure bespeaking wistful sorrow, not serenity. She was thin almost to the point of frailness.

On a map, she pointed out the location of the Bryans' hillside home and described the sylvan serenity of the neighborhood.

"There are no large front lawns, but the houses are well covered by trees along the street," she said. "If you look up at the houses, off the eucalyptus path, it is not possible to see more than a board here and there or a corner of a window."

"Were you familiar with your daughter's routine?" Coakley asked. "Did you know her customary route home from school?"

"Yes, I knew it because I chose it. I often met my children and walked home with them. The first year I met them every day."

Mary went on to explain that three "large, beautiful, heavy foliage trees" on the inside of Alvarado Road's first curve, opposite the tunnel-path rising from the Claremont, blocked the view of approaching traffic from both directions. From this hidden spot, or near it, Stephanie had been abducted.

Under law, Coakley could have bypassed the grand jury altogether in taking Abbott to trial by going directly to court on Dr. Bryan's complaint instead. Several tactical considerations, however, had influenced the prosecutor to take the indictment route. The grand jury was essentially his own creature; he could summon it at will, and in its secret deliberations it would hear only the evidence he chose to present. Abbott's lawyers could not cross-examine his witnesses nor even hear their testimony; thus the defense would get no tip-off to his strategy.

Even more valuable to Coakley, in the injunction process, was the opportunity it afforded him to subpoena reluctant witnesses and compel them to testify under oath without benefit of counsel. Not only could he draw out their stories and perhaps discover evidence for use during Abbott's trial; he also could establish a basis for impeachment of trial witnesses whose testimony might differ from what they said now.

With such considerations in mind, he had subpoenaed Georgia Abbott, and she was the first witness called after the Wednesday lunch break.

"May we have your name, please?" Coakley began.

Georgia held in her hand a declaration prepared by Whitney and Hove, and she responded by reading:

"My name is Georgia Abbott. I live at 1408 San Jose Avenue, Alameda. I refuse to answer questions on advice of counsel for the following reason: Under Section 1881, subdivision 1, of the Code of Civil Procedure, a wife cannot be examined against her husband without his consent."

"Well, are you *willing* to testify yourself?" Coakley asked, trying an end run.

Again came the rote response, in a flat voice.

"Have you asked your husband for his consent for testifying?"

The same answer again.

Five times altogether, Georgia read the prepared statement. Finally Coakley conceded defeat: "Well, I guess, Mr. Foreman, that is all we can do."

"You are excused," grand jury Foreman Wainwright told Georgia, and she left.

Unlike Elsie, who was lying low, and Georgia, who was shielded by spousal privilege, Burton's newlywed brother, Mark, had no way of evading testimony at this inquiry. He probably was closer to Burton than anyone else; moreover, he and his bride, Mary, had been with Burton at Wildwood during the crucial weekend after Stephanie vanished.

Could Mark have been an accessory to her murder? Not likely, Coakley thought, but what he knew might nonetheless throw light on how it had happened. Moreover, Burton had admitted lying to Mark about his supposed land grant inquiries. Perhaps the deception had driven a wedge between the brothers that the state could exploit.

Coakley called Mark to the witness chair as soon as Georgia left it. His first question was, did Mark know where his mother was hiding out?

Mark said no.

Consulting a paper on the table before him, the D.A. then called Mark's attention to his earlier police interrogation.

"Did you say at that time that Burton told you he had used a shovel to clear a path into the cabin garage?" Coakley asked. Placing a shovel in Burton's hands at any time during his trip to Wildwood might prove critical. It would also evoke a visceral response from the jurors, who of course had read of Stephanie's burial and exhumation.

"I might have made that statement. I don't remember," Mark parried.

"Now did you make that statement? Did you make the statement?" Anger colored Coakley's voice.

"I may have."

"Will you please answer the question yes or no? Did you make that statement to Officer Plantz and Special Agent Poole?"

"Yes, I think I did," Mark finally acknowledged.

"Well, how did you happen to be talking about the shovel? Who brought it up?"

"I don't remember. It was probably Burton himself."

Coakley's further questioning established that both Mark and Burton had used a shovel that weekend "working in the stream"—specifically while digging for hellgrammites, the large, soft larvae they were using for fish bait.

"What shovel did you use?"

"I think it was the short-handled one," Mark said.

Mark and Mary had reached the cabin about 3 A.M. on Saturday, April 30, finding Burton clothed but in his sleeping bag, in a stupor after his nine-hour boozing session with Tom Daly.

"Was he in the habit of getting drunk?" Coakley inquired.

"No, I don't think so, not if you mean going right out and deliberately getting drunk. I would say no."

"Well, was he in the habit of getting drunk for several hours?"

"No."

Again Coakley referred to Mark's earlier police interview: "In that conversation, didn't you say that on that Saturday, Burton's stomach was upset from drinking and he was taking Bromo-Seltzer?

"Not Bromo-Seltzer, Alka-Seltzer."

Next Coakley wanted to know about the long, convoy-style trip home from the cabin on Sunday, May 1—Burton in his Chevy and Mark and Mary in their Ford.

Though his preoccupation may have puzzled others, the district attorney remained obsessed with their homeward crossing of the Cottonwood Creek bridge, although it hardly seemed a meaningful site in Burton's alibi scenario.

Three or four men were working on the bridge when the two cars reached it that Sunday afternoon, Mark testified. There was only a single lane of temporary planking on which to cross, and the workmen had to step off to let them through.

The homeward route also had included Franklin Canyon, where Stephanie's French textbook was found the next morning.

"When you turned onto Franklin Canyon Road, what time was it?" Coakley asked.

"Around six o'clock, maybe a little bit later; it was still daylight."

"Did you or Burton stop anyplace along in there?"

"Not that I recall."

"At that time, who was leading?"

"I was, all the way."

"And where was Burton?"

"Two or three car lengths behind me."

"How fast were you going?"

"Oh, approximately 55–60 miles an hour."

"Did you ever look in your rearview mirror to see if he was behind?"

"Quite frequently."

Coakley turned next to Burton's movements immediately following the fishing trip. He claimed to have been hunting for cheap tires on the day after his return, when he had made a telltale gas purchase at Tank Farm Hill. As we know, the police suspected that he was then really headed back to Franklin Canyon, hoping to recover Stephanie's jettisoned French book.

Mark confirmed that Burton's tires had indeed been thin if not bald. Indeed, it was Mark himself who had finally solved Burton's problem by finding some old tires that could be purchased for two dollars apiece plus the cost of recapping.

"And when did he put those tires on the Chevrolet? Was it in May?" Coakley asked.

"I don't think so. I think it was in June sometime, or possibly this month."

What did Mark know, the prosecutor asked next, about his brother's unsuccessful effort on Tuesday, May 3, to reenter the Livermore Veterans Hospital? Was he seeking a place to lie low in the aftermath of Stephanie's murder?

Mark said Burton's reason for going to the hospital that day was a troublesome abscess on his back.

"Did he say anything about it afterward?"

"Yes, he said the doctor didn't want to touch the case right then; he wanted to wait until September. It was something about the doctor's assistants; they were back east at a conference or something, and he wanted to wait until they returned."*

Earlier in the day Mark had piqued Coakley's interest with an offhand remark that he had prepared a master list of supplies and tools needed at the cabin. Presumably Burton had used it when he packed his car for the April trip. Now, in late afternoon, the district attorney surprised Mark by asking "Do you have that list?"

"I think I could find it."

"Well, you go home now and look for it," Coakley ordered.

With that, the grand jury recessed until 7:30 P.M.

After dinner Folger Emerson took over, calling Dolores Pring and waitress La Verne Malloy to acquaint the jury with Pring's Doughnut Shop, where Abbott might well have seen or even met the girl he was now accused of slaying. The women named both Stephanie and Burton as regular patrons of the little café near Willard Junior High. Had both ever been there at the same time? Neither witness could be sure.

Arguably William Russell, the typewriter repairman, would have been a stronger witness than either of these women to tell the jury about Pring's. He purportedly had seen Abbott there within the hour that Stephanie disappeared; the Pring and Malloy testimony was vague about the time element. However, the *Call-Bulletin* had "found" Russell only one day before this hearing, and there had been little time to evaluate his story. Coakley therefore decided the two women would be amply adequate as witnesses before the friendly grand jury; he would save Russell as a heavy hitter for Abbott's trial.

After hearing about the cheerful, companionable atmosphere of the doughnut shop, the grand jury was abruptly plunged into the ugly, sordid, and horrifying.

Examiner reporter Ed Montgomery filled eight pages of the hearing transcript telling how, with Bud Jackson's dogs, he had found Stephanie's body in its forlorn grave on the Wildwood mountainside. Then, following Montgomery on the stand, Dr. George Loquvam hideously described the ex-

---

* The hospital disputed this explanation. There was no schedule for additional treatment of Abbott, either in September or later, the administrator said.

humation and autopsy, and Stephanie's dentist, Dr. Hanson, confirmed the identity of her remains.

At a late hour Mark Abbott was called back to the stand, still under oath. Had he been able during the dinner break to find his list of tools and supplies for the cabin?

"I'm sorry, Mr. Coakley," he said. "I went through the whole house in the limited time I had—through dressers, my books, my papers. If I had more time, I might be able to locate it. Actually I didn't even have time to get dinner tonight."

Hearing this, jury Foreman Wainwright addressed Mark sternly: "You are ordered to report back at nine-thirty tomorrow morning, and between now and nine-thirty will you make a diligent search for that list?"

"Yes, sir, I will."

Thus the first day of the hearing came to an end.

As the stream of testimony continued Thursday morning, Coakley's men were deployed far and wide, searching for the witness he still wanted most, Elsie Abbott.

Inspector Charles Young was in Stockton talking to Elsie's sister May and her police sergeant husband, Cy Smith—the uncle who had been a surrogate father to Mark and Burton when they were small. The Smiths were cooperative but disclaimed knowledge of Elsie's whereabouts. Cy promised to notify Young if he heard from her.

"I wish I could talk to Burton," the sergeant said. "He always confided in me, and I think I could tell if he was guilty or not. If I thought so, you'd be the first to know."

In Oakland, Inspectors Ryken and James LeStrange tracked down Rollin Haight, a lithographer who was a first cousin to Burton and Mark and was their frequent fishing companion. He had last seen Elsie three days earlier in Alameda at a meeting of the whole family—a brainstorming session for discussing the problems at hand. Where was Elsie now? He had no clue. He did not think any other relative knew where she was either.

One family member mentioned by Haight was Elsie's brother, Wilbur Moore, from whom Burton took his middle name. Ryken found him at his Hayward home, leaving for work in the blue uniform of a Pacific Intermountain Express driver. Like Haight, Moore had had no word from Elsie since the strategy meeting on Monday.

"I've tried to reach her by phone, but she doesn't answer," he said. Then he abruptly broke off the interview, telling Ryken "I'm late for work."

Much later, the name of Wilbur Moore would reappear in the Burton Abbott drama in a surprising context.

———

A key witness in the grand jury's Thursday lineup was Otto William Dezman—friend of the Abbotts and husband of Georgia's employer at the beauty shop. By a fluke, he was destined to become a major figure in the Bryan case. Had he not been in the wrong place at the wrong time, his name might never have entered it at all.

Dezman was a handsome man, forty-four years old, round-faced with dark hair, heavy brows, and an easy smile. He had retired from the navy as a chief warrant officer in December 1954. His basic skill was as an electrician.

With Georgia refusing to testify and Burton's mother eluding her subpoena, Dezman was the only available witness who had been present in the Abbott home when Stephanie's purse was found there. His description of that occasion would fill fourteen pages of the grand jury transcript. He took this opportunity to emphasize what would later become a critical point: It was he, not Burton or Georgia, who had first suggested calling the Berkeley police. What Dezman did *not* reveal, because no one asked him, was that Abbott's lawyers, Whitney and Hove, had implored him to change his story and say the police call had been instigated by Georgia or by Burton himself. He had refused.

FBI agent Nichols followed Dezman as a witness. It was he who had dug up Stephanie's books, bra, and eyeglasses from Abbott's cellar floor on July 16, several hours before the issuance of a search warrant. His interrogation now was clearly aimed at finessing an expected challenge to the admissibility of these items.

"At the time you went to the Abbott home, you had previously obtained permission from Mr. and Mrs. Burton W. Abbott to search the place, had you not?" Emerson asked Nichols.

"I understood that permission had been obtained. I personally had not," Nichols answered.

"I meant, permission had been given for the Bureau?"

"That is correct," Nichols said. He went on to tell about the whole search of Abbott's premises.

After Thursday's lunch break Mark Abbott was recalled again, for a marathon of testimony that would take the rest of that day and much of Friday. It would fill the next fifty pages of the transcript.

Having failed to subpoena Burton's mother, Coakley now set about prying from his brother the same incriminating facts Elsie might have supplied. They would still be hearsay, but at least they would be in the record.

"Now Mr. Abbott," the district attorney began, "since you were on the witness stand yesterday, have you heard from your mother?"

"No, I have not," Mark replied.

"Do you know where she is?"

"No, I do not."

"Have you tried to contact her?"

"No, because I don't know where she is."*

"Well, did you ever have a conversation with your mother about the purse found in the basement at 1408 San Jose Avenue?"

"Yes, I think I did."

"At any time did she say anything about having seen Stephanie Bryan's purse in the basement of 1408 before Georgia found it on the night of July 15?"

"I think she mentioned at a later time—it was probably around the sixteenth, and she was hysterical—that she had told one of the officers, I think Mr. Poole, that she had seen it."

"What did she say about that?"

"My best recollection is that she had seen a purse that was similar, or was the purse that was found, either on the floor or on a shelf in the basement, and that she dropped it in a box."

"Did she say anything about the girl's books?"

"Not that I can remember."

"About the girl's glasses?"

"Not that I can remember."

"About the girl's brassiere?"

"No, I don't remember any of those."

To Mary Abbott, Mark's wife, the year 1955 had brought the kind of undeserved, hellish strife that she could never have imagined beforehand. She and Mark had wed on the last day of 1954, and almost at once she had become pregnant. All was well until, just six and a half months into the marriage, she found herself blamelessly involved in this lurid spectacle. By a stroke of a perverse fate—her decision to accompany her husband on an ill-advised fishing trip—she had become a close-in witness to events bearing on the guilt or innocence of his brother. Like everyone else so involved, she had been subpoenaed by the district attorney; quite unlike any of the other witnesses, however, she would be asked to testify while in her third trimester of pregnancy.

As the grand jury hearing went into its third day on Friday morning, Mark Abbott returned to the stand, and Coakley's opening questions concerned his wife.

---

* Actually, Elsie had not fled the country, state, or even the county. She had moved in with friends in San Leandro, less than a dozen miles from the courthouse in Oakland. In a 1995 interview with the author, she contradicted her son's denial. "Oh, yes," she said, "Mark knew where I was. I didn't get in touch with him, but I just assumed he knew where I was."

"She is pregnant and very nervous," Mark told the district attorney. He asked if she could be excused from testifying.

After discussion, it was decided that Mary would not need to come to the courthouse; Emerson would take a deposition from her at home. Mark could be present, as could Burton's lawyers and Inspector Severin.

At the house, Emerson was kindly in his questioning. Mary confirmed her arrival with Mark at the cabin in Wildwood about 3 o'clock on Saturday morning, April 30. When Burton woke up about eight-thirty, she said, he appeared to be his usual talkative self. She did not think he had used the word "hangover," but he had said something about his drinking the night before.

Later that Saturday, Mary testified, everybody shot at cans for a while with a .22 caliber rifle. Then they went fishing. They went to bed early because they were tired, and all slept well Saturday night. In answer to a question, Mary said she had never seen Burton intoxicated.

After returning to the witness chair in the courthouse, Mark told Coakley, "I'm very appreciative of the way Mr. Emerson held that conference with my wife. He was very considerate, and I'd like to thank him and you also."

It was the only time, then or later, that Mark would express a kindly sentiment about his brother's prosecutors.

Inspector O'Meara, the hard-nosed Berkeley cop coordinating the Bryan probe, was the next witness.

Questioning by Emerson drew from him in great detail Burton's three contradictory versions of his route to Trinity County on April 28:

- That he had driven direct to the cabin via Highways 40, 99W, and 36.
- That he had detoured through Sacramento, stopping at the land office to inquire about filing on an abandoned mining claim (the fabrication he had admittedly told Mark).
- That he had driven around in Sacramento looking for the land office but had not found it.

O'Meara also told the jury about the phony diagram of the Sacramento land office Abbott drew while he was still claiming to have paid an actual visit there: "a poor sketch—just a square with a counter running into the center of it."

Whether by chance, by design, or by prearrangement with Coakley, O'Meara took great care to be specific about the time elements in Abbott's story. By Burton's account he had arrived in Sacramento about 1 or 2 P.M.

and left about 3. The grand jurors may not have noticed this precision of detail, but it would become important later.

O'Meara's manner on the stand was neither accusatory nor combative. He said merely that Burton changed his story "when we refreshed his memory about Mark's statement."

As the proceedings entered their fourth day on Saturday, Mark was asked again if he had heard from his mother, and again he said no.

The district attorney, however, had one other matter to bring up before surrendering his opportunity to examine the brother of the accused under oath.

"Has Burton at any time been interested in pornographic or sex literature?"

"I don't know, but I don't think he's that kind of a guy. I can only tell you what I think, and I don't think he was," Mark answered.

For a further sexually oriented inquiry, Coakley called Hilda Frakes, the Abbotts' baby-sitter, to testify briefly.

"Now did you ever hear anything said about Burton's sex relations with Georgia?" he asked.

"No, I never did. No."

"Or with any other female?"

"No, I never did."

Mrs. Frakes confirmed Abbott's recollection that he had left home about 11 A.M., bound for Trinity County, on the day Stephanie vanished. She also recalled his phone call the next afternoon, asking her to warn Mark and Mary about the snowy Wildwood weather.

As Mrs. Frakes stepped down, Coakley turned to Foreman Wainright and said simply, "That's all the evidence we have at this time."

By now it was late morning, and Coakley, his staff, and the court reporter retired from the room to let the jury deliberate. They were summoned back precisely at noon, when the jury returned a two-count indictment, for kidnapping and murder.

"Let the record show," Foreman Wainwright announced, "that the grand jury voted unanimously on both counts."

Coakley was not yet ready to discharge the jury, however. He asked that the proceedings be recessed rather than adjourned, so that it would be possible for Elsie Abbott to be resubpoenaed if he chose to do so.

With the filing of the indictment, Abbott was moved from Berkeley to the Alameda County Jail in the courthouse by the lake—a building he would not leave until his fate had been decided.

On August 15 the court was ready to unseal the grand jury transcript, which would give the avid public its first glimpse of sworn revelations by Bryan case principals. Each accredited newspaper would receive just one copy of the bulky, 317-page document, which would be released close to the afternoon papers' deadlines.

The arrangements threw the press into a frenzy. On the face of things, it appeared that the P.M. afternoon papers would be able to carry only a few highlights, but the *Chronicle* and *Examiner* could score heavily the next morning with the full transcript and in-depth coverage.

To Jack McDowell, the city editor of the afternoon *Call-Bulletin,* this was a vile prospect. He was a resourceful, imaginative, and pugnacious newsman, a Pulitzer winner, built like a Sherman tank, and now he vowed that his P.M. paper would have it all: spot news plus analysis plus the verbatim testimony.

McDowell would need to overcome a vexing production problem, however. He would have only minutes, not hours, to get the story into print, and he would require a second copy of the transcript if the Q&A was to be set in type concurrently with the news accounts.

This was still the carbon paper era; office copiers were far in the future. What instant copy machines existed were scientific curiosities. But McDowell had heard that an obscure company called Xerox had opened a San Francisco office, and he resolved to shoot the works. Well before the transcript release, he talked to the Xerox people, swore them to secrecy, and recruited them as willing conspirators in a stunt. They clandestinely set up one of their primitive machines in the *Call-Bulletin* office—a Rube Goldberg wonder filling a whole room, with vent pipes reaching nearly to the ceiling. Only the Xerox people were able to run it.

When the transcript was given out in Oakland, a motorcycle messenger sped the *Call*'s single copy across the Bay Bridge to the newspaper's shop. The binding was ripped off and the pages went first to the ponderous Xerox apparatus. Copies, not of today's quality but fully legible, were made instantly and sent unedited to the typesetters. Meanwhile the original transcript went to the city desk, where McDowell apportioned the testimony of key witnesses to designated reporters to be quickly summarized in story form.

The *Call-Bulletin* hit the streets within minutes, carrying both stories and transcript. Its ecstatic circulation people papered the city with preprinted placards as they placed the newspapers in the racks:

> **EXCLUSIVE:**
> **SECRET ABBOTT**
> **CASE TESTIMONY!**

With its clean beat, the *Call* sold thousands of extra street copies, demolishing its competition. The Xerox people were so pleased to demonstrate their machine's capabilities that they never sent the newspaper a bill. The *Call*'s venture may have been the first use of instant photocopies in the news industry—an industry that today cannot exist without them.

14

Melody

The stream of mail to Coakley's desk from the inflamed community was unabated. Few of the letters, ranging from the thoughtful to the weird, required more than a thank-you note, but four handwritten pages that arrived on August 24 demanded serious attention. This letter, on plain stationery, was from a troubled young mother who signed herself simply "Melody."

The penmanship was an open backhand, suggesting an intelligent, outgoing, friendly woman, perhaps left-handed. Her grammar, spelling, and punctuation were less than perfect, but she expressed herself clearly and believably. Her tone was sincere.

The district attorney shared the "Melody letter" with only a few of his closest aides, and never with the Berkeley police or the FBI—certainly never with the press.

Let us consider Melody's story as her own words told it:

I am writing this letter as I have thought about this since Burton Abbott was accused of the murder of Stephanie Bryan. I have fought with my conscience against my home.

I have twin daughters and . . . my husband [works] at night. I see very little of him & get very lonely. I met a man sometime ago who was a friend of my husband in the Army—we have gone together for dinner & an occasional show. I did nothing to be ashamed of and did not neglect my daughters. However, I do not think my husband would have liked it and would have left me. I would not want this. Therefore I cannot say who I am or appear in person and testify. My home & my life are more important to me.

On Apr. 28 I met my friend in Oakland or rather Berkeley at the Claremont Hotel. We were to meet at 4:15 for a cocktail & then go to dinner & then home. I was early so I strolled around. I walked up some steps & a path with bushes at the side—then I came near the end of this path but stopped. I saw a young girl with saddle shoes on walking to a young man about 25 or so I guess, and they walked up toward a car—he behind her.

I turned and walked back to the hotel. My friend was there & we carried on from there with our plans for the evening.

Melody went on to describe the "boy or man" as thin, with a mustache, wearing a leather jacket. All she could remember about the girl was that her hair was short and that she was carrying some books. Melody "thought nothing of it" at the time.

"If I could see you and talk, and you'd guarantee not to *ever* disclose my name, I'd come in," she now promised Coakley. "However, you'll have to solve or dis-solve without my testimony, were I to put my babies in jeopardy. I know it's too much to risk. I'll read the papers and if you can give me some sign of *secrecy*, I'll come see you. I believe this man may have been this Mr. Abbott and you should try everything to find out."

Coakley's inspectors spent countless hours trying to find the sender of this remarkable message. On August 26 and 27 they ran a cryptic "personals" ad in the four San Francisco dailies, the *Tribune*, and the *San Mateo Times*:

MELODY—Secrecy assured. Will protect your interest in hotel site. Write me at Oakland or advise when arriving in person.

Weeks passed with no response.

A month later, on September 26, as Inspector Severin was poring over the tantalizing letter anew, something suddenly "clicked." Quickly he shuffled through the back mail until he found the envelope Coakley had received in July, bearing just the plain white card with the rubber band taped to it. On the card someone had penned the unexplained words "Berkeley, Calif."

Bingo! The handwritten "Berkeley" was identical to the same word in the Melody letter. Severin took the letter to a Post Office Department graphologist, who confirmed the match-up.

The "Berkeley, Calif." card had arrived in the printed business envelope of a real estate woman named Alma Ogel,* to whom Severin and Inspector Donald Lynn now paid a visit. They found a small lady in her sixties, not hostile but not inclined to be helpful either.

Yes, she said, in July she had addressed an envelope to the district attorney, meaning to send him a letter with some ideas about the Abbott case. However, she had never gotten around to writing the letter. She disclaimed any knowledge whatever of the "Berkeley, Calif." card, or how it had come to be mailed in her envelope

A flaw in Mrs. Ogel's tale tipped off Severin at once that she was less than candid. She said the addressed envelope had lain on her desk for a month unsealed, awaiting the letter about Abbott that she intended to write. Yet the envelope had been postmarked on July 24, just one week after Burton's name first appeared in the newspapers (and only four days after the discovery of

---

* Fictitious name.

Stephanie's body). When Severin pointed out this discrepancy, Mrs. Ogel grew agitated and accused him of "trying to put words in my mouth."

"How do you *think* that card might have gotten into your envelope?" the inspector asked her.

"Maybe someone dropped the envelope in the mail box unsealed. Maybe a traveler picked it up in my house. Maybe it was dropped on the street and someone found it. Maybe someone at the post office was playing a practical joke."

The way Mrs. Ogel rattled off this rejoinder, propounding four theories in rapid-fire order, convinced Severin that it was well thought out and rehearsed, and that "she knew more than she was telling."

Mrs. Ogel had a daughter, a former nurse named Nancy,* but she was an unlikely Melody candidate, having only recently moved to the Bay Area from Utah. For two hours Severin and Lynn persevered in their interrogation of the realty broker, trying to pry out some clue to Melody's identity. They finally gave up.

In mid-October, with Abbott's trial only three weeks away, Coakley tried the classified ads again:

MELODY—I urgently need your help, as time is running out. Please contact me as soon as possible. Secrecy absolutely assured.

Again there was no answer.

As this is written four decades later, the "Melody letter" remains in the Alameda County archives, a haunting mystery.

Was this guilt-ridden young mother an eyewitness to the abduction of Stephanie Bryan? Was Melody, whoever she may have been, the last person to see Stephanie as she walked unsuspectingly toward bondage and death?

---

* Fictitious name.

15

Smokescreen

Reflecting upon the Abbott case much later, the last surviving lawyer of his defense team, John Hanson, told the author, "There was a lot of smokescreen." Abbott's attorneys pursued a double-barreled strategy, not only seeking evidence to exonerate him but also smearing others with suspicion when they could. Their idea was to diffuse the miasma of guilt, letting it wash over "anyone that looked like a suspect." All within sight were fair game.

Conversely, Coakley strove to keep public fury focused on Abbott alone. The opposing strategies splattered into public view in August when Stanley Whitney issued a petulant press release rebuking Coakley for seeking "to create discrepancies in Abbott's story"—as if that were not the prosecution's expected role.

In their efforts to shift suspicion from Abbott to others, his lawyers got no help from their client. "Burton never pointed a finger at anybody," Hanson remembered.

Harold Hove was the principal architect of the smokescreen tactic. He laid the groundwork four days after Burton's indictment by unveiling what the *Examiner* called his "bogey in the basement" hypothesis.

Since May, he told reporters, little Chris had refused in sheer terror to enter the basement of the family home, formerly his favorite place to play. "I'm afraid I will see that man again," the tot had screamed. At first the family had paid no attention, chalking it up to Chris's vivid imagination. Now, however, Hove declared it likely that he had actually seen some stranger in the cellar, possibly in the act of burying Stephanie's possessions.

Who? Hove would nominate several candidates in the weeks ahead.

Although hostility to Abbott was running high in the streets, many East Bay people were offended rather than convinced by Coakley's blatant declarations of his guilt. One such doubter was Georgia Nelson, who ran a rooming house on Telegraph Avenue. She had her own suspect, Amos Stanford,* a moody twenty-four-year-old restaurant worker who had been her tenant in April.

---

* Fictitious name.

On the day Stephanie Bryan vanished, Amos had supposedly left Berkeley on what he said was a fishing trip to Eureka on California's far northern coast, not far from the principal road entering Trinity County from the west. On his return, he had requested clean bed sheets, and Mrs. Nelson had discovered bloodstains on his used ones.

Soon thereafter she had found Amos on his knees, peering out through his window into the gloom of dusk. When she asked him why, he had replied, "I like the dark." He told her he had lost his job and was "trying to save a thousand dollars to buy a doughnut shop." Then he had vanished, moving out of his room in the middle of the night. Mrs. Nelson took her suspicions about him not to the police but to Hove and Whitney.

Could this be the break they were praying for? Could Abbott truly be innocent, as they kept trying to convince themselves? Was this peculiar roomer Stephanie's real killer and Chris's basement "bogey"? Rather than pursue the tip on their own, an endeavor for which they were ill equipped and ill financed, Hove took it directly to J. D. Holstrom, Berkeley's chief of police.

"What is your gimmick?" Holstrom demanded, leery of this approach from the enemy camp.

"No ulterior motive, Chief," Hove assured him. "God knows you're better set up to check this out than we are, and it might amount to something. Whether it does or not, nothing you discover can hurt our client."

Holstrom assigned the investigation to Officer Hutchins, who quickly determined that Amos Stanford had a petty police record. What caught Hutchins's eye on the rap sheet was a bench warrant for a traffic violation in Davis, sixty miles northeast of Berkeley near Sacramento. Davis was not on the normal route of a Eureka-bound fisherman, but it was a town through which Abbott claimed to have passed on his April 28 journey to the cabin. Moreover, a search of Amos's vacated room turned up several items he had left behind, including a socket wrench (like Abbott's lug wrench, a possible weapon), a black hair found on a blanket, and—most interesting of all—two map books. On one map, a line had been drawn across Alvarado Road where the Bryans lived.

As tantalizing as these clues seemed at first, they soon began to wither. At the Jolly Roger Restaurant where Amos had worked, his ex-boss confirmed that he had failed to show on the critical Thursday, April 28—but he had come in as usual at 10 A.M. on both Friday and Saturday.

Although Amos had left Mrs. Nelson's establishment in haste and mystery, Hutchins found him easily. He was now working in Las Vegas, and when he got word that Hutchins was looking for him, he returned at once. Amos remembered well the date of Thursday, April 28; it was the only full day he had ever missed while employed at the Jolly Roger.

No, there had been no fishing trip, he confessed. The truth was that he had gotten blind drunk the previous night and was badly hung over. He had prevailed upon his stepmother to lie and call in sick for him. He could account for every hour of the critical day.

Hutchins, a tenacious cop, nevertheless spent three weeks investigating Amos Stanford before satisfying himself that he was clean. When he informed Hove that the man's alibi was airtight, the disappointed lawyer said, "Just about what I figured. Thanks."

Hove sprung into action again when, early on a Saturday morning, the body of a down-and-out alcoholic was found hanging from a drapery cord in a cheap hotel room on Oakland's forlorn East Fourteenth Street. He was clearly a suicide.

Within hours Hove proclaimed the dead man a "prime suspect" in the death of Stephanie Bryan. The Sunday *Examiner* carried the story about him on page one, including provocative interviews with two of his follow residents at the hotel.

One of these roomers, Marjorie Droughman, related, "Sometime in July, I asked him why he drank so much. He said, 'If you had to live with my conscience, you would too.' Then he talked about the Bryan case; he always seemed to want to talk about it. One time I laid a newspaper before him and asked, 'What do you know about it?' He turned the paper over and wouldn't answer. He said he was too weak to pay for his wrongs."

To the other hotel guest, Albert Avilla, the dead man had confided, "I know more about this thing than they think I do. I don't want to get in a worse jam than I'm in now."

"I thought he merely had too much to drink—until he took the deep six," Avilla was quoted.

The district attorney's office shot down Hove's accusatory conjecture about the suicide victim in less than a day. The man turned out to be the discharged mental patient, Victor Louis Christy—the former Oakland upholsterer checked out in early July on the basis of a tip from an anonymous letter writer. Hutchins had found him in a cheap hotel in San Jose, where he was then employed by the Food Machinery and Chemical Corporation. His time card showed that on the day Stephanie vanished he had been on the job forty miles south of Berkeley until 4:31 P.M.

The *Examiner*'s follow-up story about Christy on Monday morning, an embarrassment after the previous day's sensational yarn, pointedly took note of Hove's continuing series of fizzled alarms. The newspaper quoted an unnamed prosecution source as boasting, "All of the defense's publicly made claims have been investigated; none has been substantiated."

As certain and outspoken as Coakley was about Abbott's guilt, he did not fall into the trap of ignoring other suspects dredged up by the defense or anyone else. His men rigorously checked out everyone suggested as culpable, no matter how improbably or irresponsibly, or by whom, or with what ax to grind.

The district attorney quietly ordered one such probe when he learned that Lloyd K. Snyder, the man who had slain Ray Latham in the Wildwood cabin seven years earlier, had been released from San Quentin on April 7. Could Snyder have murdered Stephanie on his twenty-first day of freedom and then buried her on the same desolate terrain where he had once deposited Latham's hacked-up corpse? The possibility was not necessarily far-fetched.

As it turned out, however, Snyder had been paroled to Sheriff Orrin Brown of remote Alpine County in the high Sierra, and was now managing a motel Brown owned there. It was some two hundred miles from either Wildwood or Berkeley.

Brown attested that Snyder now had religion, no longer drank, and had not left Alpine's tiny county seat of Markleeville for even one night since his release. In imparting this information to a Berkeley officer, the sheriff asked one small favor: "Don't tell anybody I've got an ax murderer running my motel."

In mid-August one Mrs. Russell Swanson went to her lawyer in San Francisco, Thomas A. Allan, with another eerie tale. For six weeks in the fall of 1953, she said, Burton Abbott had worked as a carpenter renovating her apartment. It was "exceptionally heavy work," which he had performed well despite his exaggerated claim of having only one lung. When Mrs. Swanson had offered sympathy about his health, his response—as she quoted it—had taken her breath away:

"I will have one supreme moment before I die. I will kill someone and bury the body on a high hill. It will be the perfect crime."

This was not the sort of thing attorney Allan dealt with as the sedate senior partner of a financial district law firm, so with Mrs. Swanson's permission, he called Coakley's office with her story. Inspector Russ Ryan, who was sent to interview her, obtained the name of her renovation contractor, John Geraghty, and went to see him.

"I have never employed Burton Abbott," Geraghty declared indignantly. "The man on that Swanson job was Wayne Beach. He still works for me."

Beach turned out to be a tall, thin man of thirty-one, almost a dead ringer for Abbott. No one was more deflated than Mrs. Swanson to hear the prosaic truth, which smashed her dreams of a moment of drama, even fame, on the witness stand.

On a Monday evening in September the phone jingled on the desk of Lieutenant Hank Whaley at Berkeley police headquarters. The caller was Sheriff Prentice Maddux in Fort Smith, Arkansas, who was questioning a robbery suspect—a twenty-six-year-old hoodlum named Poole. The man had been drifting around the country in places like Miami, New Orleans, and Los Angeles, and in August the FBI had nabbed him at Lake Tahoe on a fugitive warrant. Maddux had extradited him on the robbery charge.

Now, almost two thousand miles east of California, Poole was "confessing" a monstrous crime he claimed to have committed in Berkeley. He said he had picked up a girl there and, failing in a rape attempt, had slain her.

Was the girl Stephanie?

"Let me talk to the man, Sheriff," Whaley suggested, and Maddux put Poole on the line.

"You say you killed this girl?" Whaley asked.

"Yeah."

"When was that?"

"I don't really know. I was drunk most of the time. Maybe five or six months ago."

"Where were you living then?"

Poole gave two addresses in Oakland—an apartment on Telegraph Avenue and a cheap hotel on San Pablo Avenue.

"Tell me about the girl. How did you meet her?"

"I was driving around and I saw her on a street corner carrying some books. I stopped and told her I knew her, and she got into my car." Poole was unable to name the street where this had taken place.

"What kind of a neighborhood was it?" Whaley asked,

"Just a few stores, is all I remember."

"Any big buildings, like office buildings or hotels?"

"I don't remember any."

Poole described the area as on the flat, with straight, level streets.

"What kind of car were you driving?"

"A 1950 Nash four-door with Louisiana plates."

"What time of day did you pick up this girl?"

"During the noon hour, between twelve and one."

All Poole could remember about his victim's attire was that her skirt was probably light blue, and she had on some sort of blouse. She had worn eyeglasses.

"Okay, so what happened then?"

"I drove her to the mountains and tried to screw her, but I was too drunk. I couldn't get it up."

"How far was this from where you picked her up?"

"Six or seven miles."

"And then what?"

"I'm not sure. I had a fifth of whiskey in the car, and I was drinking all the time. But I hit her over the head with a tire iron and killed her."

It was now almost five months since Stephanie's abduction, so Poole's time line was about right. Having been in northern California, he had doubtless followed the Bryan case with a deranged fascination. Some of his other details were correct, but he could have read any or all of them in the papers: the abduction from the street, the books, the glasses, the bashing of the girl's skull. However, his wrong guesses about other matters betrayed him as a not-too-cunning liar. Stephanie had been kidnapped at 4 P.M., not midday, from a part of the town that was hilly, not flat. Poole could recall no large buildings nearby, although Stephanie had been snatched from the shadow of the massive Claremont Hotel.

Whaley was sizing Poole up as a compulsive confesser—one of a bizarre breed whose egos feed on criminal fantasy. Such twisted personalities, known in every cop shop, crave notoriety and derive perverted pleasure from the admission of fictitious evil.

After killing his victim, Poole told Whaley, he "drove around wondering what to do" and then left the area, heading for "either Modesto or Vallejo"— cities in diametrically opposite directions from Berkeley. Late in the day, he said, he carried the girl's body three or four hundred feet up a hill and, using a collapsible army shovel, buried her under a "red oak tree"—hardly to be confused with the lofty pine that had guarded Stephanie's actual resting place. The weather was sunny, Poole said; there was no snow on the ground.

"How far from Berkeley was that?" Whaley asked. Poole first guessed "fifteen or twenty miles" and then said it might have been a hundred miles, toward Oregon over a paved road all the way.

"How long did you drive with the dead girl in your car?"

"A couple of hours."

Now Whaley was certain Poole was lying. The actual driving distance from Berkeley to Stephanie's grave was three hundred miles, much of it over dirt roads. Under the best conditions the trip took six hours.

After burying his victim, Poole said, he returned to Berkeley and continued south to Los Angeles by a coastal route, stopping in Oxnard for his first gasoline since the start of his murderous episode. It took Whaley only seconds to calculate that if he had actually driven to Stephanie's grave and then back to Oxnard, he would have had to travel eight hundred miles on one fill-up—at a time when fifteen miles to the gallon was considered good mileage.

Despite his well-founded skepticism, Whaley asked Maddux to get as much of Poole's tale as possible in writing. There was always a chance that some small part might be true.

Another investigative flurry came when an Oakland woman named Gloria Olsen* called the district attorney with a chilling tale. When Coakley's inspector arrived to interview her, she was in bed, covered with nothing but a sheet. As the inspector entered her bedroom, he passed an unidentified man leaving.

Gloria was a former neighbor of the Abbotts, who had once thrown a pot of coffee at Georgia for allegedly chasing her ex-husband. That incident, however, had nothing do with her present story, which concerned her current husband, Carter Olsen.** He had disappeared for about five days in late April, she said, returning dead drunk "with a big lump on his head and a sore leg" on April 29, the day following Stephanie's abduction. His handkerchief and the collar of his gaucho coat were bloody, and he told Gloria, "I need $600. I'm in a lot of trouble and I have to leave town."

Carter had then fallen asleep on the couch, so his wife said, and in his sleep sometime after midnight had muttered, "I'm sorry, Stephanie, I'm sorry." He had disappeared the next day.

The FBI checked out the tale and declared Carter Olsen in the clear. As for Gloria, the inspector wrote, "In my opinion the woman is a psycho."

As the tempo of the Abbott investigation quickened, Coakley expanded his network of undercover informants. Importantly, he developed new sources on the island of Alameda in the neighborhood of the Morton Beauty Salon. From them he was now picking up vibes that Hove and Whitney, in their smokescreen campaign, had settled on one man above all to tarnish with suspicion: the Abbotts' friend, retired navy chief Otto Dezman.

Were it not for Dezman, Burton might never have been suspected of Stephanie Bryan's murder. Her body might never have been found, her fate shrouded in mystery forever. As the unexpected guest in the Abbott home when Georgia discovered the girl's purse, Otto had been the first to say, "Call the cops." Had he not been there, would the discovery have been reported at all? Very possibly not.

The reports and rumors about Dezman now reaching Coakley were varied, fuzzy, and contradictory. Those who knew Otto best sang his praises loudest.

"The Dezmans are very fine people," said Rose Lewis, their landlady at the beauty salon. "I couldn't have better tenants. Everyone in the neighborhood

---

   *   Fictitious name.
   **   Fictitious name.

loves Otto. He's an old softie; he will do anything for you." An echo came from Zella Prager, Georgia's ex–chorus girl friend: "Dezman is a fine, stable man, in love with his wife and interested in no one else."

But Otto had his enemies too—one of whom sent Coakley an anonymous note: "This case may be pinned on Burton Abbott, but the guilty ones are Dezman and Georgia Abbott. Give them the third degree. *You'll see.*"

A rumor overheard in a beauty parlor had it that Otto was framing Abbott in order to take possession of the "sharp-looking" Georgia. Whitney and Hove were said to be exploring a scenario to reverse the dynamics of the purse discovery—insinuating that Dezman's presence was not accidental but part of the frame-up plot against Burton.

In Coakley's mind this was nonsense. But the question he had to settle with certainty before the trial was: Who, if anybody, was framing whom?

On the night Georgia had come running up from the cellar with the purse in hand, the possibility of Burton's involvement had not entered Dezman's mind. He felt sure that "nobody who was there was implicated." To his eye, Burton's reactions of excitement and puzzlement appeared normal for a person suddenly cast into a nightmare.

Otto himself was just as upset. "I won't sleep tonight, couldn't if I had to," he told Burton, an avowal that led them to sit up all night with a bottle nearby, playing chess.

During the next five days, Otto and Leona Dezman gave the Abbotts unstinting support, opening their home to Burton and Georgia to shelter them from public gaze and afford them much-needed rest.

Then the discovery of Stephanie's grave gave Dezman a sickening jolt, for reasons never made public until this writing. Suddenly Otto's memory flashed back to certain events in early May—events that had seemed wholly natural at the time.

About two days after Burton's return from Trinity, he had come to Otto suggesting another trip to the cabin right away. This time it would be a stag party—Burton, his brother, and one or two others. Did Otto want to come along? Otto had declined, mainly because Leona wasn't invited, and the trip had fallen through.

"When they found the body," Dezman told the author in 1995, "all at once it struck me that Burton had intended to make me his patsy. He had needed somebody to sucker in. He had wanted to get my fingerprints on the shovels and everything else at the cabin."

With the dawning of this idea, Otto became wholly convinced that Burton was indeed the kidnapper and murderer of Stephanie Bryan. He was thankful beyond measure that he had rejected the invitation in May.

His fears of becoming Burton's "patsy" did not abate, however. Because he had had access to the Abbott basement, as did several frequent visitors, technically he was already a suspect. Moreover, it was indeed possible that Stephanie's purse and its contents bore his fingerprints; he had handled them, as had everyone present, before the police came.

It did not reduce Otto's anxiety when Whitney and Hove, Burton's lawyers, paid him a visit one evening and invited him out to their car to talk in private. There they implored him to retract what was probably the most relevant statement he had made earlier to the FBI—his positive assertion that he had been the first to suggest summoning the police. Whitney and Hove wanted him to "correct" that now and say the idea had originated with Georgia or Burton.

Otto refused.

On September 20 Inspector O'Meara took a call from a Mrs. Leonora Bowden, an Oakland apartment house owner, who said she had important information about the Bryan case. Berkeley Officer A. C. Phibbs was dispatched to talk to her. She turned out to be a stout woman in late middle age.

About six-twenty on the evening of April 28, she said, a man and a young girl had come to her looking for short-term lodging. The girl had done most of the talking and negotiating. She said they were from Long Beach, her "husband" was in the navy, and they would be shipping out soon for Honolulu. They had taken an apartment, paying $9.50 for the first week. Mrs. Bowden could not recall their name.

A few days later, the landlady said, she had seen a picture of Stephanie Bryan in the *Tribune* and at once recognized the missing girl as her young tenant. Before she could confirm this, however, the "navy couple" had moved out.

Mrs. Bowden described the "wife" as about fifteen years old, of medium build, and a little over five feet tall, with dark-brown hair, blue eyes, and extremely white skin. She had worn a white upper garment and dark skirt. She spoke with what Mrs. Bowden took to be a New England accent.

"Any facial blemishes?" Phibbs asked.

"No, definitely not."

Mrs. Bowden had failed to mention the very noticeable eczema she would have seen on Stephanie's upper lip. There were other problems, too, with her description. Stephanie's eyes had been hazel, not blue. She had been wearing a vivid turquoise skirt, not a dark one. Although the Bryans were from Massachusetts, none of them spoke with any noticeable regional inflection. Above all, it would have been totally out of character for the shy Stephanie to have taken the lead in choosing the apartment and paying the rent.

The landlady said the "husband," who wore khakis, appeared to be about forty, about five feet ten, and of medium-heavy build, with a full oval face and light-brown receding hair. He was definitely not Burton Abbott.

Phibbs showed Mrs. Bowden unidentified photographs of other men involved in the case, including Mark Abbott, Inspector O'Meara, Lieutenant Sherry, and Dezman. After careful study she declared none of them was her tenant. Then, unaware that she had just ruled out Dezman, she said, "I wish I could see Mr. Dezman's picture."

Two days later she repeated her story to Folger Emerson.

"Have you remembered the man's name yet?" he asked.

"I've been doing a lot of studying on that," Mrs. Bowden said. "It was a two-syllable word, I'm sure of that, and 'm-a-n' was the last, with an 's' or a 'z' or something like that in front of it—Desmond?"

She didn't quite have it right, but she was unmistakably pointing a finger at Otto. During the interview she let it slip that Abbott's lawyers had talked to her.

Another finger-pointer was Dezman's next-door neighbor, Mrs. Diane Westbrook, who said she heard screams from his garage about the time of Stephanie's abduction. Later, she added, her shovel and hoe were missing. A lieutenant at the Naval Air Station was spreading a false story that Dezman had been kicked out of the navy. Winifred Tyson, who also worked at the base, told an inspector she considered Otto "shady" because he was "fresh" like most navy chiefs. Mrs. Tyson turned out to be a close friend of Elsie and Mark Abbott.

Perhaps the most titillating rumor of all was that on July 15 Burton had accused Georgia of sleeping with Dezman, and her furious reaction had been to recover Stephanie's purse—of which she was well aware—and in a fit of spite bring it upstairs in Dezman's presence.

To Coakley it was becoming increasingly apparent that the Abbott defense was generating the glut of Dezman derogation. Yet, he wondered, could there be so much smoke without at least a little fire? He was considering ways to find out when Otto himself called in by phone.

"Do you people want the records of my wife's beauty shop?" he asked. Indeed they did.

"Well," Dezman said, "you had better come and get them as soon as you can. Whitney is trying to take them from us with a subpoena."

Within the hour the D.A.'s office had the records of the Morton Beauty Salon under lock and key, out of reach of Whitney and Hove. It was a major coup. Emerson, carrying the main burden of preparation for Abbott's trial, especially wanted the parlor's appointment book page for April 28. Perhaps it would list the names of witnesses who would remember what time Burton visited the shop that day.

Otto's inquiry had an important additional outcome. It cemented a productive behind-the-scenes partnership between the Dezmans and Burton Abbott's prosecutors. If indeed Hove and Whitney intended to frame Dezman, Emerson vowed to make them wish they had never tried. He was convinced of Otto's innocence, and now he fashioned a scheme to establish it beyond doubt.

"You're going to have to account for all your time from the day Stephanie disappeared until her purse was found," he informed Otto and Leona.

They readily agreed. They had done considerable traveling during that period but offered, if necessary, to retrace all their trips, gathering documentation from hotels, restaurants, and other places they had visited. Especially crucial, of course, were the days of Abbott's journey to the cabin. Coakley's inspectors were able to document Otto's movements hour by hour, minute by minute, during that four-day span:

On Thursday morning, April 28, about the time Stephanie had begun her last school day, Otto and a friend named Frank Gregory had started a concrete repair job at the home of a neighbor, Al Beyerle. Twice during the day Otto had driven to the Rhodes-Jamieson Concrete Materials Company for supplies. He had taken a short break about noon to give a ride to Hattie Clark, Leona's cleaning lady. In midafternoon Otto had arrived at the beauty parlor where a client, Bessie Wells, was fretting about an overdue parking ticket, and he had raced to the Alameda traffic office and paid it just before the 5 P.M. closing. Then he had returned to Beyerle's place to help Gregory with cleanup.

Similarly detailed reports on Otto's doings and goings were prepared for each of the three following days. For much of Friday he had worked with a helper on a remodeling job at home. During the morning he had deposited the beauty parlor receipts at the bank, and later he had taken Leona to the dentist with a toothache. On Saturday, with the tooth still aching, he had driven her to another dentist to have it pulled. On Sunday the Dezmans had rested at home.

Corroboration and documentation were ample. Traffic court records showed that Mrs. Wells's parking ticket had been paid between 3:45 and 5:00 P.M. Thursday, the critical time of Stephanie's disappearance. Leona's dental appointments were matters of record, and the Bank of America furnished Otto's deposit slip. Rhodes-Jamieson had sales slips for his cement purchases. All this evidence was brought together in a remarkable ten-page document of proof. On August 8 Emerson sent Coakley a triumphant memo: "We are now able to provide Otto Dezman with a complete alibi."

The Dezman exoneration project was top secret; Coakley was determined that the defense get no inkling of it before the trial.

On August 21 Inspector Severin got a query from *Examiner* reporter Purcell who—working on the Abbott story from the start—had taken a strong dislike to Dezman. He told the inspector he considered Otto "a prime suspect" and demanded, "Are you investigating him?"

In a memo about the incident, Severin informed Coakley, "I told Frank we were checking out all persons who could be involved, including Dezman, and will do so on anyone who may come under suspicion. I said that as of now, we felt Dezman was in the clear—but I didn't tell him how we knew it."

16

The Other Grave

July and August had been a frustrating time for the proud staffers of the *San Francisco Chronicle,* the self-styled "Voice of the West," as they suffered one humiliation after another.

First Ed Montgomery's bloodhound discovery of Stephanie's body had been a stupendous scoop for the rival *Examiner.* Then had come the *Call-Bulletin*'s "discovery" of typewriter repairman William Russell, expected to be a key prosecution witness when Burton Abbott came to trial. Finally the *Call,* with its primitive Xerox machine, had scored a clean beat on the grand jury transcript.

Now, as a new month dawned, the *Chronicle* saw a chance to get even, to break out of the dismal pattern of catch-up journalism. On Friday morning, September 2, the paper hit the streets all over Northern California with a banner headline five inches deep, in black gothic type:

EXCLUSIVE

LOOTED GRAVE FOUND IN MARIN—STEPHANIE'S 1ST?

The story below, running forty-five inches with two pictures, was written for maximum shock. It announced the discovery of an empty grave "in a lonely Marin County creekside glade that may have been the site of Stephanie Bryan's murder." It theorized that Stephanie had been buried there originally, then moved later to where her body was ultimately found uphill from Abbott's cabin in Trinity County. According to the *Chronicle* reporter:

> When the [Marin] grave was first discovered last May, it almost certainly contained a human body. When it was revisited less than two weeks ago, the grave had been opened and the body removed . . .

This fantastic new development in the already confounding mystery may well change the entire complexion of the case.

If, indeed, the grave proves to have been Stephanie's, it will mean that the prosecutors of Burton Abbott must change their entire theory. They have held all along that Abbott kidnapped Stephanie in Berkeley on April 28, drove her directly to Wildwood, and buried her body there.

Abbott has said he drove alone to Wildwood that day.

The *Chronicle*'s yarn, astonishing on its face, was in fact heavy-laden with ifs, almosts, maybes, and question marks. Without attribution, solely on its own authority, the newspaper reported that county investigators and the FBI had found "several highly significant clues at the grave, apparently linking it with Stephanie Bryan's death."

At no point did the story quote an official source firsthand, except for an unvarnished "No comment!" from Folger Emerson. Instead the piece spoke enigmatically of "the story that unfolded last night."

The reporter called attention to the fact that "soon after Stephanie's disappearance she was reported to have been seen at the San Rafael bus depot in Marin County. Those reports have never been proved or disproved."

What "the *Chronicle* learned" (a phrase prominent in its story) was that back in May a San Rafael couple, Horace and Amanda Tomlin,* had gone to the woods nearby to dig loam for their garden. The spot they chose, near the tiny settlement of Tocaloma, was "a sort of bucolic lovers' lane." There, beneath a bay tree on the brushy bank of Lagunitas Creek, they had come upon what they took to be a closed grave with a neatly rounded top. It gave off a strong stench of decomposing flesh that made both of them "violently ill."

As they returned to their car the Tomlins noticed tire tracks and a five-foot length of strap iron splotched with red lead. Close by was a puddle of black oil. They picked up the iron bar and took it home.

Later Amanda mentioned the "grave" to her sister, who exclaimed, "Maybe it's Stephanie's!" but the Tomlins made no report to the authorities at that time. Over the next weeks their sixteen-year-old son used the bar to stir their incinerator fire, bending it in the process.

On August 22 the Tomlins returned to the site for more loam and found the grave "violated." It was now an empty hole with a little water in the bottom. The excavated soil was heaped alongside.

This time the Tomlins called the Marin County sheriff, who sent Donald Midyett, his chief criminal investigator, to take a look. With Midyett went FBI Special Agent Dale Norton. They asked questions but were insufficiently

* Fictitious names.

impressed to commandeer the iron bar (which the *Chronicle* was now styling the "slayer's bludgeon").

Two evenings later, as the Tomlins returned to San Rafael from an all-day trip, they glimpsed a prowler fleeing their yard and found the screens ripped from their back door and a window. Then two days after that, they reported the house ransacked by a burglar. There was no apparent link between these intrusions and the "grave" discovery, but Amanda, fearing someone was after the iron bar, hid it in the folds of her living-room drapes. Then she placed a call to Coakley's office and told her suspicions to Emerson.

On Monday, August 29, Emerson and Inspector Russell F. Ryan crossed the bay to interview the Tomlins and then, accompanied by Midyett, went to inspect the excavation by the creek. The pit was about five feet long, two and a half feet wide, and a foot and a half deep. Its axis was east to west.

Ryan took six samples of the soil, which, like that from the Trinity grave, was reddish in hue. He also obtained a specimen of oil from the puddle the Tomlins had noticed. The inspector was mindful that Stephanie's clothing, after her exhumation, had borne traces of oil and some dirt stains that did not match the soil at Wildwood.

In his report, Ryan described the area around the excavation as one "apparently frequented by picnickers." He had found empty beer cans, paper plates, several newspapers dated June 20, and a scrap of paper apparently torn from a composition book, bearing the typewritten notation "1/4 pound of veal."

Exploring the surroundings, the officers also discovered a footprint in the bottom of a mud hole that could have been made by a girl wearing saddle shoes. Emerson and Midyett thought it was fresh, but Ryan wasn't sure. Midyett took a plaster cast of it.

In the *Chronicle* story, Mrs. Tomlin quoted Emerson as telling her, "If Stephanie's body wasn't buried in this grave, then Marin County has another unsolved murder on its hands."

The *Chronicle's* rivals took a skeptical view of the "fantastic new development" and "highly significant clues." The Associated Press compressed the newspaper's report into a few short paragraphs within its Saturday roundup on the Stephanie case, which featured another angle in its lead. The A.P., like Inspector Ryan in his report, put the word "grave" in quotation marks each time it referred to the muddy hole in Marin.

In its own follow-up story on Saturday, again under an eight-column front-page line, the *Chronicle* strove mightily to keep its sensation alive. The reporter wrote that the Bryan murder probe was "thrown into high gear" by the grave's discovery and that the investigators were in a "buzz of excitement."

To support this, the report said Marin County deputies had done further digging along Lagunitas Creek and found, among other things, a wine bottle filled with gravel, a torn leather glove, an oil can, and "a strange piece of triangular cloth" shaped like a piece found in Abbott's basement.

The best second-day angle that the *Chronicle* could come up with was an unattributed statement that Inspector O'Meara and Emerson had held a "secret conference" on the Marin developments.

No one welcomed the *Chronicle*'s sensation more than Harold Hove, who jubilantly predicted that the Marin developments would force Coakley to rethink his basic assumptions.

"I don't think the girl's body was buried in Trinity County on April 28, and I never have," Hove said. "She was probably buried somewhere else first. Maybe this is it."

The prosecution, on the other hand, draped a shroud of silence over the Bryan case. For the second day Emerson refused comment, as did criminalist Paul Kirk, to whom the Marin evidence had been given for analysis.

Confidential information in the prosecutors' possession gave them abundant reason to regard the Marin grave theory with disdain. Privately Kirk told Inspector Ryan that none of the Marin soil appeared to match the dirt on Stephanie's clothing, but he would not know for sure until he ran a spectrographic test.

Also, an entomologist had made an unpublicized study of the insects that had contributed to the decay of Stephanie's body. From their age, he had concluded that the girl had been in the ground between sixty and ninety days—an estimate coinciding with the actual term of eighty-four days between her disappearance and her exhumation at Wildwood.

On Sunday the *Chronicle* dropped its own "exclusive" like a hot potato. No explanation was given, other than two cryptic sentences near the end of a short, unsigned article about Abbott's forthcoming arraignment: "Investigative activities around the grave came to an abrupt halt yesterday. Mrs. Tomlin said she had been requested by authorities not to speak further about it."

The sensation had survived less than forty-eight hours. Perhaps mercifully for the *Chronicle,* a Richter-5.5 earthquake rattled the Bay Area Sunday evening, filling Monday's front page and diverting attention from the fact that on that day, the paper carried not a line on the Bryan case.

Neither of the Tomlins would be called as a witness by either side when Burton came to trial.

Supplemental reports filed by Midyett and Inspector Severin shed the only light on the ignominious conclusion to the "looted grave" episode.

"Reynolds Yates, retired game warden, called," Midyett wrote. "He said he had been in the Tocaloma area digging for worms about the first week of April and had noticed a small mound, as if someone had been digging topsoil or leaf mold. There was a strong odor in the area; so he investigated and found a dead black cat a few feet away."

Severin's memo, directed to Emerson, told of conversations he had had with Marin County Undersheriff A. L. Ingalls and San Rafael Police Inspector Nick Foley. Both had classified Mrs. Tomlin as a "screwball."

During the investigation of an infamous murder several years earlier, she had bombarded the sheriff's office with useless tips. In the seventeen months preceding her "grave" discovery, she had called the San Rafael cops no fewer than eight times about trivial offenses ranging from a dog nuisance to a youngster riding his bike on the sidewalk. She also had been involved in a civil disturbance.

"Inspector Foley said that Mrs. Tomlin recently moved to Novato, for which they give heartfelt thanks," Severin wrote.

17

The Road More Traveled

Three months elapsed between Burton Abbott's indictment and the beginning of his trial. In California's hot, rainless summer, the sere hills and flatlands were brown. Between Berkeley and Wildwood, the road Abbott had followed one cold day back in April—with or without Stephanie or her body—was singularly drab. Clocked from the Berkeley Police station to the lonely hillside grave, the distance was 303 miles. For about half of the way, the route was along the narrow gray ribbon of Highway 99W, running straight as a string up the Sacramento Valley to a horizon that shimmered in the dry heat.

As the trial approached, this route carried a constant stream of travelers in quest of the facts that would convict or exonerate: Berkeley cops, the D.A.'s inspectors, FBI agents, forensic scientists, lawyers for both sides, private detectives, reporters for a dozen newspapers, the rugged lawmen of Trinity County. Besides seeking evidence, the prosecutors and defenders spied on each other and seduced each other's witnesses. Each place along the highway held its own secrets.

Sacramento: Lost in the Capital

It is fairly difficult to get lost in downtown Sacramento. The north-south streets are numbered, and the east-west streets, flanking the State Capitol, are lettered in alphabetical order. So anyone who knows the alphabet and can count has little trouble finding his way around. Yet Burton professed to have become totally befuddled within this elementary street grid while looking for the land office.

His three conflicting stories about Sacramento—that he didn't go there; that he went there and stopped at the land office; that he went there but didn't stop—were of major interest to the prosecution and major concern to the defense.

Berkeley Officer Don Kent was among those who went to the capital trying to establish the truth. He spent a day in mid-September shooting several rolls of film in the neighborhood where Burton claimed to have become lost.

His pictures included aerial photos showing the simplicity of the street pattern.

Kent found no one in the land office who recognized Burton's picture—not surprising, since he was now saying he never got there. One of the officer's more interesting discoveries was that the land office was not "opposite the post office," as Abbott insisted he had been advised by the Forest Service. It was in the post office building itself, Room 352 on the third floor.

Burton's "fibs" (to use his own word) were "one of the pitfalls" for the defense, said John Hanson, the last surviving lawyer of Abbott's team, in 1993.

Dunnigan: Bill and Kathy's

According to Burton, he had paused at Bill and Kathy's Restaurant in Dunnigan for a sandwich and coffee sometime after three o'clock on Thursday afternoon, April 28. This would have placed him a hundred miles north of Berkeley just one hour or less before Stephanie's disappearance.

In mid-October Assistant D.A. Dale Stoops visited Bill and Kathy's to interview waitress Ann O'Connor, who thought she remembered Burton's visit. Her story, far from unraveling any part of the Stephanie Bryan mystery, compounded it.

The customer she remembered had entered the twenty-four-hour café not on Thursday afternoon, but about four o'clock on Friday morning, April 29. He had taken the second or third stool from the door and ordered milk or coffee. As Ann remembered him, he matched Burton's description plausibly if not perfectly: tall and slender, about thirty, wearing an "army-colored" jacket. He said he was a fisherman headed home, having caught his limit.

Ann liked the man not at all. He was surly, nervous, and fidgety, she told Stoops. He had abruptly contradicted her when she warned him that he had been fishing illegally—that the season wouldn't begin until the next day. In retrospect it seemed sinister to the waitress as well that the man's jacket, trousers, and shoes had been heavily caked with mud, which could have been acquired during Stephanie's burial.

Stoops at once perceived a major problem with Ann's memory, however. The 4 A.M. time of her customer's visit, about which she was positive, fitted neither Burton's alibi nor Coakley's hypothesis about the case. All evidence at hand indicated that Burton, whether innocent or guilty, had reached Wildwood by that early hour Friday—although no one knew for certain. Stoops reluctantly surmised that Ann O'Connor had waited on someone else.

Several weeks passed, and then (with Burton's trial well under way) the café in Dunnigan had another visitor from Coakley's office. Inspector Lloyd Jester was on his way north to check out other clues, and his stop there was more for food than for information. But in chatting with the help, he picked up a fact no one had mentioned before: Bill and Kathy's employed *no wait-resses at all* on the afternoon shift. At the time Burton claimed to have been there, all personnel were men.

Excitedly Jester went to a phone and called his boss, Captain Severin. By now it was expected that Abbott would soon testify in his own behalf, and Severin caught the note of urgency in his aide's voice.

"Cross-examine Abbott about Bill and Kathy's," Jester advised. "Ask him who waited on him. If he says it was a woman and describes her, we can prove he is lying!"

Corning: The Red Fan Belt

Corning, where Abbott said he had gassed up his car around 5 P.M. on Thursday, was a farm town of perhaps three thousand persons in 1955. Olive groves surrounded it; olive oil refining was its main industry. Its chief of police was aptly named Dick Tracy.

About November 1 Assistant D.A. William Sharon drove there, unaware that he was being followed. He stopped at the Shell station run by the brothers Craig—Jim, William, and Pete—and talked to Jim.

"Do you recognize either this man or this automobile?" Sharon asked, showing pictures of Burton and his car. Although Abbott's photo had been constantly in the papers since his arrest, Jim said no—the same reply he had given all interviewers since July.

No sooner had Sharon left—his auto was still in sight—than another car rolled into the Craigs' station, bearing Stanley Whitney and Harold Hove.

"Didn't you see the investigator just leave here?" the astounded Jim Craig asked them.

"Yes, we were down on the corner watching his car."

Although Jim's answers to Abbott's lawyers were the same he had given Sharon, his friendliness suggested that he might be converted into a useful defense witness.

"Mr. Craig," Hove said, "we'd like you you to come to Oakland to see Bud Abbott in person and look at his car. Maybe something will refresh your memory."

"Okay."

Jim's ready assent was not surprising. For anyone in the Sacramento Valley's dreary northern boondocks, a junket to bustling Oakland was an exciting prospect. One day later Whitney escorted Jim Craig to the eighth-floor jail in the Alameda County Courthouse, employing a small deception. In the register of visitors, Whitney wrote Jim's name as "J. Crane," not Craig.

If this bit of trickery was intended to keep Coakley in the dark about what the defense was up to, it was in vain. Corning Police Chief Tracy, who kept his thumb on everything in his town, was an *ex officio* part of Coakley's intelligence network. He talked to Jim Craig as soon as he was back home and sent Coakley a full report:

> He [Craig] went to Oakland and viewed Abbott, did not recognize him. He then looked at Abbott's car, under the hood and everything. They asked him if there was anything he noticed about the car, any peculiarity or anything that could distinguish it. He then said, "The only thing that I might recall is the red fan belt."

The words "red fan belt" had galvanized Hove and Whitney. "They jumped on this," Chief Tracy wrote. Clearly they were desperate for any shred of evidence, no matter how frail, that might prop up their client's alibi.

Privately Craig admitted to Chief Tracy that he had no way of telling when he had previously serviced a car with a red belt or what make it might have been. The other Craig brothers were even more forthright, telling the chief there were lots of red fan belts, certainly too many to make them important in identifying an automobile. And the Craigs' competitor, Harold Fandrich of the Standard station in Corning, said he had probably seen a thousand red fan belts in the months since Stephanie's murder.

Nevertheless, Jim Craig was destined to become an important witness for the Abbott defense.

Red Bluff: The Chuck Wagon

In his early interrogations, Burton had stumbled when asked to name the café where he had eaten about 6 P.M. Thursday in Red Bluff: "It had something to do with chicken—the Chicken Fry Spot, maybe?" he had told the FBI.

Because of this answer, the first inspector Coakley sent to Red Bluff early in September went astray. Spotting a restaurant called the Chicken Shack, he assumed it must be the place. Not surprisingly, the people there knew nothing about Abbott, so the D.A.'s man went on his way empty-handed.

Hove and Whitney had better luck in Red Bluff. Perhaps their client had given them better information, for they ignored the Chicken Shack and went to another place called the Chuck Wagon. There a waitress suggested, "Talk to Rosa Arnone. She worked here last April and may know something."

Conveniently for Abbott's lawyers, Rosa had since moved south to Alameda County and was now living with her husband in a trailer in San Leandro, about ten minutes from Whitney's office. Abbott's photograph brought an instant flash of recognition.

"Yes," she said, "he looks like a customer I served one night last spring. I

remember him because we talked a lot about fishing at Donner Lake." Rosa
further recalled that her boss had joined in the conversation and that the customer had spoken of a cabin in Trinity County. He had worn blue jeans and
a dark-brown leather jacket with fur collar, she said, and had entered the café
about 6:30 P.M. for a hamburger. She was unsure about the date, but she
thought it was the eve of her last day at the Chuck Wagon, which was Friday, April 29. She would need to see Abbott in person, not just a photo, before making a positive I.D.

Whitney and Hove, jubilant, began wooing Rosa like ardent swains. If her
recollection could be firmed up, they had their first eyewitness to a key incident in Burton's alibi. They took her to see him in jail, where again, as with
James Craig, they used minor subterfuge. Although they gave the jailer her
correct name, Whitney passed her off as his secretary. In the following weeks
Rosa developed so strong a bond with Hove that she was calling him "my
attorney."

Almost two months would pass before the prosecution, through the dig-
ging of the dogged cop Willard Hutchins, would "discover" Mrs. Arnone.
When Coakley sent Stoops and Inspector Russ Ryan to talk to her in her San
Leandro trailer on October 27, they got an icy reception.

"I have been advised by my attorney, Mr. Hove, that I do not have to disclose what I know to anyone," she said. "I will tell my story in court."

Stoops tried to reason with her. "It's true that you don't have to talk to us,"
he admitted, "but as law enforcement officers we feel that we should be
treated no differently than Mr. Hove."

"If you had found me first, I would talk to you," Rosa replied, "but I talked
to the defense first and I don't want to break my promise to them. You have
to be on one side or the other in this case, and I am on the defense side."

At this point she excused herself and left the trailer briefly to use a nearby
pay phone. It became clear that she had called Abbott's lawyers, for within
minutes Whitney's partner, John Hanson, appeared on the scene.

"Get out. Leave now!" he ordered Stoops and Ryan.

They did.

By October, California's far north had been well scouted by both sides in the
Abbott investigation, but Officer Hutchins retained an uneasy feeling that
there were still stones unturned.

"I decided to go back over the ground that everybody had covered," he
recalled much later. "I stopped at every service station and every restaurant
between Berkeley and the cabin, and I found this guy Robert Hall. Eventually I coaxed a statement out of him."

Hall, a Marine Corps veteran, was the Chuck Wagon boss whom Rosa
Arnone had mentioned earlier to Hove and Whitney. Like her, he remem-

bered the fishing discussion, but at this point he was far from ready to identify the customer involved.

"I could no more confirm that it was Abbott, or tell you the exact date of that conversation, than I could fly like a kite," Hall told Hutchins on October 25.

In the ensuing days Hall would be batted back and forth between prosecution and defense like a badminton shuttlecock. On October 29 it was Hove and Whitney who were at his door, bearing Abbott's photo. He now thought he recognized it.

"Abbott is definitely innocent," Hove assured Hall. "Someone is trying to frame him. Don't discuss the case, don't give the police another statement, and above all, don't sign anything."

Another two days passed, and Hutchins was back again. Hove's persuasion had clearly taken effect during the days since his prior visit. Now Hall was all but certain that his fisherman customer had indeed been Burton. He described the fellow convincingly, telling Hutchins his most striking characteristic was his tiny, womanlike rear end.

Although most of what Hall was now saying supported Abbott's alibi, there were critical discrepancies. Abbott had said it was daylight when he reached the Chuck Wagon about six o'clock, but Hall was certain it was after sunset and the lights were on. (That day the sun had not set in Red Bluff until 8 P.M.)

On November 2 Hall made a journey to Oakland on his own, not as a guest of the defense—but once he arrived, Burton's lawyers took him under their wing. They drove him to compare notes with Rosa in San Leandro and accompanied him to the jail to see Abbott in the flesh. He observed Burton not in a line-up but with Hove in a small jail room.

Hall had played fair with both sides, and the defense had won out, capturing his loyalty along with Rosa's.

Cottonwood Creek: Red Flag or Lantern?

As the summer dragged on, Coakley retained his exceptional interest in the Cottonwood Creek bridge en route to the cabin. His aides must have been puzzled by his fixation on this detail of Burton's itinerary.

The bridge, sixteen miles west of Red Bluff on Highway 36 had been under repair in April with traffic subject to delays. Burton thought he had crossed the span about 7:00 or 7:30 P.M. after leaving the Chuck Wagon. He said "a fellow with a red flag or lantern or something like that" had waved him on. On the way home three days later, about 1:30 or 2:00 on Sunday afternoon, he had driven across the bridge again in the opposite direction, following behind his brother Mark's Ford.

The Cottonwood repair job had been completed May 23, and the workmen had dispersed widely; so now in midsummer Coakley's inspectors and FBI agents fanned out all over the state to find and talk to them. None had any specific memory of Burton, but they did supply a few bits of information that interested Coakley a great deal. The traffic delays at Cottonwood Creek had occurred only during working hours, never after 4:30 P.M. when the crews knocked off. And never had the workmen used a red lantern or red flag to direct traffic.

One crew member, Richard Boyd McNees, was nevertheless destined to become a key personality in the Abbott trial. During the repair work he had lived with his wife and their small child in a shack in a cow pasture about 150 feet downstream from the bridge. So long after the rest of the men had left at 4:30, the husky, nineteen-year-old McNees was often there, even at the hour when Abbott claimed to have made his first crossing.

McNees was now living in Southern California, and on July 28 FBI agents found him aboard a fishing boat. Like the others interviewed, he did not recognize Abbott from a photo, nor did he recall Abbott's 1949 Chevolet. He did remember two other Chevys of that vintage that crossed the bridge, but they had belonged to local people he knew. McNees's further recollections included one significant detail not mentioned by the others: Although there had been no regular flagmen at the Cottonwood bridge, crew members sometimes guided cars across with hand signals when planks were in place to permit passage.

As the trial neared, Coakley felt the need for more specific information about this; so he sent Clarence Severin south to reinterview McNees. For the tall, thin captain of inspectors, the trip was a welcome departure from the administrative routine in which he was now trapped. Severin was cut out to be an investigator, not a supervisor. In the field he was smart, relentless, and tough as nails.

He knocked on McNees's door in Hermosa Beach early on a November afternoon and showed his credentials to Richard's wife, Alice. Richard was out looking for a job but expected home soon for dinner. From the first minute Severin knew this interview would not be easy.

"Two of Mr. Abbott's lawyers have already been here," Alice told him. "They told us not to talk to anyone, not even the FBI. Under the circumstances I feel obligated to them, and I probably shouldn't talk to you."

From her description, Severin knew one of the lawyers was Harold Hove and that he had taken the same approach to the McNeeses that he had to Rosa Arnone, in virtually the same words: Abbott was a frame-up victim.

Severin perceived, however, that Alice's reluctance to talk didn't mean she was hostile. Hove obviously had irritated her. She felt he had been less than truthful, having told her the only discovery in Abbott's house had been the red purse. He had said nothing about the bra, schoolbooks, and eyeglasses.

Both Alice and her husband had signed a two-page statement written by Hove in longhand. Hove had read it back to them, but Alice had no idea whether the read-back had been accurate. Gradually she opened up a little.

"When you were living up by the bridge," Severin asked, "did your husband ever act as a flagman? Did he ever use a red flag or lantern or wear a red coat?"

"No, never." Alice said. However, she did recall one evening when she and Richard, crossing the bridge's loose planking on foot after working hours, had scampered off to let an automobile pass. With a wave of his hand, her husband had signaled the driver to proceed, and he had waved back.

"Could this have been on April 28?"

"Maybe," Alice said, "because it was drizzling." The time conformed to Burton's supposed itinerary, but Alice said the car was a late model, newer than 1949 or 1950. She did not know the color.

"Did you get a good look at the driver?" Severin asked.

"No, I couldn't identify him."

"Was there anyone else in the car?"

"I don't know."

By this time Severin had been chatting with Alice for about forty-five minutes, and her husband was not yet in sight; so he departed, saying he would return. When he did so, Richard answered his knock and invited the inspector in—but that was as far as his amiability went. Unlike his wife, he would be a hard-nosed adversary.

"I want to discuss the Cottonwood bridge incident with you," Severin began, but got no further.

"I can't talk to you," Richard informed him. "I've given my written statement to the defense. I'm a defense witness."

"In other words," Severin said, "you are telling me as a law enforcement officer to go to hell."

"If that's the way you want to put it, yes."

"Well, we want to use you in court, Mr. McNees," Severin informed the young man, extending a subpoena. It commanded McNees to appear for the opening of Abbott's trial.

McNees waved the piece of paper away. "I refuse to accept it," he declared.

Severin then handed the subpoena to Alice and addressed her as she stood beside her husband.

"Mrs. McNees, your husband must be in court on the day indicated here, and you should see to it that he is."

At this, McNees snatched the subpoena from his wife, crumpled it up, stalked to the door, and threw it into the back of Severin's car.

"Have you been subpoenaed by the defense?" Severin inquired.

"No, and I don't need to be, because for them I'll testify on my own. Now, you'd better get out!"

"Are you ordering me from the house?"

"I definitely am!"

Severin turned and left.

His next stop was at the Hermosa Beach Police Department, where he enlisted the services of a uniformed officer to serve a second copy of the summons. From his own automobile down the street, Severin watched it done.

Wildwood: Slow Day at the Inn

If Burton, when first interrogated, had not mentioned stopping at the Wildwood Inn for a drink on the evening of his arrival, his subsequent problems might have been fewer. The rest of his alibi itinerary—Sacramento, Dunnigan, Corning, Red Bluff, Cottonwood Creek—might not be provable, but there was little to disprove it either.

However, he had been emphatic about spending twenty minutes at the tavern that Thursday night, consuming a bourbon and soda and talking to the owner, Delbert Cox. Cox, on the other hand, was equally emphatic that Burton had not come in until the following afternoon—the time of his memorable binge with Tom Daly.

Now in midsummer Burton's lawyers traveled north to size Cox up. They appeared at his bar incognito on August 6, ordered drinks, played the pinball machine, and left without a word—making Cox suspicious. He knew they weren't locals and could tell they weren't outdoorsmen; at first he pegged them as state liquor officers. The next morning they returned and began asking questions about Bud Abbott.

"What do you fellows have to do with the case?" the innkeeper demanded.

Only then did Whitney and Hove identify themselves.

By this time Cox had developed a loyalty to the prosecution, much as McNees and Rosa Arnone had committed themselves to the defense. However, he reluctantly agreed to talk to Abbott's attorneys in a shed at the rear of his bar, out of earshot of customers.

Back in Oakland Coakley learned of this interview almost before it was over. Cox, annoyed with himself for giving it, reported it at once to his friend, Trinity County D.A. Stennett Sheppard, who in turn informed his Alameda County counterpart.

For the best part of an hour Hove and Whitney had tried to make Cox retreat from his positive declaration that Abbott had not been in his tavern on the night of the twenty-eighth.

"Maybe your place was so crowded that Abbott could have been there without your seeing him," Hove suggested, grasping at a thin straw.

In response Cox went to his cash register receipts, which showed that the bar proceeds for April 28 had totaled only $34. It had been a slow day.

"I've already told my story to the grand jury," he reminded Hove and Whitney. "I can't change it now."

"Don't worry about that," Whitney said. "If you get into trouble with conflicting statements, I promise to get you off, and it won't cost you a cent."

In the end, Abbott's lawyers got part of what they had come for. Despite his unwillingness, Cox was finally persuaded to sign a statement slightly softening if not materially altering what he had testified to earlier.

"I don't remember exactly what I said to Hove and Whitney," Cox told Trinity D.A. Sheppard, "but it was something like 'If Abbott was in here on the 28th, I didn't recognize him.' "

When first questioned about the morning after his arrival at the cabin, Abbott had said:

> I awakened early. Later, perhaps between 7 and 8:30, two men and a woman came by in a covered pickup truck, light green. They asked me where they could go bear hunting . . . Oh, Bob Wetzel stopped in too, Bob Wetzel the produce man. He has a great big refrigerator truck and goes through all the hills up there selling his produce. Bob has been up there for years.

Law officers put in countless hours of unpaid overtime during the scorching summer weeks checking out such random musings by Burton. They found some hunters from Stockton who remembered seeing the green pickup truck that Friday—but later one of them said it could just as well have been Saturday.

Wetzel, who lived close by and kept a sharp eye on the neighborhood, confirmed that he had talked to Abbott outside the cabin Friday morning. But he also volunteered that he had passed the same spot between and ten and eleven Thursday night—more than an hour after Abbott's supposed arrival—and seen "no sign of life, no lights in the cabin, no smoke in the chimney, no car, no tire tracks in the snow, no person." The garage door was ajar—the only time Wetzel had ever seen it that way.

As the trial neared, Coakley sent Stoops north to size up Tom Daly, Burton's drinking buddy on the afternoon after his arrival in Wildwood, as a possible prosecution witness. Although doubt overhung Burton's claimed visit to

Cox's tavern Thursday night, there was no uncertainty about his boozing marathon there Friday.

Daly, who worked at the Wildwood Lumber Company mill, proved something of an intellectual and gave Stoops a fascinating account of the nine-hour binge. During the afternoon Tom and Burton had talked of classical music, college life, and books, notably O. Henry's *The Four Million.*

Daly clearly recalled Abbott's midafternoon phone call to warn Mark about the fierce weather and discourage him from coming to Trinity County. Burton had tried the call four or five times before getting through.

"What's your general feeling about Abbott?" Stoops inquired.

"I definitely feel he's innocent," Daly said. "A man with his personality wouldn't do the crime he's accused of."

Because of that answer, Stoops counseled Coakley against calling Daly to the stand, despite the helpful testimony he might supply.

"It would be better," Stoops suggested, "if he were called by the defense and cross-examined by us."

Later, in Oakland, Coakley had his own chat with Daly, and they hit it off well. The tone of the surviving transcript suggests that they both thoroughly enjoyed it. Among other matters, Coakley was much interested in whether Hove and Whitney had tried to intimidate Tom.

"No," Daly said.

"Well, they did try it down here, with some of the witnesses."

"I heard that. Several people up there talked to both Whitney and Hove before I saw them, and the general opinion was that neither of them was really a top attorney. In the community up there you have no secrets."

"I have heard," Coakley said, "that when Hove and some other fellow were up there, they dressed up in pretty rough clothes like they were natives or loggers. But of course the flaw in their act was when they ordered Gibsons or martinis or something like that."

"Martinis?" Daly howled. "If a logger ordered a martini at Cox's bar, he wouldn't even know what to start with! If you have been working in an office all summer, you can't put on rough clothes and pretend you are an outdoor man. We see that all the time when the hunters come up. Twenty-five percent don't know one end of the gun from the other."

"Well, apparently Hove did quite a bit of drinking up there anyway," observed the D.A.

"That's what I heard," Daly said. "The story got around that he was just damned near as pie-eyed drunk as you can get. As the saying goes, he couldn't find his ass with both hands if his pants were on fire."

Talking to the droll Daly gave Coakley a great lift. Nonetheless, he accepted Stoops's advice to let the defense, if anyone, summon Tom to testify in the upcoming trial.

What did they all add up to—the stories, recollections, accusations, and hints gathered during the hot summer and fall along the road to Stephanie's grave?

Not until the case reached court, if then, would they be sorted out.

18

"No Lothario"

Awaiting trial, the talkative Burton Abbott regularly welcomed reporters to his cell, and they vied ferociously for exclusive interviews with him.

On September 20 in the *Chronicle*—the most friendly toward Burton of all Bay Area dailies—he discoursed at length on his case, his life in jail, his marriage, his religion, and his health. Far down in the story, he hotly disputed widely published statements by police psychiatrist Kelley asserting that his reading habits betrayed a preoccupation with kinky sex. The *Chronicle's* reporter wrote:

> Bud Abbott, with a quick, nervous laugh, said he could not remember ever taking any book on abnormal sex from the library.
>
> "I did not have an abnormal interest in this subject," he said soberly. . . .
>
> Abbott was asked whether he had known many other girls before he met and married the red-haired Georgia.
>
> "I'm no lothario," he said with a wink, "but I'd known a number of girls."

In the district attorney's office a secretary retyped these remarks for ready reference. Coakley had decided at the outset to prosecute Stephanie's murder as a sex crime, so anything Burton said about his sex life was germane.

Because of the decomposition of Stephanie's body—virtually all of the pubic area and reproductive organs were gone—it would be impossible to establish by physical evidence that she had been raped.* The D.A. was therefore building a psychiatric case to convince the jury that Abbott was a sadistic pervert. He had little to build on at first, but little by little, as tips were pursued and facts surfaced, an image of a sexual psychopath was taking form.

---

* The same would have been true even with today's DNA technology, according to forensic scientists. The DNA of a rapist's semen would have been destroyed by bacterial action during the time Stephanie lay in her moist grave.

With good reason Abbott feared Dr. Kelley, who had originally interviewed him in tandem with lie detector expert Al Riedel. On the day after Stephanie's body was found, a *Tribune* article had quoted the psychiatrist at length in a story clearly based on the premise of Abbott's guilt.

The article posed the supposedly hypothetical question, "How can an apparently mild, inoffensive sort of a man, the studious type, head of a family, become involved in a fiendish crime?" Kelley's printed response considered essentially no other motive than a carnal one. He talked about "deviate sex," "distorted sex," and "symbolic sex," any of which, he said, could lead to murder by a person with a twisted personality. Such a person might be activated by ego or feelings of inadequacy. The doctor's thesis was the foundation on which Coakley was now building his case.

It was a tip from a part-time page at the Alameda Free Library that led Coakley to order a probe of Abbott's reading tastes and his supposed preoccupation with erotica and pornography. The boy recalled that several months earlier Burton had asked him to open the "restricted" case where adults-only books were kept under lock and key. When Inspector Mark McDonough tried to check this out, however, he ran into a buzz saw in the person of the head librarian, a Mrs. Killinger, who flatly refused to cooperate.

"If you want any information, go to the Berkeley Police," she snapped. "I'm tired of the bad publicity the library has been getting in the Abbott case. Everybody reads sex books, and there is something wrong with anyone who doesn't."

Mrs. Killinger not only denied McDonough's request for a list of the books Burton had borrowed; she also refused to let him interview library staff members except in her presence.

In his report, the zealous McDonough nonetheless listed a sampling of books in the "restricted" case, including *Sex Problems of Returned Veterans, Sex and Religion, The Folklore of Sex,* Kinsey's *Sexual Behavior of the Human Female, The Book of Marriage, Facts of Life and Love, Sin and Divorce,* and *Essays by Havelock Ellis.* From a 1990s perspective, it is hard to perceive why such titles should have stirred any great prosecutorial interest. In the 1950s, however, mores were different, and Folger Emerson told the press such books were "not the type for average, normal laymen's reading."*

---

* When Coakley ultimately obtained a list of some eighty books Abbott had checked out since 1953, it included *Bugles in the Afternoon,* by Haycox; *30 Days to a More Powerful Vocabulary,* by Funk; *Fly-tying,* by Sturgis (borrowed three times); *The Follett Spanish Dictionary,* by Fricilla; *Building or Buying a House,* by Johnstone; *The Story of Civilization,* by Durant; *Rome,* by Gibbon; *The Crusades,* by Lamb; *Kiss Me Deadly,* by Spillane; *Contract Bridge for Everyone,* by Culbertson; *The Best-known Works of Edgar Allan Poe; Algebra,* by Bartlett; and art books on Renoir, Gauguin, and Degas. No obvious sex books were listed.

A family named Beyerle was well known in the close-knit Alameda neighborhood where the Abbotts lived. The father, Alvin, was a druggist*; the mother, Marie, a regular at the Morton Beauty Salon and at the Lewis Store where everyone shopped for groceries.

In mid-August, acting on a confidential tip, Dale Stoops and Inspector Russ Ryan visited the Beyerle home to talk to the children, ten-year-old John and six-year-old Sharon. Interviewed both separately and together, the youngsters consistently and convincingly told a dreadful story.

Back in May or June, as they were riding their bikes near Franklin Park (which faced the Abbott residence on San Jose Avenue), a man in a new-looking green-and-yellow car had driven up beside them and opened the rear door.

"Sharon," he called, "I have six new dimes in my hand. Come with me and I'll give them to you."

The little girl accepted the coins.

"Don't get in, Sharon," her big brother commanded. "I'll tell Mommy."

Enraged, the driver turned to the boy and threatened, "I'll kick you in the mouth if you do!"

Sharon started to climb into the automobile despite John's warning, but withdrew when her brother repeated his threat to tell on her. The driver then sped off down the street, and Sharon went to the Lewis Store and spent her six dimes on candy.

By the time she got home, her mother knew of the adventure, and not just from John. Rose Lewis, proprietor of the store, had thought it odd that the six-year-old should have so much money in hand. She had called Marie Beyerle and asked, "Did Sharon rob the piggie bank?"

John was unable to tell the D.A.'s men what make of car the man with the dimes was driving.

"Was it a Pontiac?" they asked—the Abbotts having taken delivery of Georgia's new Pontiac, green and yellow to be sure, on May 13.

The boy wasn't sure. But he was certain that the driver knew Sharon because he had called her by name. Sharon herself told the investigators she and the man were good friends and they had met before. It was the second time he had offered her shiny dimes.

Sharon said her "friend" had dark hair, a mustache, and glasses, and was wearing a white shirt but no hat. Not a perfect description of Abbott, whose hair was light brown—but could a six-year-old be expected to recall everything perfectly after two or three months had elapsed?

---

* The reader may recall Beyerle also as the friend for whom Otto Dezman had done some concrete work on the day Stephanie vanished.

Later, when Sharon saw Abbott on the TV news, she cried out, "Holy Toledo! There's my boyfriend. He shaved off his mustache." John, who had never seen the driver except during the encounter near the park, also recognized TV shots of Burton.

As the weeks passed, many others came forward to tell of being crudely approached, stalked, or propositioned in Alameda or Berkeley by someone who looked much like Abbott.

Diane Thompson, a fourteen-year-old Alameda high school girl who once had been introduced to Burton by a friend, told police he had tried to lure her into his old gray Chevy in June 1954. He had stopped as she was walking along along the street at about two-thirty on a weekday afternoon and called, "Do you want a ride home, Diane?" The girl, only a block from her home at the time, had declined the invitation.

In the last week of March, a month before Stephanie vanished, Nancy Hickox had been working on a high school term paper at the Claremont branch of the Berkeley Library—the very branch where Stephanie would later check out her last books. As Nancy left, a slender, blond-haired man in his late twenties had intercepted her as she approached her car.

"I've seen you before walking down College Avenue," the stranger said. "I want a date with you."

Nancy replied that she was busy.

"Let me take you to dinner."

"No, I have to go home."

"I know where you live," the accoster persisted. "I won't leave until you give me your name and phone number."

By now badly flustered, Nancy complied truthfully in the hope that the man would leave. She was not thinking clearly enough to give him a phony address.

"I will call you," the man said. But he never did.

Nancy's description of him matched Burton Abbott closely, but she could not make a positive identification. One of Coakley's inspectors noted that Nancy herself bore a striking resemblance to Stephanie Bryan.

An experience even eerier than Nancy's, likewise in the Claremont neighborhood, was reported by a young mother named Gladys Thurston. In the spring of 1954, she and her small son had been strolling along a tree-shaded street near the hotel when a strange man had begun began tailing them in a car throttled down to three or four miles an hour. He stayed behind them until they entered a drugstore near the Berkeley Tennis Club, where they had lunch at the counter.

When they returned to the street, the automobile followed them again.

Three times they returned to the pharmacy, trying to lose it, but each time it fell in behind them. Finally Mrs. Thurston and her boy walked to John Muir Grammar School nearby to pick up her teenage daughter, and from there the suspicious car followed the three of them all the way home before it vanished. At no time did the driver leave the vehicle or speak to them.

In a similar episode reported by a Mrs. Newman, however, a stalking driver finally had pulled up beside her with an offer of oral copulation.

Another incident had taken place in Alameda not far from Abbott's home. The mother of sixteen-year-old Virginia Payne ran a cleaning establishment there, and one evening in mid-June she had sent Virginia to deliver a sailor's uniform nearby. In front of the cleaning shop a man was sitting in a dark-colored car with a sun visor (a 1950s accessory that Abbott's old Chevy boasted). The man, judged by Virginia to be about thirty, got out and followed her to the corner, where he extended an invitation much like the one Nancy Hickox had received in Berkeley in March:

"Take a ride with me. I'll take you to dinner. I'll pick you up in a few minutes after you deliver that uniform."

Virginia, who rebuffed the stranger, described him as well-spoken and courteous in manner. A month later, when Abbott's picture first appeared in the newspapers after his arrest, she told her mother he looked like the man who had tried to pick her up.

On October 30 the victims in the foregoing and other encounters gathered at the Alameda County Jail at the invitation of the police and Coakley to view Abbott in a lineup. Mrs. Thurston and both Beyerle children identified him positively as their stalker. The others weren't sure.

Whether any of this stalking evidence would be usable in court was highly doubtful, as Coakley was well aware. Some of it was hearsay. In other cases victims' memories had dimmed over time, and their recollections, though believable, were understandably flawed. Some of the descriptions of stalkers, while closely matching Abbott, were wrong in critical details. The Beyerle children were too young to be wholly dependable on the witness stand, and furthermore, their father was vigorously opposed to their appearance at the trial. Likewise, Virginia Payne's mother wanted to keep her away from the courtroom.

In the face of such problems, Coakley needed a totally different approach to plant the seeds of sexual suspicion in the minds of Abbott's jurors. He kept returning to a key piece of physical evidence that Hove and Whitney could neither deny nor explain, the size 34-A brassiere dug up from the sandy floor of Abbott's basement.

That the bra was Stephanie's there could be no doubt. It was the one item of apparel missing from her body in the grave at Wildwood. Her mother had identified it and produced the $3.50 sales tag for its purchase at I. Magnin's on August 13, 1954. Helen Wales, a Magnin's buyer, had confirmed the identification.

Early in the preparation of his case, the methodical Coakley had assigned deputies to prepare forty-eight meticulous memoranda, some up to fifteen pages in length, exploring issues and points of law that might conceivably arise during the trial. Now he turned to Memorandum #13, dealing with fetishism. The question it was designed to answer, as couched in his turgid legal prose, was:

> Can the People, in their case in chief, put on the stand a psychiatrist or expert to testify that it is common medical knowledge that in fetish sex crimes, it is an ordinary practice for the perpetrator to keep certain items of the victim, such as books, pants, brassieres, etc.?

The memo writer's answer was yes, and he went on to expound at length on fetish phenomena:

> Fetishism is a fixation of erotic interest on an article of clothing.* The fetishist is an individual who obtains sexual pleasure and excitement by touching or viewing some bit of female apparel. He may not desire the woman but can achieve gratification simply by fondling the fetish. Fetishists are classified as psychopathic personalities. Such individuals are unable to manage their emotions, instinctive strivings, or impulses. No matter how brilliant the psychopath may be, or what his position in society, he will not consider it beneath him to commit a "shady act" if by doing so he can gain a greatly desired objective.

On August 31, acting on another tip, Inspector McDonough knocked on the door of Mrs. Doris Guernsey at a rural crossroads in the San Joaquin Valley a hundred miles east of Berkeley. Although taken by surprise, she knew instantly why he had come.

"How did you find me?" was her first question.

"We checked the records of the power company," McDonough replied. Then he inquired about an incident that had taken place in Stockton sixteen years earlier. In 1939 Mrs. Guernsey had resided there in the same neighborhood as Elsie Abbott and her two young sons. Burton was not yet a teenager.

"The first time the Abbotts ever came to my attention," Mrs. Guernsey

---

* Other items can be fetishes also.

told McDonough, "was when a neighbor, Mr. Davies, came and asked me if any of my lingerie was missing. I hadn't noticed up till then, but I checked and discovered that panties, brassieres, and nightgowns—both mine and my daughter's—were gone."

The intimate apparel had not been stolen from Mrs. Guernsey's clothesline but from within her house. She had found an imprint of corduroy trousers in the dust of her bedroom windowsill.

Other women in the neighborhood, it turned out, were missing the same kinds of things, and Davies had found a cache of such items in a room above a garage where the Abbott boys often played. Lewd pictures had been discovered there too. Davies told Mrs. Guernsey the intimate feminine undergarments were so "befouled" that they had to be burned.

If Mrs. Guernsey's account was accurate, Burton might have had fetishist tendencies even before puberty, but there was no official record. She thought that Burton's police sergeant uncle, Cy Smith, had intervened to hush up the incident. Even if it had gotten as far as juvenile court, which was doubtful, juvenile proceedings were sealed under California law. Thus there was scant possibility that Coakley would be able to bring the Stockton events into the open at Abbott's trial.

Not long after the episode, Elsie and her boys had moved to Oakland.

Fetishism had surfaced in several celebrated criminal cases cited by Coakley's memo writer, one being the Chicago prosecution of the notorious William Heirens in the 1940s.

In 1946 Heirens had murdered two women, then kidnapped Suzanne Degnan, a six-year-old girl, choked her to death, and dismembered her body for no apparent reason. After his arrest, forty pairs of women's panties were discovered in his grandmother's attic, where he had spent much of his time. From the possession of such items, stolen from clotheslines, he had derived deep sexual gratification.

Heirens also had committed many burglaries in which, besides things of value, he had stolen odd and worthless items, such as old neckties, socks, handkerchieves, buttons, belts, cuff links, birth certificates, and college pennants. These he had hidden in his parents' home.

Similar in some ways was the case of Robert Irwin, a New York sculptor who in 1937 had murdered an artist's model, her mother, and a roomer in their house. The two women had been strangled and the roomer stabbed five times. The model's body, nude, had been found in her bed, with her mother's body underneath.

Three months later Irwin walked into a newspaper office and voluntarily surrendered. Still in his possession was a small, cheap alarm clock he had taken from the home of his victims for no apparent reason. It was the chief clue that confirmed him as the murderer.

A psychiatrist, writing about the Irwin case, noted a linkage of the murderer's fetishism with another abnormal phenomenon, "flight into custody," an unconscious emotional drive to surrender. Over a period of years, Irwin had repeatedly turned himself in to state mental hospitals.

Another "flight into custody" case was that of Albert Fish, who had murdered and dismembered an eleven-year-old girl in New York in 1928. Six years later, in a letter to the child's mother, he had confessed the crime. Although the letter was unsigned, the envelope bore a return address that Fish had inked out so imperfectly that it could still be read. It led directly to his capture.

Coakley, pondering these historic cases, likened them to the one he was about to prosecute. Beyond a doubt, he decided, Stephanie's purse, wallet, schoolbooks, eyeglasses, and especially her bra were Abbott's fetishes. Also, on the fifth day after Stephanie's disappearance, Burton had fled toward the custody of Livermore Veterans Hospital, which had been his safe haven in the past. But his doctor had turned him away.

Yes, Coakley decided, Abbott fit perfectly into the classic psychiatric mold of Heirens, Irwin, and Fish, and his prosecution would be conducted accordingly.

19

Georgia's Torment

From day to day, as trial time neared, Georgia Abbott lived in a fishbowl. Watching her became a spectator sport. The Bay Area buzzed with talk that she was going to dump Burton at trial's end, win or lose. Her announced intention to stick with him was dismissed as blather for the press. The word got around that her estrangement was not only from Burton but from his family as well.

"She is being left out in the cold more and more," one of Coakley's undercover snoopers reported from a bar where newsmen gathered. "About all she can do now is go along and protect her son, who seems uppermost in her mind . . . There is a story here, and the press boys feel like they will get it sooner or later, as Georgia will crack up under the strain."

From Georgia herself came mixed signals. The Berkeley police picked up a hearsay report that she had asked a beauty shop customer, while doing her hair, "Do you think I should stay by my husband for the sake of the child, if I no longer care for him?" This conversation supposedly had taken place within days after Stephanie's disappearance—long before Burton had become a suspect.

Chronicle columnist Herb Caen fueled the talk of an imminent split-up with an (accurate) item about Georgia visiting a nightclub with friends. She had asked the band to play "One for My Baby, and One More for the Road."

Yet in another day's *Chronicle* she was quoted as saying "Bud is gentle and kind and good. No woman could ask any more in a husband, and I am not easy to live with. I am Leo-born. I am the lion. He is an Aquarius, the gentle one."

Georgia's response to the stresses working on her was not that of a recluse. When Inspector Lloyd Jester went to the Abbott home looking for Burton's mother, he walked in on a party in progress, with Georgia "dressed in toreador pants and seeming to be in a jovial mood." Jester saw "several women lolling around on the floor, davenport, and ottomans, together with several men." The latter he assumed to be business acquaintances, adding the gratuitous comment, "My independent information is that Georgia has been surrounded by male hairdressers who for the most part are alleged to be homos."

In mid-October Georgia returned to the Livermore Veterans Hospital for a checkup and ran into William Smiley, who was there for the same purpose. He had known both Burton and Georgia when all three were patients at the same time.

To Smiley, Georgia appeared despondent. Over a cup of coffee he asked her, "Do you think Burton would do something like that?" She paused, shook her head, and said quietly, "I don't know."

Among the most useful of Coakley's intelligence sources was a waitress at an Alameda restaurant called Tim's. She knew both Georgia and Leona Dezman well, having attended beauty school with them. Her main value, however, lay in the fact that she served lunch almost daily to Hove and Whitney, who were Tim's regulars. Toward the end of August she reported them to be highly optimistic, professing total belief in their client's innocence.

Such outward confidence, however, belied increasing turmoil beneath the surface of the defense. More and more, infighting was setting in, much of it stemming from the squeeze Hove and Whitney were putting on the Abbotts for money.

Burton's lawyers faced prodigious expense in trying to compete with the prosecution's limitless investigative capability. In a rare moment of candor, Hove acknowledged this during a conference with his foe, Folger Emerson.

"Hove made a couple of remarks of interest," Emerson reported to Coakley. "For one thing he said that if he ever became convinced that Abbott was guilty, he would personally endeavor to get him to plead guilty. He also said that there were several defense leads he might ask our office to investigate, in view of the fact that their resources were limited."

The Abbotts were not well-to-do, and the money for Burton's defense came in uncertain dribbles from diverse sources. Whitney arranged a $4,000 personal loan and had all members of the family cosign the note. Mark, who took charge of the fund-raising effort, negotiated a loan from the credit union at the Naval Air Station, where both he and Elsie worked. Burton's policeman uncle in Stockton, Cy Smith, dug into his savings to put up $10,000. Elsie paid the lawyers $500 at a time, as often as she could. The beauticians at the Morton shop got a few hundred dollars together. Georgia chipped in between $600 and $700—a fund she had been saving for a vacation at a cosmetologists' convention.

Georgia probably had slimmer resources than the rest. Her friend Rose Lewis, of the grocery store, told Severin and Stoops, "Burton never worked that I know of, but he seemed to have plenty of time to run around. Georgia is the one who did all the work; she would make good money, but they lived up to everything they made. She is up against it."

In late October Whitney asked Georgia for another $200.

"Where am I going to get it?" she asked. "I've borrowed all I possibly can from my friends."

"I don't care where you get it—just get it," the lawyer snapped.

Georgia's worsening finances and her deteriorating relations with friends and family became increasingly visible as time passed. A salesman who called regularly at the beauty parlor informed Coakley that Leona Dezman had fired her old friend. The next day, however, Georgia was reported back at work and in good spirits, laughing heartily at a joke along with Mrs. Dezman and a customer.

On August 22 the newsletter of the Oakland Cosmetologists Association carried a poignant letter over Georgia's signature:

Dear Members:

It is with the deepest regret that I must resign my post as president of our Oakland Unit #14, as of this date.

I find continuing my office a physical impossibility at this time. . . . It is unfair for me to hold this office while not being able to act, and I know the other officers you have elected will continue to keep our unit the wonderful organization it is. Perhaps in the near future I may be able to take my place with all of you. . . .

Support your officers in the future as you have supported me. My very best wishes to each and every one of you, and again thank you for your graciousness.

Sincerely yours,
GEORGIA ABBOTT

As Georgia stepped down, Leona Dezman took her place as president of the Oakland cosmetologists.

Severin cultivated several information sources within the beauty salon clientele, and from them he learned that Mark Abbott had appeared at the San Jose Avenue house and taken away all of Burton's clothes. When Georgia had protested, Mark had told her—apparently on his own—that even if Burton got out of his present trouble, he wouldn't be living there any more. She was given to understand that she and Burton "were all through." Perhaps sparked by this rebuff, but more likely because her funds were low, Georgia gave up the roomy comfort of the house on October 11 and moved to a modest apartment nearby.

There was an even more rancorous confrontation between Georgia and Elsie, who resurfaced after Coakley's subpoena threat blew over. A substantial part of Georgia's income since Burton's arrest had been his veteran's disability pension. Then, summarily, Elsie informed Georgia she would no longer receive it; Burton had signed it over to his mother to help defray the defense costs.

"How do you expect me to get along and support Chris?" Georgia demanded.

"That's your problem," Elsie replied.

Georgia was upset and angry, moreover, because Burton's lawyers had been avoiding and ignoring her, except when seeking their fees.

"I am never consulted," she told a beauty shop customer. "I am completely in the dark as to what is being done." She suspected the worst—that she was being used by the defense attorneys, with four-year-old Chris as the pawn.

"Mark Abbott is said to have contacted Georgia and asked for the custody of Chris," Severin reported to Coakley, "and Georgia was given to understand that if she did not relinquish Chris, the Abbotts would find legal ways of taking the child away from her on the basis of her background. It was suggested that Georgia take this matter up with the police, but she said she was afraid to because the Abbotts had told her that if she did, a word from them would cook her goose as far as her child was concerned."

If Elsie's treatment of her daughter-in-law seemed mean-spirited, it may have arisen from the intolerable pressure under which she too was surviving from day to day. The prosecutors, smarting from her evasion of their grand jury subpoena, still wanted to question her about her sighting of Stephanie's purse in early May, two months before Georgia found it.

"I had quite a talk with Harold Hove about getting Mrs. Elsie Abbott to come in for an interview," Emerson wrote in one of his progress reports to Coakley. "He stated that he would contact her and see whether or not she would come in voluntarily, but I have not heard from him."

The discomforts and pressures of the police probe were felt far beyond Abbott's immediate family and circle of friends. Over time the investigators hunted down and repeatedly interrogated his uncles, aunts, cousins, and in-laws in all directions, throughout California and beyond. Some of them knew Burton barely if at all.

In mid-August Officer Phibbs was sent to reinterview Elsie's brother, Wilbur Moore—Burton's namesake uncle. Moore already had been quizzed briefly during the grand jury hearings, when Elsie was hiding from the subpoena servers. At that time he had denied knowledge of her whereabouts. Phibbs now discovered that the relationship between Moore and Elsie was strained, to say the least.

During the 1940s, when Wilbur and his then-wife, Claudia, had occupied an Oakland apartment across the hall from Elsie and her sons, Claudia and Elsie had become fast friends. They became even closer after the Moores' year-old son was stricken with tuberculosis of the spine. Wilbur, taking his cue from pessimistic doctors, wanted to put the child in a state institution to die, to cut costs. This Claudia refused to do, and Elsie sided with her against Wilbur, her own brother. In this trying episode it was Elsie who had sustained Claudia's faith in her child's recovery.

Wilbur and Claudia had split up over the issue of the child's care. The divorce was bitter, but happily the infant survived and recovered. Eventually Claudia remarried, but her friendship with Elsie remained intact. It was because of this, Phibbs surmised, that Wilbur now distanced himself from his sister and her family.

Phibbs asked Wilbur point-blank, "Do you think your nephew could have murdered Stephanie?"

"No, definitely not," he replied—but Phibbs noted that he took no umbrage at the blunt, cruel question. Of all Burton's relatives, Uncle Wilbur seemed the most dispassionate and objective with regard to his troubles.

"Do you have any theories about the case?"

"No, I don't," Moore answered. "I've had very little contact with the family in recent years. I don't even know Georgia. I don't want to be drawn into the matter."

But "drawn into the matter" he would be, much later on.

On August 3, four days after his indictment, Burton was brought before Superior Court Judge Donald Quayle for arraignment. The hearing was brief. He entered no pleas, and the judge continued the proceedings until August 12. Three additional continuances would ensue.

Each time Abbott returned to the courtroom, reporters closely studied his face and demeanor. At this first appearance he was reported to be "in apparent high spirits, talking and laughing," but three weeks later on August 26 the *Berkeley Daily Gazette* would report him to be "extremely grim and serious-faced . . . [His] voice was high-pitched." Outside the courtroom that day, Whitney doused growing conjecture that Burton would plead an unsound mind.

"He's as sane as anyone," the lawyer told reporters, burning behind him the bridge of an insanity defense.

Later, when the defense retained the expert witness services of Dr. Joseph Catton, an eminent Stanford psychiatrist, Whitney emphasized anew that there was no retreat from the "Abbott is sane" position. Catton was coming aboard only to rebut the insinuations by Dr. Kelley that Burton fit the sexual psychopath mold.

At the next hearing on September 8, Abbott's mood was better. He posed cheerfully for photographers for five minutes and joked with his attorneys.

Perhaps his improved disposition reflected misplaced confidence in a motion Whitney and Hove filed that day calling for dismissal of his indictment. It was a transparent ploy, reviving the already-rejected argument that only Trinity County could try Burton because Stephanie's body was found there.

Even if such a contention had arguable merit with regard to the murder charge, it was absurd with regard to the kidnapping. There was no doubt whatever about the place of Stephanie's abduction—the immediate environs of the Claremont Hotel.

Coakley, who knew the law was on his side, would not countenance a change of venue in any event. Apart from his own emotional involvement in the case, he had practical reasons for keeping it on his own turf. Inflamed public sentiment demanded it. Furthermore, Trinity County had literally a one-man prosecuting staff, in the person of District Attorney Sheppard, and virtually no investigative capability.

There was still another consideration—a secret that could never be discussed in the open. In San Francisco some years earlier, an official had come under suspicion of child molesting and had fled to the state's northern mountains. He had acquired a dude ranch there and had since become an esteemed member of the local gentry. Now he was a member of the Trinity County Grand Jury and might well become its foreman. Coakley was not about to surrender jurisdiction over Burton Abbott to a grand jury headed by a suspected molester.

Ultimately the defense effort to shift the case to Trinity County would be rejected at every level, up to the State Supreme Court.

On September 21, Burton finally stood in Superior Court as the clerk read the first count of his indictment, the kidnapping charge, and asked him, "What do you plead, guilty or not guilty?"

"I am not guilty," he answered firmly.

The clerk next read the murder charge and repeated his question.

"I am completely innocent of any crime that is charged," Burton replied this time.

Emerson, who was present for the state, spoke up. "I think the defendant should enter a plea to the second count instead of making a statement, your honor."

"So do I," the judge concurred. But he did not press the matter, and Abbott's declaration was entered into the record as a simple plea of not guilty to murder.

In the courtroom as Abbott entered his pleas was one George Achison*

---

* Fictitious name.

of Oakland, who buttonholed Inspector Russell Ryan, one of the officers present. Achison slightly knew the inspector, who in another case had once investigated *him*.

"Mr. Ryan," he said. "I have some information you should know."

"Yes?"

"You see, I died in 1924."

"Really?"

"And I went to heaven, Mr. Ryan, and then I was reborn, and now I can talk directly to God. I recently asked God about Burton Abbott, and He told me that Burton is innocent."

Other well-meaning mystics and devotees of the supernatural continued to inject themselves into the Abbott case. Among such was Simon Baylor* of San Francisco, who appeared at Coakley's office and insisted on seeing the person in charge. He told of having a vision: the seas and clouds and a wooded canyon with a sawmill in the background and the name "Anderson." This scene had dissolved into a circle of people conducting a burial service for Stephanie in a language that Baylor believed to be "Czechoslovakian." He did not know whether Anderson was the owner of the mill or whether it was situated in the town of Anderson, east of Wildwood. At any rate, Baylor was sure that the name Anderson was the clue that would solve the case.

Another offer of help came from Frank Trask,** a water witcher from remote Lake County, who believed he could find the place of Stephanie's death with his forked divining rod.

Both the prosecution and defense experienced such distractions as the trial neared, but the defenders found the most expeditious means of dealing with them. A woman who showed up at Whitney's office, saying she had seen Stephanie's murder in her dreams, was told, "We think your information is very important, and you should take it up at once with the district attorney's office. Call Mr. Folger Emerson." As the woman headed for the door feeling important, she was further instructed, "Don't let them foist you off on some minor deputy. Your information is too critical for that. Insist on talking to Mr. Emerson, who is in charge of the Abbott case." This treatment not only flattered the tipster but effectively distracted Emerson, taking up time he much needed to hone his case against Whitney's client.

On October 20, with the trial less than three weeks away, Whitney and Hove unveiled important details of their planned strategy. The *Tribune* reported: "Burton W. Abbott definitely will take the witness stand in his own defense

---

  *   Fictitious name.
 ** Fictitious name.

when he goes to trial . . . Several members of the family will also take the stand, but it has not yet been determined whether Abbott's mother, Mrs. Elsie Abbott, will be summoned."

In a follow-up statement, Whitney announced that Elsie would "be available" if the prosecution wanted her. In so reporting, however, the *Examiner* noted that she would be a hostile witness if called by the state and quoted both Coakley and Emerson as saying they had no further interest in serving her with a subpoena.

That news must have come as a great relief to her.

20

Down to the Wire

From its first day the Bryan investigation had taken on a life of its own at Berkeley police headquarters, dwarfing all others. It drained resources and diverted manpower from other work, and disrupted other essential duty. By mid-August the case's document file stood four feet eight inches tall and was growing daily. The index alone filled two thousand 3 by 5 file cards.

A companion file of similar size was taking shape at the district attorney's office. Before the Bryan case was over, Inspector Charlie Ryken would put in 1,150 hours of overtime, for which he would be paid "not a penny." Others worked equally hard.

Late one September afternoon Folger Emerson's telephone rang, and he heard the voice of Harold Robinson, an assistant to California's attorney general, Edmund G. "Pat" Brown. Emerson sensed at once that the call was politically inspired.

Pat Brown and Coakley had been natural rivals since the 1940s, when they had occupied the respective D.A.'s offices in San Francisco and Oakland, across the bay from each other. In many ways the two men were alike: both local natives, both devout Irish Catholics, both politically ambitious. Coakley was a Republican who had once been a Democrat; Brown a Democrat who had once been a Republican. Coakley, at fifty-eight, was eight years Brown's senior.

Reminiscing in 1994, Coakley's son Tom recalled, "My father was very jealous of Pat Brown. Pat had got lucky and become attorney general, and my father had always wanted that job. My father thought that Pat Brown would stab you in the back if he could get ahead politically, but he didn't hate Pat; he thought of him more as a buffoon than anything else."

Robinson's phone call that afternoon was on behalf of Brown, who was traveling in the East, and intended personally for Coakley, who was out of the office. So Emerson took notes from Robinson's dictation:

> Although Brown realizes you and he may have had personal difficulties in the past, he wants you to know that his office is willing to give you all possible assistance in connection with the Abbott case . . . You are to consider him as "standing at your right hand."

To the astute Coakley, the message carried an additional significance: Pat Brown realized that with public revulsion against Abbott running so high, it was wiser for him politically to be the ally rather than the foe of the man who coveted his job.

As the trial neared, the prosecutors intensified their probe into the depths of Abbott's psyche. What made this fellow tick?

In their endeavor to answer that question, Coakley's men had an unknowing collaborator in Abbott himself. Compulsively and endlessly he talked about himself to anyone who would listen—fellow prisoners, jailers, visitors, reporters.

"People have asked me whether I'm worried," Burton said in a long *Chronicle* interview on September 19. "I am not, because I have faith that everything will be all right. Each night as I lie on my jail cell bunk I make this prayer: I pray that the person who did this thing gets caught. I don't get down on my hands and knees in the usual sense. I just lie on my bunk there and think this prayer."

The reporter wrote that Burton answered questions with "a ready grin, an easy laugh, and a quick, congenial way of talking."

"I've never been an overly religious person," he was further quoted as saying, "but a situation like this makes you more religious or definitely more thoughtful. You're going along in a nice normal life, and all of a sudden everything blows sky-high. It's just been one mad race since then."

Burton was asked about a widespread perception that his protestations of innocence "lacked a ring of indignation."

"There is no reason to be immature and jump up and down and scream and yell," he replied, "so I've tried to reason with the officers rather than make wild protestations. After all, I've spent several years in the hospital and have learned to keep myself under control looking death in the eye. I've always been easygoing and I've never had a chip on my shoulder. I've found that if you try, you can get along with anyone. Even the prisoners here are just swell fellers. They've all been decent to me."

Burton used the interview to lash back at Dr. Kelley, the police psychiatrist who had concluded that he had an immature superego—or conscience—and that his personality was compatible with the act of murder.

"He's all wet," Burton said. "My conscience is quite well developed. If anything, I am rapidly developing a persecution complex. Dr. Kelley seems to be impressed with his own importance. I just can't understand how he could reach such a conclusion on the basis of a short examination lasting only an hour."

Was all of this an honest baring of Burton's inner feelings, or was it self-serving flimflam? One of Coakley's informants within the jail said Burton's "swell fellers" characterization of his fellow jailbirds was nothing but blatant showmanship. Actually Abbott mixed with other inmates reluctantly, often shunning the jail dayroom in favor of his cell.

He sometimes played chess with his fellow prisoners, he told the *Examiner,* "but not for too long a time. It's too tiring." It was becoming apparent that chess, the game he had played until dawn with Otto Dezman after Stephanie's purse was found, was something of a compulsion with him.

As a jail inmate Abbott was fussy and demanding, just as he had been as a hospital patient. Frequently he went on sick call. He asked for a high-protein diet, and he occasionally got streptomycin and terramycin shots. On October 21 he complained of pains in his left upper chest when he moved. Examination showed a rapid pulse of 125 to 130 and about one degree of fever, but his lungs, which had given him so much grief, were clear.

Several investigators were talking to people who had known Burton at the University of California. Officer Kent, after interviewing seventy-three students who had been in classes with him, reported that, on balance, "a question as to his reputation would probably have to be answered, 'good.' "

"A real normal guy," said a youth who had sat next to him. Adjectives like "pleasant," "quiet," and "nice" kept popping up in Kent's interviews. Several students remembered Burton as an immaculate dresser who came to class in slacks and sports clothes, white shirts and sometimes a tie—seldom if ever in jeans.

Yet there were discordant notes. Abbott was "what the layman might call a pansy," said a male student, and there was speculation about his sexual orientation. Another student told Kent, "I never thought of him as being effeminate or queer, but just a small, weak guy."

Two male students used virtually identical words, calling Burton a "lone wolf, with no friends."

Students in his speech class remembered Burton as a forceful and convincing public speaker. In one talk he had discussed the capital punishment issue, but the girl who mentioned this couldn't remember which side he had taken.

Two female students had diametrically opposite opinions of Burton.

"He was very, very nice, very friendly," said nineteen-year-old Sherry Klobas of San Pablo, who sat near him in the speech class. "Never argued with anyone. He showed me pictures of his youngster; he never talked about his wife that I can recall, just the little boy."

By contrast, twenty-year-old Barbara Simpson, who was in the same class, told Kent, "He seemed to have contempt for other people's ideas. He would look at you as if to say, 'How could you be so stupid? I'm right and you're wrong.' "

Abbott with his defense team: (from left to right) Harold Hove, John F. Hanson, Abbott, and Stanley Whitney. *(Courtesy of San Jose Mercury News)*

Abbott (third from right) in County Jail lineup, October 30, 1955. *(Courtesy of Alameda County District Attorney's Office)*

At the end of one of his first days on trial, November 15, Abbott leans over to ask his wife, Georgia, for money to spend in jail. She left five dollars with a jailer. *(Courtesy of San Jose Mercury News)*

Coakley makes his opening argument to the jury. *(Courtesy of* San Jose Mercury News*)*

Mary Ann Stewart, who accompanied Stephanie on her last homeward walk. *(*Oakland Tribune *photo courtesy of Alameda County District Attorney's Office)*

Burton's brother Mark Abbott with Georgia in the courthouse corridor. *(*Oakland Tribune *photo courtesy of Alameda County District Attorney's Office)*

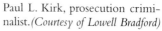

Paul L. Kirk, prosecution criminalist. *(Courtesy of Lowell Bradford)*

Mary Bryan, Stephanie's mother, enters court to testify. *(Courtesy of San Jose Mercury News)*

Bud Jackson indicates the location of Abbott's cabin and Stephanie's grave on the courtroom mockup of the burial site. *(Courtesy of Alameda County District Attorney's Office)*

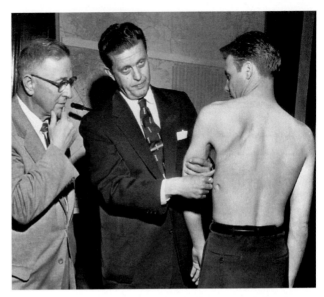

Dr. Elmer J. Shabart of Livermore Veterans Hospital points to scars from Abbott's lung surgery; Stanley Whitney is at left. *(Courtesy of* San Jose Mercury News*)*

Abbott is questioned on the stand by Harold Hove. *(Courtesy of* San Jose Mercury News*)*

Georgia Abbott takes the stand. *(Courtesy of* San Jose Mercury News*)*

Elsie (left) and Georgia Abbott at the trial. *(Photo by Bill Regan courtesy of* San Jose Mercury News*)*

As the jury returns from their deliberations, Abbott and his attorneys await the verdict. *(Courtesy of* San Jose Mercury News*)*

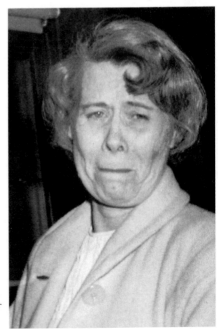

Elsie Abbott leaves the courthouse after the guilty verdict. *(Courtesy of* San Jose Mercury News*)*

In a press conference the day after his conviction, Abbott appeared distraught one moment, thoughtful the next. *(AP photos; courtesy of Palo Alto Historical Association)*

WEATHER FORECAST
ay Area: Mostly fair Satur-
AY, cloudy Sunday. Little
nange in temperature. Low
aturday 40-47, high near 50.
Full Report, Page 22

YEAR No. 75   CCCCAAA

San Francisco Chronicle

THE VOICE OF THE WEST

FINAL

SATURDAY, MARCH 16, 1957   10 CENTS   GArfield 1-1112

ABBOTT DIES
GOVERNOR'S CALL
TOO LATE

Mideast Tension
Egypt Proclaims Gaza Strip Rule

GAZA, March 15—New Egyptian Governor Ma-General Hassan Abdel Latif today proclaimed his ministration in power in the Gaza Strip and empha-ed that the United Nations Emergency Force was a guest status here.

Latif told newsmen the only duty of UNEF was patrol his armistice line.

The Egyptian administra-h was in power in Gaza el- time from my arrival last d," the governor said.
Ha attitude met with wild

After talks with administra-tors sent in from Cairo by President Gamal Abdel Nas-ser's regime, U. N. officials agreed they would move out of the modern Gaza police headquarters to make way for

Teamster Boss Admits 'Borrowing'

WASHINGTON, March 15 UP—Teamsters' Union officer Frank W. Brewster acknowledged today he drew on the Teamsters' treasury for the traveling expenses of his horse trainer and jockey. He said he intends to repay the money.

Brewster, boss of the 11-State Western Confer-ence of Teamsters, came before the special Senate rackets committee to deny testimony that he schemed with other high-ranking Teamsters officials to take over gambling and vice in Portland, Ore.

Under questioning by the committee Brewster acknowl-edged he had used union funds to pay for travel by Mel Eisen, the horse trainer, and Jockey Richard Cavallero. He didn't say how many trips or how much money was in-volved. A member of the committee's staff said the trips were taken in 1954

The Late Stay
Knight Assails Defense

By Charles Raudebaugh

Burton W. Abbott was given a stay of execution yesterday two minutes too late.

By radio telephone at 11:20 a. m. from the Navy aircraft carrier Hancock, Governor Goodwin J. Knight asked Warden Har-ley O. Teets if the execu-tion could be halted.

It couldn't.

The deadly cyanide pellets had been dropped two min-utes before — precisely at

Gas Chamber
Stephanie Bryan Slayer Executed

By George Draper

Burton W. Abbott, one of the most amusing figures in message and murder of prison, was executed in San Quentin Prison's gas cham-ber yesterday for kidnaping and then murder Stephanie Bryan almost two years ago.

The petulant young man, who had infuriated police and prosecutors with his quips and jibes and vague replies, breathed the cyanide fumes and was pronounced dead seven minutes later.

With him died the secrets of the 14-year-Berkeley schoolgirl's death because, to the very end, Abbott maintained that he was innocent of the crime.

Abbott's flair for the dramatic was honored even at the moment of his death. He might still be all

The execution: Governor Knight called to offer a stay, but the execution had already begun. *(Courtesy of* San Francisco Chronicle*)*

After a class discussion of religion, Barbara had concluded Burton "didn't believe in church or God."

While Berkeley officers were hunting down Burton's U.C. classmates, Coakley's deputies were talking to his professors and counselors. What they learned was eyebrow-raising. The Veterans Administration, which was paying for his schooling, had been pleased with his progress until April, when his grades had suddenly plummeted. However, the downhill slide had not started with Stephanie's murder; it had begun more than a month earlier. On business administration exams taken March 21 and April 6, Burton had scored dismally—47 and 48 out of a possible 100. He had flunked another test entirely. His midterm grades in two of his four subjects were Ds (though he had managed to raise one of them to a C by the end of the semester). Midway through the term, the university had permitted him to drop an accounting course, after he persuaded a doctor to say that his streptomycin shots were interfering with his concentration.

Burton had failed to turn in a term paper when it was due on May 2, his first day back after his trip to the cabin, but he had made up the work later.

"I just don't know what's wrong with me this semester," he had plaintively told his V.A. counselor, Eugene Evans, sometime in May.

"This term was by far Abbott's worst showing in any semester at the university," Deputy D.A. Laurence Horan concluded in a memo to Coakley.

On October 4 a team of lawyers and cops returned once more to the cellar of the Abbott home on San Jose Avenue, which had produced such damning evidence three months earlier.

What were they looking for this time? They didn't say, but another "box in the basement" caught their attention. This one, just to the left of the furnace, held a stack of old newspapers, one of which was a clipped copy of the *Hayward Daily Review* for May 10, carrying an article headed "Schoolbook a Vital Clue to Lost Girl." There were also copies of the *San Francisco Examiner,* the *Oakland Shopping News,* the *San Leandro Morning News,* the *Alameda Times-Star-Advertiser,* the *Alamedan,* and the *Oakland Tribune*—all in the basement of a home where, according to Burton, the news was seldom read.

Abbott's incoming mail was watched carefully by his jailers. A curious letter dated August 25, which drew their special attention, was on the printed stationery of an unfamiliar group calling itself World-War Veterans Welfare & Service (ALLA) Inc. The return address was a post office box in Richmond. Flawlessly typed, the letter was signed in the smooth, flowing hand of one Arnott J. Williams, identified as the organization's secretary:

Dear Mr. Abbott:

We hold a strong belief in your innocence and are trying to do something about it. Have interested a noted criminologist in your case and he is making a private investigation.

We would like to arrange for a personal interview with you by our public relations representative . . .

Keep your chin up, fellow, for Mr. Coakley will do more to free you than he will to convict you, once he is convinced that you are innocent or holds a reasonable doubt of your guilt. He is a fair man. Advise us when our man may see you and we will make the arrangements for same.

In the district attorney's office, this strange missive was studied carefully. The name Arnott J. Williams rang a faint bell—which would clang louder later.

In the second week of August, Professor Paul Kirk began assembling his conclusions about the vast amount of physical evidence he had gathered in July, from the Abbott house and cars and from the grave site. Not a word about his findings was leaked; Whitney and Hove could only wonder what surprises awaited them in court.

In some respects, Kirk's data was disappointing to the prosecutors. It shed no light on one of the great puzzles still unsolved: exactly where the murder of Stephanie Bryan had taken place.

Kirk's examination of the girl's saddle shoes had produced another enigma. They were heavily blotched with oil, which he thought was the result of dripping, not immersion. It was likely, he believed, that Stephanie's body had lain under an automobile for a considerable period of time. Acting on this theory, Inspector O'Meara took another trip to the cabin and ripped up the garage floorboards, but found no great sign of oil leakage.

Within the D.A.'s office, Kirk's reports went first to Folger Emerson, who was handling the day-to-day burden of the investigation—and sometimes they compounded his problems.

"He [Kirk] has gone over the Abbott Chevrolet as thoroughly as possible and had found absolutely no sign of blood," Emerson wrote in a memo to Coakley on August 8. "He is convinced that Stephanie was not killed in the automobile."

More welcome to the prosecutors were Kirk's findings about the field boots that Abbott had worn during his April trip to the cabin. They were heavily smeared with mud, some of which appeared to be identical with soil samples taken from the grave.

Among the odds and ends Kirk had found in Abbott's car was a green-and-yellow pencil, which stirred great excitement among the investigators.

It was of an obscure brand, "Apache," manufactured by the Linton Pencil Company in Lewisburg, Tennessee. One of the few outlets in Berkeley that carried Apaches was the Elmwood Dime Store near Willard Junior High— the same place Stephanie had purchased the spiral notebook unearthed in Abbott's basement.

The pencil was shown to Stephanie's schoolmates, several of whom re-called seeing a similar one among her possessions. One girl pointed out that its colors approximated Willard Junior High's green-and-gold school colors— a significant observation because Stephanie was a loyal Willardite. A Paper-mate ball-point pen found in her purse also carried out the green-and-gold motif.

Because it is sometimes possible to identify pencils by their sharpener markings, Apache samples were put through each of the sixty-four sharpen-ers at Willard school and sent to the FBI laboratory in Washington for com-parison with the pencil from the automobile.

With a mountain of physical evidence moving in on him, Coakley felt the need for further education in criminalistics. On October 20 he put through a call to Donald Parsons at the FBI lab to ask some questions. A transcript of their conversation ran to thirteen typed pages.

The district attorney especially wanted to know whether it was possible to identify the "Kleenex" found in the pack rat's nest near Stephanie's grave. (He loosely misused the brand name in a generic sense.) This could be im-portant, he explained, because "the defendant is a great user of Kleenex. His automobile was full of Kleenex, and his clothes."

Parsons was doubtful that the brand of the rats' nest tissue could be proven conclusively.

"Sometimes," he said, "we have found on those cellulose fibers that there is more difference between two runs by the same manufacturer than between two pieces from different manufacturers."

"How about sputum?" Coakley asked. "Is there any kind of identification that can be made if you get sputum on a Kleenex?"

"If it isn't decomposed, the sputum from some people can be grouped. In other words, you can tell what a person's blood group is by his sputum. Some people have in their sputum the same secretions which permit the grouping of blood. Other people do not."

Parsons explained the capabilities and limitations of several blood tests in common use—the benzidine, Luminol, Teichmann, and malachite green tests, and spectrophotometric examination. The most certain of these, he said, was the Teichmann.

"What does it mean if you get a positive reaction?" Coakley asked.

"It means it probably is blood. You cannot say for sure."

Compared to the virtually infallible DNA blood identification tests of today, the technology of the 1950s was crude indeed.

Coakley also quizzed Parsons about chemical and microscopic soil identification.

"Soil varies so much," Parsons told him, "that two samples taken only a few feet apart might be different."

In detail, Coakley wanted to know what could and could not be determined from fabric fibers and hairs. It was possible, Parsons said, to distinguish head, arm, leg, and pubic hairs from each other and often to prove that two hairs had *not* come from the same person. But it was impossible to say with certainty that they had.

As the trial neared, Coakley was keenly concerned about a weakening link in his chain of prosecutorial evidence. His only witness who could definitively place Abbott in Berkeley on the afternoon of April 28 was William Russell, the balding, bony-faced school typewriter repairman. Russell's testimony of seeing Abbott in Pring's Doughnut Shop a half hour before Stephanie vanished was obviously going to be pivotal. But now his life was coming unglued, as he was alternately courted by the prosecution and hounded by the defense.

Russell was sized up by Berkeley Officer Kent, who interviewed him at length, as a good prosecution witness; his honesty was unanimously confirmed by all who knew him. Yet he was terrified by the thought of appearing in court. He retained a small, nagging doubt about the date he had seen Abbott at Pring's, after delivering a repaired typewriter to Willard Junior High. In his own mind he was sure it was Thursday, April 28, but could he be mistaken? It was possible. He had visited Willard both Wednesday and Thursday during that last week in April.

Doubts about the time element were magnified when the police checked Russell's time cards at the Berkeley School Department. They showed him at Willard on Wednesday, April 27, but at Berkeley High School, far across town, all day Thursday—the critical Thursday. Russell explained that he filed his time reports with no pretense of accuracy—such fabrication being tolerated as long as the total number of hours was right. To Kent this explanation rang true, but it would sound devastatingly fictitious from the witness stand. Kent determined that the defense had made no effort to see the payroll records, and he instructed the school people not to release them without a clearance from the D.A.

No fewer than five times was Russell interviewed by officers trying to shore up his flawed story. Finally he remembered that the day he had gone to Pring's was overcast, and since Wednesday that week had been clear, he at last felt certain that he had seen Abbott on the twenty-eighth.

Russell, a recovered polio patient, was acknowledged by his superiors to be a good typewriter mechanic, but he was a cranky individualist with a history of personality clashes on the job. Now that he was in the limelight, his boss, Frank Thomas, was miffed that he had come forward as a witness in the first place. Thomas felt that Russell was giving the school department a bad name, and proceeded to make his life miserable.

First Russell was told he would be docked two hours' pay for the time required by his original police interrogation. This was ultimately rescinded, but Russell was forbidden to take any further coffee breaks at all. He was also informed he would no longer be compensated for the stops he made on his way to and from work, picking up typewriter parts from wholesalers. Finally, feeling pushed, he quit the school job and took a lower-paying one at the Caterpillar Tractor plant in San Leandro. The work there was monotonous, and he resigned after a month.

While Russell's financial security was thus crashing, Hove and Whitney were working behind the scenes to undercut his credibility. In late August they showed up at the door of Eleanor Rice, the Willard typing teacher for whom Russell had fixed the broken-down machine in April.

Russell had said consistently that Mrs. Rice's room was not in use when he had returned the typewriter about two-thirty Thursday afternoon, so he had not seen her that day. Now Hove and Whitney wanted Mrs. Rice to declare definitively that Russell had *not* come to the school on April 28. When she refused, Hove wrote out a two-page statement, the gist of which was that "to the best of my knowledge Mr. Russell was *not there* on Thursday." Under Hove's pestering, Mrs. Rice had finally signed the statement, an action she would regret immediately.

At one point during their visit to Mrs. Rice, Hove and Whitney strayed from the matter of Russell and the typewriter repair.

"What kind of a girl was Stephanie Bryan?" Hove inquired.

Was he looking for something to tarnish Stephanie's wholesome image? Suspicious, Mrs. Rice told him she did not know Stephanie and referred him to another teacher, Elizabeth Ivelsky.

On August 31 Hove and Whitney paid a visit to Mrs. Ivelsky, who had signed the privilege card found in Stephanie's wallet. They found a self-confident, no-nonsense, sixtyish woman who had taught at Willard for twenty-five years. Privately she believed Abbott "guilty as sin."

"We have just about come to the conclusion," Hove began, "that Stephanie had a boyfriend or boyfriends, and that she may have gotten into a car willingly."

"I'm sure she wouldn't do that," Mrs. Ivelsky snapped, "She was far too intelligent. If you are looking for derogatory remarks, I have none. If you want information, go see the Bryan family."

"Of course we cannot do that," Hove replied. Then, turning to Whitney, he said, still within Mrs. Ivelsky's earshot, "We might as well go. This girl knows the law."

Russell quickly got the word that Hove and Whitney had paid surprise visits to Mrs. Rice and Mrs. Ivelsky, and he correctly guessed that he would be next. Indeed, the defense attorneys soon appeared at his door, "barged" (Russell's word) into his living room, and grilled him for two hours. As he would testify later, they offered him a deal, and when he turned it down, they threatened to "tear him apart on the witness stand."

At the end of August an interior decorator with a spectacular goatee, dubbed a "bearded Bohemian" by the *Chronicle,* appeared of his own accord at Berkeley police headquarters. His name was Alexander Marten, and like Russell he had been a regular at Pring's. Briefly he had been a potential suspect in the Bryan case himself—one of scores interviewed and cleared by the FBI. Because of what he was now telling the police, however, Coakley thought he might become a much-needed witness who could corroborate and augment Russell's testimony.

Marten's story was that at three-thirty on the afternoon of April 28, his GMC pickup and Abbott's 1949 Chevrolet had nearly collided when Abbott ran a red light at College and Ashby Avenues. The intersection was on a direct route between the doughnut shop, where Russell claimed to have seen Abbott about three-twenty, and the Claremont Hotel, where Stephanie had vanished about 4 o'clock.

To support his tale, Marten produced two items: an appointment book showing he had been en route to a nearby customer that afternoon and a packet of Dill's pipe cleaners. In anger after the near accident, he said, he had taken the license number of the offending car and written it in pencil on the inside of the pipe cleaner packet. It was 1L53486, the correct number of Abbott's plates.

Marten's information was vital if true, but it would not be easy to prove. The fact that he had Burton's license number right proved nothing, for it had been printed in the newspapers. The critical question was, when had he written it? If his penciled notation could be shown to have been written in late April, it would be powerful evidence; if written later, it was probably a fraud. Perhaps something akin to carbon dating could reveal how long the pencil lead had been on the paper? Was there a way to tell?

Apparently not. The Dill's packet was sent to the FBI laboratory for whatever testing was possible. But within six weeks it was back in the Berkeley Police Department's evidence locker, the puzzle of when the number had been written still unsolved.

On October 18 Mary Bryan was drawn back into the pretrial investigation when she took a call from Ed Montgomery, the *Examiner* reporter who had found her daughter's body.

"Mrs. Bryan," he asked, "was Stephanie acquainted with any of the maids who worked for your neighbors?"

"I really don't know," Mary replied. "Why do you ask?"

Montgomery told her an unidentified woman, apparently a maid in her neighborhood, was now claiming to have met Stephanie on the street, virtually at the time she vanished. Supposedly they had talked about a birthday cake Stephanie had made for the woman's daughter. According to Montgomery's information, the conversation had taken place on Alvarado Road, just where the shortcut from the Claremont opened into it. For this to come to light now, six months after Stephanie's death, was overwhelming for Mary Bryan.

"Who told you this, Mr. Montgomery?" she asked.

"My source has to be confidential for the present. I'm sorry."

Mary wracked her brain trying to imagine who the unknown domestic might be.

Montgomery's source was, in fact, Harold Hove, who had received an unsigned letter from the maid detailing her supposed conversation with the kidnapped girl. Hove had given the reporter a photostatic copy.

Why had the maid kept her encounter a secret for so long? The letter explained that she had informed her employers of the conversation when it occurred, and they had admonished her not to go to the police.

"We do not wish to be involved in this case," they had told her, "and we do not want anyone who works for us to be involved." Their meaning had been clear: If she talked, she would be fired. Finally, however, her conscience had compelled her to write anonymously to Burton Abbott's lawyer.

Apparently she had revealed her secret privately to others also. A few days later Laura Hogue,* a sixty-seven-year-old widow who sometimes worked as a housekeeper, appeared at Berkeley police headquarters and asked to speak to someone about the Bryan case.

Mrs. Hogue had visited the station often in the past and was known there as a compulsive informer. Often her reports had proved well founded and resulted in arrests. Once she had even turned in her former husband for abortion conspiracy. This time her tip concerned the maid whose employer had forbidden her to talk. Mrs. Hogue said she was a black woman named Helen, who now worked for a doctor in Walnut Creek.

But that was not the only information Mrs. Hogue imparted. She herself, while descending from Alvarado Road to the Claremont parking lot via the

---

* Fictitious name.

woodsy shortcut on the afternoon of April 28, had watched a young man intercept a dark-haired girl attired in a blue skirt, white blouse or sweater, and something red near the neck. Her accoster had worn faded denims and a brown jacket. The girl had tried to avoid him, Mrs. Hogue said, but he had blocked her and pulled her behind some shrubbery. Then there had been a muffled scream and the couple had driven off in a gray-green "two-seater."

At the time Mrs. Hogue had thought it was high school horseplay. Later, reading about Stephanie's disappearance, she had become so unnerved as to avoid calling the police, hoping someone else would do so. Now, six months later, she was finally making her report.

There was a haunting similarity, though not a perfect match, between the incident Mrs. Hogue described now and the meeting of a man and girl reported months earlier by the mysterious letter-writer who signed herself "Melody."

Going into the trial, Coakley was determined to anticipate and be ready for any trick Whitney and Hove might have up their sleeves. He labored night and day to tighten his case.

He still worried especially lest the defense convince the jury that Abbott was too frail to have climbed the hill to the grave site, either with or without the dead weight of Stephanie's body. On November 2, therefore, with the trial's opening gavel only five days away, Coakley sent two inspectors back to Wildwood, taking with them a 100-pound sack of wheat. Several times they dragged it from the cabin to the grave by different routes, until they ascertained the easiest one. At the time of her death, Stephanie had weighed between 108 and 111 pounds.

Her desiccated remains, in a refrigerated crypt at McDonald's Chapel in Redding, weighed but a fraction of that now. One afternoon Stephanie's mother took a call from Rudy Balma at the mortuary.

"Are you ready to dispose of your daughter's body?" he inquired.

Mary Bryan replied that the family desired cremation.

"We have no cremation facilities here. Stephanie must be taken to Sacramento for that."

Mary referred Balma's call to Folger Emerson.

"I can't anticipate any further need for pathological studies," he said, "but it would be desirable to retain the body if it doesn't cost too much."

The charge would be $25 to seal a receiving vault at Redding's Lawncrest Memorial Park, plus $3 a month for storage. Stephanie would lie in that vault for the next eighteen months. The trial of Burton Abbott and its aftermath would all be history before she would go to her final resting place.

PART FOUR

In Court

21

"We Will Prove . . ."

The *Chronicle,* which prized brightness above all else in its presentation of the news, carried a cheery weather box atop its front page on Monday morning, November 7.

> This Riviera-type weather began taking on a nice look of permanence yesterday, with still no break in sight. Today will again be gloriously autumnal—blue skies, balmy mid-day, gentle afternoon winds.

Two columns to the right of this buoyant forecast, the page was dominated by a menacing portrait of Burton Wilbur Abbott, who at 10 A.M. would go on trial for his life. Whoever had selected the photo must have chosen it for its sheer malevolence. Abbott's brooding eyes glowered straight at the reader from beneath arched brows conveying the look of a vampire. His lips were set in a cruel line extending nearly the width of his gaunt face.

Outside the courthouse in Oakland, would-be spectators began gathering before the sun's first rays struck the shimmering surface of Lake Merritt. When the doors opened at eight o'clock they sprinted for the elevators, which took them to the fifth floor, where they queued up again outside the richly appointed courtroom of Judge Charles Wade Snook. By 9:15 their number had grown to two hundred. Their exertions on this opening day would be for naught, however, because prospective jurors would fill all of the courtroom's nonreserved seats.

To accommodate the working press, three rows of spectator seats had been removed, and in their place were specially built benches with space for thirty-two reporters. In addition, four chairs inside the rail were reserved for newspaper artists; under Judge Snook's rules, photographers would be barred from the room while court was in session. The glass doors of the courtroom had been frosted to prevent the snapping of pictures from the corridor. Radio broadcasters were prohibited from bringing their microphones into the room. Television, in 1955, was not even a consideration.

Courtroom security, a major concern in later decades, was accorded short shrift. Metal detectors at the doors were unheard of.*

Never before had an Alameda County trial attracted such attention. A jury room on the fourth floor, below Judge Snook's court, had been converted into a press room, with typewriters and direct phone and teletype lines to newspaper offices and radio stations. The press corps was studded with Pulitzer winners, including Montgomery for the *Examiner* and cameraman Joe Rosenthal, (who ten years earlier had taken the Iwo Jima flag-raising picture) for the *Chronicle*. The *Examiner* had also retained Erle Stanley Gardner, Perry Mason's creator, for background and color pieces.

A ripple went through the corridor crowd at nine-fifteen when Georgia Abbott arrived and took one of several rear seats reserved for the defendant's family. One reporter described her as "calm and very trim—a beauty operator who served as a good advertisement for her trade." Soon she was joined by Elsie and Mark.

Burton entered through a side door exactly two minutes before the trial was to start. He was well barbered and flawlessly groomed in a dark-blue suit, white shirt, and black tie, with a white handkerchief in his coat pocket. The *Chronicle* would contrast the cheerful accents of his attire with the "prison pallor" of his face. As he came into the room, twenty-five flashbulbs went off simultaneously, creating a blinding light. One photographer popped a bulb so closely under Abbott's nose that he jumped back, startled. A minute later he was serious and poker-faced as he seated himself between his attorneys at the defense table. His slender hands held a stenographer's notebook and pencil.

The cameramen withdrew, and at ten-twelve a bailiff rapped his gavel. The courtroom assemblage rose as Judge Snook entered from his chambers and took his seat.

For more than six decades Snook had been a name to be reckoned with in the law enforcement and jurisprudence of Alameda County. The judge's father had served for six years as district attorney in the 1890s, and in the early 1920s the judge himself had been assistant district attorney under Earl Warren. Within the D.A.'s office, Snook and Frank Coakley had worked together closely. Later it was Warren who, as governor, had given Snook his judicial appointment.

---

* In 1955 a retired Berkeley police officer revealed to the author that there had been "concern" about the daily trial attendance of Dr. Charles Bryan, Stephanie's father. The doctor was known to be bitter, angry, and grieving, and there were fears that he might be carrying a gun.

The judge was now a heavyset man of middle age with a pleasant, double-chinned face and wire-rimmed glasses. He was customarily soft-spoken on the bench. In view of his background, it was probably inevitable that he was widely perceived as having a prosecutorial bias. (In private the defense lawyers called him "schnook.") Yet his ability and knowledge of the law were unchallenged.

With few preliminaries, he addressed himself to the panel of prospective jurors.

"There has been a death penalty asked," he said, "and you must in your own minds be able to pass fairly on this request. Be entirely frank with yourselves."

A bailiff called the roll of the fifty-six venire members present, and twelve names were drawn from a big spinning drum that resembled a gambling device. The seven men and five women who tentatively took seats in the jury box ranged from a fellow in a racetrack-plaid sport coat to a young women with severely swept-back hair and the grace of a ballerina. Abbott turned slightly toward the jury box, nodded, and tried to smile but didn't quite make it.

Now began the process of voir dire—the questioning of the prospective jurors by the attorneys and the judge to determine their suitability. Any juror could be excused by the judge "for cause," such as prejudice, conflict of interest, acquaintance with any of the principals, health problems, or major inconvenience. In addition, under California law each side had available twenty "peremptory" challenges, to excuse jurors without stated reasons. In exercising these, the sides would take turns.

Anonymity of jurors, today so diligently guarded in sensitive cases, got no serious consideration in the Abbott trial. The newspapers not only printed jurors' names and pictures but also their addresses, occupations, descriptions, and family connections.

The venire lists being public records, both sides had made efforts to check out the potential jurors well before the trial began. In this endeavor, however, the prosecution had held tremendous advantage, not only by reason of its manpower resources but because of its easier access to information. Many panel members had served on earlier juries, and the deputy D.A.s trying those cases had routinely taken notes on their feelings, faculties, and foibles. Also, the cooperative I.D. bureaus of the sheriff's office and local police departments had apprised the prosecutors that several of the veniremen had criminal records of their own. When Coakley and Emerson took their seats at the prosecutors' table, they had before them astonishingly detailed dossiers on all potential jurors.

- "Do not accept this juror in any case," a deputy D.A. had warned regarding a thirty-one-year-old former seaman who had once been invited to join the Communist Party. He had not joined but was deemed unreliable nonetheless.

- "Overly sympathetic, quite certain she voted (in a prior trial) to acquit defendant" was the evaluation of a woman on the panel.
- "(Colored) Clerk: U.S. Postal Worker. Undesirable—best holdout on 11–1 jury for 1 1/2 hours," a deputy wrote following another woman's name.
- "Mrs. Dorothy Garrison:* Husband, John, in November 1946 subscribed to *People's World*" was the notation for another possible juror (the *P.W.* being a West Coast Communist newspaper that had enjoyed some popularity during World War II).
- "Fine, objective woman" was the unexplained evaluation of another panel member, presumably conviction-oriented.
- More specific was a deputy D.A.'s favorable evaluation of another woman with past jury service: "A 'nodder'—seemed very friendly to me and possibly pro-prosecution."
- "Bounce this juror," a deputy recommended regarding a female panelist with past service. "While jury rendered guilty verdict, she cried. Is colored and very easily swayed by defense counsel."

One panelist was deemed a good prosecution bet because he had a relative in the Colorado Highway Patrol. Likewise a woman was looked upon favorably because her father was the grand tiler of a Masonic Lodge. By contrast, a woman who had signed a petition to the State Legislature, opposing a loyalty oath and wiretapping bill, was blackballed.

One of the few panelists with his own rap sheet was a man with "six arrests for Chinese lottery." This individual, perhaps not surprisingly, would pass muster with both prosecution and defense and serve diligently on the jury determining Abbott's fate.

Seven of the first twelve panel members called were eliminated before the trial was two hours old. By the end of the day three more had been excused. Some of the defense's worries and fears came blurrily into view as Whitney interrogated other men and women in the jury box:

Did they have children? Boys or girls? How old? Did they wear glasses while driving? [The car struggle sightings would be crucially in dispute.] Did they object to social drinking? Did they hold any bias against students receiving tax-financed education under the G.I. Bill of Rights?

---

* Fictitious name.

At the noon break Abbott was whisked back to jail, five floors above the courtroom, for a lunch of beef stew and hash-brown potatoes. He returned for the afternoon session wearing his horn-rimmed spectacles for the first time in public since his arrest.

"The glasses added ten years to his face," the *Chronicle*'s reporter wrote.

Judge Snook's appearance was altered as well. He returned to court wearing a red carnation given him at a Kiwanis Club luncheon for twenty-five years of membership. The judge had a somber announcement to make, however: Lawyer Harold Hove's brother had died, and the trial would be in recess Tuesday morning during the funeral.

At midday Tuesday Georgia Abbott had a forty-five-minute visit with Burton via talking tube in the jail. "We spoke of love and affection," she told reporters. Soon thereafter her husband reentered the courtroom seeming relaxed and optimistic. But within minutes a daring tactic by Hove, his own attorney, transformed him into a figure of tension and fear.

Hove had been watching for the right moment to take a calculated risk. It came when prospective juror James Jensen, a well-dressed Oakland exporter, described himself as a "small-print" newspaper reader, not merely a reader of headlines.

"In your reading of the small print, Mr. Jensen, did you read that a purse was found in the Abbott basement?" Hove asked.

"Yes."

"Did you read of other articles belonging to Stephanie being found?"

"Yes."

"Do you think it was true?"

"I had to believe it was true. It was presented as news."

"Did you read that the remains of the Bryan girl were found in Trinity County?"

"Yes, certainly."

"Well, did you form any impression from that?"

"I usually form an impression."

"Would it take special evidence to erase that impression?"

"Things are not erased from the mind," Jensen observed.

Hove's maneuver was intended to spike Coakley's guns. He had brought the most damaging elements of the prosecution's circumstantial case into the record early, in a straightforward but low-key manner. When the time came for Coakley to introduce these matters later, Hove hoped, little of their punch would remain. The intentions behind this strategy eluded Burton, however, and the acknowledgment of the books-bra-and-body evidence left him shaken and fidgety.

Moreover, Burton was taken by surprise when Judge Snook had explained to the jury panel that "the law makes no distinction between circumstantial and direct evidence." That evening he confided his consternation about this to his cellmate, a logger awaiting sentence for selling marijuana.

"He was surprised to learn that circumstantial evidence was enough to convict a person," the cellmate told a reporter. "He had thought it required witnesses to send a man up."

The trial's first clash between opposing lawyers came on Wednesday, when Hove was questioning Dolores Anderson, a young housewife. In answer to a question, she acknowledged reading about Georgia's discovery of Stephanie's purse.

"Have you read that it was Abbott's wife who then telephoned the Berkeley police?" Hove inquired.

Emerson was on his feet objecting before the woman could answer.

"The defense is attempting to introduce evidence that in no way has been proved actual," he charged. "No one knows whether this is fact or fantasy."

Judge Snook upheld the objection, but Hove was not cowed. As the screening of jurors continued, either he or Whitney asked the same question twelve more times, until Snook angrily admonished them to "stop flying in the face of the court."

Their purpose was plain enough. The fact that the original police call had been made *by Abbott's wife, from Abbott's house, with Abbott's consent,* was a matter to be impressed on the jurors at every chance. The judge's anger notwithstanding, Hove and Whitney were spectacularly successful in doing that.

Not since the trial's opening session had Burton's gray-haired mother or his brother appeared in the courtroom, so the press made a beeline for Elsie and Mark when they showed up on Thursday morning, accompanied by Elsie's sister, Mona Marsh.

"Where have you been?" the reporters wanted to know.

"We have to work," Elsie said. "We're government employees and we get docked when we take time off. We can't afford it." The cost of Burton's defense, his mother volunteered, already exceeded $15,000, and she expected the figure to double before the trial was over.

"When the testimony starts we'll need investigators, plenty of them, but they cost $250 a day." She went on. "How are we going to hire them at that price? Justice is based on money. It's a terrible thing to say, I know, but I'm convinced of it. The family has already gone into debt for at least the next seven years. We wouldn't want Bud to know this, but actually we're desperate."

Elsie's final admission was a sad slip. It must not have occurred to her that her son would read her words in the next day's newspapers.

Just before Thursday's proceedings began, Mark Abbott slipped past the rail to where his brother was sitting, bringing a set of glossy color prints with him. Some of the pictures showed four-year-old Chris reading a book; others were of Mark's own son, David, only seven weeks old. Abbott and Hove viewed the pictures together, the defendant smiling and pointing to details.

Elsie's sister Mona would become a courtroom fixture for the remainder of the trial. A skilled stenographer, she had taken a six-month leave of absence from her job in order to record every word said in court. Each night she would brief the family from her shorthand notes.

Georgia Abbott did not join her in-laws in court that Thursday. She and Elsie, who had sat together on the trial's opening day, would seldom be seen together thereafter.*

Among courtroom observers, a perception was growing that Hove was working himself into a hole with his bellicose style. Coakley and Emerson were easygoing, friendly, and for the most part brief in questioning jurors. By contrast Hove often seemed to badger them.

It became apparent Thursday morning that someone had relayed this concern to Hove himself. Overnight his whole manner had changed. He modulated his previously strident voice and engaged in little jokes. When prolonged questioning was necessary, he went out of his way to explain the need for it.

He gave a hint of things to come, though, while questioning Lucille Hull, a panel member who mentioned having a son at Marin Junior College. The word "Marin" was the fuse that set Hove off.

"Have you ever lived in Marin County?" he wanted to know. "Have you ever had any contact with the Marin sheriff's office?" "Do you know anyone who lives on Lagunitas Road?"

Clearly the defense had not abandoned the discredited conjecture of a "first grave" for Stephanie Bryan in Marin County, where a San Rafael couple claimed to have detected the odor of death around an open pit under a bay tree.

To the courtroom press, Hove's revival of the Marin speculation added a welcome touch of mystery and excitement to the voir dire, which in its fourth day was beginning to drag. To the prosecutors, however, it was a sign that Hove was grasping at a straw. The stench had emanated from a dead cat.

Coakley ridiculed the "first grave" theory when questioned about it out-

---

* In 1995 Elsie Abbott told the author, "We weren't getting along at all. I don't know why." In the trial's aftermath, however, Georgia and Elsie would become good friends.

side court by a reporter for the *Chronicle,* which had given it big play back in September.

"The fact that a metropolitan paper should have fallen for a phony like that is preposterous," he said with a snort.

Dolores Anderson, the first panelist to whom Hove had directed his touchy question about Georgia's phone call to the cops, was a stunning brunette of thirty-two. She had captured the eye of a photographer for the *Chronicle,* which had run her photograph on this Thursday morning. Late in the day she was excused from serving, after pleading that she had two small children to care for.

"My mind would not be on the case when the time came each day for them to return from school," she said.

That was only half the story, however. After her picture appeared, she told the judge, she had received a phone call from a strange man who first asked to speak to "Hazel."

"There is no one here by that name," she had replied.

A pause had followed, and then the man said coldly, "I know that. I saw your photograph in the paper, and I don't want to see another picture of you until you're in the cemetery."

In excusing Mrs. Anderson, Judge Snook ascribed the menacing call to an anonymous psychopath and said he had received several crank calls himself.

The call to Mrs. Anderson exemplified a cowardly tide of meanness and maliciousness rising in the Bay Area as the trial captured its attention. Poison pen letters streamed into the courthouse, the jail, and the homes of participants on both sides.

"We were constantly threatened," Harold Hove's wife, Alice, remembered forty years later. "—a gravelly voice in the middle of the night: 'Get your husband off the case or something will happen to your children.' "

Mrs. Hove suspected that one of the callers was a shyster lawyer envious of her husband's high visibility.

By the time Judge Snook recessed court for the long Veterans Day weekend, the endless dismissals and challenges of the trial's first four days had exhausted the original fifty-six-member jury panel. A new sixty-five-member venire was ordered to report on Monday morning. Conceivably jury selection could go on for a long time yet, because the defense still had twelve of its twenty peremptory challenges left; the prosecution, fifteen.

Burton looked forward to a lonely weekend of "light reading" in his cell. Because of the holiday, the jail's usual Friday visiting hour had been canceled.

Refreshed after the long weekend, Abbott entered court Monday morning in new garb—a freshly pressed gray flannel suit. He smiled as his eyes met those of his red-haired wife, also wearing gray, in the rear of the room.

Soon after jury screening resumed Abbott got his biggest lift of his trial. Panel member Richard Cavagnaro, a Berkeley cost accountant, acknowledged having once told a friend, "From what little I have read, I don't think a jury could convict him." Burton flashed a big grin to his lawyers, who were also beaming. Cavagnaro added, however, that he had no fixed opinion and was still "open-minded." Neither side challenged him.

As the morning recess began, Abbott whispered to Bailiff J. H. Fitzpatrick, who in turn cupped his hand and called: "Hey, Georgia!"

Leaning forward toward the rail, Abbott asked, "Can you bring me some money, honey?"

Georgia smiled back and nodded as her husband was led from the courtroom. She proceeded at once to the jail upstairs and left a five-dollar bill with the jailers. Abbott told reporters he needed the money for candy and cigarettes and to pay a trusty for pressing his suit.

"We don't have any coat hangers," he complained. "I have to keep my suit rolled up in a box."

Completion of the jury came with surprising suddenness on Tuesday afternoon, midway through the trial's sixth day. Of seventy-seven venire members who had been called and questioned, sixty-three had been rejected. Coakley had just passed on his turn to challenge another one, indicating he was content with the dozen who filled the jury box at that moment. There was a brief, whispered conversation at the defense table, Abbott gave a jerky nod of his head, and Whitney addressed the court:

"The defense will pass, your honor."

The words set off a scramble as thirty reporters bolted for telephones to flash the word that Abbott's jury was fixed for the remainder of the trial—or so everyone thought.

The seven men and five women who were sworn in ranged in age from their late twenties to about sixty. All but one were married; six had children. Eleven were Caucasians, the twelfth was a Chinese-American. The men included an accountant, a naval supply supervisor, a warehouseman, a sheet metal worker, a mechanic, a milk truck loader, and an electronics technician.

Before recessing for the day, Snook gave them the mandatory admonition against discussing the case, reading about it, listening to radio or TV reports about it, or visiting the sites involved.

"I would suggest," he said, "that you have members of your families clip the trial stories from the newspapers before you are given them to read. You can save the clippings and read all about it when the trial is over."

On Wednesday morning, for the first time, the courtroom's spectator seats—no longer needed for jury panelists—were opened to the public, first come, first served.

The prosecution's opening statement, lasting forty-five minutes, was for the most part a low-key recitation. In a loose-fitting gray suit, Coakley took a comfortable stance just a few feet from the front row of jurors and lectured in slow, determined tones. For emphasis, he gestured occasionally with his right hand, leaving his left in his pants pocket. His matter-of-fact outline of the people's case was devoid of incendiary prose but nonetheless crafted for maximum impact—to horrify the jury and terrify the defendant.

"We will prove . . ." was Coakley's motif. He repeated the phrase no fewer than forty-two times as he outlined the crimes against Stephanie Bryan.

Somewhere in the courtroom, little noticed, sat one of the district attorney's aides with pencil and notebook. This anonymous person's assignment was to watch Abbott and his lawyers and record their reactions minute by minute as Coakley shed the first glimmer of light on the surprises he held in store. In the following account of the prosecutor's remarks, excerpts from these notes are interspersed in parenthesized italics.

Coakley began by describing the victim as an "extremely shy" girl who held her school privilege card by virtue of "outstanding scholarship and good conduct." He traced her homeward route on her last afternoon: her stops at the library, the pet store, and the Dream Fluff Donut Shop, and her parting with her friend Mary Ann Stewart at the Berkeley Tennis Club.

"We will prove," he declared, "that Mary Ann Stewart never saw Stephanie again and that Stephanie never reached home. We will also prove that the reason she never reached home sits right there in the person of Burton Abbott."

In detail Coakley described the dense foliage surrounding the Claremont Hotel and the forbidding shortcut through the wooded buffer between the hotel and Alvarado Road.

(*"Both Whitney and Hove seemed particularly interested in the description of the Claremont Hotel grounds and the time Stephanie arrived there."*)

Next the district attorney promised evidence that would cut the heart out of Abbott's alibi: "We will prove that around the time the last class at Willard Junior High School was dismissed, the defendant was in the vicinity of the school; that his Chevrolet automobile, oxidized greenish-gray or grayish-green in color, was parked on the east side of Telegraph Avenue about 160 feet south of Stuart Street [which bordered Willard on the south].

"We will prove that around 3:15 P.M. the defendant was in Pring's Doughnut Shop, a place frequented by students from the junior high school, located about half a block south of the school on Telegraph Avenue."

(*"Abbott began writing in his tablet from the moment his car was described as being in the vicinity of Willard Junior High School at 3:15."*)

"We will prove," the district attorney continued, "that the defendant left Pring's and drove away at about 3:25 P.M.; that shortly thereafter, around 3:30, an automobile exactly like his was seen traveling easterly on Ashby in the direction of College Avenue and the Claremont Hotel; that this automobile ran through a red light in crossing College Avenue and continued up Ashby; that the driver will be identified as a person who looks like the defendant."

(*"Hove smiled and shook his head with satisfaction during the portion of the statement dealing with the near-accident and Abbott's running a red light at the intersection of Ashby and College, as if he had expected that and was ready for it."*)

In vivid language Coakley went on to promise that "several witnesses" would tell of seeing a man beating a dark-haired young girl at about 4:15 in a car on Mt. Diablo Boulevard, a girl who "was looking out the left rear window with a terrified expression and seemed to be screaming."

In roundabout but positive fashion Coakley next approached the main puzzle for which a solid answer still eluded him: Where had Stephanie died?

"We will prove," he said, "that a short distance beyond where this [beating] incident took place is an area known as the Orinda Crossroads, where a road goes westerly toward the San Pablo Reservoir; that from this road one can drive on a number of roads in a northerly and westerly direction to the vicinity of Tank Farm Hill or Pinole; that along some of these roads are a number of places relatively secluded and isolated, where the defendant could have assaulted Stephanie and killed her."

This part of Coakley's narrative was only hunch and hypothesis, but it served to link the car struggle with the still-secret findings of lie detector expert Al Riedel, who was convinced that Stephanie had been slain in the hills near Pinole.

Pressing on, Coakley covered the undisputed facts of Abbott's April visit to the cabin, his drinking binge, the arrival of Mark and Mary Abbott thereafter, and the caravan-style homeward trip along a route that partially followed Franklin Canyon through Contra Costa County.

(*"Both Hove and Abbott seemed quite surprised and concerned about that portion of the statement dealing with Abbott driving directly behind his brother Mark to Franklin Canyon."*)

"We will prove," Coakley declared, "that on the next morning, Monday, May 2, a Mr. Tyree was driving along Franklin Canyon Road [and] stopped to relieve himself. Upon returning to his automobile, he saw a book on the shoulder of the highway and picked it up. Investigation proved that it had been issued by Willard Junior High School to Stephanie.

"We will prove that that same day, Abbott drove out alone to the vicinity of Tank Farm Hill, where he purchased gasoline on a credit card at a Standard Oil station, and that this station is on the route to Franklin Canyon where Stephanie Bryan's French book was found that morning by Mr. Tyree."

Coakley went on with his damning step-by-step revelation of the evidence to come: "We will prove that on the next day, Tuesday, May 3, the defendant drove to Livermore Veterans Hospital and demanded immediate admission as a patient, expressing a willingness to submit to any kind of surgery and to cooperate in every way—an attitude quite contrary, incidentally, to that which he had exhibited on prior occasions. At this time he was regularly enrolled as a student at the University of California with a whole semester's work drawing to a close and final examinations to be taken. To enter the hospital at this time would have meant his loss of the semester's credits and failure to receive his degree before his educational rights under the law would expire—that is, his rights to receive a college education at the expense of the United States Government."

("Abbott showed a marked reaction by looking up and swallowing and seeming alarmed when Mr. Coakley mentioned that he returned to the veterans hospital on May 3 and demanded entry and offered to cooperate where he had failed to cooperate before.")

Coakley made it clear that even in the absence of physical evidence, he would treat the murder of Stephanie Bryan as a gross sex perversion. After describing in ghastly detail the condition of her body when exhumed, he said:

> With the exception of her brassiere, which was found in the basement of the defendant's home, and her panties, which were tied around her neck, she had on the clothes which she was wearing on April 28.
>
> We will prove that the brassiere had been carefully removed from Stephanie; that the straps were intact and that the fastener in the back was not ripped or torn, thus indicating that her sweaters and her slip had been removed and put on again before her body was buried.

Approaching the end of his discourse, Coakley gave the jury and the defendant their first veiled glimpse of the physical evidence amassed by Professor Kirk—until now the prosecutor's most closely guarded secret.*

---

* Much has changed in criminal law during the four decades since the Abbott trial. Followers of the O.J. Simpson trial in 1994–95 will recall vividly the endless confrontations over discovery rules that compelled each side to disclose its evidence to the other. In the 1950s "discovery" was a concept alien to California criminal courts, so the adversaries guarded their secrets and "surprise witnesses" abounded. Changing standards of courtesy and "political correctness" have also impacted courtroom behavior. At one point Abbott's attorney Whitney addressed a female court reporter as "honeychild." Imagine the uproar that would have ensued if one of O.J.'s lawyers had addressed Marcia Clark that way.

Choosing his words for surprise and shock value, he announced: "We will prove that Stephanie Bryan was in the defendant's Chevrolet automobile before she was murdered by him, and that the defendant was at the grave on the hill near the cabin, and that the defendant dug that grave and buried her body."

("Abbott paused in his writing and swallowed when Mr. Coakley stated he would prove the defendant took Stephanie up to the grave dead or alive.")

Coakley's peroration was a slashing attack on Abbott's character as determined by Dr. Kelley, the police psychiatrist who also had plumbed the souls of Hermann Goering, Joachim von Ribbentrop, and Rudolf Hess.

The defendant, the D.A. asserted, had "a mentality of extreme vanity, egotism, and selfishness; a mentality which enabled him to kill and lie without shame and then to rationalize and justify his conduct, to lie and keep on lying about it until he believed or almost believed his own lies, and eventually to eject all of it blandly from his mind as if it never happened. In brief, we will prove the guilt of the defendant not only beyond a reasonable doubt but beyond the peradventure of any doubt—and having done so, we will expect you to find him guilty as charged."

As Coakley sat down, Hove patted the arm of his "tense and gray" client, according to the *Chronicle,* "much as a second might do for a battered prizefighter." The newspaper's eight-column front-page banner the next morning proclaimed:

ABBOTT SHAKEN AS D.A. CLAIMS PROOF OF GUILT

Beyond the courtroom doors, Coakley's opening statement sent a surge of excitement throughout the state. It set nerves on edge and loosened tongues. At 4:04 the next morning, the desk sergeant's phone rang at the Berkeley Police department.

"My name is Fred Leidecker," the caller announced. "My wife and I have some information that perhaps you should know about."

22

An Accusing Finger

A hush settled over the courtroom as the small girl entered. In green sweater, black-and-white plaid skirt, white scarf, bobby socks, and saddle shoes, she could have been an incarnation of Stephanie herself. She was the same age, fourteen, and her dark hair was cut to ear length, just as Stephanie's had been.

This was Mary Ann Stewart, the chum who had accompanied Stephanie on her final homeward walk—the last friend to see her alive. Coakley had chosen Mary Ann as an appealing witness to open his case against the man accused of slaying her.

The girl took the stand nervously. At first, seemingly fascinated, she stared at the ashen-faced Abbott, who peered at her from the corners of his eyes. After a few minutes she gained composure and spoke in a clear voice as she recalled her last parting with Stephanie by the Berkeley Tennis Club. Later in her testimony, she solemnly identified the purse and wallet found in Abbott's basement as the ones Stephanie had been carrying then.

Hove, cross-examining Mary Ann gently but at length, seemed to be searching, without success, for something to combat Coakley's declaration of a sex motive in Stephanie's slaying. He wanted to know whether Mary Ann had looked into Stephanie's purse, and if so, had she seen a brassiere? The obvious inference, if she had, would have been that Stephanie had remained braless after her gym class on April 28 and that she had not been undressed while in captivity as Coakley claimed. It was a clumsy theory at best, and Mary Ann demolished it.

Yes, she said, she had seen the contents of the purse when Stephanie opened it in the library, but they did not include a bra.

For unclear reasons, Hove queried Mary Ann in great detail about which arms Stephanie carried her books and her purse in, and whether she wore her eyeglasses all the time during the walk. Mary Ann couldn't recall how Stephanie carried the books and purse, but said yes, she did wear her glasses. After court, puzzled reporters asked Hove what he was getting at with this line of inquiry.

"It was calculated" was his enigmatic reply.

Next Coakley called to the stand four of those who had observed the car struggle east of the tunnel on Mt. Diablo Boulevard. He chose them as much for shock impact as for their descriptions of the old Chevrolet or Pontiac, its driver, and the victim. Lieutenant Allen Hill, the red-haired navy pilot who with his wife had been approaching the tunnel from the east, painted a vivid word picture for the jury:

"I saw a young girl appear in the left rear window, which was partially open. She had brown hair, rather short, and appeared to be wearing something dark over something light. The girl's face had a terrified expression, and she screamed 'No!' so loudly that I could hear it over the roar of the traffic. We could hear it very distinctly. The driver of the car—I couldn't tell whether it was a man or a woman, honestly—crawled over into the back, put an arm around the girl's chest, and pulled her down away from the window."

Whitney's cross-examination of Hill was severe, probing for weaknesses in his account. He seized on the lieutenant's estimate that his car traveled about 125 feet between the time he heard the girl scream and the time her head disappeared from view.

"So you're telling this jury you drove on in this heavy traffic for 125 feet without looking to the front?" Whitney sneered.

"Yes" was Hill's instant rejoinder, which caught the lawyer off guard. "My pilot's training has taught me to observe details rapidly and to estimate the speeds of moving objects. I am perfectly capable of driving a car and observing something while I maintain my position on the highway."

Jacqueline Hill, the pilot's wife, followed him on the witness stand, corroborating his account in all essentials. Two others who had observed the car struggle, Emma Lee Van Meter and Sam Marshall, also reinforced his testimony. None of these eyewitnesses had stopped to investigate the scuffle, and all registered remorse for not having done so.

"What I saw imprinted itself on my mind so much that it took weeks to get it out, just a little bit," Mrs. Van Meter told the court.

On the stand Mrs. Van Meter, the Hills, and Marshall were credible, logical, and impressive, but nonetheless inadequate for Coakley's grand strategy. What he needed, but lacked at this point, was someone who could positively identify the driver of the suspect car as Abbott.

Now the district attorney produced his first surprise witness.

When, in his opening statement, Coakley had promised a witness who would place Abbott at College and Ashby Avenues on the afternoon Stephanie vanished, Hove had snickered. He had doubtless assumed (as did the *Chronicle's* reporter in print) that this would be Alexander Marten, the "bearded Bohemian" interior decorator, a shadowy character on the fringes of the Bryan case. The newspapers had given big play (though not necessarily credence) to Marten's tale that he had recorded Abbott's license number inside a packet of Dill's pipe cleaners, after a near collision on April 28 at the College-Ashby corner.

Now, however, it was not Marten that Coakley called to testify but instead, a grandmotherly woman named Marian Morgan—a new character in the Stephanie Bryan drama. Coakley had been holding her on ice since early fall. Until she took her oath, not the defense, or the press, or the public at large had ever heard of her.

With her well-coiffed gray hair, light-rimmed spectacles, long blue coat, and jeweled hat, Mrs. Morgan exuded dignity, honesty, and common sense. She carried a large manila envelope as she made her way to the witness stand.

She identified herself as an insurance underwriter who had resided in Berkeley twenty-three years. At three-thirty on April 28, while driving north on College Avenue, she had stopped for a red light at Ashby—at the same corner Marten had mentioned. That intersection, of course, was on the route Stephanie and Mary Ann had walked about the same time that afternoon.

"And did you see anything unusual?" Coakley asked Mrs. Morgan.

"Yes."

As the light turned green and she prepared to cross the intersection, she said, an eastbound car was "coming down Ashby pretty fast." She thought the driver would stop but he did not. As she slammed on her brakes, he ran the Ashby red light "like he was going to a fire," cutting her off and barely missing a pickup truck (Marten's?) in the intersection.

"Did you observe who was driving this car?" Coakley asked.

"Yes, it was my impression he was a young college student, kind of light-complected."

"And have you seen the young man since then?"

"Yes, I saw a man who looked like him in a lineup at the jail."

"I call your attention to Mr. Abbott. Does he look like the man?"

"That's right."

With assurance, Mrs. Morgan went on to describe the offending vehicle.

"I'm familiar with automobiles," she said. "My husband and I used to have a General Motors agency. The car was a 1949 or 1950 Chevrolet with a sun visor in front and a torpedo back. It was greenish-gray."

"How can you pin down the date of this incident?"

From the manila envelope Mrs. Morgan withdrew her appointment book. It bore two notations for April 28: a 3 P.M. business appointment with someone named "Evelyn," from which Mrs. Morgan had been returning when the incident occurred, and a cryptic note reading "Call Gertrude Nelson about Mark Clark, This is Your Life, Darryl Zanuck."

As the district attorney had independently confirmed, a *This Is Your Life* segment about General Mark Clark, a top army commander in World War

II and Korea, had aired on local channel KRON-TV the previous evening, April 27. Mrs. Morgan testified that she had written herself a reminder to call her friend Gertrude about it. (Gertrude, incidentally, had been riding with her when the speeding Chevy cut her off.)

As the evidence against him mounted, Abbott's courtroom demeanor disintegrated.

"His pallor is increasing. His smile is less ready," wrote Carolyn Anspacher in the *Chronicle*. Observers were laying odds that he would crack under the strain. In the jail, he briefly threatened a sit-down strike—a refusal to go to court—when tomato juice was withheld from his breakfast. He sat for a long time in the jail's bullpen with his head in his hands staring at the floor.

Next Coakley called on William Russell, the school typewriter repairman, to tell of seeing Abbott in Pring's Doughnut Shop on the afternoon of April 28. If his timing was right, his sighting had taken place only a few minutes before the near accident Mrs. Morgan had described a few blocks away.

Russell, thirty-one, seemed haggard and harried as he came forward in the courtroom. His deep-set eyes stared apprehensively from his gaunt face, and his receding hair was disheveled. This was the day he had been dreading since late July, when the *Call-Bulletin* had "discovered" him. Since than he had lived in a pressure chamber.

As he seated himself in the witness chair, he glared at Abbott, whom he said he knew well, and Abbott glared back. Under Coakley's guidance, Russell recited the particulars of his encounter with Burton on April 28: how he had gone to Pring's for coffee about two-forty-five, after returning a repaired typewriter to Willard Junior High, and found Abbott sitting at the counter wearing a brown leather jackets and jeans.

From a box, Coakley produced the jacket Abbott had worn on his April trip to Trinity.

"Like this?"

"That looks like it."

"Did you have any conversation with Mr. Abbott?"

"I didn't talk to him because I didn't feel good and didn't want to talk to anyone. About 3:15 I got up to leave. Just a minute before that, he had passed next to me as he paid his check. He went out the door just ahead of me and got into his car—a gray Chevrolet which was parked in front. I was parked a few spaces back, and I got into my car. I drove away before he did."

Hove's cross-examination of Russell was fierce. His tactic, which he would use again in the weeks ahead, was to paint the witness himself as a suspect in Stephanie's death.

Harking back to mid-August, when the defense lawyers had "barged" into Russell's living room and grilled him for two hours, Hove asked, "Do you recall telling us that you yourself were under suspicion in this case, and that you had 'put a noose around your neck' because you had left work early that day?"

"No, that's not true," Russell replied emphatically.

"Do you recall telling us that your own mother had accused you of this crime?" (Here Hove was imputing sinister significance to a kidding remark Russell's mother had made. The police were fully aware of it.)

"I most certainly did not. There was no such conversation!"

"You deny it?"

"Yes, I do."

As this accusatory line of questioning ended, Emerson was instantly on his feet to counterattack.

"What else did the defense attorneys have to say when they interviewed you?" he asked Russell.

Russell's answer electrified the courtroom: "They offered me a job."

Their proposition, the witness said, was that if he would water down his testimony, they might employ him as an expert witness in future cases.

"And did Mr. Hove say anything else?" Emerson asked.

"He said he could make it kind of tough on me. He threatened to 'tear me apart' on the witness stand."

At the next recess, reporters converged on Abbott's lawyers for their reaction to this damning accusation. They did not seem dismayed.

"We know Mr. Russell. He hasn't finished testifying," was Whitney's cryptic comment.

Two hundred persons, mostly women, were on hand as the trial went into its third week on Monday morning, November 21, drawn by newspaper speculation that Dr. and Mrs. Bryan would be the next witnesses called. Only about a third of the would-be spectators got into the courtroom, and those who did were disappointed. Instead of the Bryans, the district attorney called Delbert Cox, the proprietor of the Wildwood Inn.

Until now Coakley's key witnesses had been chosen to show—if not prove—that Abbott had been in Berkeley at the hour Stephanie vanished. Cox's complementary role was to show—if not prove—that Abbott had *not* been where he said he was that night, in Cox's tavern far to the north.

Del Cox was was a ruddy, rough-hewn man in his fifties, with gray hair and at least two chins under his jowly face. For his big-city court appearance he had exchanged his mountain garb for a three-piece blue serge suit with an elk's tooth on a gold chain across the vest. His tie was a gaudy plaid.

The defense, knowing the verdict might hinge on Cox's testimony, tried to block it from the moment he started to speak.

"Just a minute," Whitney protested. "We feel in the interest of justice the corpus delicti should be established before the defendant is connected up with this crime."

Judge Snook allowed Cox to proceed, reserving the right to strike his testimony if a corpus delicti was not established.

Coakley's temper flared. "I can assure you, your honor, that we will establish one in no uncertain terms," he shouted.

Cox retold his story that he had not seen Abbott in his bar on Thursday, the night of Stephanie's disappearance. The first time he had seen the defendant that year, he insisted, was the next afternoon when Burton arrived for his drinking marathon.

"When he came into my place, I was busy at the cash register," Cox recalled. "My back was to the door. I heard a voice say, 'Hi, Del.' Mr. Abbott was there. I shook hands with him and said, 'What are you doing up here?' He said he was there for the opening of the fishing season, and he sat down at the bar and ordered a drink of Old Hermitage, ninety proof."

Abbott kept reordering at intervals of fifteen to twenty minutes, Cox testified, and eventually "chummed up" with Tom Daly. The two men talked and drank until near midnight, each spending between ten and fifteen dollars on liquor alone. A $15 check Daly had cashed at the time was introduced in evidence.

Coakley now shifted to a new line of inquiry, asking Cox about a later visit by Abbott to the Wildwood Inn, in June, with Georgia's sister Florence and her husband, Edwin Jeppesen.

"Was the defendant dancing?"

"Yes, sir."

"What kind of music?"

"We call it up there 'okie hokie.' "

"Jitterbug?"

"I don't know what *you'd* call it."

"Was it fast?"

"Yes."

With this brief exchange, Coakley sought anew to undercut the major defense theme that Abbott, missing a lung lobe, was too frail to have committed the crime of which he stood accused.

Hove launched his cross-examination of the innkeeper with a disarmingly simple question: "Are you absolutely certain you did not see the defendant prior to April 29, Mr. Cox?"

"Yes, sir."

Having elicited this unconditional declaration, Hove produced the statement he and Whitney had pried from Cox back in August, in the tool shed confrontation behind his bar. The document was in Hove's handwriting but Cox had signed it.

Examining the paper, the innkeeper had to acknowledge several remarks that watered down the positive testimony he had just given. At one point, when asked if Abbott had been in the bar on Thursday night, he had replied, "He may have come in, but I didn't see him."

A shouting match broke out between the lawyers when Cox was forced to confirm that Hove had read the statement to him before he signed it.

"Oh, he purported to read it. That's probably what happened," Coakley interjected, snarling.

Whitney instantly demanded that the district attorney be cited for misconduct. Then he roared at Cox, "Did anyone force you to make that statement?"

"No, sir."

"Did you make it freely and voluntarily?"

"Yes, sir."

"Did you look over Mr. Hove's shoulder when he read it to you?"

"I did, sir."

If Coakley lost ground and stature during the cross-examination of Cox, he nevertheless had little cause for despair. He had another surprise witness waiting in the wings with testimony calculated to devastate the defense. She was Reva Leidecker of Oakland, whose existence had been unknown to the district attorney until ten days into the trial. It was Reva's husband, Fred, who had placed the mysterious 4 A.M. phone call to the Berkeley police the previous Thursday, telling them "We have some information you should know."

Reva, after reading Coakley's opening statement in Wednesday evening's *Tribune,* had become so haunted by suppressed memories that she had lain awake all night.

At age thirty-three, Reva was a woman of ample girth but barely five feet tall. Her mop of long, straight, dark hair fell well past her shoulders in what the *Chronicle* called an "Alice in Wonderland hairdo." She lumbered to the witness stand late on Monday, November 21.

What would her testimony be? No one in the courtroom, save the prosecutors, had the slightest clue.

The previous April the Leideckers, contemplating a possible move to Contra Costa County, had driven there on the afternoon Stephanie vanished, passing through the Broadway Tunnel sometime after four o'clock.

"We were driving on the outside right lane and were talking," Reva testified. "Suddenly my husband put on the brakes and cried out, 'Look at that crazy bastard!' This car, the second car ahead of us, had suddenly stopped. The guy just behind him had to swerve to the left to get around him, and my husband had to put on the brakes to keep from hitting him. We didn't completely stop but slowed down to about fifteen or twenty miles per hour.

"There was a girl in the back of that car, sitting on the edge of the seat with her head way down. As we came alongside, she turned toward the window and raised her head. The man in the front seat turned toward the left, toward me. He had his arm way up by the ceiling of the car and shoved the girl down out of sight. The man was tall and slender and had long arms and slender hands, like a doctor's."

Reva kept repeating "Those hands, those hands." She told of screaming at her husband, whose eyes were on the traffic, "Honey, he's hitting her!"

"Wives get beat all the time," Fred had replied. "Don't pay any attention to it."

Reva remembered "fussing about it all the way to Orinda Crossroads." She said she had stared momentarily into the face of the driver from "only about three feet away" and described him as "very fair complexed [sic] with light brown hair sloping down from the center on both sides."

The girl, Reva said, had dark hair "hanging loose around her shoulders," and her upper garment was "dark—black or maybe navy blue." She seemed to be about the age of the Leideckers' own daughter, Carol, who was four-teen.

When Stephanie's picture first appeared in the papers, Reva testified, she "couldn't be sure whether it was the same girl or not." But when she read Coakley's "we will prove" declaration about the car struggle, the whole episode had popped vividly back into her mind.

Up to this point Reva's story, for all its detail, had added little to the earlier testimony of the other tunnel witnesses. But now, after her graphic description of the assailant, Coakley startled the jury by asking: "Do you see that man in the courtroom?"

"Yes, sir," Reva replied in a high, girlish voice.

Coakley ordered Abbott to stand and face the witness. His face was white, drained of blood. His facial muscles were taut.

Reva Leidecker leaned forward, extending her fleshy right arm, and pointed an accusing finger at him.

"The man in the blue suit," she said.

23

Flimflam and Poison Pen

In the trial's opening days, Abbott's brother Mark had been in the courtroom as a spectator. Now, under subpoena, he was there in a new role—as a reluctant witness for the prosecution. He couldn't have been in a more unenviable situation. He was totally loyal to his brother and committed to his innocence; yet his testimony could help send Burton to the gas chamber. Not only was Mark known to be truthful by nature,* but he had no choice about truthfulness now. He was to be questioned about matters already well established, not only by his closed-door testimony to the grand jury but by Burton's own words to the FBI.

Mark's time on the stand was brief but crucial. Coakley had him trace, in red pencil on a map, the route he and Burton had taken on Sunday, May 1, returning caravan-style from Trinity County in their separate cars. In Contra Costa County, as had been established, Mark's red line followed Franklin Canyon Road, which they had traveled at around 6 P.M. If the significance of this eluded the jury at first, it soon became clear with the testimony of Coakley's next half-dozen witnesses, who appeared in quick succession.

• David and Ernest Tyree, father and son, recounted their discovery of Stephanie's French textbook beside Franklin Canyon Road on the following morning, Monday, May 2.

• Evelyn Prisk, Stephanie's French teacher at Willard, identified the book, *Modern French Course* by Dondo, bearing the girl's scrawled signature.

• Two U.S. Weather Bureau men, David Powel [sic] and Robert Dale, presented Franklin Canyon's weekend rainfall data, proving that the book (which was dry when found except for some dew) had been left by the roadside close to the time Abbott passed there.

• Finally John Kreutzer, a Standard Oil accountant, produced Abbott's credit card records, establishing that he had purchased gasoline in San Pablo,

---

* Inspector Charles Ryken told the author in 1994, "Mark wouldn't volunteer anything, but as far as I know he never lied."

not far from Franklin Canyon, the same Monday the book was found. Had he driven out there on a sneak trip to recover the telltale book he had jettisoned the night before? That's what Coakley wanted the jury to surmise.

The book itself was introduced into evidence. Its pages had been ripped loose from the binding and their edges turned reddish brown by iodide fumes during fingerprint tests. No prints of Abbott's had been found, but there were some small ones that could have been Stephanie's.

Miss Prisk described Stephanie as an "extremely capable student, very conscientious," but often self-conscious and uncomfortable when reciting. While cross-examining the teacher, Hove elicited what might become a telling point for the defense: In the days immediately preceding her murder, Stephanie's grades had fallen from A-plus to C-plus, indicating possible emotional turmoil for some reason unknown.

Kreutzer's oil company records also established, besides Abbott's trip to San Pablo, his gasoline purchase at Twentieth and Harrison Streets in Oakland on the Thursday of Stephanie's disappearance. This cast into doubt his original story that he had gassed up in Alameda the night before.

The poignant moment that trial spectators had been avidly anticipating came on Tuesday afternoon when Mary Bryan, Stephanie's mother, entered the courtroom. Her quiet voice marked her as a woman of culture and self-control. As she seated herself in the witness chair, she stared momentarily at Burton Abbott (her first view of him) and then turned to the jury and smiled. Abbott returned her gaze unblinkingly.

Abbott's lawyers were keenly aware of the sympathy this tiny women evoked. It was in their interest to keep her appearance before the jury as brief as possible. Before Coakley could ask his first question, Hove rose and addressed the court.

"Your honor, knowing the trials this witness has been through, we will stipulate to her testimony as given before the Grand Jury, so that she may be excused."

Coakley was having no part of this.

"I think this jury would like to hear Mrs. Bryan's story, Mr. Hove," he snapped, "so we'll proceed."

Mary Bryan related the familiar story of how the family's initial puzzlement, when Stephanie failed to return from school on April 28, grew to anxiety, dread, horror, and grief. She explained her children's customary homeward route through the woodsy Claremont Hotel shortcut—a path she herself had chosen.

The mother's testimony was effective not so much for its content (there were few surprises) as for its emotional nuances depicting Stephanie in a happy family setting. After identifying her daughter's picture, she described the girl lovingly:

"She was almost five-feet-two, weighed about 105 pounds, and her hair was dark brown, very fine and very heavy." Mary's voice cracked. "She had the most hair I've ever seen on any child's head."

Mary remained before the jury for a half hour.

"We have a wonderful, happy home," she concluded. "My other children have not been told of the crime by us. The older ones may have seen head-lines, but we do not talk about it. When I say 'no' now to my children, I think three or four times. I don't want to overprotect them. Fear should not be used as a wrap-around."

After this testimony Abbott told reporters, "I had the urge to stand up and tell her, 'Mrs. Bryan, I didn't kill your daughter.'" However, he followed his lawyers' admonitions to say nothing and refrain from spontaneous outbursts in court.

Dr. Charles Bryan, following his wife on the stand, presented an opposite image. At age forty-four, he was a towering, wavy-haired man of athletic build, square-faced with jutting chin. Just as Mary's eyes projected grief, the doctor's flashed anger as he described the family's vain seach for Stephanie on the night of her vanishing. As he stepped down, reporters asked him if he believed Abbott guilty.

"I have no doubt about it," he coldly replied.

When Coakley called Otto Dezman to the stand on Wednesday morning, both of them knew he faced an excruciating ordeal. The retired navy chief had angered Whitney and Hove early in the game by refusing to "correct" certain damaging references to Abbott in his original statements to the police. Now he was convinced he was Abbott's selected "patsy." Since mid-summer Coakley had known, via his intelligence network, of the defense's intention to paint Otto as Georgia Abbott's illicit lover and convert him from witness to suspect in the jurors' eyes.

Clad in a tan suit, Otto was conspicuously nervous as he began to testify. He perspired freely, often mopping his face with a white handkerchief. He avoided looking at his former friend Burton.

Dezman was essential as a prosecution witness, to tell what had happened in the Abbott home on the night Georgia discovered Stephanie's purse. He had been the only "outsider" there, the others present being Abbott, his wife, and his mother.

Coakley led Otto through the events of that evening—a story now known to everyone who read the newspapers. He told of Georgia screaming "Abbott! Abbott!" as she came running up the stairs from the cellar with the purse in hand. He described the family's consternation and how they passed the

purse, wallet, and contents around, possibly contaminating them with fingerprints. He related how Georgia summoned the police at his suggestion,
bringing them to the house within half an hour. Finally he told of playing
chess with Burton until dawn and of their consumption of a pint of whiskey
during the game.

Small sidelights enlivened Otto's recitation, such as Burton's seeming de-
tachment, to the point of working a crossword puzzle while the police interrogated him.

Dezman's testimony also enabled Coakley to inform the jury of Elsie Abbott's "secret"—that she had noticed Stephanie's purse in the basement early
in May, within days after the girl disappeared. Otto said that a day or two after
Georgia found the purse in mid-July, he overheard her scolding her mother-
in-law for telling the FBI about seeing it earlier.

The defense lawyers, taking over on cross-examination, were unaware of
the D.A.'s secret investigation back in August, meticulously checking out
Dezman's history and confirming his innocence in Stephanie's death. Whitney therefore wasted no time in launching his expected character assassina-
tion effort.

"Why did you retire from the navy after twenty-seven years, when thirty
years is the regular retirement time?" he demanded.

"I just figured I had enough," Otto replied.

"Did you have any trouble when you were in the navy?"

"No, sir."

Coakley, angered both as a lawyer and a navy man himself, grew red in the
face and jumped up.

"I will say this, if the court please," he roared. "I will stipulate right now
that this man's entire record of twenty-seven years in the navy can go into
the record of this case. I have seen it, and it is very honorable."

Furious, Whitney demanded that Coakley be cited for misconduct. "The
district attorney might as well take the stand himself," he complained.

"Do you accept the stipulation?" Judge Snook asked him.

"I will make the decision on that later, you honor," Whitney answered. He
next moved into what had until now been the exclusive province of gossip-
mongers—the rumors of a steamy affair between Otto and Georgia.

"When did you first meet the Abbotts?" Whitney asked.

"In 1949–50 or so."

"Did you meet Georgia first?"

"Yes, I did. I met her through my wife. Burton was then in the hospital."

"How much later was it that you met the defendant?"

"About a year."

"Have you ever had meetings with Mrs. Abbott alone?"

"I guess so, but mostly in the company of my wife."

"Isn't it a fact, Mr. Dezman, that you lived in the apartment right next door to the Abbotts in Alameda?"

"Yes, sir."

"And did you ever visit with Mrs. Abbott while her husband was away in the hospital?"

"I would say yes."

"And was Mrs. Dezman around?"

"Sometimes yes, sometimes no."

"How many times did you visit Georgia Abbott?"

"I would not estimate that, sir." Dezman's voice turned icy.

"As many as ten times?"

"Possibly."

"More?"

"I don't know."

Whitney wanted to know how often Dezman had visited the Abbott house on San Jose Avenue where Stephanie's possessions were found.

"I would say two or three times, maybe more, but I think Burton was present."

"Did you not do extensive wiring for the Abbotts when they moved into the house on San Jose Avenue?"

"Not extensive wiring. I put a light in the breakfast nook for them."

"And were you not in the basement of the Abbott home and thoroughly familiar with the layout of that basement and subbasement?"

"No, sir. I went into the attic to install the wiring for the light."

Whitney, who had hoped to make Dezman admit familiarity with the cellar, registered acute disappointment. The electrician had neatly sidestepped his trap.

"Do you know Georgia Abbott's present address?" Whitney asked.

"It's on Encinal Avenue, but I don't know the number."

"Well, since Georgia Abbott has been living at her new address—since Burton's arrest—have you ever gone there?"

"I went there one night to pick up Chris—to baby-sit for her."

"Did you ever take any sort of a trip with Mrs. Georgia Abbott, Mr. Dezman?"

"I did not."

This line of grilling went on and on. Dezman was finally excused after three and a half hours on the stand, and reporters converged on him wanting to know how he felt.

"I feel fine and dandy," he said.

"How do you feel about the cross-examination?"

"I stood up under it, and I'm laughing."

"Would you like to punch Whitney in the nose?"

"I'll reserve that privilege for someone else."

Leona Dezman, Otto's wife, later dismissed Whitney's adultery insinuations as "the biggest bunch of bull I've listened to yet." She still had Georgia working for her at the beauty shop.

Now Judge Snook recessed the trial for the four-day Thanksgiving weekend. For prisoners on the tenth floor of the courthouse, the holiday fare was turkey with giblet gravy, cranberry sauce, candied yams, peas and carrots, Waldorf salad, bread and butter, choice of pumpkin or mince pie, and coffee. But Abbott, his public relations knack having deserted him, was one of two prisoners who refused to sign a note thanking the inmate chef for the exceptional menu. He thus gave the papers cause to report that he passed the holiday "sulking in his cell."

Georgia spent Thanksgiving not with the Abbotts but with friends. A confidential source told Inspector Severin, "Georgia has been informed by Whitney and Hove not to appear in court as a spectator, as she may have to testify later. When they asked her whether she thought Bud was guilty, she answered, 'If you don't know whether he is or not, who does?' "

On Friday Abbott was visited by his mother and Mark. The latter replied with a cold "no comment" when asked about rumors that Burton and Georgia were splitting up.

As the trial resumed after the Thanksgiving break, Inspector O'Meara settled his six-foot frame into the witness chair. He was at home there, having testified often during his nineteen years on the Berkeley force as beat cop, traffic officer, sergeant, and detective.

O'Meara's unspectacular role as a prosecution witness was to confirm events that followed the finding of the purse. When the time came for Hove to cross-examine him, however, tension gripped the courtroom. It was cop-versus-cop as the ex-FBI defense lawyer tried to make O'Meara look incompetent. For a time he had little success, and the shadowboxing seemed to bewilder the jurors, who grew fidgety. Then Hove scored when he asked O'Meara about the detergent box in which Stephanie's purse had been found.

"Did it ever occur to you that there might be fingerprints on that box?" Hove inquired.

"Yes, sir." O'Meara said Lieutenant Roland Sherry, his department's fingerprint expert, had examined the box.

"And was it dusted for prints?"

"He made whatever examination he does with objects of that type."

It was a valiant try at evasion, but what it boiled down to was that the vaunted Berkeley cops had bungled. As Sherry himself reluctantly confirmed later, they had failed to look for fingerprints on this key piece of evidence.

On Tuesday morning, November 29, an unsigned letter typed in red capitals, bearing an Oakland postmark, arrived at the county jail addressed to Abbott. Sheriff H. P. "Jack" Gleason opened and scanned it:

YOU LEPROSY-BRAINED HORRENDOUS CREEP—
IF IT IS THE LAST THING I EVER DO ON EARTH, AND NO MATTER HOW LONG IT TAKES, I AM GOING TO KID-NAP THAT 4 YEAR OLD BRAT OF YOURS, BAT HIS HEAD IN, AND THROW HIS BODY UP IN THE WOODS WHERE YOU THREW STEPHANIE'S.
THE LAW OUGHT TO KILL YOU THE SLOW, HARD WAY, NOT EASY IN THE GAS CHAMBER!
IF THE LAW DOESN'T EXECUTE YOU, I WILL. I WILL BE WATCHING AND WAITING TILL YOU GET OUT AND KILL YOU OFF (PARDON ME, I WILL EXECUTE YOU), SO PER-HAPS YOU BEST CONFESS AND DIE EASY IN THE GAS CHAMBER.
WHERE DO YOU GET YOUR MAGGOTY-BRAINED CONCEIT TO THINK YOU CAN JOUNCE YOUR 4 YEAR OLD SON ON YOUR KNEE AND WATCH HIM GROW TO MANHOOD, AND THEN TAKE A DOCTOR'S CHARMING YOUNG DAUGHTER OUT AND KILL HER OFF WITH A CLUB LIKE SHE WAS A RAT, AND THROW HER BODY IN THE WOODS. I'LL LEARN YOU IF THE LAW DOESN'T.

Gleason showed the letter to Abbott, who read it with a blank expression before leaving for the morning session in the courtroom. Then the sheriff re-leased it to the press before turning it over to the postal inspectors.

"Are you going to place a guard on the boy?" a reporter inquired.

The sheriff said no.

Life was growing more hellish by the day for Georgia. More and more, as the people's case against her husband unfolded, she found herself terrified, be-sieged by doubts, bothered by conscience, deserted by friends, and snubbed by Burton's family and lawyers. She was fair game for gossip and was regu-larly assailed in the newspapers and in public discourse.

One of the few people in whom she confided was Lou Kirkpatrick, who worked alongside her at the beauty shop. As Georgia unburdened herself, she had no inkling that Lou was passing on what she said, almost daily, to Inspector Severin.

"Georgia is once again on friendly terms with Elsie Abbott as the result of the threatening letter concerning harm to her son Chris," Severin reported in a memo to Coakley on December 4. "This letter has had the effect of cementing family relations. Georgia has permitted Elsie to take Chris to see Santa Claus."

Continuing, Severin wrote that "Georgia's relations with Whitney and Hove are definitely unfriendly. She told Lou she 'wouldn't waste a nickel on them.'* She stated that she can't even talk to Burton anymore because he just gives her one lie after another."

Georgia was wondering at this point whether Burton's lawyers would ask her to testify. If they did, should she fall back on the same rote refusal she had invoked before the grand jury? She knew that if she testified, she would be put on the spot about the time of Burton's brief visit to the beauty shop on April 28, before his departure for the cabin. Was it in the morning or afternoon?

"Georgia still believes that Burton was in the beauty shop at 11 A.M., but she is *NOT SURE* of this, and it is bothering her," Severin noted. "Lou has told Georgia not to testify about it unless she is sure, as she may get herself out on a limb. Georgia is very much puzzled about this situation and doesn't know what to do. Being a Catholic, she is going to see a priest about it, hoping that he will point out to her what she should do under the circumstances."

In another vein, Georgia had confided to Lou that despite his Methodist upbringing, Burton was now a professed atheist.

"Georgia and Burton have had some terrible arguments about religion," Severin wrote. "Burton doesn't believe in baptism nor in original sin, and although Georgia wants Chris to be baptized, Burton won't permit it. Burton doesn't believe in God, only in himself."

The improved relations between Georgia and Elsie, generated by the poison pen letter, were short-lived. They waned again after a day or two when Georgia, for whom one of the three family seats in the courtroom was reserved, authorized her sister, Florence Jeppesen, to occupy it. Elsie's sister, Mona Marsh, protested that Florence was "not a member of the family" and stopped her from doing so.

---

* In a 1994 interview, the author questioned Georgia about this:

  Q. Did the lawyers kind of freeze you out of the picture?

  A. Yes, they did; they sure did. That whole case was so badly done by the attorneys.

  Q. On which side?

  A. Both sides.

The twelve jurors sat entranced as Tuesday's first witness, FBI agent Richard Nichols, held up Stephanie's white nylon, lace-trimmed bra, deeply stained with mud.

"I first saw this brassiere in Burton Abbott's basement shortly after I had dug up some books and a set of eyeglasses," he testified. "It was in the same immediate area and it was also buried."

Assistant District Attorney Emerson, who was examining the witness, handed the bra to Whitney and Hove for inspection. Abbott, sitting with them, blinked and declined to touch or examine it.

Nichols, a sturdy, prematurely gray man in his forties, displayed the books and glasses next. As he presented each article, it was deposited on the court clerk's desk within sight of the jurors.

Under cross-examination by Hove, Nichols admitted that no casts had been made of the numerous footprints in the basement, but he defended this, saying it would not have been feasible because officers had walked and crawled all over the sandy floor during the digging.

In the afternoon, two muscular detectives marched into the courtroom bearing a mysterious package of irregular shape, four or five feet across and more than a foot thick. They deposited it on a table directly in front of the jury. As Coakley tore away its brown paper covering, he revealed a plaster of Paris model of Abbott's cabin site. On a scale of one inch to ten feet, it bore true-to-size miniatures of the cabin and its outbuildings, with Hayfork Creek to the rear and the mountainside across the road. A tiny reddish depression near the top represented Stephanie's grave, and spongy rubber, dyed green, indicated the manzanita growth around it.

In deepest secrecy, the model had been built by Bill Brockett of the Alameda County Surveyor's office. He had worked on his own time, using materials that cost only $44.70, after a $975 bid from a private firm had been rejected. Clearly this exhibit was Coakley's delight. With its introduction he was at last taking his first step toward the establishment of the corpus delicti.

Caught by surprise, the defense reacted with outrage. Abbott and his lawyers instantly grasped Coakley's purpose—to demolish further their contention that the tubercular defendant was too frail to have dragged or carried Stephanie up that hillside.

To introduce the model, the district attorney called on O. E. Anderson, the county's chief deputy surveyor, who had reconnoitered the site for three days in September, Under a withering cross-examination by Hove, Anderson acknowledged that the hillside's heavy forestation was not shown. Missing too were fallen timber and stumps that would have made climbing difficult. Only the landmark pine near the grave site was represented.

"Were you given instructions to put in that one tree and leave out all the others?" Hove asked.

"Yes, sir."

"And who gave you those instructions?"

"The district attorney." Anderson said the trees were left off so that the contour of the hill could be clearly seen. The grading was precisely accurate, he emphasized.

"Why didn't you show the deer trails on the mountain?" Hove demanded.

"I am not familiar with the deer trails. There are some paths, but many of them seem to start nowhere and end nowhere."

Hove next asked Anderson about the one path clearly indicated on the model, running from cabin to grave: "Do you know if it existed on April 28?"

"I have no knowledge of that."

After the judge rejected a defense motion to bar the use of the model, Whitney moved that the jurors be taken to Trinity County to view the scene for themselves. On the ground, the distance from cabin to grave was 339 feet by way of the trail and the vertical rise was 85.5 feet.

"The slope doesn't look steep on that model," Whitney complained. "Actually it's a darn tough climb, and the first jump from the road up to the slope is about five feet. All we care about is showing the terrific climb up that hill."

The estimated cost of an overnight trip to Trinity County for fifty persons, including Abbott, jailers, judge, and jury, was $1,000.

"Motion denied," Judge Snook said dryly.

During the afternoon recess, Abbott inspected the model at close range. When he returned to the counsel table, wrote Carolyn Anspacher in the *Chronicle,* "his face was almost as gray as his suit."

Having focused the jurors' attention on Stephanie's lonely burial spot, the prosecution now brought before them the man who, with his hounds Shorty and Spot, had discovered it. Harold "Bud" Jackson, by coincidence, shared the nickname of the defendant. Their gazes briefly met as Jackson settled his thin, wiry frame in the witness chair.

When tracking bears and bobcats on his home ground, Jackson usually wore cowboy garb. Today the forty-three-year-old mountain man was attired in a rumpled suit, white shirt, and a necktie of green, yellow, and purple. He chewed gum as he took his seat and made himself comfortable by throwing his left leg over the chair's spindly arm.

Jackson's story was known by now to most persons in Northern California, but it took on new reality as he told it in his backwoods twang. In the cabin basement, he said, "the dogs picked up the scent and crossed the road to the left and went up the hill into the manzanita." Soon thereafter "the black dog," Shorty, returned and led the way up to the grave where Spot was standing guard. Jackson could see bits of Stephanie's clothing exposed.

"When I saw those clothes sticking out of the dirt, I hollered to the rest of the party to come up there," Jackson recalled. At this point he walked to the plaster model and placed his finger on the reddish depression near the hilltop.

"I took a shovel and dug down six inches and uncovered a shoe," he continued.

"Did you find anything in the shoe?" asked Emerson, who was conducting the examination.

"Yes." Jackson tapped his own ankle with his forefinger. "It looked as if it was an ankle or a bone."

In further testimony, Jackson identified three shovels from the cabin basement, including the nick-bladed one, which he had used in his exploratory digging. At that time, he said, the red clay of the grave was dried hard and cracked, but it had certainly been very wet when the pit was dug. Jurors cringed as the cat hunter told of the odor of the grave.

Jackson took on the role of an expert witness when questioned by both sides about the habits of Trinity County wildlife, reiterating his judgment that the grave had likely been disturbed by a bear. Although the earth right around the grave had borne no bear tracks, Jackson had noticed some nearby. He believed that an animal about two years old and weighing between 125 and 150 pounds had left them.

Trinity Sheriff Harold Wilson and his deputy, Charles Wyckoff, followed Jackson on the stand.

The latter was a husky man who had done the heavy digging to exhume Stephanie's body. His grim storytelling took the jury back to the wooded hillside on that torrid July morning. He told how the brush had been chopped away to enlarge the grave clearing and how pathologist George Loquvam had labored for three hours under a scorching sun to remove the surrounding dirt with his fingers. Wyckoff identified a clod of red clay taken from Stephanie's right shoulder, bearing strands of her hair and a weave imprint of her blue cardigan.

On cross-examination Hove asked the deputy, "Isn't it possible the condition of the body was altered by the hatchet when the brush was chopped away?"

"No, because the hatchet wasn't used anywhere near the body itself," Wyckoff firmly replied.

With the testimony of Sheriff Wilson and Berkeley officer Willard Hutchins, who followed him, Coakley extended to the grave site the tissue trail that followed the tubercular Abbott everywhere. The two witnesses told of digging two pieces of cleansing tissue from the pack rat's nest forty or fifty feet from Stephanie's crude burial place. A discernible path ran from the grave to the nest, Wilson said.

Were the tissues Burton's? Perhaps the highly anticipated testimony of criminalist Paul Kirk would shed light on that. For the district attorney's purposes at the moment, the implication was enough.

For the three mountain lawmen who had come so far to testify—Jackson, Wilson, and Wyckoff—further adventures were in store that evening. By now the forty-odd members of the trial's largely male press corps had become a close-knit gang. As happens on every big running story, they traded tips, interviewed each other, and dined, drank, and caroused together in off hours. On this night they had a special event planned for the three rustic celebrities from Trinity. A hot attraction then on the San Francisco amusement circuit was Tempest Storm, an abundantly endowed stripper, and she was to appear at a backstage party for the trial's press platoon. The backwoods witnesses were invited.

Forty years later, in his eighties, cat-hunter Jackson still marveled at the "naked topless show" that night. It was not what mountaineers were accustomed to.

"Tempest Storm was there and a whole bunch of gals," he remembered. "I didn't like it at all. It's a wonder they didn't all go to jail. The reporters were in there, a bunch, in the dressing rooms. Some of 'em went back there to get a good picture of Tempest Storm, and they got in a fight with a bouncer, whoever he was. Then they got Harold Wilson and they took a picture of him peekin' in there—Sheriff Wilson, Peeping Tom on Tempest Storm! They didn't put it in the paper, but they said they was goin' to. I come out on the street and got the hell out of there, 'cause I knew that hell was gonna pop pretty soon. We'd all be in jail. A lot of women in there was topless besides Tempest Storm."

One of Coakley's undercover sources, as the trial progressed, was a new Abbott cellmate, a bad-check writer named Cober who had two priors and three holds against him from California to Michigan.

Taking any inmate's information at face value was chancy, of course, because jailbird stool pigeons often concocted their stories to win favor or clemency. However, Cober's reports carried a ring of truth to the night jailer, a deputy named Calvin Wyatt. As fellow ex-marines, Cober and Wyatt shared a bond of confidence. Because of what he was hearing from Cober, Wyatt summoned him to the jail dispensary on some pretext, to be interviewed secretly by Deputy D.A. William Sharon.

"I'm convinced Abbott is guilty," Cober told Sharon. In their cell he had led Abbott into theorizing about Stephanie's murder, and with the slips of the tongue to which Burton was prone, he had often trapped himself.

"How could that girl have been grabbed in broad daylight, at a place like the Claremont, without dropping her books or causing a scene?" Cober had asked. Burton had come up with a ready scenario:

"Well, whoever did it could have caught her eye in that doughnut shop a few times, so that she would recognize him. Then he could have waited for her, and when she approached he could have gotten out of his car, maybe with some college books of his own, and offered to take her home, saying he was going in that general direction."

"Well, why would she have gotten into the backseat of his car?"

"He could have suggested that if her mother saw her in the car, she could say that he had taken a whole car full of girls home from the open house at school, and that she was the last of them."

Another time, Cober said, Abbott had shown increased worry as criminalist Kirk's testimony neared. In one slip-up, he had told Cober, "Dr. Kirk can link me to Stephanie."

"Well, how could a person carry Stephanie all the way to Trinity County in his car without being noticed?" Cober had mused. "Would he put her in the trunk?"

Without thinking, Abbott had replied, "I couldn't put her in the trunk. It was full of camping gear."

"Christ, man," Cober warned, "don't say that or you're a gone goose."

"Oh, I was just using that as an example" was Burton's reply.

Abbott's most damaging slip, however, had come just before the testimony of the pathologist, Dr. Loquvam. In a discussion with Cober he had theorized about how the killer might have carried Stephanie to the grave.

"Well," he had said, "he would have to take two trips because the body was in rigor. The body would have to be taken up first, and then the person would have to come back for the shovel."

Up to that time, there had been no public disclosure whatever about Stephanie having been buried in a state of rigor mortis.

24

Hair, Fiber, Dirt, and Blood

For the first time there were empty seats in the courtroom. By noon on Friday, December 2, about half of the spectators had left, having sickened as pathologist George Loquvam took Stephanie Bryan's death clothing, item by item, from a cardboard box. An overpowering stench of decay, scarcely dissipated in the months since the girl's disinterment, spread heavily across the room.

Bits of skin still clung to the garments. Loquvam carefully unfolded Stephanie's panties and held them before the jury, pointing to the knot with which the murderer had bound them around her neck. Abbott's face seemed to crumple at the ghastly display—but it was a reaction shared by all present, especially the jurors.

The testimony of Loquvam, an intense man with dark shadows beneath his eyes, was horribly graphic, as he twisted his own limbs to show the position of Stephanie's contorted corpse in its grave. He described the two gaping holes inflicted with a "hard object" in her skull—each between two and three inches in diameter.

"I recovered within the cranial area numerous small bones that could be fitted into the holes like a jigsaw puzzle," the pathologist said. In his opinion the blows to the skull were the primary cause of death. Because the girl's tissue had decomposed into a "glutinous mass," he could not determine whether the knotted panties had strangled her. For the same reason he could not tell whether she had been raped.

Now, and only now, came the first courtroom disclosure of Loquvam's opinion that Stephanie had been dumped into her grave while in a state of rigor mortis—as Abbott had prematurely told his cellmate Cober. Loquvam explained that this muscle stiffening usually occurred about six hours after death and lasted between eighteen and twenty-four hours, after which the tissues became soft again. But in cases of death under great emotional stress, he added, rigor might set in instantly. Stiffened bodies of soldiers were sometimes found holding weapons in firing position or grenades ready to throw. Stephanie's right arm, cocked above her head, suggested to Loquvam that she had died fending off a blow by her killer.

He concluded that she could have been buried within minutes after death but no more than a day thereafter. How long had she been in the ground? At least sixty days, he estimated, judging from the gelatinous adipocere covering her left shoulder; the waxy substance took that long to develop. (Eighty-four days had elapsed between Stephanie's disappearance and her exhumation.)

During cross-examination, Hove thought he saw a chance to revive the "second grave theory," that Stephanie had first been buried for an unspecified period in Marin County.

"Dr. Loquvam," he said, "you have testified your findings are consistent with burial at Wildwood as of April 28. They would also be consistent with burial on May 15, wouldn't they?"

"No," the pathologist declared emphatically, "not when you take into consideration the position of the body, which I am sure was due to rigor. By May the rigor would have completely passed off and the body would have been flaccid."

Hove's try had been bold, but it hadn't worked.

The defense lawyers, aware that the pathologist was a powerful witness, sought to divert the jury from his testimony at every turn. Whitney objected when a hideous picture of Stephanie's decomposed body was offered in evidence.

When Loquvam produced a piece of dried clay removed from Stephanie's thigh, bearing the imprint of her skirt and bits of decayed tissue, Hove objected that it bore no identifying mark.

"How do you identify that clod, Dr. Loquvam?" the judge asked.

"By the looks of it and the smell of it, your honor," the pathologist replied, handing the clod to the jurors, several of whom winced as they passed it from hand to hand.

When Snook's gavel fell that Friday afternoon, finally releasing those present from the courtroom's necrotic miasma, a quiet weekend was foreseen. The lawyers therefore were mystified on Sunday when the judge summoned them to an extraordinary conference in his chambers.

"Gentlemen," Snook announced, "a matter has arisen concerning one of the jurors, Mr. Rettig."

For two weeks Snook had been aware of a possible problem with August Rettig, a sober-faced, thirty-nine-year-old electronics technician. He had received letters from two of Rettig's fellow employees at the Alameda Naval Air Station, apprising him that Rettig worked in close proximity to Burton's brother Mark. Their desks were only twenty-five feet apart.

Upon receipt of the letters, Snook had ordered an investigation by Sheriff Gleason, whose report now lay before him. When interviewed, both of the letter-writers had said Rettig discussed the pending case with them, though without expressing an opinion about it. However, a third employee had quoted Rettig as saying he thought Abbott was being framed.

Snook informed the assembled lawyers of his intention to dismiss Rettig and ordered them to return for a formal hearing on the matter at nine-thirty Monday morning. Stunned, Whitney and Hove phoned Mark Abbott as soon as the conference broke up.

"I don't know the man, never met him, never talked to him," Mark assured them.

Rettig's first inkling of the uproar surrounding him came when he was summoned to Snook's chambers before court convened Monday.

"Do you know Mark Abbott?" the judge asked him.

His answer jibed with Mark's: "I have had no dealings with him. I have never talked to him. I recognized him when he came to court, but up to then I didn't even know who he was."

Nonetheless, in open court Snook announced that "to save Mr. Rettig any embarrassment or criticism, the court has decided to excuse him."

Hove, sensing that he was losing a friendly juror, immediately offered a mistrial motion, which Snook summarily denied. Whitney denounced the juror's dismissal as "arbitrary, contrary to the rights of the defendant, extremely prejudicial, and unfair."

Rettig was replaced on the jury by alternate Edmond T. Harrison, an aircraft mechanic. As he left, Rettig was pursued by reporters: Did he think Abbott was innocent or guilty?

"At present I don't think they have a case against him," the ex-juror replied.

The next witness was Dr. Elmer Shabart, the tall, sad-eyed chief of surgery at Livermore Veterans Hospital. It was he who had removed a lobe of Abbott's tubercular left lung in 1951. Calling him to the stand was a move Coakley would regret before the day's end.

Coakley had two purposes in summoning the doctor: to further undercut the defense contention that Abbott was too sickly to have committed the crime against Stephanie and to picture him as a classic flight-into-custody case.

Under the D.A.'s questioning Shabart told of Abbott's coming to Livermore on May 3, five days after Stephanie vanished, and pleading for additional surgery. Burton had formerly been a rebellious patient, the doctor said, "but on May 3 he appeared almost over-anxious to enter the hospital." Shabart, seeing no need for an operation, had refused to admit him.

At this point the prosecutor introduced U.C. records to show that if Abbott had been hospitalized, he would have lost a full semester's credit. Welcoming admission to Livermore at that time, therefore, was "just part of his guilty conduct," the prosecutor asserted, with a contemputous glance at the defendant.

Coakley next asked Shabart, "Would a person's energy be impaired by the type of surgery Mr. Abbott underwent? Is Burton W. Abbott a respiratory cripple?"

"No," Shabart answered categorically.

Hove opened his cross-examination of the doctor with a disarming question: "Were any of the defendant's back muscles cut when you operated on him?"

Shabart began a highly technical reply, which Hove soon interrupted. "Doctor, can you show me? We have a real live model here. Let's use him."

On cue, Abbott rose from the witness table, stripping to the waist with obvious enjoyment. Dramatically bared was his spindly torso, deeply scarred, with the chest grotesquely caved in.

In the jurors' eyes, the demonstration was enough to offset all the prosecution could say about the defendant's supposedly robust health.

During the trial's first month, Coakley had fallen into the habit of visiting the press room late each afternoon to answer reporters' questions and clue them about his plans for the next day. From these sessions, which were often convivial, he got helpful feedback as well as good press most of the time.

"Sometimes he'd get to talking and maybe one of the reporters had a bottle there," Inspector Ryken remembered much later. "Coakley would have a couple of drinks with the boys, and he would talk and talk and talk. But he was a smart one, you know; he never overdrank."

After joshing with the newsmen, Coakley would head for some favored restaurant with Ryken, Folger Emerson, and sometimes others, and over a predinner cocktail they would consider tactics and strategy, with the district attorney bouncing ideas off his underlings. One such brainstorming session took place now, on the eve of Coakley's plunge into the final, hard-evidence climax to his case.

Waiting in the wings to testify was Edwin Deiss, a scholarly FBI fingerprint expert who had flown in from Washington. The newspapers were agog over his anticipated appearance. Certainly, they suggested, he would confirm Burton's prints on Stephanie's possessions, or hers in his car or cabin.

The D.A. and his dinner companions knew better. The FBI's best efforts had failed to find fingerprints anywhere that established direct contact between the defendant and his alleged victim. For that reason, some of Coakley's men didn't want to put Deiss on the stand at all. Why show the jury a negative result?

Coakley and his men went round and round on this question. The next morning, having slept on it, the prosecutor followed his own instincts and summoned Deiss to testify. In the press seats, reporters had their pencils poised. At the defense table, Abbott appeared anxious. After establishing Deiss's credentials, Coakley showed him Stephanie's red purse.

"Did you find any fingerprints on it?"

"No, sir." Those who had handled the purse the night it was found had apparently done so carefully.

Deiss gave the same clipped reply when asked about the girl's wallet and its contents, her eyeglasses, and her parakeet book. Eight prints had been found on *Sue Barton, Staff Nurse* and eighteen on *Two's Company,* but none could be identified. Stephanie's French book bore several prints matching others lifted from a jar, a piggy bank, and a mirror in her bedroom. But nowhere had Abbott's prints been discovered.

It was not surprising that few relevant prints were recoverable, Deiss testified, considering the time lapse: "A fingerprint is left by sweat from tiny pores on the skin ridges," he explained, and in humid conditions this moisture "tends to migrate, resulting in a smear. Some people, known as nonsecretors, leave no marking at all."

Abbott was visibly relieved when Deiss stepped down. Yet Coakley was content. Had he failed to call the FBI man to the stand, skirting the fingerprint question altogether, Hove and Whitney would have had a field day: Why was he ducking it? What was he hiding? But now the matter had been faced squarely and disposed of. No way remained for the defense to make hay with it.

Since the start of the trial, all had known that the prosecution's climax would be Dr. Kirk's secret accumulation of physical evidence. Coakley had fed the excitement, telling reporters that the criminalist would be the "exclamation point" for his case. Now he began setting the stage for this with a series of preliminary witnesses introducing bits of this evidence—hair from Stephanie's head, yarn from her sweater, soil from her grave, Abbott's muddy garments, boots, and shoes.

Berkeley Police Inspector William Robinson, whose role was to identify soil samples he had collected in Trinity County, proved an unfortunate choice as the first of these introductory witnesses. On cross-examination, Hove made him admit that he had not cleaned his own shoes between the cabin and the grave, the clear inference being that he could have tracked "foreign" dirt into Stephanie's burial pit. Hove also extracted an admission that Stephanie's garments, removed at the mortuary at Redding, had been left unguarded overnight in an outbuilding.

Next, for the second time in the jury's presence, Stephanie's pitiful garments were removed from their carton. Pathologist Loquvam had described them earlier in clinical language, but it now fell to the girl's mother to relate them intimately to her child's daily life. Mary Bryan had prepared beforehand for this soul-wrenching duty. Before coming to court she had been shown the garments and had handled them, so that now she could retain her composure.

"I recognize this bra," she said quietly, holding up the lace-trimmed brassiere that the sand of Abbott's basement had yielded. "It is exactly like the one I bought for Stephanie, and she wore it many times."

Mary went on to identify her daughter's navy-blue cardigan, white Orlon sweater, turquoise cotton skirt, bouffant petticoats, tricot slip, shoes, and bobby socks. At last she picked up the panties. "She wore Kayser knitted nylon panties that fitted anyone. She always wore them. I bought them at Magnin's."

Quickly Mary went through the dead girl's books and her purse and wallet, recognizing snapshots of her schoolmates and her little black poodle, Jolie, and the unfinished letter to "Teddy," a girl in Massachusetts named Theodora Bliss.

Finally the mother identified several strands of dark hair, displayed on a cleansing tissue: "I took them from the heavy woolen blanket on Stephanie's bed. They were easy to find."

During Mary's thirteen minutes on the stand, Abbott sat transfixed. His eyes never left her. Whitney and Hove chose not to cross-examine.

At last Professor Paul Kirk, Coakley's promised "exclamation point," entered the courtroom carrying a fat briefcase and a flat package of photo-enlarged microscope slides. The peppery little chemist, wearing a gray tweed suit, clenched a pipe in his teeth whenever possible. At age fifty-three, he was the author of three books and 151 articles in scientific journals. A dozen years earlier, he had helped build the first atomic bomb. On the stand he smiled easily and spoke confidently at a rapid clip. His testimony, which would last five days, began in low key.

Kirk captured the jury's full attention with his first disclosure: that in the fabric of Stephanie's panties he had found thirty of her short, dark eyelashes and eyebrow hairs. They suggested that the undergarment had served as a blindfold before it became a garrote.

Emerson asked the professor next about the facial tissue found in the pack rat's nest near Stephanie's grave. On one piece, he said, he had discovered a brown spot which proved in a benzidine test to be blood. Although the FBI lab had cautioned Coakley that there was little chance of determining the brand of the tissue, Kirk had tackled that problem with some success. Using microscopic technology he had pioneered himself, he had compared the bloodstained tissue with samples of twelve commercial brands and was able to find differences between it and all but the Kleenex sample. By process of elimination, he thus established a strong probability (though not a certainty) that the rat's nest tissue was Kleenex, the brand which had been found in Abbott's car and leather jacket.*

For the second day of Kirk's testimony, would-be spectators began appearing at 5:30 A.M.—the earliest arrivals yet. By the time the courtroom opened, 350 persons were in line for the fifty-seven seats available.

On his first day the professor had presented exhibits visible to the juror's eyes—clay clods, clothing, and Kleenex. Today he would be dealing with what he called the "microscopic debris" of the crime—tiny grains of soil, infinitesimal blood spatters, hairs and fibers that his powerful vacuum cleaner had sucked from Abbott's car.

Emerson, conducting Kirk's examination, showed him three specimens of Stephanie's hair: one from her grave, one from the mortuary table, and one that her mother had recovered from her bed blanket.

"On your microscope slides," Emerson asked the scientist, "have you found any other hairs matching these specimens?"

Yes, Kirk said, two hairs in his sweepings were "completely indistinguishable" from Stephanie's, and six others were "extremely close."

"Where did those hairs come from?"

"From the rear compartment of the Chevrolet."

The professor next testified that the car had also yielded "a fair number" of fabric fibers. Under his 110-power microscope, ten of them matched the wool of Stephanie's cardigan in diameter, color, scale surfaces, and curvature from knitting, although their dark-blue dye had faded somewhat. Eight of the ten matching fibers had been recovered from the Chevy's rear compartment, two from the front. Three white Orlon fibers, matching "precisely" those of Stephanie's pullover sweater, also had been recovered, as had one turquoise fiber matching her skirt.

"What about blood?" Emerson asked.

When Kirk had first examined the Chevrolet, he said, he had found no blood. Later, however, the rear floor mat had been "subjected to a soaking process, using filter paper which would remove blood down deep in the nap." The result was a positive benzidine test, turning the invisible blood spatters bright blue.

"There was a region about two inches in length and an inch and a half wide that showed approximately a dozen such spots on the paper," Kirk testified. "It was a typical blood reaction. The benzidine test was immediate and

---

* Kirk associate Lowell Bradford (who will appear soon in this book in another role) said in 1997 that Kirk's micro and submicro examination techniques were "little known to the legal profession or the press" in 1955, and "consequently the revelation of this new technology in a scenario that had nationwide press coverage had an electrifying effect."

strong." Later a Luminol test causing latent blood to glow in the dark had confirmed the finding.

"Did you find blood anywhere else?"

"Yes, there were some additional small spots to the right of this region in the floor mat, and there were approximately twenty small spots on the back of the front seat, low down, just above the floor."

Why, Emerson wondered aloud, had there been no sign of blood on the floor mat surface?

It was Kirk's belief that the mat had been washed.

After the lunch break the professor presented his most damning evidence. Emerson showed him the boots Abbott had worn to the cabin and a pair of Abbott's brown oxfords. Inside the latter Kirk had found sand, and from between the heel and sole of each boot he had recovered coarse sand, subsurface clay, and surface soil.

"Were you able to draw any opinion from studying these deposits?" Emerson asked.

"Yes, the soil on the inside of the oxfords was identical with the basement sand at 1408 San Jose Avenue in Alameda."

After a pause, to let these words sink in, Kirk continued, "There was the further opinion that the soil from the left and right boots was identical to the subsoil from the edge of Stephanie's grave at approximately the nine-inch level."

How had Kirk determined this?

Explaining, he told the jury that soil in the cabin area varied widely. That of the hillside was much different from that near the cabin or in the creek behind it. Kirk had therefore gathered forty-six dirt samples from the vicinity, to be compared with the specimens from Abbott's shoes and boots and Stephanie's saddle shoes. The comparisons had been made by the density gradient technique—a method developed several years earlier by Kirk himself. It involved filling several test tubes with eight layers of fluids having progressively lighter densities (much as a skilled bartender would pour a poussecafé, with layers of varicolored liqueurs in a glass). When bits of soil were dropped into the test tubes, each sank to the level at which the liquid equaled its own density. The sand from Abbott's oxfords, the professor said, had fallen to precisely the same level as a sample from his basement floor. Likewise, the soil from his boot soles matched a specimen from the nine-inch level of the grave.

On that incriminating note Kirk stepped down, smiling tightly, and court adjourned for the afternoon.

Abbott, whose demeanor often betrayed his inner storms, seemed oblivious to the fact that the day had been a disaster for him. He joked with the bailiff and told reporters, "I feel fine!" Had he lost touch with reality or was he putting on an act?

Certainly the working press grasped the ominous import of Kirk's testimony. "Burton W. Abbott was nudged a step closer to the gas chamber yesterday," wrote the usually cautious George Draper in the *Chronicle,* under an eight-column banner proclaiming:

'ABBOTT AT GRAVE
. . . GIRL IN HIS CAR'

Whatever Burton might have been feeling, his lawyers were in shock. Whitney and Hove were untrained and unready to cope with the scientific discourse. In vain they moved to strike Kirk's testimony from the record on the ground that back in July, Abbott's Chevrolet had been inspected and seized without a warrant. The judge held that none had been needed, however, because of the written permission Burton and Georgia had given for the search. Moreover, Whitney himself had been there that day and helpfully backed the car into a better position to be photographed by the police. He had told Berkeley Officer Richard Young, "We have no reason not to be cooperative. We have an innocent man."

The defense attorneys also struck out when they asked Snook for a four-day recess to prepare to cross-examine Kirk. He gave them half a day. The following afternoon Hove drew on his FBI training in a brave cross-examination effort to weaken the impact of the professor's testimony, but with limited success. He managed to establish that a number of substances—copper, cobalt, dried beef, fish, tincture of iodine, asparagus, carrots, dandelion roots, potatoes, and citrus, to name a few—sometimes yielded "false positive" reactions to the benzidine or Luminol tests. However, Kirk insisted, their degree of positivity differed markedly.

"In the case of the floor mat, I feel quite certain the tests indicated blood—not potato juice or anything else," the scientist declared.

"From your tests, can you tell positively whether the blood was that of Stephanie Bryan?" Hove asked.

"No, I certainly cannot," Kirk acknowledged. "As a matter of fact, there is no technique by which that can be done at present—although I'm working on one." (DNA testing would accomplish that goal years later.)

At one point Hove appeared to have undercut the prosecution's case by making Kirk admit that his hair evidence did not "definitely and positively" identify either Burton or Stephanie in the way that fingerprints could have. Two substantially identical hairs could come from different heads.

However, upon redirect examination by Emerson, Kirk said the hairs from Abbott's car matched Stephanie's as to six different characteristics: color, scale, diameter, pigment distribution, density, and refractive index. Each match increased the chance of a correct identification.

Emerson then asked, "Doctor, can you estimate the odds?"

"As a minimum estimate," Kirk said, "the chances are 125,000 to one that my identification is correct."

Emerson paused momentarily to let Kirk's declaration register. Then, to the judge, he said: "Your honor, the prosecution rests."

No one had followed Kirk's testimony with more fascination than Lowell Bradford forty miles to the south. He was the young criminalist for Santa Clara County, and a few years earlier Kirk had been his professor at U.C. Bradford still regarded Kirk as his mentor. He was more than a little amused by the defense's evident consternation in the face of his old prof's discoveries.

Two days after Kirk had left the stand, the phone rang in Bradford's basement lab at Santa Clara County Hospital.

"This is Stanley Whitney," the caller announced. "Can you do a consulting job for us?"

25

Perry Mason Revisited

Whitney and Hove opened their case on December 13 with a scene from Perry Mason, not just figuratively but almost literally—for it was crafted by Erle Stanley Gardner, Perry's creator.

Seated in the courtroom press section, Gardner represented the *Examiner,* which had retained him for background stories. But like Ed Montgomery and several other reporters, he had crossed the line between observer and player in the Burton Abbott drama.

The defense presentation began with a grizzled sea captain in the witness chair. This goateed ancient mariner was sworn in as Walter Raleigh Bethel—his real name, as far as anyone knew. But he had used many names, one of which had already come up briefly in the Abbott investigation.

Four months had elapsed since the curious keep-your-chin-up letter had arrived for Abbott at the jail, signed "Arnott J. Williams" on stationery of "World-War Veterans Welfare and Service (ALLA)," telling Burton that a noted criminologist was interested in his case. Williams had suggested he would be heard from again but had made no follow-up contact.

Burton had turned the letter over to his lawyers, and in their efforts to track down its writer, they had shown it to an *Examiner* reporter. Three months passed, and then, just as the trial was getting under way, the newspaper had run a tantalizing story headed:

LONG MISSING WITNESS FOR ABBOTT FOUND

Located by Gardner With Help
Of Examiner Reporter

Alongside the story was a photo of the mystery witness with his back to the camera, surveying the car struggle site near the tunnel. The *Examiner* explained that it could not name the man yet, because he was currently dodging process servers. However, Erle Stanley Gardner had found him "in an East Bay city," and he had "turned himself in to the defense lawyers at a prearranged rendezvous." He was supposedly prepared to refute key testimony upon which Abbott's indictment was based.

"We feel he is a very credible and reliable witness," Whitney claimed in the article. The *Examiner* promised to name the man within two weeks.

It did so in an interview on November 30. Walter Raleigh Bethel, now pictured full face, related that on the afternoon of Stephanie's disappearance he had been driving behind the so-called struggle car on Mt. Diablo Boulevard. It had suddenly veered, he said, forcing him off the road, and he had come to a stop a few feet behind it. Bethel claimed he had observed the driver and the female passenger at close range for three or four minutes, and there had been no altercation at all, just "a friendly hair mussing." The gaunt seafarer promised that when he got to court he would identify the driver.

In a signed story the following day, Gardner disclosed that he and "Captain Bethel" were old comrades from a bygone time when both had written detective fiction for pulp magazines at three cents a word. During Prohibition Bethel had "enjoyed a certain elevated social status because of his seafaring opportunities in regard to uncut whiskey." Soon after Abbott's arrest, Gardner had received a letter from his nautical chum, telling of the Mt. Diablo Boulevard incident and imploring him to investigate.

"The main thing," Gardner emphasized, "is that Bethel insists the man driving the car was not Bud Abbott. He certainly promises a highly dramatic scene in the courtroom."

Now that scene was about to be acted out.

Hove's first questions to Bethel were intended to establish him as a person of substance, authority, and credibility—not easy to do.

"How old are you, sir?"

"About seventy."

"And you are a licensed Merchant Marine officer?"

"I am licensed to sail vessels of any tonnage on any ocean."

In his ensuing testimony the old skipper failed to name the scuffle car driver as he had promised. But he insisted that the automobile was a Pontiac, not a Chevrolet, and that he had seen the man's face clearly.

"Can you describe that face?" Hove asked.

"About the same as yours."

Laughter rippled across the courtroom, for Hove's blunt features were as different as imaginable from Burton's. Hove asked Abbott to stand and, turning to Bethel, he asked, "Did the driver resemble the defendant?"

"No, sir!"

Bethel went on to describe the driver as "an older and heavier man" in a brown-and-gray checked sport coat.

"How you fix the date as April 28?" Hove inquired.

Bethel said he had been returning from the errand of paying his dues to the Steamfitters Union in Oakland.

Emerson was more than ready to cross-examine the old skipper, whom he recognized as a longtime East Bay character with a thick police file and many aliases. Sometimes Bethel accorded himself the military rank of colonel. His rap sheet went back to 1931, when he had been charged with drunken driving and drawing a gun on a cop. There were at least three later alcohol violations and a $10 fine for cavorting on a public beach with a "partially nude woman." Other accusations included impersonating a U.S. marshal and an FBI agent, libel and slander of his ex-wife, and attempted blackmail of a congressman.

During the Depression-ridden 1930s Bethel had fluttered on the fringes of politics, serving a term as a Democratic county committeeman and running twice for the Oakland City Council. In the same era he had been involved with "Ham and Eggs for California," a pie-in-the-sky pension scheme touted by political charlatans. With the approach of World War II, he had joined the fascist, anti-Semitic Silver Shirts organization of William Dudley Pelley, and about ten days after Pearl Harbor he had taken command of the Silver Shirts in San Francisco. Publicly he listed himself as an "engineer, author, and editor" with five years of college and two of postgraduate law, but his credit file showed high school only.

In short, Whitney's "very credible and reliable witness" was a known con artist with the hokum instincts of Phineas T. Barnum.

"What other names do you use?" was Emerson's first question to him. "Did you ever use the name of Sam O. Betts?"

"Only in writing."

Emerson asked Bethel to recall a visit two Berkeley police inspectors had paid him on November 28: "You denied you were Walter Bethel then, didn't you?"

"I'd been instructed by Mr. Whitney not to talk about this case."

"You told the officers your name was Sam Betts, and that Walter Bethel was in Texas, didn't you?"

"Yes, I guess I might have. I told them a lot of things. I didn't tell them the truth about much of anything."

"Have you ever used the name of Arnott J. Williams?"

"He's a Kentucky colonel. I was mixed up with him." Bethel said both he and "Williams" used P.O. Box 1146 in Richmond—the return address on the keep-your-chin-up letter Abbott had received.

By the time the old sailor left the stand, Abbott's agonized lawyers knew Erle Stanley Gardner's "discovery" had turned into a disaster for them.

Hove did not have much better luck with two other witnesses he called that day to impeach the prosecution testimony of typewriter repairman William Russell. Both were waitresses at Pring's Doughnut Shop, where Russell claimed to have seen Abbott just before Stephanie's disappearance.

The first of the two was Elmyra Mills, who had known both Russell and Abbott as customers. From her, Hove coaxed a statement that she didn't remember seeing Abbott in the shop on the crucial afternoon.

Coakley made short work of Mrs. Mills on cross-examination: "When you say you don't remember seeing Abbott on April 28, you mean he either might or might not have been there, is that right?"

"Yes." The one-word answer corroborated Russell's testimony as much as impeached it.

"Isn't it true," Coakley prodded, "that you told me on November 8 that to the best of your memory Abbott *was* in the shop between 3:15 and 3:45 on the afternoon in question?"

"I could have said that," the flustered witness admitted.

The second waitress, La Verne Malloy, gave equally shaky testimony. As for April 28, she had no specific recollection at all.

Next Cyril Smith, Burton's police sergeant uncle from Stockton, took the stand. He was a member of Stockton's inner circle, at the time the exalted ruler of the Elks lodge there. In his dark-blue suit he was physically impressive: tall and stalwart, with graying hair, piercing eyes, and gold-rimmed glasses. As we know, Cy Smith had been a second father to Burton, and under Hove's questioning, he scored a strong point for his nephew.

Five days before Stephanie had vanished, he testified, Burton had invited him to come along on the fishing trip to Wildwood. So obviously the trip had been well planned and was no last-minute flight from the law. The invitation had been extended, Smith said, while the Smiths were visiting the Abbotts in Alameda on April 23, and he had later "made arrangements" to take the trip but they had fallen through. This disclosure took Coakley by surprise, and he battled to keep it out of the record, but too late; the jury had already heard it.

Smith also remembered that during the April 23 visit, he had seen his nephew enter the sandy-floored portion of his basement to obtain some wooden blocks stored there. With this testimony, the defense sought to defuse Kirk's discovery of cellar sand in Burton's shoes.

––––––––

For their next witness, Whitney and Hove had two possibilities, either of whom purportedly could place Stephanie in the company of men other than Abbott on the night she vanished. One of them was Leonora Bowden, the Oakland landlady who had told of renting a cheap apartment to a teenage girl and her sailor "husband" that evening. Mrs. Bowden itched for the glitz and renown of a witness-stand debut. "I want to provide the climax that will blow the case wide open," she had told a reporter.

The alternative available witness was Charles Munds, the San Pablo fruit stand operator who said he had sold cigarettes on the night in question to two Mexicans accompanied by a "black-headed" Caucasian girl in a battered jalopy.

Which of the two, Mrs. Bowden or Munds, would the defense use? The dilemma was that although either might divert suspicion from Abbott, they canceled each other out. Stephanie could not have been in Oakland with a sailor and in San Pablo with two Mexicans at the same hour. Whitney and Hove could call one witness or the other, not both. They chose Munds, leaving Mrs. Bowden frustrated and furious.

Munds was a wiry, gray-eyed man of middle age who told his story in a country drawl. He said he had seen the girl with the Mexicans a little before nine o'clock, at which time Stephanie had been missing about five hours. Hove showed him Stephanie's picture and asked, "Does that resemble the face you saw?"

"Yes, sir, that's the face," the fruit seller declared emphatically.

Hove ordered his client to stand.

"Was the defendant one of the two men in the car?" he asked Munds.

"No, I never seen him."

"Did you notice anything further?"

"One thing, the girl was sitting in the car between the men, looking right straight ahead. She never made a move. Looked like she was worried."

Taking over on cross-examination, Emerson jumped on this remark: "You never saw anything except the girl's profile, did you?"

"No, that's all I see."

The photo of Stephanie that Munds had previously recognized was a head-on shot. He denied that he had identified her only after seeing the $2,500 reward offer.

Munds could not recall what the girl with the Mexicans had worn. She might have had a hairnet on; he wasn't sure. (Back in May he had called it a scarf.)

Hove sought to mitigate the damage Emerson had inflicted on Munds's credibility by calling to the stand Richard Cox, a tall, brawny truck driver. He had been at Munds's establishment buying a quart of milk when the two men and girl drove up. Unlike Munds, Cox declined to characterize the men as Mexicans, although their skins were dark. But also unlike Munds, Cox said he had caught a good full-face view of the girl, "a very attractive young lady."

"Is this the face you saw?" Hove asked, showing Stephanie's picture again.

"Yes, sir, it is," Cox said. "I'm satisfied in my own mind she was the Bryan girl."

As Munds stepped down Hilda Frakes, the Abbotts' baby-sitter, replaced him and confirmed that on April 28 Burton had left home about 11 A.M. Over Coakley's loud objection, she recalled a tender scene at Abbott's parting with his four-year-old son: "He leaned down to give Chris a kiss goodbye. He put his arms around him and told him to be a good boy. He said he'd bring him back a big fish."

The baby-sitter had next seen Abbott on Tuesday, the second day after his return from Wildwood.

"How did he appear?" Whitney asked her.

"Just the same as on any other morning, just as good-natured and natural as any other time I've seen him."

By coincidence, the witness following Mrs. Frakes was, like Munds preceding her, a produce dealer, but in a much different venue. Robert Wetzel ranged the back roads of Trinity County selling his wares from a refrigerated truck.

On April 28, Wetzel said, his route had taken him past Abbott's cabin twice, at about 9:30 A.M. and between 10 and 11 that night. On the first pass, he said, he had noticed the garage door locked and chained, but on the second it had been ajar. This agreed with Abbott's claim to have reached the cabin about a quarter to nine that night after a brief stop at Del Cox's bar.

Under cross-examination, however, Wetzel acknowledged that on his nighttime trip, he had observed no car, no lights in the cabin, no smoke in the chimney, and no fresh tire tracks in the snow. All this suggested the opposite—that no one was there.*

Of all the stops Burton claimed on his way to Wildwood, the one in the little olive grove town of Corning was possibly the most critical to his alibi. He said he had stopped for gas there between 4 and 5 P.M.—less than an hour after Stephanie was last seen in Berkeley far to the south.

---

* The reader may wonder how a peddler passing in a truck could credibly testify to such small matters. The answer lies in the clannish attitudes of Trinity County at midcentury. The whole sprawling county was essentially one neighborhood, often a dangerous one, in which the neighbors looked out for each other and strangers were suspect. It was natural for Wetzel to observe every person, landmark, and structure on his route. Moreover, Abbott's garage fronted on its narrow dirt road without a foot to spare; its open door would have been a traffic hazard.

Now Whitney called on James Craig, who with his brothers ran the Shell station in Corning, to confirm that part of Burton's timetable. As we know, Craig had journeyed to Oakland in November to view Burton in jail and examine his car. He had failed to recognize either but had remarked that he "might recall" the car's red fan belt.

Whitney now asked him, "What is your best recollection, Mr. Craig, of the number of months between the time you first saw the red fan belt and the time you saw the car with one in the county garage?"

"Around six months, something like that."

"In a period of six months you only saw two red fan belts?"

"So far as I know."

With every question, Craig's answers were becoming fuzzier, but the lawyer plowed on: "You have no idea what date it was that you saw a car with a red fan belt?"

"No."

"Or what time of day?"

"No."

Hardly a help to Abbott's alibi.

Emerson perceived a chance during cross-examination of Craig to show the defense as sneaky and underhanded.

"You visited the defendant in the county jail, did you not?" he asked.

"That is correct."

"What name did you use?"

"I didn't give any name."

"Did you not sign the name of 'J. Crane' in the jail register, Mr. Craig?"

"No."

Whitney, who had supplied the phony name to the jailer, now realized he had been caught in his trickery and sheepishly interrupted to admit "For your information, Mr. Emerson, I did that."

From Corning, Burton said he had continued north to Red Bluff, where he had stopped for supper about six o'clock at a place called the Chuck Wagon. The defense now called Rosa Arnone, who had worked there in April, who would become possibly Burton's strongest witness. Rosa, a trim, bright-eyed brunette of thirty-seven now living in San Leandro, took the stand in a gray outfit and a white hat.

"Mrs. Arnone," Hove asked her, "do you know the defendant, Burton W. Abbott?"

"Yes, I do. He's sitting directly beside you in the blue suit."

"You have seen him before?"

"Yes, at the Chuck Wagon on April 28 at approximately 6:30 in the evening."

A smile lit up Burton's usually cheerless face.

Rosa told her story of his entering the restaurant in blue jeans and a leather jacket and ordering a hamburger.

"Did you have a conversation with Mr. Abbott?"

"Yes. He said something about going fishing in Trinity County, and I think I asked him if he had ever fished in Donner Lake. Then he said something about having a family cabin in Trinity County."

"Was anyone else in the restaurant at the time?"

"Yes, there were four truck drivers in a booth, two men at the end of the counter, and another couple. And the cook, he was sitting at the end, too." (The "cook," as she called him, was Robert Hall, Rosa's boss.)

Folger Emerson's hostile cross-examination of Rosa, calculated to reveal her as a biased witness, set courtroom tempers boiling. He first brought up the brush-off she had given the D.A.'s men at her San Leandro trailer in October.

"In that conversation," he demanded, "did you not say that Mr. Hove had instructed you not to talk to us?"

"He told me not to discuss the case with anyone."

"In that same conversation did you not say, 'You have to be one side or the other in this case, and I am on the defense side?' "

"I might have said that."

"How can you be sure of the date on which you supposedly saw the defendant?"

"I remembered it was the night before my last day at the Chuck Wagon, which was April 29."

To Emerson, this answer meant nothing. *"How* did you remember?" he shouted. *"How, how, how?* Did you go around from April to September saying over and over to yourself that 'I saw Abbott on the day before I quit'?"

At this, Whitney erupted like a volcano. "You have no right to treat the witness like a woman of the streets!" he roared at Emerson.

Judge Snook turned livid, slapped the bench, and ordered, "Stand up, Mr. Whitney." When the defense lawyer did so, the judge cited him for contempt, giving him a choice between a $25 fine or five days in jail at the end of the trial.

The question about the date of Abbott's supposed restaurant visit was further explored when the defense called Hall, the Chuck Wagon proprietor, to corroborate Rosa. It was he who, back in October, had told Officer Hutchins, "I could no more confirm that it was Abbott, or tell you the exact date of that conversation than I could fly like a kite." Now, two months later, Hall backed up his waitress all the way and, glancing at Abbott's picture, announced assuredly, "That's the fellow who was there."

How did he explain his miraculous recovery of perception? By talking with Rosa and consulting payroll records, he said.

Unbelieving, Emerson demanded the records. At first Hove balked, but finally he pulled them from his pocket and handed them over with a sardonic "There you are, sir, and a Merry Christmas."

From the Chuck Wagon, Abbott claimed to have headed west toward Wildwood on Highway 36, crossing the South Fork of Cottonwood Creek between 7:00 and 7:30 on a bridge then being rebuilt. To substantiate this, his lawyers now summoned Richard McNees, who, like Rosa Arnone, had been courted by both sides but had cast his lot with the defense.

Since April, when he had been a workman on the bridge, McNees's status had changed; he now wore the uniform of a soldier. Wrote George Draper in the *Chronicle,* "Pvt. McNees, who vaguely resembles Marlon Brando, settled himself on the witness stand with a surly air and appeared ready to do battle with all comers." He began by telling how, during the Cottonwood job, he had lived with his wife and baby in a cabin 150 feet downstream from the bridge.

"Did you observe any particular automobile on the evening of April 28," Hove asked him.

"Yes, my wife and I were crossing the bridge in the rain about 7:30 when a car slowed down and came to a stop on the approach from Red Bluff. I waved the car on."

"Did you have anything in your hand when you waved it on?"

"I had the baby's diapers in my hand."

Hove showed McNees a photo of Abbott's 1949 Chevrolet. "Is this similar to the car you saw?" he asked.

"Yes, it is." Like Abbott's auto, McNees noted, the car he waved across the bridge had a sun visor.

As we have noted, Abbott's Cottonwood bridge crossing was a detail of his alibi that held a curious, consistent fascination for Coakley. At this point, however, the D.A. left the cross-examination of the soldier to Emerson, who pounced at once. "Well, Mr. McNees, there's been quite a change in your story since you talked to the FBI."

Emerson forced McNees to admit that when interviewed in July, he could neither remember Abbott's car nor identify his picture. Nor could he then recall anything special about April 28.

Asked next about his hostile reception of Inspector Severin later in Hermosa Beach, McNees confirmed that Hove and Whitney had admonished him to tell the prosecution nothing—as they had with Rosa Arnone.

"Mr. Severin tried to serve you with a subpoena, didn't he?" Emerson asked.

"He gave me a piece of paper, but I didn't know what it was and put it back in his car."

"You mean you crumpled it up and threw it into his automobile, didn't you?"

"I did," McNees said, with defiant pride showing.

The soldier's young wife, Alice McNees, followed him on the stand. In the main she duplicated his testimony, also recalling a car with a sun visor.

In Hermosa Beach Alice had been far more cooperative than her husband, although obviously under his thumb. Emerson reciprocated now, speaking softly as he questioned her. Had she not told Severin she was sorry about signing a statement for Hove and Whitney?

"I don't remember, sir."

"But you didn't tell Captain Severin anything you had said in your statement, did you?"

"I didn't think I should."

"Why not?"

"Because I was told not to."

"By whom?"

"By Mr. Hove and Mr. Whitney."

"Let me ask you just this question, Mrs. McNees: Isn't it true that when you talked to Captain Severin, you couldn't describe the car, couldn't state what color it was, didn't think it had a visor, and remembered only that the windshield wipers were going?" (Emerson took his phrasing, word for word, from Severin's report, which lay on the table before him.)

Alice considered the question momentarily before responding with obvious unease, "I told him that I knew the windshield wipers were going, and I didn't tell him anything else."

"All right, Mrs. McNees, that's all." Emerson said, and the soldier's wife stepped down.

For days the press had been in a ferment as the word got around that Whitney and Hove had retained their own criminalist, Lowell Bradford, to challenge the world-famous Dr. Kirk. Would Bradford be able to overcome the damning physical evidence Kirk had developed? The reporters exploring this tantalizing question, however, were not privy to certain events transpiring offstage.

Whitney's initial phone call to Bradford in San Jose had been an S.O.S. He and Hove had been caught totally unequipped to deal with Kirk's brilliant exposition on blood, fiber, hair, and soil. Not that they could be blamed; they were lawyers, not scientists.

Their proposal to hire Bradford placed him on an uncomfortable spot.

Under his contract with Santa Clara County, he was permitted to take consulting jobs on the side if they did not create conflicts of interest. But working for the Abbott defense would be sensitive because Bradford's boss, Santa Clara County D.A. Napoleon Menard, was Coakley's counterpart, and the two prosecutors were friends.

"It would be a conflict of interest for me to work for you unless Nap Menard authorizes it," Bradford informed Whitney.

A lot of telephoning between Alameda, San Jose, and Oakland ensued. Whitney called Menard. Menard called Bradford. Then Menard called Coakley, asking "How do you feel about this?"

"Well," Coakley said after some thought, "they're going to get somebody to examine the evidence sooner or later, and we know there are a lot of charlatans around. Really we'll be better off if they get somebody who will give straight answers. Go ahead and have your man do it."

"So I went up to the cabin," Bradford related much later. "I took my own soil samples from the grave and various places near there—something like twenty samples altogether. I put them through the soil density sedimentation process—which Kirk had taught me—and I confirmed his work right down to the last decimal place."

It was the same with Kirk's hair and fiber analyses. Bradford caught no mistakes by his ex-professor.

With the courtroom showdown on the physical evidence at hand, Bradford sat down with Hove and Whitney to talk about his findings.

"Don't call me as a witness, because it's going to backfire," he warned them at the outset. "If I have to go down the list of everything I've done, it will confirm everything Paul Kirk did."

Like Kirk, Bradford had detected a slight difference in color between the soil specimen from the grave and that from Abbott's boots, the grave soil being redder. But, also like Kirk, he did not consider the variation meaningful—certainly not sufficient to offset the sedimentation evidence. The color difference could be due to stain material from the boot or to a trace of oil or floor wax.

Under the microscope Bradford also had found some "little dots" of dark color, unmentioned by Kirk, on one of the hairs recovered from Burton's car. There was no such discoloration on the specimens from Stephanie's head. But again, it was a picky difference that Bradford did not think significant. Overall, he considered his findings weak stuff to put before the jury. Not only weak, but dangerous. But the impetuous Hove turned a deaf ear to the warning and decided to go for broke.

"Well, we have these differences and I want you to expound on them," he instructed Bradford. In Hove's view any deviation at all, no matter how insignificant, was better than none.

A flashbulb barrage nearly blinded Bradford as he entered the courtroom. Despite misgivings, he projected confidence and modesty as he seated himself in the witness chair, and at first his testimony went well. More than Kirk, he emphasized the color variation between the grave and boot soils, adding a new fact: He had run tests showing the boot sample to be blood-free.

Bradford also described the dark particles of foreign matter his microscope had found on the hair from Abbott's car. He showed the jury a blown-up view of the slide in full color.

"Is it possible to come to an absolute, personalized identification of hair?" Hove asked.

"I don't know of any way that hair can be individualized," Bradford replied—essentially what Kirk had said.

"What about Professor Kirk's estimate that the chances are 125,000 to one that the disputed hair is from Stephanie's head?"

"I could not make such a calculation myself."

Bradford next took up the fiber evidence. In Abbott's fly-tying kit, he revealed, he had found a blue fiber "indistinguishable" from those of Stephanie's cardigan sweater. He also had recovered a matching blue fiber from Mark Abbott's car. He thus undermined Kirk's opinion that the sweater had to be the source of the ten blue fibers found in Abbott's Chevrolet. There were numerous sources of such fibers in his family environment, he said; they could have come from anywhere.

So far so good. If Bradford's first day on the stand had failed to nullify his old prof's findings, it at least had raised some significant questions for the jury to ponder. Bradford knew, however, that he was not yet out of the woods. On the morrow, he would have to duel with the brilliant Folger Emerson.

"Oh, Emerson was sharp!" Bradford told the author in 1994. "It was interesting to watch his cross-examination develop. When he started out, he was afraid I was going to trap him somewhere, because in those days there was a lot of cat-and-mouse play between technical witnesses and attorneys. He was walking on needles. Then, the more he began to get affirmative answers out of me, the deeper he would go. And finally he popped the key question— *exactly what I told Whitney was going to happen.*"

Eight lines of the trial transcript tell the story about that:

Q. [by Emerson].. You are familiar with his [Kirk's] findings in this case, are you not?

A. I think that I am, yes.

Q. Now is it not a fact, Mr. Bradford, that with respect to the physical evidence in this case, there is *no disagreement* between your findings
and those of Dr. Kirk except in the instance of one hair which has the
black spots on it, which you showed us in the picture?

A. *I think that is precisely correct, yes.*

With those words from Bradford's lips, the reporters went wild, scrambling
madly from the courtroom to file their stories.

26

Burton Abbott and Sigmund Freud

Now the defense lawyers took their boldest gamble. Addressing the court, Hove said, "Call Burton W. Abbott to the stand."

A gasp went up as Abbott, wearing his well-pressed blue suit, walked forward, raised his hand, and swore before God to tell the truth.

At first he spoke so softly that Hove had to admonish him to speak up. However, as Carolyn Anspacher would write in the *Chronicle,* the former drama student "immediately appeared the expert performer, certain of his lines, up on his cues, polished in his technique." Hove's first questions were contrived to elicit his explicit denial of every aspect of the crimes charged.

"I will show you People's Exhibit 12, which is a red purse," the lawyer said, "and I will ask you if you had ever seen that purse at any time prior to the night of July 15?"

Burton took the purse in his hands and examined it for several seconds.

"No," he said.

Staring straight ahead, the defendant repeated his unadorned one-word denial twenty-seven times as Hove produced other key exhibits and fired more questions:

- "Did you bury those glasses in your basement?"
- "Did you bury those books in your basement?"
- "Have you at any time had those books in your automobile?"
- "Has that brassiere has ever been in your possession?"
- "Did you take that brassiere off the body of Stephanie Bryan?"
- "Were you in Berkeley at any time on April 28?"
- "Was Stephanie Bryan ever in your car?"
- "Did you at any time take Stephanie Bryan to your cabin?"
- "Did you murder or kidnap Stephanie Bryan?"
- "Did you at any time bury Stephanie Bryan's body up on the hill?"

Finally Hove handed his client a grisly color photo of Stephanie's rotted corpse being exhumed from her grave.

"I will ask you," he shouted, "did you do this horrible crime to Stephanie Bryan?"

One last time Abbott answered, without emotion, "No."

Next he retold his well-known version of his April trek to Trinity. Emphatically he insisted that he had made the journey alone. In his recitation he had to deal with his previously admitted lie to the police about stopping in Sacramento, so he tried to pass it off now as a piddling thing, almost comical. "I went to Sacramento to go to the state land office and find out about a cabin site for my brother. I couldn't find the land office; so I became disgusted and left. I didn't stop. I'm afraid I told the Berkeley police I did, but I didn't."

"Why did you tell them that?" Hove asked.

"Because I had already given Mark the false story," Burton said. "I didn't want my brother to know I had fibbed."

At this point Coakley took over for what all knew would be a merciless cross-examination. The decision of Abbott's lawyers to have him testify had opened for the prosecutor a cornucopia of opportunity. Suddenly Burton was fair game for questions that otherwise might never have been asked or answered.

His attorneys had drilled him for hours the night before. "Give straight answers. Be humble," they had instructed again and again. Four decades later John Hanson, the last surviving lawyer of his team, sadly recalled, "He said yes, yes—and then he did everything opposite in the first hour."

From the start Coakley was bent on showing the defendant to be a habitual liar. Assuredly he was not going to let Burton get away with his light-hearted explanation of his "fibbing" about Sacramento. Had he gone to Sacramento at all? Coakley doubted it.

The D.A. now produced the diagram Abbott had drawn in July for FBI agent Hallahan—the hastily faked sketch purporting to show the interior layout of the Sacramento land office.

"Is this the picture you drew?" Coakley inquired.

"I don't know—*sir.*"

"What do you mean you don't know?"

"It doesn't have my signature on it—*sir.*"

Abbott's repetitive, patronizing use of the appended "sir" betrayed his intense personal hatred of the district attorney. Coakley repeated his question, and as he did so, the composure that the defendant had so far maintained deserted him.

"It looks like my picture, but I wouldn't trust our law officers as far as I can throw them right now!" Burton hissed. Coakley's florid face reddened deeper.

"And you say that, sir, after all the United States Government has done for you?" he shouted at the witness. Whitney and Hove loudly objected, and the remark was stricken.

Burton admitted trying to deceive Hallahan by drawing a diagram of the San Francisco land office, which he actually had visited once, rather than the one in Sacramento.

"Yes, I was compounding the prevarication," he whimpered, "and I have gone ahead and told you I prevaricated on three occasions, and you continue to badger me about it!"

Whether his euphemism was "fib" or "prevaricate," Burton seemingly could not let himself admit a deliberate "lie."

Using early interrogation transcripts, Coakley showed the jury that Burton had not, as he now claimed, corrected his misstatements about Sacramento at the first opportunity. His original lie to the FBI had been not only repeated but elaborated when he went before Coakley later that night. Not until the next afternoon, after conferring with Whitney, had he confessed that he had never visited the Sacramento land office at all.

Abbott's memory blanked out again when Coakley asked him about landmarks on the road by which he claimed to have entered Sacramento. He could not recall, for example, the approach to the State Capitol. This was a significant lapse, for the highway entered the city over an impressive bridge across the Sacramento River, with the Capitol dome looming straight ahead.

Coakley's interrogative style was marked by sudden changes of pace, as Abbott had learned when arrested. Now he encountered this trait again as the district attorney asked him without warning, "On what date were you inducted into the army?"

Abbott couldn't remember, other than that it was in late October 1947.

"Don't you know it was just two days before the G.I. Bill expired?" The question's obvious intent was to portray Abbott as a leech on the government, and both Whitney and Hove jumped up again objecting. When Judge Snook ordered them to speak one at a time, Whitney glared at Coakley and replied, "It takes two of us to shut him up!"

Abbott also pleaded loss of memory about where the army had inducted him—was it Oakland or San Francisco?—and whether he had been processed at Camp Beale, a huge post north of Sacramento. All he remembered, he said, was going somewhere on a bus.

"Did you attend college in 1946?" Coakley asked.

"To the best of my knowledge, no," was Abbott's reply.

"What was the date you entered college?"

"I don't know the precise date—*sir.*"

Coakley produced an army qualification card bearing Burton's signature, purporting to show that in 1946 he had taken university courses in chemistry, physics, and accounting. Actually, he had not entered the university until 1949, more than a year after his army discharge. Although he now admitted signing the card, he denied that he had personally written the misleading entries.

Sparring with the district attorney, Abbott seemed to be enjoying himself. But how was this playing with the jury?

On another form Burton claimed to have been a lieutenant in the junior ROTC at Oakland's Fremont High School.

"Did you fill out that form?" Coakley demanded.

"I just don't recall—*sir.*"

"Can't you tell us whether you did or didn't—not this 'I don't know' stuff all the time? Were you in the junior ROTC?"

"I don't remember—*sir.*"

Coakley turned again to a transcript of his own first interview with Abbott, in which he had identified himself as a U.C. graduate student although he was actually an undergraduate, a junior. From the witness stand Abbott denied he had ever made such a claim, implicitly accusing Coakley of doctoring the transcript.

It was a bad moment for Abbott, and Whitney tried to dampen its impact by demanding exactly when the contested statement had been made.

"It was July 16," Coakley shot back. "That was the night you threw the ashtray at the photographer, remember?"

Another abrupt shift now: "How often have you traveled Franklin Canyon Road?"

"I don't know," Abbott said. Nor would he give an estimate of the time at which he had traveled that road, convoy-style behind his brother, on their return from the cabin May 1. (Mark Abbott had already established the time as about 6 P.M.)

"Do you know where Tank Farm Hill is located?"

"No, *sir.*"

"You don't know?"

"I don't know it as Tank Farm Hill—*sir.*"

To Coakley this rang false, for FBI reports of Abbott's early grilling mentioned the landmark hill by name.

"Well, did you or didn't you buy gasoline on May 2 at a gas station on Tank Farm Hill?"

"I purchased gas on May 2 at a Standard service station on San Pablo Avenue."

"Where were you going?"

"I was looking for tires—*sir.*" Abbott said he had stopped at seven or eight wrecking yards but could not remember their names.

Mindful of earlier testimony that Abbott was broke when he returned from the cabin, Coakley asked, "What were you going to use for money?"

"The legal currency—*sir.*"

"Isn't it a fact," the infuriated prosecutor roared, "that the reason you went out to Tank Farm Hill on May 2 was not to buy tires, but to look for Stephanie's textbook, which you had thrown from your car in Franklin Canyon on May 1?"

"No, that is not a fact," Abbott answered firmly.

For his next day of cross-examination, Abbott arrived looking fatigued. His thin hands dangled limply from the arms of the witness chair.

"Why did you go to Pring's Doughnut Shop?" was the first question Coakley shot at him, without explanation or preface.

"To get doughnuts—*sir.*" Burton smirked.

Since becoming a suspect, Abbott had given at least two versions of his daily commute to and from the U.C. campus. Both routes were logical, but one passed Pring's and one did not. Coakley now sought to exploit the inconsistency.

"How far is Pring's from Willard Junior High?" he asked.

"About a block."

"As a matter of fact, isn't Pring's on the same side of the street as Willard, just a half-block down Telegraph Avenue?"

"It could be—*sir.*"

"Well, don't you know, Mr. Abbott?" Coakley's voice dripped sarcasm.

At this point, by chance or by intent, Abbott glanced momentarily toward his lawyers, and Coakley instantly challenged, "What are you looking over there for? Are you getting signals?"

Whitney demanded that the remark be stricken, and this time Snook sustained his shouted objection.

Now at last, confronting the accused in front of the jury, the prosecutor imparted the reason for his fixation on Burton's crossing of the Cottonwood Creek bridge on the road into Wildwood. Back in July, while questioning Abbott about his route to the cabin, Coakley had caught what he thought to be a Freudian slip. Speaking of the workmen at the bridge, which had been under repair, Burton had used the phrase "They waved us through."

"*Us*"—the plural pronoun! And yet the heart of Abbott's defense was that he had taken the trip by himself.

"Who were 'us'?" Coakley now demanded.

"I don't know—*sir.*"

"Was Stephanie Bryan in your automobile, or was her body in your automobile at that time?" the D.A. bellowed.

Burton was caught off guard. There were several seconds of silence before her replied, "No, sir. I must have meant my brother and me when we were coming home. We passed the same spot."

Did the jury buy this explanation? No one could tell.

After four arduous days, Abbott was finally excused as a witness. He drooped as he rejoined his lawyers at the defense table.

Had his time on stand served him well or ill? Throughout the trial no reporter had been kinder to him than Carolyn Anspacher in her *Chronicle* color stories. Repeatedly she had remarked on his trim appearance, poise, and courtesy and had chided the district attorney for his lapses into fluster and abuse. But now she wrote:

> In his verbal jousting with Coakley, Abbott appeared to forget that it was a jury of seven men and five women who would ultimately decide whether he was guilty. . . . Neither the jury nor the courtroom spectators found his evasions or sarcastic little gibes entertaining.

Late on Thursday, December 22, Judge Snook wished the jurors "a happy and enjoyable Christmas" and recessed the trial for five days. Abbott took the courthouse elevator five floors upward to begin a dreary holiday weekend with his cellmate, John Cober—the same who was covertly informing the D.A. of much that Burton confided.

Cober had a puckish sense of humor, and on Christmas Eve suggested to Burton, "Let's hang up our stockings!"

Whether Abbott did so we don't know, but Cober left his sock dangling from the corner of his mattress. In it, the next morning, he found a note written on toilet paper:

> *To Whom It May Concern: I hereby bequeath and decree that John Douglas Cober be invited to witness my execution as my Christmas present.*
>   *Burton W. Abbott,*
>   *Christmas, 1955,*
>   *Alameda County Jail.*

27

The Appointment Book

Coakley's rebuttal plan was simple, direct, and brutal: a sledgehammer attack to demolish the defense case piece by piece like a jalopy in a wrecking yard. His first blows were aimed at the old sea dog Walter Raleigh Bethel—Erle Stanley Gardner's friend.

Coakley took aim at the heart of the mariner's testimony, which had contradicted six prosecution witnesses to the vicious car-beating near the Broadway Tunnel. Bethel, claiming to have seen the incident himself at close range, had insisted it was just a "friendly hair-mussing." If anything, he had said, the woman was attacking the man, not the other way around. Moreover, he had described the driver as "an older and heavier man" wearing a checked sport coat, not hunting clothes.

On only one matter had Bethel agreed with the state's witnesses: the time of the incident—about a half hour after Stephanie's disappearance. How had he fixed the date? Easily, he had testified; he had just left the Oakland office of the Steamfitters Union that afternoon, after paying his dues to the secretary.

Now that secretary, Kay Vodopich, took the stand for the district attorney. Did she remember Bethel's visit?

"No," she said, "I did not go to work on April 28. My nephew was having surgery, and I was at the hospital."

"Did Captain Bethel pay his dues that month?"

"Yes, his check for seven dollars came in by mail."

"Who signed it?"

"It was signed 'Arnott J. Williams.' "

There was that phony name again—the same one signed to the strange keep-your-chin-up letter Abbott had received in August. As Miss Vodopich stepped down, Hove and Whitney were painfully aware that she had obliterated whatever credibility their salty old skipper might have had left.*

---

* To be thus publicly discredited was embittering for the old mariner, but it scarcely mattered. A month later he was found dead of a heart attack. In a letter to a friend soon after his testimony, he had written, "I wish I'd kept my big mouth shut. However, Erle Stanley Gardner insisted that I tell it on the stand, and I did. It didn't help me a damn bit, and I don't think it helped Abbott any, but if he is innocent I'm glad, and if not I'd be very glad to take care of him myself."

The next rebuttal witness, Berkeley Officer Hutchins, took aim at Robert Hall, who ran the Chuck Wagon in Red Bluff and had backed up Abbott's story of stopping there about 6:30 P.M. on April 28. Hutchins had interviewed Hall in October, and the transcript quoted him as saying then that Burton had entered the restaurant "after sunset." On the day in question, sunset was at 8:01, with twilight lingering one hour and forty-three minutes thereafter. This could have given Abbott as much as six hours to have covered the 244 miles between Berkeley and Red Bluff after Stephanie was last seen at four o'clock.

Hutchins also heaped doubt on the testimony of San Pablo produce dealer Charles Munds, who had told of a girl visiting his fruit stand with "two Mexicans" the night she vanished. The officer affirmed what Munds had denied: that he had been unable to identify the girl as Stephanie until he saw her picture on a $2,500 reward poster. Only then had he said, "That is the girl. I'm sure of it."

At the defense table, listening to Hutchins attack his witnesses, Hove felt his anger rising. By the time he was allowed to cross-examine, he was furious—primed to expose Hutchins as a prejudiced, gutter-language cop out to get Abbott by fair means or foul.

"When you showed Hall a picture of Abbott," Hove asked, "did you say 'Can you identify this S.O.B.?' "

"Maybe, in part," Hutchins acknowledged.

"To speak in plainer language, did you say, 'Can you identify this son of a bitch?' "

Again: "Maybe I did, in part."

"Well, just what did you say?"

"I believe I told him, in part, 'Of course the bastard's guilty.' "

Hutchins's repetition of the phrase "in part" was getting under Hove's skin. A wiser lawyer might have sensed that the crafty cop was baiting a trap, but in his rage Hove ignored the crucial courtroom maxim: "Never ask a hostile witness a question unless you know the answer."

"Well, what was the other part?" he demanded.

"I told him we had reports of Abbott molesting other children."

The cat was out of the bag. In that moment Burton Abbott lost one of his few remaining assets—the widespread belief that he had never been in trouble before. Instantly Whitney and Hove demanded that Hutchins's answer be stricken as nonresponsive, and Snook ordered the court reporter to delete the incriminating words—but the jury had heard them. The damage was done.

Forty years later Hutchins still remembered giving the telltale answer: "See, I didn't blurt anything out. This guy Hove pulled it out of me. He just kept pressing and pressing and pressing."

Were it not for Hove's overzealousness, the prosecution could not have even hinted at the sex file on Burton Abbott—the lingerie thefts in Stockton, the little girl who had been offered six new dimes to enter his car, the teenage girl he had tried to pick up in Alameda, the woman stalked in Berkeley.

Coakley next called the officer Abbott despised and feared more than anyone else he had encountered in custody. Burton grew visibly tense as Inspector Riedel approached the chair. The D.A.'s reason for calling him was to clean up some unfinished business.

Riedel was the officer who had administered Burton's polygraph test and later grilled him five more times without the machine. Earlier in the trial Coakley had read into the record five pages from the transcripts of these interrogations, including such accusatory statements by Riedel as "I know you're guilty and you know you're guilty. Tell me why you did it." Upon Whitney's vigorous objection, Judge Snook had ordered such remarks stricken; so now Coakley brought Riedel before the jury in person to put some of this material back into the record. (In his testimony Riedel skirted mention of the lie detector, because polygraph evidence was inadmissible.)

It was once again Hove, bent on demonstrating "third-degree" tactics by Riedel, who ironically gave him his best opening. During his cross-examination Hove referred to the post-midnight grilling of Abbott by several officers after his arrest, and asked, "Didn't you at that time tell him over and over that you thought he was guilty of the murder?"

"No, I told him I *knew* he was," Riedel answered.

Incredibly Hove again seemed not to sense the trouble he was courting. He went over this ground several times, and each time Riedel corrected him, substituting "knew" for "thought."

"Didn't you go into great detail in telling Mr. Abbott about the body, just to upset him?" Hove demanded.

"No. The purpose of telling him was to try to impress upon him the seriousness of the situation and to make him stop laughing and making jokes all night long. That session was terminated when Abbott stood up, after he was told about Stephanie's body and how it was removed from the grave, and said, 'Damn you, O'Meara, where's that ham sandwich you promised me?' "

Inspector O'Meara returned to the stand next to relate a similar exchange with Abbott four days before the body was found. O'Meara had urged Abbott to "be a man" and tell what had happened to the girl, to spare her family anguish. His reply then had been "I don't give a damn about the Bryan family. They mean nothing to me. When do we eat?"

The rebuttal appeared to be running out of steam now. News stories were conjecturing that the state's testimony would end within a day. The courtroom was stunned therefore on January 6 when Coakley summoned the first of three surprise witnesses who would undercut Abbott's alibi more severely than all who had gone before:

"Call Mrs. Alma Stegall."

A large, well-dressed woman in her forties came forward, took the oath, and identified herself as an employee of the state land office in Oakland. Her testimony was plain-spoken and explicit:

Q [by Coakley]. You know who the defendant is in this case, Mrs. Stegall?

A. Yes, that man over there [nodding toward Abbott].

Q. Did you see him on April 28 of 1955?

A. Yes, I talked to him in my office between one and two o'clock in the afternoon—I think it was about 1:30.

Q. Please tell us the circumstances.

A. Well Mrs. Abbott, his wife, had called in to the office in the morning and asked for information about tax-deeded lands in Trinity County. I told her she was talking to the wrong office and that she would have to contact the state land office in Sacramento. I asked her if she wanted me to mail her a form letter we have which tells how to go about acquiring such lands.

She said she would be very glad if I would send it. I put it in an envelope, addressed it to her, and put it on the pile of letters to be mailed. She told me the address, 1408 San Jose Avenue in Alameda.

Q. Then what happened in the afternoon?

A. Well, this man came in. I was the only one in the office at the time. He said his wife had called that morning and that I had promised to mail her a letter about getting lands. He said he would like to pick it up so I went to the mail pile, dug it out, and gave it to him. He took it and left.

Q. And how do you fix the date of April 28, Mrs. Stegall?

A. That was an unusual day for me. I was talking with our district manager in the morning about a transfer. The call from Mrs. Abbott came during that conversation and interrupted it. I have since checked the separation papers [filled out that day] and they are dated April 28.

Q. And how do you know this defendant is the man who came into your office?

A. I picked him out of a lineup of seven men on November 4. He has the same build and the same general appearance. I am reasonably sure he is the man.

Hove, reeling as he launched his cross-examination, asked when Mrs. Stegall had first gone to the district attorney with her story.

On November 2, she said—only five days before the start of the trial. "Why did you wait so long?"

Shortly after Abbott was arrested, Mrs. Stegall said, she had talked the matter over with her boss, and he did not want her to testify. Likewise, her husband had admonished her not to "become involved in this business." She had accepted their counsel at first, but later changed her mind.

Not only did Mrs. Stegall's story challenge Abbott's alibi timetable; suddenly his admitted lie about visiting the Sacramento land office had also been cast in a new light. It appeared Abbott had indeed visited a land office on the afternoon Stephanie vanished. But if guilty he could not acknowledge doing so in Oakland; so he had moved the locale to the state capital. The roots of his "fib" had caught up with him.

If Abbott had been in the Oakland land office at one-thirty and in Pring's Donut Shop at two-forty-five (as Russell had testified), where had he been in between? With his next surprise witness, Coakley sought to supply the answer. She was Mrs. Bessie Wells, who operated an accounting business with her husband. A small blond woman, she testified in a sprightly manner.

As we know, back in August Otto Dezman had turned the Morton Beauty Salon appointment book over to Folger Emerson, frustrating efforts by Whitney and Hove to subpoena it. A 2 P.M. appointment for "Bess" had been discovered on the April 28 page. Mrs. Wells was more than just a client; she was also the salon's bookkeeper and had known the Dezmans, Georgia Abbott, and Burton for years.

On the afternoon of Stephanie's disappearance, she told the court, she had kept her appointment—and, while sitting under a dryer about 2:15, she had seen Burton enter the shop and say hello to Leona Dezman.

"He was in a leather jacket," Mrs. Wells said, "and I leaned out and asked Leona where Bud was going. She said he was going up to Trinity County to open the fishing season."

About 3:30 or 4 o'clock, the witness continued, Otto Dezman had come in and offered to pay an overdue parking ticket she was fretting about. She had given him a dollar to do so, and he had left to make the payment before the Alameda traffic office closed at 5 o'clock. To support her testimony, Mrs. Wells produced two documents dated April 28: her parking ticket receipt and her canceled check to the beauty salon in the amount of $17.78.

Whitney and Hove demanded that Coakley also produce the appointment book.

Coakley growled back, "You'll get it when I'm ready to bring it in."

Mrs. Wells was still on the stand when the trial recessed late Friday afternoon, January 6. Whitney, besieged by reporters, sought to deprecate the day's devastating testimony: "It is so beautifully timed that it smells like a slightly spoiled herring."

Burton left the courtroom doleful and in shock. In the jail upstairs, taking a step his family had been urging, he signed a power of attorney giving his brother Mark full authority to act for him. By so doing, he stripped Georgia of any control she might still exercise over his affairs.

For Georgia, the day's events had brought a triple jolt of misery and fear.

Until now, despite all that had occurred since July, she and Leona Dezman had kept their friendship alive. It had survived Otto's testimony for the prosecution early in the trial as well as the innuendos of adultery between Georgia and Otto. Georgia was still working at the beauty shop, and that's where she took an unexpected call from John Hanson, Stanley Whitney's law partner, on this Friday afternoon. From him she got her first news of Bessie Wells's disastrous testimony. Moreover, he said, the word was out that Leona Dezman would take the stand next to back up Bessie's story. It was essential that Georgia huddle with the defense team right away.

Hanson's call carried three meanings for Georgia, all bad: (1) Burton's defense, and his alibi especially, were in deep trouble; (2) her trusted friend and employer, Leona, was about to drive another nail into Burton's coffin; and (3) she could no longer elude the ordeal of testifying. Burton's lawyers, who had snubbed her for months, now needed her urgently to declare that Bessie and Leona were liars.

By the next day, thanks to his undercover contact with Lou Kirkpatrick in the beauty shop, Severin knew of the storm that had followed there after Georgia hung up the phone. She had, in Lou's words, "flipped her lid" and quit on the spot. The next morning she had returned to pick up her cosmetologist's license, collect her pay, and turn in her key. Now, in the deepest crisis of her life, Georgia's income was cut off.

For others, the weekend held no less terror. About eleven that Friday night, Bessie Wells's husband, Fred, was working alone at their accounting office in a deserted building when he saw the doorknob turning slowly. He jumped up and snapped the deadbolt and then called the police. Although the prowler was not caught, Wells took the incident as an attempt by someone to silence further testimony by his wife.

On Saturday afternoon the phone rang at the Morton Beauty Salon. The cosmetologist who answered heard a woman's voice say, "Leona had better watch out when she is on the stand Monday." Later Leona took another call: "This is just fair warning. You've said enough. Now we are going to burn your place down." A third caller warned that if Abbott was convicted, the Dezmans' heads would be "bashed in."

Otto applied for a gun permit. Clearly, someone familiar with the beauty

shop was waging the fear campaign. Two neighborhood women with scheduled appointments were warned by phone not to keep them, lest their heads
be "bashed in" too.

An innocent victim of the terror was Wade Gaskin, a young bank teller
who stopped at an Alameda bar for a couple of beers after work. Leaving the
place, he noticed a car following, and as he was parking in front of his house
about six-thirty, a stranger accosted him, demanding "Are you Otto Dezman?"

"No, I'm not," replied Gaskin, who was fifteen years younger, sixty pounds
lighter, and much shorter than Leona's husband.

"I believe you are," the man insisted, and slugged Gaskin on the jaw,
knocking him cold. He was later treated at Alameda Hospital for a possible
broken jaw, a broken nose, and facial bruises.

Anger was thick in the courtroom as the trial resumed on Monday morning
and the prosecutors called Leona as their next witness. Her hair perfectly
coiffed, she wore a gray suit with pink gloves. Abbott eyed her sullenly.

Folger Emerson, conducting her examination, lost no time in getting to
the crux of the information he sought: "Did you see the defendant, Burton
Abbott, on April 28?"

"I did," Leona answered, "in my beauty salon."

"How many times did you see him that day?"

"I saw him twice."

"When was the first time?"

"In the morning, after ten o'clock."

"And the second time?"

Leona was unequivocal as she gave the answer that snipped the essential
thread of Abbott's alibi: *"It was in the afternoon, somewhere after two o'clock, approximately 2:15 or 2:20."*

"What were you doing at the time?"

"I was removing the fingernail polish from Mrs. Wells."

"And what was the defendant doing?"

"He just walked in as he did normally, to the middle or back part of the
room."

"How long did he remain there?"

"A matter of seconds, a matter of minutes. I don't know exactly how
long."

"Did you speak to the defendant?"

"I did."

"What did you say to him?"

"I asked him how lucky could he be, to be going fishing at the opening
of the season, because I wished I could go. I'm a past fisherman myself."

Hove's clear tactic when he cross-examined Leona was to destroy her credibility by besmirching her character. It was the same tactic Whitney had used earlier with Otto. Insinuations of vice and adultery lurked in question after question:

- "Have you ever used any name other than Mrs. Dezman?"
- "Do you know a Joe Hagen* [the owner of an Alameda watering spot]?
- "In the past six months or year, did you at any time reside above the [tavern]? Did you have the key?"
- "Have you at any time used the name of Mrs. Joe Hagen?"
- "Have you ever been in any other business besides operating a beauty parlor?"
- "Have you ever had any other occupations?"
- "Did you ever have an establishment on Fruitvale Avenue in Oakland?"

Leona was not required to respond; each of Hove's inquiries into her intimate affairs brought a shouted objection from the prosecution, sustained by Judge Snook. As Leona withstood Hove's salvos, her face tightened with mounting fury.

Now Hove revived his stratagem of casting Otto Dezman as a suspect rather than a witness in the crimes against Stephanie. Referring to Georgia's blow-up the previous Friday in the beauty shop, he asked: "Is it not true that you told Georgia at that time, 'I'm going down there to testify to protect my own husband—and little Leona'?"

"I did not!" Leona screamed in a loud voice full of anger.

Hove would have been well advised to forgo his demeaning attack on Leona. When he finally dropped it in favor of straightforward questioning, he extracted from her a significant admission: Her current story of seeing Burton after 2 P.M. was at odds what she had been telling other people for months.

"Did you not tell Mr. Whitney last July that you saw Mr. Abbott in the beauty shop only on the morning of April 28?" Hove asked.

"I did tell him that," Leona acknowledged. She had made similar statements to Attorney Hanson and even to the prosecutors. She now said, however, that her memory had been refreshed about Abbott's afternoon visit by the appointment book. Seeing the 2 P.M. entry for "Bess" brought to mind her hair-dryer conversation with Mrs. Wells about Burton and her own envious remark to him about his fishing trip.

Coakley concluded his rebuttal with still another witness who caught

---

* Fictitious name.

the defense off guard: tall, mink-coated Kathy Green, the "second half" of Bill and Kathy's Restaurant in Dunnigan. There, more than a hundred miles north of Berkeley, Abbott said he had stopped to eat about 3 P.M. on April 28.

During his earlier cross-examination of Abbott, Coakley had asked him about the Dunnigan stop, but so casually that few reporters had mentioned it in their stories: What had Burton ordered? A sandwich and a cup of coffee, he said. Who had taken his order? A "dusty blond" waitress. How old was she? In her late twenties.

Coakley now asked Mrs. Green, "How many waitresses did you employ last April?"

"Five."

"Would any of them be called a 'dusty blond?' "

"No."

As Coakley already knew, from the report of Inspector Jester months earlier, all on duty at Bill and Kathy's on the afternoon of April 28 had been men.

Now the trial went into a phase that is usually a mere postscript: surrebuttal—literally, rebuttal to the rebuttal. In this case, however, anticipation was escalating, for by now it was clear that Whitney and Hove were going to put Georgia Abbott on the stand. The testimony would be her first formal public statement since the case began.

As a prelude to Georgia's appearance, Whitney and Hove called Anne Adams, a harpist with the San Francisco Symphony, to testify briefly. On April 28 she had kept an appointment at the Morton Beauty Salon at two-thirty, a half hour later than Bessie Wells's. She had remained there until about five o'clock, she said, and at no time had she seen Burton.

Popping flashbulbs greeted Georgia at the courtroom door, just as they had met Burton on the trial's first day. Her serenity impressed all who watched; nothing betrayed the dread she felt. *San Jose Mercury* reporter Charles Cruttenden called her "the picture of composure" in her navy-blue suit and small beige hat with matching gloves. Georgia and Burton exchanged brief smiles as she seated herself in the witness chair.

Hove, conducting her direct examination, dealt first with Mrs. Stegall's allegations.

"Mrs. Abbott," he began, "did you on April 28 or at any other time place a telephone call to the state office of tax-deeded lands in Oakland?"

"No, sir, I did not," Georgia replied firmly.

"Also, with regard to April 28, did you see your husband that day?"

"Yes, I saw him before I left for work about five minutes to nine, and when he came into the beauty shop to say goodbye around eleven o'clock."

"Did you see him at any other time on April 28?"

"No, sir, I did not."

"Did Leona Dezman say to you that the only reason she was going to be a witness was 'to protect her husband . . . and little Leona?' " This was the question to which, in fury, Leona had literally screamed her denial two days earlier. Now, however, Georgia replied, "She did."

"And before last Wednesday, did Leona Dezman repeatedly tell you that she only saw Burton on the morning of April 28?" Hove asked.

"Yes, that's correct."

Emerson's cross-examination of Georgia was brief and merciful overall, though at one point he observed that she seemed "a little overtrained" as a witness. He asked her only eight questions, one of which harked back to her FBI interview on July 16, less than twenty-four hours after she had found Stephanie's purse. Had she not, at that time, told Agent Marvin Buchanan that "due to the relationship existing between them," her husband would not have stopped at the beauty shop to tell her good-bye?

Georgia denied such a statement, although it was in Buchanan's notes. She was excused after a little less than half an hour on the stand. Outside court she spoke briefly with reporters, one of whom commented on her calmness.

"I could be very composed because I was telling the truth," she said, "and also because I know my husband is innocent."

Then she grasped what seemed a chance to lay at rest the whispering campaign she had endured since the case began.

"We are as friendly as ever," she declared. "There will never be a divorce in our lives."

28

"We the Jury Find . . ."

In all, 106 witnesses had testified in the first forty-two days of the trial, stretched over nine weeks. The transcript had reached a million words, filling four thousand pages. Now would come additional thousands of words—the oratory of the attorneys' final arguments.

Throughout the trial the journalists had used contrasting sets of adjectives for Frank Coakley and his right-hand man, Folger Emerson. For the former, the terms were robust: "two-fisted," "bulldog," and "unrelenting." By contrast, Emerson was described as "intellectual," "astute," "scholarly," "severe."

The manner in which these teammates blueprinted their finale confirmed the reporters' distinctions. Emerson was to go first, putting the prosecution case together brick by brick, as a mason builds a wall. Then, after Abbott's defenders had had their say, Coakley would deliver the state's emotional appeal.

For the best part of a day Emerson would hold the jury transfixed, as he lectured in low key from handwritten notes filling forty-seven pages in a three-ring binder:

> Ladies and gentlemen of the jury, the time has come for us to talk to you. As the myriad of evidence has been introduced, we have wanted to turn to you and say, "Look, look! See how this fits in. See how it all dovetails." So now we want to fit all the pieces together.
>
> It was Providence which placed Otto Dezman in the Abbott home when Stephanie's purse was found there. Had this not been the case, Burton Abbott probably would never have been brought to trial.
>
> I think it is time to say that the original intent of the defendant was to commit a sex crime. When a girl is kidnapped and her panties and bra are removed, there is only one reason, ladies and gentlemen, only one. And there is no doubt that Stephanie was murdered with premeditation, because the kidnapper could not run the risk of being identified by her.

Emerson heaped scorn on Abbott's alibi. Showing the jurors a picture of rugged, isolated San Pablo Dam Road, not far from the tunnel struggle scene, he told them:

There! There was the time, the place, and the opportunity to do what was done to Stephanie! At the time it was happening, the defendant told you he was between Dunnigan and Corning. This was a figment of his imagination. When he made up this alibi, he had to account for a three-hour time lapse—which was taken care of by his imaginary trip to Sacramento.

At this point Emerson veered sharply into pure conjecture, purporting to read Abbott's mind. He advanced a theory which, while neither proven nor indicated by evidence on record, was nonetheless consistent with the prosecution's case:

The question comes up, why wasn't Stephanie's body disposed of somewhere else? The answer is, Abbott was not sure whether Stephanie was dead or alive. He could not take a chance on stopping his car hurriedly, dumping her into a culvert, and speeding away.

Now consider the remote, isolated community of Wildwood, where Abbott's cabin is. In Trinity County any stranger would immediately be noticed, but Abbott could be there without arousing suspicion. It was a place he could run away and hide, where he would feel safe temporarily. It was a place which would give him the time he needed to gather his thoughts and plan his alibi. It was the place where Stephanie was buried that weekend. It was the place where she was found.

Displayed on a table near the jury were the purse, wallet, books, glasses, and brassiere, to which Emerson now pointed. Clearly his aim was to land an emotional punch that would dispel whatever squeamishness the jurors might retain about invoking the death penalty:

Here lying before you, ladies and gentlemen, is the legacy of Stephanie Bryan. You and I have never seen her, but we know her. Visualize a typical American schoolgirl and the kind of girl the future of America depends upon. Whatever she was to us, she was more than that to her family.

The law regards some murders as worse than others, some kidnappings as worse than others. Try to imagine a worse one than this. If there ever was a crime that fitted the punishment of death, this is it. Often it is easier to find ways to acquit a defendant than find him guilty when a death penalty is involved. But the whole system of justice and protection would break down if we shunned the unpleasant tasks.

The State of California endeavors to take a life in the most humane way possible, in the gas chamber. Let me ask you this: Wouldn't it almost have been a blessing *if Stephanie could have died the painless way, as long as she had to die, rather than suffered in agony? And what happened to Stephanie before her death was, in my opinion, worse than death itself.*

In closing, Emerson told the jury that the state's case rested on five basic facts:

• Stephanie's body was found 339 feet from Abbott's Trinity County cabin.

• Abbott went to the cabin the weekend she vanished.

• Her brassiere and other possessions were found in Abbott's basement in Alameda.

• Fibers and hairs matching Stephanie's were found in Abbott's car, and soil matching that of her grave was found on his boots.

• He had admitted lying to the police.

The professorial approach Emerson had taken was not the style of Burton Abbott's chief lawyer, Stanley Whitney. Despite his kindly, grandfatherly mien, he was sometimes described as "bombastic," and this was the trait in evidence as he now came forward to open the final plea for Burton's life. Like a desperate soldier with a machete, Whitney slashed in all directions:

The state's case is a fairy tale! The prosecution grabbed a patsy when Abbott was arrested on July 20, and since then they have moved heaven and earth to pin this crime on him. I don't know how much money they've spent, but they've spent thousands and thousands of dollars and many thousands of hours of manpower. They haven't tried to find the real killer of Stephanie. All of the state's evidence points so patly at Abbott that it's ridiculous. Somebody did it and tried to make it look like Abbott did.

Whitney dripped ridicule and contempt in a broad-brush denunciation of prosecution's witnesses, especially those who had seen the car struggle or otherwise placed Abbott in Berkeley or Oakland that afternoon:

Mrs. Leidecker [was] the sob lady who looked into a crystal ball.

Mrs. Marian Morgan hypnotized herself into believing all these things she saw must have happened. . . .

Sam Marshall is again an individual who thought he saw something and saw nothing. . . .

Mrs. Van Meter didn't see the driver at all. . . .

Do you remember Mrs. Jacqueline Hill, the little lady? Very vivacious, very nice, but wanted to give her whole testimony in one breath? She had been properly prepared on the ninth floor [the District Attorney's office] so that her testimony could come out like a gush of water. . . .

Mrs. Leidecker, Lieutenant Hill, Mrs. Hill and Mrs. Van Meter are not liars, but they magnified what they saw into a beautiful piece of fiction. What possible reliance can you place on that kind of testimony? How can you give it any validity or any credence when a man's life is at stake?

Seeking to neutralize the ruinous prosecution testimony of Leona Dezman that placed Burton in the beauty shop in midafternoon April 28, Whitney again painted Otto Dezman as a suspect:

You watched his testimony; you listened to him; you saw. Why was Mr. Dezman so nervous? Why was Mr. Dezman constantly taking his handkerchief out of his pocket and wiping the perspiration from his hands? Is he concealing something? Why was it necessary to produce an alibi for Mr. Dezman? And that is all that Leona Dezman's testimony amounted to.

Whitney reserved his deepest scorn for the prosecution's pivotal witness, Dr. Kirk:

They told him what was needed, and he produced for a price. Dr. Kirk brought into court only those portions of his findings which fitted into the pattern set up by the district attorney. Dr. Kirk came and tried to sell you something. Yet all he could find were two hairs, and he couldn't personalize them.

The testimony of Dr. Kirk that soil on Abbott's boots matched soil taken from the 9-inch depth in Stephanie's grave is absolutely unbelievable. [Whitney picked up Abbott's boots and waved them before the jury.] Mud in front of the cabin on April 28 was four or five inches deep—and yet Dr. Kirk could only find soil from the grave impacted under the heels.

Repeatedly throughout his long oration, Whitney reverted to a dubious premise—that Burton was too smart to have made the mistakes that Stephanie's killer did:

Is it reasonable to say that Abbott would gamble for eight hours with the girl's body in plain sight in the back seat? What if he blew out a tire—and they were bad—or what if a policeman flagged him and said, "Hey, you only have one light. Let's see your driver's license?" Is it reasonable to say that he would be so completely without understanding or reason that having done such a thing, he would bring all this property back to his home and put it in the basement? It doesn't make sense.

We know Burton Abbott is a man of intelligence. You have seen him here. He gives no indication of being idiotic or stupid or unbalanced. He gives the impression of a man who knows what it is all about. Is a man like that going to leave a trail of evidence leading right to his own back door? I say to you, "No!"

In similar vein, Whitney argued that it was preposterous to impute a sex crime to Burton Abbott. Why? Because he had no reason to commit one:

The only motive the people have been able to develop for the commission of this crime is a sex motive. Well, now, nobody commits a sex crime like that unless there is a background for it. There is a reason for everything people do unless they are complete lunatics. There is no evidence that this man [pointing at his client] is a lunatic! You have observed that Burton Abbott in all respects is a completely sound, moral, intelligent man. He is not a man capable of committing these crimes. He is a married man. He lived with his wife and his 4-year-old son Chris right up to the time he was taken into custody. Even on the day he was departing for Trinity County, he took his little son Chris into his arms; he kissed him and told him to be a good boy and Daddy would bring him a fish. Is that the act of a man who has in the back of his mind the commission of an atrocious crime? It is not.

With Whitney's utterance of this line, Coakley perceived an unforeseen opportunity: "Objection, your honor! Mr. Whitney knows we couldn't bring out any sexual aspect of Mr. Abbott's background unless the defense opened the door. If they had opened the door, we jolly well could have!"

Now Hove took over. If sarcasm and scorn were Whitney's hallmarks, Hove leaned to bare-knuckle attack strangely mingled with pathos and bathos. His way with words was extravagant. He loved puns, similes, and metaphors and was not loath to mix them:

The state's case is like a big block of Swiss cheese, with so many holes you can drive a truck through it. There are only threads that purport to tie it together. Is life so cheap you can hang it by a thread?

Do you imagine for one moment I could sit here next to this boy for all these months if I thought he was guilty of doing this crime to Stephanie Bryan? No, I have a 14-year-old daughter myself.

On the football field they have an expression: "When in doubt, punt," and that's exactly what the district attorney's office did in this case. They punted by charging Burton Abbott on suspicious circumstances alone. On July 20 they had no proof, and up to this day they have no proof, and they have been punting ever since.

Hove labeled Riedel, O'Meara, and psychiatrist Kelley—the interrogators Abbott feared and hated most—"the Unholy Three."

These were the men who interrogated Abbott the night of his arrest. He was subjected to every abuse possible. I wouldn't treat a dog the way the prosecution treated defense witnesses in this case. There is such a thing as a psychological third degree. This defendant has been worked over by experts. In Latin they say *ad infinitum*. With reference to this, I say *"ad midnitum,"* because they questioned him many times after midnight.

The element of fair play and sportsmanship has been abandoned in this case. The prosecution's theory has been, "When you get a man down, kick, kick, kick!" Everything that is derogatory, that is nasty has been said concerning this defendant. But no matter which way you turn this case—upside down, backwards, or how—you'll see reasonable doubt sticking out all over.

You have had the opportunity to observe the defendant over a period of a couple of months, and at no time has he ever exhibited anything to give you any indication that he was guilty. Why doesn't he show some emotion, some feeling? What good would it do for him to beat his head against the wall?

Hove reminded the jury that when Georgia had discovered Stephanie's purse, she had reported it at once with Burton's consent:

There wasn't a bit of hesitancy about calling police, and they told them what they'd found as good, honest people. But what has happened since that date? This boy, this young man has been accused of every possible vile thing in the books. Mr. Emerson has demanded the death penalty as lightly and easily as an undertaker.

The facts point directly to a frame-up. What about the shallow grave? Would anyone dig a shallow grave if he wanted to conceal his evidence? No, he'd dig it deep. Maybe the man who dug it didn't want to hide the body too thoroughly; maybe he wanted it to be found. It looks to me and a lot of other reasonable people that someone wanted the circumstances to point to this defendant. Maybe we've heard that person's name in this court. Maybe we've seen his face here; I don't know. There is a motive for the testimony by Leona Dezman and Bessie Wells, and that motive is to take the heat off of Otto Dezman!

The lies that Abbott had admittedly told remained a troublesome problem for the defense. Another lawyer might have chosen to ignore them at this point, but not Hove.

I wonder how many of us have told little white lies. Any one of us who has not fibbed at something is not normal. Look at Burton Abbott. Is there anything abnormal about him? Is there anything sinister, anything that looks violent or mean? Absolutely not.

Perhaps Hove's FBI background gave him credence in the jurors' eyes when he renewed the defense assult on criminalist Kirk:

They had all the king's horses and all the king's men to work with on this case, and they overlooked so many fundamentals it is really a shame. Dr. Kirk is a buffalo artist playing Russian roulette with Abbott's life. A lot of flimflam and malarkey has been given you. Speculation? Yes. Guesswork? Yes. Conjecture? Yes. But is that the type of evidence you consider taking a man's life on? Some people are from Missouri. You still have to prove it to them.

This case, to the public, has assumed the stature of a Perry Mason novel, a whodunit. [Perhaps Hove was getting even with Erle Stanley Gardner for the Skipper Bethel fiasco.] The prosecuting attorney can take a fiber, something you can't see with your eye, and say, "Let's take a life on it." Life is a God-given thing, something not to be taken lightly and rolled off your tongue with ease and callousness. Has the prosecution sustained the burden of proof? No, not a way you look at it!

Consider the witnesses we have brought before you. Take Rosa Arnone, the waitress; Robert Hall, the Red Bluff restaurant owner; Robert Wetzel, the Trinity County fruit peddler; Richard McNees, the boy who came in here in an Army uniform. Each one alone projects reasonable doubt, each one alone projects innocence. Taken together, they are definite.

We ask this. Seek in the back of your conscience such help as you can. Consider every fact; consider every word said by the witnesses;

consider every bit of the evidence, and on the basis of that we ask that you come in with a verdict of acquittal.

Thank you.

While Whitney and Hove were lecturing the jury, Coakley had been weighing several strategies for his response. His opening, in a rasping, biting voice, seemed as spontaneous as it was explosive:

> I hadn't intended to start this way, but counsel for the defense has asked, "What is the motive for this crime? What is the reason? Why? Why? Why?"
>
> THIS is the motive!

At this point the prosecutor whipped out Stephanie's brassiere and the knotted panties and waved them before the jury. With violent motions, he simulated the way the murderer had cut the panties from the girl.

> The killer slashed from the waist to the crotch, and then again from the waist to the leg. Two times the knife slashed through the panties, and that is the way they were taken off of Stephanie Bryan sometime during the afternoon or night of April 28, taken off by none other than this defendant!
>
> Do I have to dwell on that? Stephanie was kidnapped and killed, brutally murdered by a sexual psychopath, a sex pervert. The burial of her body on the hill, on a knoll marked by the pine tree where the defendant could easily look up from the cabin and re-live again and again the awful experience which gave him some perverted satisfaction—there could be in this a fetish symbolism. I also believe he was fondling the purse and the bra in the basement occasionally.

Coakley refreshed the jurors' memory of Abbott's crass reaction when Inspector O'Meara had described to him the anguish of Stephanie's parents: "I don't give a damn about the Bryan family . . . When do we eat?"

> What do you think of that? What kind of a person would say that under those circumstances? I will tell you what kind of a person: the exact type of psychopathic personality that this defendant is—the kind of personality who could do what he did to Stephanie Bryan. He had been through a terrific experience, and he'd had perhaps the greatest sexual satisfaction and orgy in his life, and he went down to the bar in Wildwood to drink and drink and drink and celebrate for ten hours!

Although rough on the surface, Coakley was devout enough to flavor his speech with scripture, and scholarly enough to invoke Shakespeare, as his passion grew:

Mr. Whitney and Mr. Hove are hopelessly insolvent, bankrupt, without assets of any kind. Their case is just an empty shell, a sounding brass or a tinkling cymbal,* or as Shakespeare says, "a tale told by an idiot, full of sound and fury, signifying nothing."**

The psychology of the defense is that if they throw enough mud, maybe some of it will stick. So they keep throwing mud. And what was the psychology of the Nazis and the communists? Keep telling the big lie in the hope that if it is told often enough, somebody might believe it. I say advisedly that the arguments of the defense counsel constitute the most extreme, the most glaring, the most outstanding exhibition of blowing hot and cold that I have ever witnessed.

Coakley now came up with a final surprise. He told the jury that Burton, in reciting his itinerary to Wildwood, had made not one but two Freudian slips. The first, brought out in court, had been Abbott's plural phrasing— "they waved *us* across"—when he told of crossing the Cottonwood Creek bridge supposedly alone. The second slip Coakley now identified was Burton's claim that he left Sacramento without going to the land office because "it was getting later and later and darker and darker."

That came out of his subconscious mind. What time was it when he was at the land office? According to his own story it was the middle of the day. But at the time when he was actually in the latitude of Sacramento, up there someplace, it really *was* getting later and later and darker. It *was* dark, and in his car was the body of Stephanie Bryan!

Now let's add it up. We have Abbott's conduct from the time that the purse was found right down to the present—his consummate vanity and arrogance. We have his appearance here in the courtroom, his mannerisms on the witness stand. You know that he can smile and smile, ladies and gentlemen. I have noticed this during the trial, how he would stand as you would have to go by him, smiling at you, smiling at you. I am reminded of the line from *The Merchant of Venice:* "The devil can cite scripture to his purpose. An evil soul producing holy witness is like a villain with a smiling cheek; a shining apple rotten at the heart."†

---

*   I Corinthians 13:1.
** *Macbeth,* Act V, Scene v.
†   *The Merchant of Venice,* Act I, Scene iii.

At this point Coakley picked up the unfinished letter to Stephanie's Massachusetts school friend Teddy, among her belongings as Georgia found them. He began to read:

Dear Teddy,

I am writing this letter on notebook paper because I am at school with some extra time. . . .

I have had my hair cut fairly short. I like it better this way. It's much easier to take care of.

How are you doing in school? I won a gold pin for superior scholarship during the time I have been here. Fifteen other people got them.

We are already planning our summer trip. We had hoped to come home [to Massachusetts] until we found out the cost of transportation. We are planning a camping trip to different places in California.

It's spring here. The fruit trees have all bloomed, and the trees that lose their leaves in the winter are getting them back again. I planted some seeds, and now the plants are quite big.

This hasn't been a very eventful winter. I can't think of anything else to say . . .

There was no closing phrase or signature. Poignantly the letter thus dramatized the abrupt termination of the life of its writer. As Coakley broke off his reading, he turned to the jurors, at least two of whom were crying. He whipped out a handkerchief, and blew his nose to clear his choking voice before continuing:

Do you want to hear any more? She'll never make that trip! Never again will she put on those little shoes which you saw here. She will never romp and play again with her sisters and brother. She was a good girl. She would have been a fine woman and a wonderful mother. She deserved a better fate.

Are you going to set Burton Abbott free to sing again his siren song of sex and sink his fangs into some other unsuspecting child? Or are you going to give him that which he so justly deserves by bringing in two verdicts—guilty of kidnapping with the death penalty, and guilty of murder of the first degree with the death penalty?

Thank you.

Judge Snook declared a fifteen-minute recess. In the corridor Coakley approached Georgia and said, "I feel very sorry for you. I really sympathize with you."

"How can a rattlesnake be friendly?" she spat at him as she turned away.

The judge took an hour and a quarter to instruct the jury. With care he explained the presumption of innocence: "A defendant in a criminal case is not required to prove his innocence. It is the state's burden to prove guilt to a moral certainty and beyond a reasonable doubt."

Proof of motive, though desirable, was not essential, Snook told the jurors. He explained the distinction between direct evidence, actually perceived, and circumstantial evidence, requiring an inference. The law recognized each type, he said, "for such convincing force as it might carry."

The fate of Burton Wilbur Abbott was placed in the jurors' hands at thirteen minutes past noon on Thursday, January 19—just nine days short of nine months after the crime with which he was charged. Deliberations began after a long lunch at Villa de la Paix, a fashionable restaurant near the courthouse.* By acclamation the jury chose Harry A. Whitehead, a lean-faced ex-marine with an eighteen-year-old daughter, as its foreman. During the trial the members had gone home each night, but now they would be sequestered under guard at the Leamington Hotel, arguably downtown Oakland's finest.

The waiting began. For Georgia, Elsie, and others of Abbott's family, keeping vigil in a courthouse corridor was hell. Georgia went to a church to pray. Upstairs in the jail, Abbott played pinochle with fellow inmates.

Newsmen covering the trial filled their Friday stories with empty conjecture: "Courthouse observers" were speculating that the verdict could come in hours—or days. "Great significance" was attached to a jury request for a rereading of certain testimony. One report had the jury split nine to three for conviction, with a trio of soft-hearted women in dissent.

Abbott's lawyers were asked the inevitable question: Would they still represent him if a new trial was needed? Hove said it would be a "financial burden." Whitney said, "I'll cross that bridge when I come to it." The lawyers' fees were estimated at $22,000 to date.

In midafternoon on Sunday, the fourth day of deliberation, Elsie Abbott broke down for the first time during the trial. She was keeping her stoical vigil in a front-row courtroom seat when a photographer's flashbulb triggered her collapse.

"He's innocent! He's innocent! Oh, I'm so frightened," she shrieked, slumping her her seat. Later she told a reporter she had had no sleep; she had spent the night praying.

On Monday morning Burton rose smiling and asked a jailer, "Well, what do you know today? What do you hear?"

---

* 1955 restaurant prices were modest. For the thirteen jurors including the alternate, the lunch check was $37.90. Their dinner tab at another restaurant was $69.21.

"I've got a couple of rumors from the newspaper," the turnkey answered. "I understand the jurors are split at eleven to one."

"For me, of course?"

"No, for conviction."

Burton's face darkened, Sheriff Gleason later told reporters, "as if a window shade had been pulled down."

At midafternoon Wednesday, the seventh day, it appeared there would be no verdict soon. In the courtroom die-hard spectators kept watch. A few reporters had a gin rummy game going, and others snoozed in the jury box. A copyboy was sent out for coffee and sandwiches. Abbott's lawyers dropped in to chat. Court clerk Robert Snyder, his feet propped on his desk, was reading a book. At ten minutes to four the jury sent word that it wanted to work until at least eight o'clock before retiring.

Then suddenly, only thirty minutes later, Bailiff Jack Fitzpatrick emerged from Judge Snook's chambers to announce "We've got a verdict!" The jury had reached it after fifty-one hours and fifty-six minutes of deliberation.

Quickly the playing cards disappeared and order settled over the room. Uniformed deputies and plainclothes officers appeared, taking up stations throughout the assemblage. Within minutes the lawyers arrived and Abbott, in his blue suit, was brought down from the jail. Georgia and Elsie, who had been waiting two floors below, entered separately and took seats in the front row. Though seated side by side, they spoke no word to each other, nor did they exchange any sign of recognition.

Judge Snook took the bench at 4:42 with a stern warning against any outburst when the verdict was announced. At 4:50 the jury filed in, led by Mrs. Mary Altomare, who had been rumored to be a holdout; her face was sober. Next came the other four women jurors, all with grim expressions, and the seven men, tired and stooped. None looked at Abbott. They took their chairs and stared straight ahead.

"Have you reached a verdict, Mr. Foreman?" Judge Snook inquired.

"We have, your honor."

The twin written verdicts were handed to the judge, who glanced at them briefly before passing them to Clerk Snyder to be read aloud. He read the finding with respect to kidnapping first.

"We the jury find the defendant, Burton W. Abbott, guilty of felony, violation of Section 209 of the Penal Code as charged in the first count of the indictment. We further find that the person subjected to such kidnapping suffered bodily harm and we fix the punishment as death."

Elsie, leaning forward, beat her head against the courtroom railing as Snyder intoned the word "death."

The verdict with regard to the second count, murder in the first degree, was similarly worded.

Snook ordered next that the jury be polled, and Snyder asked each juror in turn, "Is the verdict rendered in this indictment your true verdict?" Each answered "Yes" or "It is."

Abbott was white-faced and expressionless, but remained under control. He bit his lip slightly. Much later, however, he would tell *Oakland Tribune* reporter Bill Fiset, "My blood turned to ice water. Inside I was shaking so hard I thought I'd faint."

Fifteen minutes after the verdict, he resumed his card game in the jail upstairs. By 11 P.M., jailers reported, he was in deep slumber.

At the verdict Georgia Abbott ran from the courtroom, her hands over her face, fleeing the press. Outside the building, where dusk was gathering, Hove's wife Alice sat in her parked car, waiting for him. "The most awful sight I've ever seen," she said in 1993, "was a band of reporters chasing Georgia Abbott up the middle of Twelfth Street."

Georgia herself retained little memory of that moment.

"When I think of that whole court thing," she said later, "I feel I was somewhere else. I was in another life or something. It just wasn't happening to me. And I think if you can take that attitude, you can get through most anything. It's like living at another place at another time."

The *Chronicle* sent reporter Art Hoppe to the Bryan home on Alvarado Road to learn the reaction of Stephanie's parents.

"I don't think the gas chamber is much of a punishment, really, for that fellow," Dr. Bryan said. "I feel his ego will protect him right through to the end."

PART FIVE

After the Verdict

29

On the Row

Abbott's sentencing on Friday, February 10—a formality in view of the mandatory death verdict—took only minutes, but in a supercharged atmosphere. Judge Snook had received an unsigned bomb threat, and a score of deputy sheriffs stood guard in his courtroom and its corridor. Among the spectators sat Georgia and Elsie Abbott and at least three of Burton's other relatives.

"We will tolerate no demonstration of any kind," the judge warned as the proceedings began. "Anybody demonstrating will be taken into custody."

Flanked by Whitney and Hove, Burton rose and stood pale and mute as Snook intoned the words the law demanded:

"It is hereby ordered, adjudged, and decreed that the penalty of death be inflicted upon the said defendant, Burton W. Abbott, by the administration of lethal gas within the walls of the State Prison of the State of California at San Quentin."

As the last words were uttered, a deputy tapped Burton on the shoulder and led him silently from the room. His transfer to Death Row was set for the next morning.

Not everywhere was the scene so grim. That night, across the bay in San Francisco, journalists who had covered the Abbott story gathered at the Press Club to eat, carouse, and stage a mock trial. *Examiner* photographer Seymour Snaer portrayed "District Attorney A. Crank Jerkley," Terry Hansen was defense attorney "Manley Spitney." The *Chronicle's* hard-shelled sob sister Carolyn Anspacher, who had milked the case for every tear and whimper, played "Hey Baba-Reba Slydecker." A hilarious time was had by all.

The turreted walls of San Quentin Prison rise from a stubby peninsula on the Marin shore of San Francisco Bay, across the water from the East Bay cities. It is California's oldest prison, a place of dread since 1852. Historically it has been the death site for the state's condemned felons—on the gallows until 1937, after that in the gas chamber, and since 1996 by lethal injection. As the seagull flies San Quentin is only about sixteen miles from the courthouse in Oakland where Abbott was incarcerated, but delivering him to the prison in 1956 required a roundabout ride about twice that long across the bay to San Francisco and over the Golden Gate Bridge to Marin County. The Richmond–San Rafael Bridge, a direct link between the East Bay and Marin, was not yet in service.

Burton was nothing if not vain. On the night of his arrest back in July he had primped before a mirror as the cops waited to take him to jail. Now, preparing for what might well be his last automobile ride, he did the same. He donned the blue suit seen so often in court, and with it a white shirt and a dark tie, carefully knotted. His hair was combed neatly.

From the courthouse, a basement tunnel for official vehicles emerges at street level into the heart of downtown Oakland, and from this exit at nine thirty-five Saturday morning rolled a gray Buick sheriff's sedan carrying the prison-bound Abbott. Two convicted holdup men, between whom he was manacled, shared his journey.

As every TV viewer knows, journalists often ask questions that are not only stupid but mean-hearted, and it was thus when the car rolled to a stop at the prison gates. A reporter shouted to Abbott, "How does San Quentin look to you?"

"Well—fine, I guess" was Burton's reply, before the gates clanged shut behind him. The stupid question deserved the pallid answer.

Inside the prison, within minutes, Burton surrendered his civilian garb and donned the condemned men's uniform of blue coveralls and denim slippers. He was fingerprinted, photographed with his new San Quentin number A-35539, and deposited in Death Row Cell 2437, a cubicle four and a half feet wide and eleven and a half feet long with a seven-foot ceiling. In this space he would spend twenty-two hours of each day alone thereafter. His isolation was total, the abutting cells both being vacant. Only during the midday exercise period, from eleven-thirty to one-thirty, would Burton mingle with the twenty-seven other men on the Row. He would get two meals a day; the daily cost of his rations was 58.5 cents.

He would have access to the prison library and could receive mailed books, magazines, and newspapers. Cell 2437 had radio headphones with a choice of two stations. He was authorized to receive censored mail from anyone on a ten-name list, and specified visitors could converse with him through a thick screen three times a month. He would be allowed to study, but if he tried to write his memoirs (as had another celebrity occupant of the Row, the "red-light rapist" Caryl Chessman), the manuscript would be seized and shredded.

Even on Death Row the rigmarole of official bureaucracy went on. During Burton's first weeks there he was interviewed, examined, prodded, and tested by a medical officer, a psychiatrist, a classification officer, a clinical psychologist, a chaplain, and—what irony for a condemned man—a probation officer. Con-wise by now, he managed to please most of them. After interviewing him, classification officer Joseph Tobin wrote:

> Recorded past history of subject points to a picture of a healthy, outgoing, happy, confident, and comparatively well adjusted and well-liked child and young man. [He] participates in the interviews in a courteous, cooperative, cheeerful manner. He supplies answers to questions with little hesitation and no apparent evasiveness.

Abbott's "apparent flippancy and often jocular manner," odd for a Death Row inmate, puzzled Tobin at first; but he decided the attitude stemmed from "his expressed conviction of innocence and confidence in eventual freedom."

San Quentin's clinical psychologist, Dr. Arthur Davidson, also found much interesting in Abbott's character:

> Subject was pleasant and cooperative during psychological testing procedures. Testing suggests an individual with very superior intelligence [I.Q. 130] who is rather guarded and evasive. He is rigid and constricted with great emphasis on exactitude and accuracy. He has an active fantasy life and shows potential for creative thinking.

Burton may have been smart, but he didn't fool Dr. David Schmidt, San Quentin's chief psychiatrist, who wrote:

> Our explorations have shown that he not only considered himself bright, but considered himself much brighter than he actually was. He has a psychoneurotic personality, but he is not insane.

Because Burton had been raised as a Methodist, it was the prison's Protestant chaplain, Byron Eshelman, who was sent to comfort him. Eshelman found not a repenter but a cynic:

> The subject has always responded in a polite and cheerful manner. He smiles a great deal during the conversations. He expresses skepticism about the conventional beliefs of Christianity and a resurrection and a life hereafter. He appears to be aware of no great weakness in himself as needing forgiveness or moral transformation.

Georgia, though estranged from Burton's family, remained loving and promising in her letters to him. On April 17 she wrote:

My darling:

Just another night to put behind us. I've just finished my daily chores, and if there was ever a boy like his father, this one [Chris] is definitely it. I cleaned out his trousers to wash them, and it looked just like yours—old wadded-up Kleenex,* used gum wrappers, empty boxes, etc. I don't know what he does with all that nose-blowing, but I guess like his dad, just a wet nose all the time. . . .

I miss you so much. I'm back on our old song again, "What'll I Do?"— remember? I sure wish this was over and you were home. Chris and I need you.

Well, Sweet, I have to say goodnight. Why don't you write? I look every day for your letters.

Love forever,
Wife.

As time passed, Abbott's keepers at San Quentin came to recognize the great deficiency in his makeup—a virtual absence of emotion. He drew a curtain between himself and those he should have loved, except perhaps his mother. Between August 1956 and January 1957 he did not mail out a single letter.

As Burton settled into the Death Row routine, events elsewhere kept his name on the front pages. On Sunday afternoon, April 1, the grisly history of the cabin at Wildwood ended when it burned to the ground. Two drunken lumbermen on a lark admitted torching the place as a rowdy April Fool's joke. "We figured two murders were enough," they told the sheriff.

Although Abbott's conviction had appeased majority public opinion, a hardy band of dissenters remained. One of these, an Oakland divorcée named Elaine Jellison,** told a strange tale to the FBI in early April.

She suspected that her estranged husband, Wilkie Jellison,† not Abbott, was Stephanie's true slayer. During their marriage he had taunted her by devising fanciful plans for killing her and disposing of her body. Also, he had once shown high anxiety after the rape-murder of a young girl in Hayward. Elaine had no solid evidence connecting him to the Bryan case, but one part of her tale was chilling.

She and Wilkie had separated in July 1955—the same month Stephanie's body was found. At that time he had been involved with another woman, who was pregnant with his child.

---

* When Georgia wrote this, did she remember or even know that Burton's trail of Kleenex—in his jacket, in his car, and in the pack rat's nest near Stephanie's grave—had helped convict him?
** Fictitious name.
† Fictitious name.

In mid-March Elaine received a phone call from a man whose voice she did not recognize, who told her, "You might be interested in checking out what your husband has named his new son."

Elaine therefore obtained a copy of the baby's birth certificate. Born on January 28, three days after Abbott's conviction, the boy had been christened *Stephen Bryan* Jellison.*

Around the end of March Whitney stopped at the Alameda County Clerk's office and asked to see the Abbott case file. The response—that the file had been "misplaced"—touched off an uproar that kept the courthouse on edge all summer.

Nothing about the incident became public right away. The *Tribune* learned of it but, for unknown reasons, chose to sit on the story. Not until Whitney got the same reply to a second request a month later did the storm break. This time, within minutes after he left the clerk's office, the *Alameda Times-Star* was on the phone demanding answers: Where was the file? Was it under wraps? Has someone stolen it? With Burton's appeal pending and his life in the balance, the questions were more than academic. The sheriff put detective Larry Waldt on the case.

The Abbott file had contained forty-one documents, including the indictment, jury instructions, verdict, sentencing records, court orders, and numerous affidavits. Also gone was the fictitious diagram Abbott had drawn of the Sacramento land office.

Over the next three weeks Waldt grilled a score of clerks, janitors, painters, and carpenters who worked at the courthouse. Everyone was a suspect. There were no signs of forced entry.

Little by little the truth unfolded. On March 26 a trusted secretary, a spinster who had worked in the clerk's office thirty years, had checked out the Abbott file in order to answer a letter of inquiry. At that time some remodeling was under way, and with her desk space cramped, she had propped the file across the top of her wastebasket. Had it fallen in?

"If the folders were in a wastebasket, they would have been thrown out like everything else," the janitor said.

Waldt went to the Oakland Scavenger Company and talked to the man who bundled the waste paper from the courthouse. He remembered no file folders, but in any case he could not have identified them because he couldn't read. His daily bundled went to a fiberboard plant where the paper was dumped directly into the pulp vats. By now the Abbott file had doubtless been recycled into wallboard.

---

* Fictitious name.

"Will this cause a mistrial?" excited reporters demanded of Coakley when the story broke.

"It will have absolutely no effect," the district attorney declared. "The trial transcript was perfected and accepted as correct before the file disappeared."

Coakley had checked the law before giving his answer. The penal code contained an explicit provision that photostats of missing documents, from the separate files of the lawyers, could be substituted for the originals with "the same force and effect."

California law provides for the automatic appeal of every death sentence to the State Supreme Court. The burdensome process imposes a monumental drain on the resources of both sides; so it was small wonder that Abbott's lawyers, who had doubtless lost money defending him, now sought to turn his case over to others.* On April 2 the withdrawal of Hove, Whitney, and Hanson was approved by Judge Snook, and Burton became the client of Leo A. Sullivan, a longtime scrapper in local criminal courts. The Abbott family welcomed the change.

On July 16 Sullivan filed a 75,000-word brief with the State Supreme Court, supporting Abbott's appeal. Mostly it rehashed matters already debated: It challenged anew the jurisdiction of Alameda County to try the case. It charged again that Snook had erred in discharging juror Rettig. It condemned as improper Coakley's cross-examination of Abbott about the "accusatory statements" hurled at him by Riedel and Dr. Kelley.

Sullivan also advanced a plausible new theory about the hair and clothing fibers found in Abbott's car. He noted that O'Meara and Lieutenant Sherry, who had examined the car, had previously gathered evidence from Stephanie's room in the Bryan home. Unwittingly, Sullivan argued, these officers could have picked up the girl's hair and fiber particles on their clothing and deposited them later in the automobile. This was pure conjecture, but it was a possibility not previously explored.

On November 23 the State Supreme Court rejected Abbott's appeal unanimously. The justices concurred in only one of Sullivan's points: that the accusatory statements had been improperly admitted, but they found "abundant evidence of guilt" nonetheless. Burton's double death sentence was affirmed.

Sullivan petitioned for a rehearing, but on December 19 this was likewise denied. On January 10, 1957, Snook fixed Abbott's death date as March 15. His statement with the execution warrant was devoid of such softening observations as were characteristic of the San Quentin analysts.

---

* "For us it was love's labor lost," John Hanson said in 1993. "If we'd have won, we'd have enjoyed it more."

"The defendant is a psychopathic personality, a pathological liar, and an extreme egotist," the judge wrote. "He deserves no clemency."

Burton's life expectancy was now just two months, but a final desperate battle to save him still lay ahead. On January 21 careful readers of the *Chronicle* noticed a ten-line ad in the personals column:

> REWARD
> $2500 reward for information establishing the innocence of Burton Abbott in connection with the kidnapping and death of Stephanie Bryan. Please contact W.J. Linhart Detective Agency, 12485 San Pablo Avenue, Richmond, Calif. Phone BEacon 2-8631. All information confidential.

The ad represented Elsie Abbott's boldest effort yet to forestall her son's doom. Detective Linhart, representing her, had been flitting around the edges of the case almost from the start. Now he enigmatically told reporters, "We have two suspects on the string. They're interesting. They've never been mentioned before."

A few days later Linhart went to the San Pablo police with a tantalizing tip that Stephanie had been murdered by a member of the Abbott family, but not Burton. Naming no sources, he also claimed to have information that Stephanie had had an abortion, which was why her grades had fallen during her final weeks at Willard.

On January 28, 1957, the *Chronicle* greeted its readers with an eight-column headline that took up most of page one above the fold:

EXCLUSIVE
'BUD ABBOTT TOLD ME HE'S GUILTY'

Abbott's Cellmate Talks: 'He
Made it Plain He Killed Her'

Below was a copyrighted story under the by-line of John Douglas Cober, the bad-check artist who had relayed Abbott's jailhouse musings to the D.A. during his trial. Cober had first tried to peddle his story to the *Examiner,* which had rejected it in October, deciding it had "nothing new to offer." Now the *Chronicle,* the *Ex*'s archrival, was making hay with it. Cober's lead pulled out all the stops:

> Burton W. Abbott is as guilty as hell of the kidnapping and murder of Stephanie Bryan.
>
> I was his cellmate day after day during his long trial, and he gave me everything but a written confession. I can see him now, sulking and petulant after I told him the crime was that of a dingbat.
>
> "What's a dingbat?" he asked.
>
> "A nut," I said. "A lunatic. A psychopath. Just a psychopath."

Cober went on in like vein throughout five long articles that the *Chronicle* ran as a series. In Abbott's view, he declared, there was "no such thing as good or evil." He quoted Burton as saying: "The Bible is for those who don't know any better." Cober wrote further:

> I never once heard him express sympathy for the family of Stephanie Bryan. Stephanie was never anything to him but a means to an end. He never referred to her in any words other than "the girl."
>
> Even his own kid meant little to him. When his family sent him some colored drawings of animals by the kid, Bud paid no more attention to them than to yesterday's newspaper.

The Cober stories fell short of justifying the *Chronicle*'s extravagant first-day headline. Never had Burton come close to an outright confession. However, Cober said he had made some bad slips. On the eve of Dr. Kirk's testimony, Cober had asked Abbott, "What's he going to try to prove?"

"That the girl was in my car."

"Well," Cober had observed, "they'll convince even me that you are involved if they can prove that."

"He's the only one who can," had been Abbott's unguarded reply.

During another jailhouse conversation, Cober had told Burton, "You'll get a ticket to the gas chamber if they find any dirt from the grave on your boots."

Abbott had answered casually, "I'm not worried about that. We brushed the boots before we turned them over to the police."

Another slip had occurred, Cober wrote, after testimony about Stephanie's bra being found in Abbott's basement. Back in his cell Abbott had protested,

"Do they think I undressed the girl and took off her brassiere? Her last class that day was gym, and she didn't put it back on."

Over time Cober had concluded not only that Abbott was guilty but that his motive was not essentially sex, but to gratify his overpowering ego:

> Bud Abbott planned murder for years. He plotted the specific ab-duction and killing of Stephanie Bryan for months. It was to be a spec-tacular murder. He wanted it to be a famous case. Abbott will never confess publicly, not even when the moment comes for him to step into the gas chamber. In fact, that moment will be his highest pinnacle, in his own sick mind.

As the *Chronicle* hoped, the Cober stories held the Bay Area spellbound. Not all reaction was favorable, however. A journalism professor on Burton's old campus, U.C.-Berkeley, was outraged and denounced the series as the epitome of hateful, irresponsible, yellow journalism.

The frenetic last phase of the battle for Burton's life commenced after Leo Sullivan received a telegram from Joe Babich, the governor's clemency sec-retary, on March 4:

> GOVERNOR KNIGHT HAS THOROUGHLY REVIEWED THE CASE OF BURTON ABBOTT AND HAS CONCLUDED THERE ARE NO GROUNDS FOR EXECUTIVE CLEMENCY.

At age sixty, Goodwin J. "Goodie" Knight was a handsome, ebullient, forceful politician—a Republican governor whose background included eleven years as a Superior Court judge in Los Angeles. He respected legal processes, but he was determined to exclude himself well in advance from the process of Abbott's execution.

He was not to have his way, however; Goodie Knight would remain un-comfortably in the hurricane's eye until the final moment.

30

The Ides of March

On March 4, the day Governor Knight announced his clemency denial, the state's calendar decreed that Burton Abbott had eleven days left to live. During those days Leo Sullivan bombarded all courts in sight, state and federal, with pleas, motions, and petitions. He advanced every conceivable ground for a stay of execution: to correct a "denial of due process," to await legislation suspending the death penalty, to avoid executing an innocent man, to consider "meritorius points of law," to permit another appeal. Sullivan also had Abbott sign a pauper's oath, in order to waive the $100 fee for an appeal copy of his trial's 4,000-page transcript.

It was all in vain. Out of hand the State Supreme Court denied a stay of execution, and other rejections followed, one after another. Every door Sullivan sought to open was slammed in his face. Even liberal U.S. Supreme Court Justice William O. Douglas, who had once courted impeachment by granting a stay to atomic spies Julius and Ethel Rosenberg, refused to act.

With Burton's time fast running out, Sullivan crossed the bay on March 11 to see George T. Davis, an icon among California defense lawyers. It was he who in 1939 had won freedom after twenty-three years for Tom Mooney, a socialist labor agitator convicted of murder on perjured evidence. The Mooney case, arising from a San Francisco bomb plot that left ten persons dead in 1916, had been a worldwide cause célèbre during World War I. An implacable foe of capital punishment, Davis was presently representing Caryl Chessman, another Death Row denizen with an international following.

"You've pulled them out of the hat before, Davis," Sullivan said when they met on March 11. "Will you try for Abbott? Just for a stay so I can have a little more time to work on it. There's no money in the case."

"Money's not important."

"Then you'll come in?"

"Of course."

Davis had no miracles at hand. For the next seventy-two hours he searched the Abbott trial transcript for error, while his private detectives vainly pursued the flimsiest leads for new evidence. In a last-ditch maneuver on execution eve, Davis filed a habeas corpus petition with Judge Walter L. Pope of the Ninth U.S. Circuit Court of Appeals. In it he argued that the so-called "accusatory statements" by Riedel and others had forced Abbott to incriminate himself. Pope promised to study the petition overnight and rule on it before execution time.

Unlike his frantic lawyers, Abbott passed his last days serenely. Two weeks before his gas chamber date, the Death Row watch officers began keeping a preexecution log that detailed his conduct, attitude, and activities, virtually hour by hour. They consistently described him as "friendly," "quiet and courteous," "cooperative," and "pleasant and cheerful."

Burton passed his time reading, listening to the radio, watching television, and visiting, when he could, with other inmates. At least eight times he resorted to chess—the game in which he had also lost himself after the discovery of Stephanie's purse. Most nights he slept well; several times he was given warm milk at 1 A.M.

The prison red tape never stopped, and the approach of the final day imposed on Burton unending chores. On February 27 he signed a form instructing that his body be turned over to the U.C. School of Medicine to be used "as may seem most desirable for medical teaching and research." He instructed that he be delivered to the university "unembalmed and unautopsied." On another form he ordered that the $67.48 balance in his canteen account be given to his mother. Georgia was to get his personal property.

On Wednesday, March 13, as law required, Warden Harley O. Teets designated "two physicians in good standing" and "twelve reputable citizens" as official witnesses to Abbott's execution. In addition he authorized the attendance of others, mostly police officers and newspapermen, bringing the witness roster to fifty-eight names in all.

Elsie was bitter when she saw the list. "By letting in all those people, they are turning Burton's execution into a Roman holiday," she cried. "If they are going to kill Bud, I want to be there with him. There are two seats in that gas chamber, and I will gladly take one of them. It will be the end of the world for me if they kill Burton."

The demand for tickets to the gassing was brisk. At midmorning Thursday a telegram from David Segan, the president of Radio KOBY in San Francisco, was delivered to Teets's desk:

REQUEST PERMISSION TO MAKE DIRECT BROADCAST EXECUTION OF AB-
BOTT. DUE TO IMMENSE PUBLIC INTEREST WE FEEL DIRECT RADIO BROADCAST
WILL SERVE AS LESSON TO ANY WOULD-BE CRIMINAL.

Teets curtly wired back that the proposal was impossible.

Abbott had given much consideration to the menu for his last meal, and submitted his request formally:

Dear Warden:

I would like to respectfully request that for my last meal March 14, I be served the following:

French fried butterfly jumbo prawns (with cocktail sauce, not tartar sauce).
Ravioli (one order).
Tossed green salad (composed primarily of romaine lettuce) with vinegar and oil dressing.
Chocolate cake

I would like to further request a package of Salem cigarettes (unobtainable at canteen), the cost of which may be deducted from my canteen account.

Thank you
B.W. Abbott
A-35539

Georgia, driven by one of her sisters, arrived on Thursday morning to bid her husband good-bye. This time they did not have to talk through a screen; they were together for fifty-eight minutes in a special visiting room. Among other matters, they talked about the future of Chris, who would be five and a half years old in two more weeks. Georgia told Burton she planned to leave the state, taking Chris with her.

"And change his name," Burton said, though he refrained from suggesting what the new name should be. Georgia left the prison as she had come, crouched out of sight below the windows of her sister's car.

Meanwhile Elsie Abbott had appeared at the prison gates with Mark and her sister Mona. Mark, watching Georgia speed away, made no effort to conceal his bitterness.

"There goes Georgia. You can see she's hiding on the floor," he said to nearby newsmen. "I'm sure she knows something that could help us. She held back during the trial, and she's holding back something now."

Elsie and Mona followed Georgia in the visiting room. When they left an hour later, Elsie told the reporters, "Bud was very cheerful. We avoided talking about a stay of execution because we didn't want to torture him. Instead, we joked about some of the atrocious TV commercials he had seen last night."

Mark, who would be Burton's final visitor, then went in alone for seventeen minutes, reporting "He's calm on the outside, but shaky on the inside."

Abbott spent the afternoon cleaning and scrubbing his cell. At 4:30 two guards appeared with a leather belt and handcuffs, and he was marched to an elevator that took him from the fifth-floor Row to the death cell, close by the green-walled gas chamber on the first floor. He surprised his guards by asking that Catholic Chaplain Edward Dingberg—not Protestant Chaplain Eshelman—be with him at the end.

"Entered death cell at 4:45 P.M. in very good spirits," the watch officer wrote in the log.

At six o'clock, with evident enjoyment, Abbott consumed the prawns, salad, and ravioli he had ordered, plus coffee, milk, and rolls and butter. During the meal he browsed through a science magazine and a copy of *Esquire*. He saved his chocolate cake for a midnight snack. After dinner he chatted until past midnight with his guards and visitors (all prison personnel) and then read magazines for an hour. At one-twenty he fell asleep.

The sun rose at six-nineteen on March 15—the ides of March, destined to be Burton's last day on earth. He awakened at five-twelve and asked the time, then turned over and went back to sleep; at six-thirty he woke up again. With three and a half hours yet to live, he breakfasted heartily on eggs, bacon, ham, hash browns, orange juice, tomato juice, and coffee. Then he asked that the radio be turned on for the seven-fifty-five news roundup. There was nothing in the broadcast to give him hope. Judge Pope had turned down his habeas corpus plea.

George T. Davis arose at seven o'clock in his San Francisco home overlooking the bay and pondered the situation. Having run out of courts in which to battle, he grasped at the only straw in sight. Maybe Goodie Knight, up in Sacramento, would still give him a break. At eight-fifteen he put through a call to the Executive Mansion.

"The governor is not available," he was informed.

On this day of many ironies, not the least was that the U.S. Navy brass had chosen it to entertain Governor and Mrs. Knight on a coastal cruise aboard the aircraft carrier *Hancock*—which was to embark from a pier at the Alameda Naval Air Station, the workplace of both Elsie and Mark Abbott, literally within walking distance of Burton's home. At the minute Abbott was to die, the governor—the one person with power to intervene—would be afloat offshore. Knight had accepted the navy's invitation realizing the risk involved but had nonetheless decided to rely on ship-to-shore phone to stay in touch.

The cruise posed an additional problem for Knight—a legal one. Under an anachronistic clause of the California State Constitution, the governor may exercise his powers only when physically within the state. If he crosses the state line, all authority passes instantly to the lieutenant governor. Because of this, the *Hancock's* navigator was ordered to keep the ship within California's three-mile jurisdictional limit until Abbott was gassed.

Whoever had answered Davis's call to the governor's mansion had informed him that the Knights were at that moment airborne, bound for Alameda. By now Burton had less than two hours to live.

Dejectedly Davis hung up, but hardly had he done so when the phone rang. It was George Wolfe, host of the *Today* show, on the air at that moment from the NBC Studios in Burbank, four hundred miles to the south. The program was seen in the Bay Area on the network's local TV outlet.

Wolfe wanted to know the latest on the Abbott case, and asked for a live interview. For the moment Davis declined the latter, but even as he did so, an idea began to take shape in his mind. He dialed the Alameda Naval Air Station. Was Governor Knight there yet?

"No, but he's due in ten minutes," a junior officer said. On arrival the Knights would be taken first to a dining room for coffee before boarding the ship. Quickly Davis explained his predicament to the young officer, and pleaded that the dining room TV be turned to NBC at high volume when the governor arrived. The young man, caught up in the drama, agreed to do his best.

Today had only six minutes of air time left. Davis recontacted NBC in Burbank just before nine o'clock and talked to the producer, who listened briefly and told him to hold the phone. Seconds later, on his living room TV, Davis saw the producer enter the picture and hand Wolfe a note. Then he heard Wolfe's voice, from both the phone and his TV set:

"What is the latest, Mr. Davis?"

"There is only one hope now, and that is Governor Knight. Within the last few minutes it has come to my attention that he is within earshot of your program. May I use your show to make a plea directly to the governor?"

"Of course!"

"Governor Knight," Davis said earnestly, "Burton Abbott is scheduled to die in San Quentin Prison within the hour. A stay of execution must be granted in order that I may explain to you an aspect of this case that I am sure has not been brought to your attention. Will you please call me as soon as possible, in time to save this boy's life?"

Davis then gave his home number, hung up, and waited. Two minutes later his phone rang.

"What new evidence has come up, Mr. Davis?" Knight demanded. He sounded unhappy at having been put on the spot with the TV audience listening.

"The evidence against Abbott is too pat," Davis told him. "Detectives are now working on the theory that it could have been planted. I need just a little more time to draft the necessary brief."

"I'll give you one hour."

What was the possibly "planted" evidence? It was Elsie's mere suspicion that the brassiere and panties introduced at the trial were fakes. (Coakley later called the idea "absurd.")

At San Quentin Warden Teets appeared at the death cell at 10:02 to tell Burton he would live at least another hour. He could do nothing but wait, Father Dingberg at his side.

During the first minutes of Abbott's hour of grace, Davis sped to his office, dictated a short petition for another stay of execution, and delivered it in person to California's Chief Justice Phil Gibson—to no avail. Upholding the stance his court had taken consistently, Gibson denied the stay.

Now it was ten-forty. Davis grabbed a phone to call the governor once more. The *Hancock* had already sailed and Knight was on the water. Because of jammed ship-to-shore frequencies, twenty-nine minutes ticked away before Davis's call went through.

"What now?" Knight asked.

"I need another stay. I'm taking another appeal to federal court."

The governor sighed. "You understand it's twelve minutes after eleven now?"

"I understand."

"Very well, I'll call my clemency secretary."

At the prison, preparations were in their last stage. At 11 o'clock Teets informed Abbott that he would die in fifteen minutes. At eleven-ten the bucket of sulfuric acid was set in place below the death chair and Abbott was summoned. He embraced Father Dingberg and then, accompanied by three guards, walked quietly the short distance to the two-chair gas chamber.

11:14: The assembled witnesses caught their first glimpse of the condemned man through the chamber's five thick windows. He wore a clean white shirt, open at the neck, and new blue jeans. His hair was combed. His eyes were moist but he seemed calm.

"The three guards were incredibly fast," wrote Ralph Condon, who covered the execution for the *San Jose Mercury* and *News*. "One knelt before Abbott's knees and strapped his legs to the frame of chair 'B.' The other guards put the chest strap around him, working together, and then each took an arm to strap down. The guards then moved out, the last man giving Abbott the customary pat on the back."

Almost two years before, one of Abbott's nurses at Livermore had told the police, "He always said 'please' and 'thank you.' " Now, at the end, Abbott corroborated her. As the guards left the gas chamber at 11:16, he gave them a small smile and said, "Thank you."

His smile, however, masked turmoil within. Before Abbott left the overnight death cell his pulse rate, which should have been 72, had climbed to 120, and his respiration, which should have been about 14 breaths per minute, had reached 22. And within the past five minutes his pulse had speeded up by half again and his breathing by a third. His heart was now racing at 180 beats per minute and his respiratory rate was 28.

11:17: The death chamber door was locked. Burton stared straight ahead, making no eye contact with the witnesses outside. Pulse 180, respiration 26.

11:18: The mechanical arm lowering the cyanide pills into the acid started to move. Burton closed his eyes and took a deep breath. Pulse 160, respiration still 26.

11:18:30: He grimaced as the first fumes reached his face. Pulse 90, respiration 24.

11:19: His head fell forward, his face contorted. Pulse 60, respiration 8.

11:20: He swallowed hard and gasped three times as if seeking clean air. Pulse 60, respiration 3.

In a small room not far from the death chamber a telephone jangled. Warden Teets answered.

"This is Joe Babich, Governor Knight's clemency secretary. Has the execution started yet?"

"Yes."

"Can it be halted?"

"Too late. The pellets just dropped."

Over the next four minutes the remaining life within Burton Abbott faded swiftly away. He lifted his head once; then it fell forward again, and saliva oozed from his mouth. Tremors shook his shoulders. His pulse dropped successively to 54, 48, 24, and zero. By 11:24 all visible movement, pulse, and breathing had ended. Dr. M. D. Willcutts, San Quentin's chief physician, pronounced him dead at 11:25.

"Gentlemen, that is all," Teets announced to the witnesses. "Thank you, and please file out."

Later the warden said Abbott's self-control at the end had been "an extreme effort, which succeeded by a narrow margin."*

---

* Abbott's time on Death Row was one year, one month, and four days, a remarkably short stay by 1990s standards.

Georgia Abbott received her confirmation of Burton's death at the home of her sister in San Anselmo where she was in seclusion, barely five miles from San Quentin.

Elsie and Mark were with Mona at her apartment in Alameda, with reporters crowding the corridor outside. When the newsmen got the flash that Burton was dead, one of them knocked on the apartment door. Mona opened it a little.

"Is it over?" she asked.

"Yes, that's the word we have." Inside a woman was heard crying.

Four decades later Elsie still recalled that agony. "When the news came to us, all I could do was say 'No!' My son Mark turned his back; he couldn't take it. And what was the worst? The attorneys. Whitney sent me a flower arrangement; can you imagine that? I refused to accept it."

Epilogue

Late on execution day a hearse rolled away from San Quentin, carrying Burton Abbott's corpse to the University of California School of Medicine in accordance with his wishes.

In Redding, two hundred miles to the north, the humble remains of Stephanie Bryan still reposed in a Lawncrest Memorial Park receiving vault. Only now were they released to her family for cremation and burial. A family plot in Pelican Rapids, Minnesota, is her final resting place.

Although the execution spelled an end to the Stephanie Bryan case legally, the story went on. For her family, closing the door on the tragedy was not easy, nor even entirely possible. In part, it was dealt with through rejection.

"My sisters and I never talk about it—or we talk about it peripherally," Stephanie's brother Sam told the author in 1993. "We've all had very difficult times. From the time I was eleven to my early twenties, I was very withdrawn; I think it was a symptom of the family suppression of this subject. I don't think the public understands how something like this affects family relationships over decades."

"My older sister and I have felt at times that it should have been one of us [instead of Stephanie]. My parents wouldn't have had their favorite taken. Stephanie was the model, the ideal child in my parents' eyes."

Reading had been one of Stephanie's great joys, and not long after her death a special collection honoring her memory was established at the Willard Junior High School library. For a long time her mother, Mary, visited the school often, bringing new books her daughter would have enjoyed.

Within three years, tragedy struck the Bryans anew, after they moved from the Alvarado Road house with its unhappy memories to a new home nearby. In 1958, without warning Dr. Bryan fell dead of a heart attack as he was painting the back fence. Sam attributes the misfortune wholly to the stress and sorrow his father had endured.

After his father's death Sam lived for several years with his godparents in Omaha, outside the lingering shadow of the crime against his sister. He later attended U.C. Berkeley, went to law school, and served for a time as a clerk in the district attorney's office that had prosecuted Abbott. Ultimately, though, he turned away from the law in favor of horticulture; at this writing he is the proprietor of a popular nursery in Oakland. His three remaining sisters, Cheryl, Estelle, and Beatrice, live nearby. Mary Bryan died of pulmonary fibrosis in 1983.

In May 1957 a court hearing was convened to decide the recipient of the $2,500 reward posted by Stephanie's family. Several claimants came forward, including an elderly widow who said her "intuitive powers" had yielded the first description of the girl's abductor (which incidentally proved quite accurate). However, the money was awarded to Harold "Bud" Jackson, the wilderness rancher whose hounds had found Stephanie's grave.

"What are you going to do with the money?" he was asked.

"I'm going to feed those dogs real well," he said.

Jackson has proved the hardiest of the Trinity County characters in the Stephanie story. In 1994 he was still lean, wiry, and spry in his eighties, still ranching and still tracking down marauding mountain lions with his hounds.

Contrary to predictions, there was little political fallout from the Abbott trial. Coakley considered running for California attorney general in 1958 and 1962, but for reasons having nothing to do with the Abbott case he did not. He continued as district attorney until his retirement in 1969, having occupied the post an unprecedented twenty-two years. Edmund G. "Pat" Brown, his longtime rival in prosecutorial affairs, was elected governor of California in 1958 and served for eight years, as did his son, Governor Edmund G. "Jerry" Brown, later. Pat Brown died in 1996.

Two other lawyers in the Abbott trial—one on each side—became Superior Court judges. Folger Emerson was elected to the bench late in 1956, and Harold Hove was appointed by Governor Ronald Reagan in 1968.* Stanley Whitney remained in private practice. Of the bench-bar principals in the case, Judge Snook died first in 1965, followed by Coakley in 1983, Hove and Whitney in 1984, and Emerson in 1989.

At the instant of Burton Abbott's last breath, the doubters and taunters of Georgia Abbott stood discredited. They had predicted that she would desert him, but she had made good on her declaration at his trial: "There will never be a divorce in our lives." Now, however, she needed escape. On the day after the execution, taking young Chris with her, she departed California for the state of her birth, Kansas. An eventful future lay before her.

She was broke, but earning a livelihood in her new surroundings was not

---

* Otto Dezman sent a contribution to Emerson's campaign, but it was returned. When Hove was appointed, Dezman sent Reagan a letter of protest.

a worry. Her hairdresser's skill was in demand, and she was soon employed by the salon in the Muehlebach Hotel in Kansas City, Missouri. If her clientele at the Morton salon had been Upper Crust Alameda, at the Muehlebach it was Upper Crust America.

This hotel was a starred location on the political map—a place frequented by dignitaries, including former President Harry Truman, whom Georgia met several times and found "very charming." Bess Truman did not patronize the Muehlebach salon, but Georgia did Eleanor Roosevelt's hair when she passed through town.

Within a few years Georgia met and married a wealthy Kentucky cattleman with dealings throughout the Midwest and South. Their travels took them to barbecues at Lyndon Johnson's LBJ Ranch in Texas, and they were in Dallas on fateful November 22, 1963. From their hotel window Georgia watched President John F. Kennedy pass in his motorcade two or three minutes before he was assassinated.

In keeping with what Georgia and Burton had decided, she changed their son's name. The surname she chose was from neither her family nor Burton's, nor was it the name of her new husband. It belonged to a friend she admired and respected.

Time healed the estrangement between Georgia and Elsie, and both helped raise the youngster formerly known as Chris Abbott. He grew up to become a career soldier, serving in many parts of the world. In 1995, retired from the military, he was a public official in a city far from Alameda.

Georgia's new marriage eventually ended in divorce, and she returned to California under her new name, resuming her cosmetology career. In 1994 her residence was a spotless mobile home in a park for seniors, with a noisy green cockatiel as her only companion. The furnishings were expensive and tasteful.

Only a few of her oldest friends were aware of the tragedy in her past. She recalled one occasion when unsuspecting fellow employees got into a lively argument about the Abbott case in her presence. Without disclosing her involvement, she told them, "When you don't know about anything, don't try to guess. You'll always be wrong."

Did she still believe in Burton's innocence?

"It's been a long time ago," she told the author. "Every once in a while when I can't sleep, I think, what in the world really happened? I've always believed that it was not him. If he did anything, he took the fall for somebody else."

Georgia died in 1995.

For Otto and Leona Dezman of the Morton Beauty Salon, drawn into the Abbott case by capricious fate, it was a disaster.

"We had a thriving business until this happened," Otto said in 1995. "The business went to hell after the trial. We sold out three or four years later."

The Dezmans resettled first in a small community in the Sierra Nevada, then in a larger town in the Sacramento Valley. Leona died of cancer in 1987. Otto eventually remarried and was still active in 1996.

Certain mysteries on the fringes of the Bryan case have never been resolved. To this day no one knows whose fingers (if any) were seen by Mack Jensen protruding from the trunk of the old Pontiac at his service station in Keyes near Modesto. Could they have been Stephanie's? The theory suggested by Officer Hutchins—that someone was playing a joke on Jensen—is widely accepted.

Burton's execution did not stifle the public's obsession with his case. His cult of defenders remained vocal—an embittered alliance embracing thoughtful doubters as well as a lunatic fringe.

An unlikely fanatic in the cult was a person who signed herself Joanne. She first came to Coakley's attention in late 1958, when she began pestering Abbott trial witnesses with letters and questionnaires, challenging their testimony. She also wrote to Judge Snook and Governor Pat Brown, and ultimately to Coakley himself, declaring "My aim is to crack this case and to prove that this man was innocent of the murder for which he was accused."

Coakley assigned Inspector Russ Ryan to determine the identity of this woman—as she was assumed to be. Instead, he found an adolescent at San Francisco's Mission High School. Had Stephanie lived, the two girls would have been the same age.

At the school Ryan was told that "Joanne" (a name she had made up) was unstable but not a disciplinary problem. She was credited with a "dull-normal" I.Q. of 86 (which seems far too low, for her grammar was good, her prose clear, her typing almost flawless, and her penmanship excellent). She was summoned to a counselor's office for questioning.

"Why are you using a false name?" Ryan asked her.

Because, she said, her parents had no knowledge of the secret battle she had been waging to clear Burton Abbott's name. It had consumed virtually all her free time for the past three years, and if they found out about it, she would be in deep trouble at home.

Why was she doing this?

"Five or ten years of my life is nothing if I can prove that Burton is innocent," she said. "To me he is the sun, moon, and stars."

Joanne had scarcely followed the Bryan case while it was happening and had known little about it in 1956 when she heard Abbott's death verdict announced. But the next day she had begun carrying Burton's picture in her purse. In her own words, she "thought of nothing but the Abbott case. When I went to bed I thought of Mr. Abbott. When I ate, I thought of Mr. Abbott. When I dreamed, I dreamed Abbott; talked, Abbott; took a shower, Abbott; went shopping, Abbott."

After Burton's execution, the girl's infatuation with him progressed to passionate fantasy. To a friend she wrote, "I loved Burton so much that I wanted to take him in the bushes and love him until he was hard as a f---."

Joanne created voluminous files on the Abbott case. She ran want ads in the *Chronicle* and the *Tribune* seeking "help, information, opinions, and witnesses." She rummaged through the clips and photos in the *Chronicle* library, disrupting operations, until she was told, "You've worn out your welcome here."

The girl hung out in office buildings, buttonholing noted criminal lawyers. She was working on a twenty-chapter manuscript about her crusade. Unlike other Abbott "fans," Joanne bore no grudge against Coakley or his men for convicting him. Instead she basked in their attention and sought to recruit them as conspirators in her clandestine cause. Once she tiptoed to the edge of bribery, telling Ryan in writing that "twenty-five dollars will be given" if he would use his position in her behalf. To Captain Severin Joanne wrote, "Dear Clarence, I have adopted you as my father." She called him monthly to talk, a habit he did not discourage because she kept him abreast of what the Abbott underground was doing.

During one of their conversations in 1961, with Joanne approaching her twenty-first birthday, Severin suggested it was high time she had some social life, which she had all but abandoned during her five-year obsession with the dead Burton.

"No," she replied. "I don't like to go out with men particularly. All they think about is squeezing me and pinching me."

Burton's vindication also became a never-ending effort for his mother, Elsie—an endeavor far more poignant than Joanne's. Elsie never lost faith. She hired private detectives when she could, and she became an investigator herself. She sought the ear of Governor Pat Brown and laid her case before the State Legislature.

In May 1960, three years after Burton's death, Elsie sent the Alameda County Grand Jury a demand for an investigation of Coakley's office. Her eleven-page, single-spaced document charged Coakley and eight others with "conspiracy to commit deliberate murder." She also accused ten key prosecution witnesses of perjury. The purse, wallet, and brassiere introduced in court were fakes, she asserted, and Stephanie's "Teddy" letter was a forgery. The Grand Jury unanimously rejected the allegations.

Elsie's sad life grew lonelier in 1968 when her remaining son, Mark, died of a heart attack.

In 1995 the author, after considerable searching, found Elsie Abbott at age ninety-one, living at home in a town far from the scenes of her midcentury anguish. Her mind was active, her memory good. Although feeble, she still tended her own garden. Her belief in her son's innocence was undiminished.

"The nights are the worst," she said. "I just don't sleep. I go over and over and over it all, constantly, night after night. For the last thirty-five or forty years I've never had any rest."

Although a frame-up had been implicit in Abbott's defense, he had never personally suggested the name of an alternate suspect. So I put the question to his mother: "Do you have a theory as to who could have framed Burton?"

Her answer was astonishing: "Yes, my brother Wilbur was the guilty one. There's no doubt about it."

Wilbur Moore was the uncle from whom Burton Wilbur Abbott had taken both his middle name and his nickname "Bud." A bus and truck driver, he had never been anything but a footnote in the Abbott story. As we know, Wilbur had lived across the hall from Elsie and her boys for a time in the 1940s, and there had been a cooling between brother and sister when he divorced his wife, Claudia, of whom Elsie was fond. None of this had ever seemed pertinent to the Stephanie Bryan murder, however. Like all of Abbott's relatives, Moore had been questioned about it, but only routinely. He had told the police, "I don't want to be drawn into the matter."

Now, forty years later, Elsie was saying *He did it.*

Why?

"Everything indicates that," she said "My brother went haywire. He came home from work and found his wife [Claudia's successor] in bed with another man. He went berserk." But there is nothing in the record to support such a scenario.

About the time of Stephanie's abduction, Elsie related, Wilbur had visited the Abbotts in Alameda. It could have been then, according to her theory, that he had secreted the girl's possessions in their basement. Elsie further recalled that during their conversation, Wilbur had talked about visiting the Trinity cabin and asked how to get there—"so we sat there like stupid idiots and told him." It was after that, Elsie now believed, that her brother had taken Stephanie or her body to Wildwood and buried her.

Elsie's conjecture also touched on the three bouffant half-slips—white, pink, and green—removed from Stephanie's body. Two of the "extra skirts," she said, had belonged to Wilbur's wife (though they had been identified by Stephanie's mother).

Had Elsie ever confronted Wilbur with her hypothesis? Yes, she said, many years ago, and he had denied it all. Elsie's suspicions can never be tested; Wilbur Moore died in 1978.

Gradually the Stephanie Bryan murder faded from public consciousness in the late 1950s, but it suddenly returned to the front pages four years after Burton had paid with his life.

The story's revival was unplanned. In September 1961 San Quentin's chief psychiatrist, Dr. Schmidt, was testifying at a sanity hearing for another Death Row prisoner and was asked by the district attorney, "Do condemned men often admit their guilt in confidence to their doctors or psychiatrists?"

"All but ten or fifteen percent of them do."

"Did Burton Abbott admit it?" the D.A. queried, probably because of his own curiosity.

"He admitted it, not directly but indirectly, to me." Schmidt blurted out. At once he wished he could swallow the words. "I wouldn't like this to get to his mother," he added, but it was too late. His statement was in the public record, and the newspapers were all over it. Street sales in San Francisco jumped thirty thousand overnight.

Elsie Abbott was furious. "It's absolutely false!" she screamed.

Schmidt's unintentional disclosure triggered a flurry of comparable revelations by others.

Private detective Linhart, who had aided Elsie's campaign to clear Burton's name, came forward with a story he attributed to the late Death Row denizen Caryl Chessman—Abbott's fellow prisoner there.

"In a nutshell it went like this," Linhart said. "Stephanie was killed by someone very close to Abbott, someone Abbott felt obligated to. There was a good possibility Stephanie had been seeing a lot of this person. At any rate, when the girl was killed, Abbott felt a desperate need to help his friend by disposing of her body; so he placed the body in his old car and headed for the cabin. The rest is an old story."

This outbreak of 1961 hearsay touched off a political storm. In Sacramento Governor Pat Brown demanded a full report from the Department of Corrections, and at San Quentin the warden called Dr. Schmidt on the carpet. As the heat rose around him, Schmidt fanned the flames by giving the *Chronicle* a detailed reconstruction of his critical talk with Abbott, not long before Abbott died:

SCHMIDT. Burton, why don't you come out and admit your guilt and throw yourself on the mercy of the governor and ask for executive clemency?

ABBOTT. Doc, I can't admit it. Think of what it would do to my mother. Doc, she could not take it.

The Department of Corrections was quick to disavow Schmidt, announcing that a search of Abbott's entire file had disclosed "nothing whatsoever about a confession." That's what the governor was told, and that's what the truth was believed to be—for the next thirty-four years.

But the governor had been lied to—at best not told the whole truth. Abbott's Death Row files eventually became public records in the California State Archives, and there the author examined them. They show that on February 20, 1957, twenty-three days before Abbott's execution, Dr. Schmidt had noted in his file:

"(I can't admit g because of my m)"

Schmidt had read this to represent the phrase "I can't admit guilt because of my mother"—virtually the same words he had recalled for the *Chronicle*.

Perhaps Whitney's law partner Jack Hanson, the only lawyer of Abbott's team alive at this writing, put the fairest perspective on his case when interviewed by the author in 1993. Asked his opinion of Burton's guilt or innocence, Hanson said: "I will never know in my own mind. One day I thought he was guilty, the next day not. I think we'd have won it if he had done what we told him to. He thought he was a smart student, playing games with Coakley. He was a little too smart for his britches."

"Did Abbott get a fair trial?" Hanson was asked.

"Oh, yeah," his last surviving attorney answered without hesitation.

AUTHOR'S NOTE
AND
ACKNOWLEDGMENTS

My fascination with the Stephanie Bryan story began when it happened—when I worked on it as a *San Jose Mercury News* rewrite man. Our reporter at the Burton Abbott trial was Charles Cruttenden, who sat through the courtroom sessions gavel to gavel, while I remained in the office to take his frequent dictation and get the story down on paper. Because of exceptional reader interest, our orders were to freshen it up for each edition, and we had about six a day.

The Bryan case had a cruel impact on the lives of many people with no direct involvement in the events themselves. A bizarre coincidence made it a nightmare for a young San Jose widow named Steffi Abbott, for example, who had a teenage daughter named Stephanie and a small son named Burton after his late father. She was hounded mercilessly by the curious for as long as the case was in the headlines.

Four decades have elapsed since then, but the memories of those caught up in the case have hardly dimmed, and their emotions and convictions have diminished not at all.

In retelling the story now, I have striven for accuracy. I acknowledge recasting some direct and indirect quotations in the interest of clarity or brevity or to achieve a conversational flow. I have had to guess at certain obscure time sequences or compress the time element. None of this has altered the essential facts of the case, however, or their significance.

All names are real unless otherwise indicated by footnote.

I am deeply grateful to many persons touched by the Stephanie Bryan tragedy who told me candidly of matters that must have been painful for them to recall.

Sam Bryan, the victim's brother, provided exceptional insights into the effects of her death on her family. The recollections of two of her childhood friends, Lesley Emmington Jones and Lois K. Thomas, gave me a clearer understanding of her shortened life.

Three members of Burton Abbott's family granted much-appreciated interviews: his late wife, Georgia, his mother, Elsie, and his son, Chris.

Several other surviving players in the Stephanie Bryan drama also talked with me. They include Harold "Bud" Jackson, who with his hunting dogs found Stephanie's grave; Otto Dezman, whose late wife, Leona, was Georgia's employer; and criminalist Lowell W. Bradford, the defense expert on forensic evidence.

I have had unstinting assistance from the family of the late District Attorney J. Frank Coakley, including his late widow, Kathleen, his son, Tom, his daughter, Clare Coakley Klinge, and his son-in-law, Ronald A. Klinge.

Abbott's principal courtroom attorneys, Stanley Whitney and Harold Hove, are deceased, but the last surviving member of the defense team, Whitney's partner John F. Hanson, granted me a full day of his time. Hove's widow, Alice, also discussed the case with me at length.

The book profits greatly from the record-keeping diligence of the Alameda County District Attorney's Office, which gave me access to its exceptional file on the Bryan case. This material enabled me to write more authentically than otherwise possible, with enormously enhanced detail. My special thanks go to former District Attorney John Meehan, Assistant District Attorney William W. Baldwin, former Captain of Inspectors Charles Ryken, Tammy de le Cruz, Jennifer Larson, and the late Richard W. Reid.

Likewise, I have had the invaluable help of the Berkeley Police Department and several of its present and former members, including Deputy Chief Roy L. Meisner, Richard Young, Ralph Schillinger, Willard H. Hutchins, and Leonard Schifsky. Other important law enforcement sources include the late Jack Fink, the Alameda police officer who arrested Abbott; Alameda County Sheriff Charles C. Plummer (who was also on the Berkeley police force in 1955); and Sergeant Jim Knudsen of the Sheriff's Department.

Needless to say, I an indebted to many journalists living and dead who covered the Bryan story or otherwise had special knowledge of the case. A partial list (with apologies to others overlooked) includes Charles Cruttenden, Ralph Condon, Bob Crabbe, Carroll Hurd, and Bill Regan of the *San Jose Mercury News;* Ed Montgomery, Gale Cook, and Bob Bryant of the *San Francisco Examiner;* Jack McDowell of the *San Francisco Call-Bulletin;* George Draper, Carolyn Anspacher, Charles Rodebaugh, and Bernice Freeman of the *San Francisco Chronicle;* Bill Fiset, Virginia Dennison, Gayle Montgomery, and Ralph Craib of the *Oakland Tribune;* and Everett Johannes of the *Berkeley Daily Gazette* and the *Alameda Times-Star.*

I have had important assistance from several librarians, archivists, and researchers, including the late Bill Strobel of the Hayward Area Historical Society, Peggy Conaway and Carmen Newby of the San Jose Public Library, Gary Lance of the *San Jose Mercury News* library, Gloria Brown and Steven Staiger of the Palo Alto Historical Association, Alden Maberg of the Oregon State Library, and Carol Moore of the Trinity County Historical Society. Other agencies that have been helpful include the California State Archives, the California State Library, the Trinity County Library, the Josephine County (Oregon) Library, and public libraries in Oakland and Redwood City.

I appreciate the support of Cal Morgan, my editor at St. Martin's Press, and my agent, Maria Theresa Caen. Three friends who have given steadfast encouragement, assistance, and counsel throughout my research and writing— Grace Elaine Matthews, Joanne Grant, and Cathie Calvert—have my special gratitude.

Others who have helped in many ways include Mr. and Mrs. Smith Anderson, Thomas Baker, D.D.S., Berndt I. Brauer, Orrin Brown, Jr., Mary Castagnetto, Jay Clark, Joanna Correll, Bernice Cotella, Vincent Dell 'Ergo, Dorothy Duckett, George William Treat Flint, Jeanne and Stan Fowler, Jack Gorman, Pat Hicks, Judy Jameson, Barbara Jones, Ray Lewis, Mack Lundstrom, Dick Morris, Page and Patty Nelson, Bruce Newby, Jade L. Petznick, Nancy Thornburg, and Angie Torres.

San Jose, California
July 18, 1997

BIBLIOGRAPHY

Books and Pamphlets

Catton, Joseph, M.D. *Behind the Scenes of Murder.* New York: W.W. Norton & Company, 1940.

Coakley, J. Frank. *For the People.* Orinda, Calif.: Western Star Press, 1992.

Gallagher, Paul E. *California Blue Book 1954.* Sacramento: California State Printing Office, 1954.

Gentry, Curt. *Frame-up.* New York: W.W. Norton & Company, 1967.

Kelley, Douglas M., M.D. *22 Cells in Nuremberg.* New York: MacFadden Books, MacFadden Publications, Inc., 1947.

Melendy, H. Brett, and Gilbert, Benjamin F. *The Governors of California.* Georgetown, Calif.: The Talisman Press, 1965.

Mello, the Rev. Edward. *Trinity Yearbook 1955.* Weaverville, Calif.: Trinity County Historical Society, 1955.

Parker, Alfred E. *The Berkeley Police Story.* Springfield, Ill.: Charles C. Thomas, 1972.

Reynolds, Quentin. *Courtroom,* New York: Farrar, Straus and Company, 1950.

Rolle, Andrew F. *California, A History, Third Edition.* Arlington Heights, Ill.: AHM Publishing Corporation, 1978.

Stone, Irving. *Men to Match My Mountains.* New York: Doubleday & Company, Inc., 1956.

Walker, Keith. *A Trail of Corn.* Santa Rosa, Calif.: Golden Door Press, 1995.

Williams, Brad. *Due Process.* New York: William Morrow and Company, 1960.

Articles and Documents

Bradford, Lowell W. "Paul L. Kirk, 1902–1970." *Police Science,* Northwestern University, 1971.

Coburn, Hugh. "The Death That Stays Alive." *Front Page Detective,* January, 1962.

Grodsky Morris; Wright, Keith; and Kirk, Paul L. "Simplified Preliminary Blood Testing, An Improved Technique and a Comparative Study of Methods." *Journal of Criminal Law, Criminology, and Police Science.* Northwestern University, May–June, 1951.

Martinez, Al. "City Editor: RECK of The Tribune combined humanity with efficiency and made it work." *Editor & Publisher,* July 6, 1963.

"Spots of Blood, Bits of Metal, and Traces of Powder." *California Monthly.* November, 1964.

Newspapers

Alameda Times Star. July 27, 1955, and August 30, 1955.

Berkeley Daily Gazette. July 23, 1955, and August 27, 1955.

Los Angeles Examiner. July 25, 1955.

Oakland Tribune. July 18–28, 1955; August 4, 1955; January 25, 1956; and February 11, 1956.

Palo Alto Times. January 23–May 1, 1957; and September 22–27, 1961.

Redwood City Tribune. October 14–28, 1955; November 4, 1955–January 26, 1956, January 10, 1957; March 8–15, 1957; September 22–27, 1961; and April 28, 1965.

San Francisco Call-Bulletin. December 7, 1955.

San Francisco Chronicle. April 30–May 6, 1955; July 17–19, 1955; November 6, 1955–January 28, 1956; February 4–12, 1956; April 23, 1956; November 23, 1956; January 28–29, 1957; March 5, 1957; and March 13–16, 1957.

San Francisco Examiner. July 22, 1955, and September 22, 1961.

San Francisco News. July 23, 1955.

San Jose Evening News. September 8, 1955; November 7, 1955–January 26, 1956; March 16, 1957; and September 22, 1961.

San Jose Mercury. May 1–19, 1955; July 17–22, 1955; November 7, 1955–January 16, 1956; March 15–16, 1956; May 8, 1957; and September 22–29, 1961.

Trinity Weekly Journal. July 21 and 28 and August 11, 1955.

INDEX

Alameda County, 77, 119, 190, 282
 County Clerk's Office, 281
 Courthouse, 67, 116, 150, 189
 District Attorney's Office, 38, 68, 176
 Grand Jury, 115–125, 298
 County Jail, 125, 164
 Sheriff's Mounted Patrol, 25
 Superior Court, 173
 Surveyor's Office, 218
Alameda Hospital, 258
Alameda Naval Air Station, 48, 55, 140,
 169, 224, 289–90
Alameda Sporting Goods Store, 75
Alameda Times-Star, 179, 281
Alamedan, 179
Algebra (Bartlett), 161*n*
Alka-Seltzer, 64, 118
"All box," 3, 4, 85, 215
Allan, Thomas A., 134
Alpine County, 134
Altomare Mary, 273
Alvarado Park (Richmond), 38
Alvarado Road (Berkeley), 6, 11, 22, 34,
 96, 116–17, 132, 185, 198, 274, 294
Anderson (California), 174
Anderson, Chesley, 71
Anderson, Dolores, 194, 196
Anderson, Jean, 71
Anderson, O. E., 218–19
Anspacher, Carolyn, 205, 219, 246, 251,
 277
Apache brand pencils, 181
Arnone, Rosa, 151–53, 154, 146, 268
 testimony, 239–41
Ashby Avenue (Berkeley), 8, 12, 13, 67,
 84*n*, 184, 199, 203–4
Associated Press, 145
Atlas Imperial Engine Company, 50
Avilla, Albert, 133

Baker Memorial Hospital (Boston), 26
Balma, Rudy, 186
Bank of America, 141
Barnum, Phineas T., 235
Barthol, Robert, 47–57
Barton, Lydia, 116

Bauman, Maxine, 44
Baylor, Simon (fictitious name), 174
Beach, Wayne, 134
Benton, Amelia (fictitious name), 35, 35*n*
Benzidine test, 181, 228–29
Berkeley, ix, 8, 107, 112, 113, 129, 148,
 163
 Parks Department, 22
 Police Department, 5, 10, 11, 84, 90,
 107, 176, 184, 201
 Public Library, 12, 163
Berkeley School Department, 113, 182
Berkeley Daily Gazette, 10, 11, 13, 172
Berkeley Municipal Court, 18
Berkeley Tennis Club, 12, 163, 198, 202
Bertrand, Joseph, 90
Best-known Works of Edgar Allan Poe, The,
 64*n*
Bethel, Walter Raleigh, 179–80, 233–34,
 252, 252*n,* 268
 testimony, 234–236
Betts, Sam O. *See* Bethel, Walter Raleigh
Beyerle, Alvin, 141, 162
Beyerle, John, 162, 162*n,* 163
Beyerle, Marie, 162
Beyerle, Sharon, 162–63
Bibbee, Arthur, 52, 53
Bill and Kathy's Restaurant, 61, 149–50,
 260
Bischop, Sergeant Ralph, 17, 30–32
Bliss, Theodora, 4–12. *See* "Teddy"
Boardman, Howard, 23
Bob's Service Station, 29–30
Boccaccio, Giovanni, 6–12
Bolton, Ebba, 42–43
Book of Marriage, The, 161
Boston, 9–26
Bowden, Leonora, 139–40, 237
Boy Scouts, 25
Boyington family, 19
Boyington, Karen, 19
Bradford, Lowell, 229*n,* 232, 242–43,
 testimony, 244–45
Brando, Marlon, 241
Brewster (fictitious name), 35*n,* 36
Briggs Stadium (Detroit), 39